Library of
Davidson College

BETWEEN SIGNS AND NON-SIGNS

CRITICAL THEORY
Interdisciplinary Approaches to
Language, Discourse and Ideology

Series Editors
Iris M. Zavala
Myriam Díaz-Diocaretz

Advisory Editorial Board:

Jonathan Culler *(Cornell University, Ithaca)*
Teun A. van Dijk *(University of Amsterdam, Amsterdam)*
Fredric Jameson *(Duke University)*
Teresa de Lauretis *(University of California, Santa Cruz)*
Jerome McGann *(University of Virginia, Charlottesville)*
Cesare Segre *(University of Pavia)*
Gayatri Ch. Spivak *(University of Pittsburgh)*
Mario Valdés *(University of Toronto)*

Volume 10

Ferruccio Rossi-Landi

BETWEEN SIGNS AND NON-SIGNS

BETWEEN SIGNS AND NON-SIGNS

FERRUCCIO ROSSI-LANDI

Edited with an introduction by

SUSAN PETRILLI

JOHN BENJAMINS PUBLISHING COMPANY
AMSTERDAM/PHILADELPHIA

1992

Library of Congress Cataloging-in-Publication Data

Rossi-Landi, Ferruccio.
　Between sign and non-sign / Ferruccio Rossi-Landi ; edited with an introduction by Susan Petrilli.
　　p.　cm. -- (Critical theory, ISSN 0920-3060; v. 10)
　Essays, written directly in English, which were previously published 1953-1988.
　Includes bibliographical references and index.
1. Semiotics. I. Petrilli, Susan. II. Title. III. Series.
P99.R58 1992
302.2--dc20   92-24183
ISBN 90 272 2419 6 (Eur.)/1-55619-177-4 (US) (hb; alk. paper)   CIP

© Copyright 1992 - John Benjamins B.V.
No part of this book may be reproduced in any form, by print, photoprint, microfilm, or any other means, without written permission from the publisher.

John Benjamins Publishing Co. · P.O. Box 75577 · 1070 AN Amsterdam · The Netherlands
John Benjamins North America · 821 Bethlehem Pike · Philadelphia, PA 19118 · USA

Table of Contents

Introduction by *Susan Petrilli*   ix
    Notes   xxiii
    References   xxvi
Sidelights by *Ferruccio Rossi-Landi*   1

I.   Signs and Masters in Semiotic History

1. A Fragment in the History of Italian Semiotics   7
       Premise   7
       1.1   Communication in the History of Ideas   7
       1.2   Flour from My Own Mill   11
       References   15
2. Signs about a Master of Signs   17
       2.1   A Personal Premise   17
       2.2   Remarks about This Selection   18
       2.3   Semiotics and Philosophy   20
       2.4   At the Threshold of "Social Practice" in *FTS*   25
       2.5   Semiotics as a Biological Science in *SLB*   29
       2.6   Sign-behavior vs. Behavior-as-communication   30
       2.7   Sign-vehicles, *Signifiants*, and Signs   35
       2.8   Meaning and the Three Dimensions   39
       2.9   Summary and Conclusions   43
       2.10 Writings by Charles Morris   46
       Notes   51
       References   54
3. On some Post-Morrisian Problems   59
       3.1   Introduction   59
       3.2   Semiotics and Philosophy   61
       3.3   Signs and Values   64
       3.4   Charles Morris and Social Practice   65

	3.5 Semiosis and Meaning	69
	3.6 Behavior and Communication	74
	3.7 Behaving and "Moving About"	79
	3.8 Conclusion	81
	References	83
4.	Wittgenstein, Old and New	87
	4.1 Foreword	87
	4.2 Wittgenstein's Iceberg	89
	4.3 Wittgenstein and Semiotics	93
	4.4 Ideas for a Common Approach to Marx, Freud, and Wittgenstein	100
	4.5 Wittgenstein and Alienation	103
	References	106

II. Signs as Cognitive and Evaluative Instruments

5.	Toward an Analysis of Appraisive Signs in Esthetics	111
	5.1 Morris's Behavioral Approach	111
	5.2 Draft of an Operational Approach to Esthetic Values	117
	Notes	126
	References	128
6.	On Absurdity	131
	Head Note	131
	6.1 "Category Mistakes" and the *Reductio Ad Absurdum* According to Linguistic Philosophy	136
	6.2 Ryle's Procedure	138
	6.3 General Weakness of the Appeal to Absurdity	140
	6.4 Various Types of Absurdity, from "Linguistic" to "Real"	142
	6.4.1 Unknown Words and Their Combinations	142
	6.4.2 Odd Combinations of Words	143
	6.4.3 Difficult or Contradictory Combinations of Words	144
	6.4.4 Illegitimate, or Spurious, Combinations of Words	147
	6.4.5 Strangeness in the Thing Reported or Spoken About	148
	6.4.6 Self-effacing Combinations of Words	150
	6.5 Absurdity and Logical Types	151
	Notes	153
	References	154
7.	On the Overlapping of Categories in the Social Sciences	157
	7.1 Some Cases of Paired Terms	158
	7.2 Instances of Overlapping Categories	160

	7.2.1	Production and Consumption	160
	7.2.2	Public and Private	162
	7.2.3	Communication and Behavior	164
	7.2.4	Language and Thought	165
	7.2.5	Thought and Social Institutions	166
7.3	A Hint at the Dialectic of Essence and Phenomena		167
Note			168
References			168

III. Signs, Linguistic Alienation and Social Reproduction

8. Introduction to *Semiosis and Social Reproduction* — 171
   - 8.1 Foreword and Outline — 171
   - 8.2 Does Semiotics Exist? — 173
   - 8.3 Social Reproduction in General — 176
   - 8.4 Social Reproduction vs. Reality — 184
   - 8.5 Three Complementary Approaches — 186

9. Articulations in Verbal and Objectual Sign Systems — 189
   - Foreword — 189
   - 9.1 Artefacts and Work — 190
   - 9.2 Homology of Production — 194
     - 9.2.1 First Level: Presignificant Items — 194
     - 9.2.2 Second Level: Irreducibly Significant Items — 197
     - 9.2.3 Third Level: "Completed" Pieces — 199
     - 9.2.4 Fourth Level: Utensils and Sentences — 203
     - 9.2.5 Fifth Level: Aggregates of Utensils — 206
     - 9.2.6 Sixth Level: Mechanism — 208
     - 9.2.7 Seventh Level: Complex and Self-sufficient Mechanisms — 214
     - 9.2.8 Eighth Level: Total Mechanism or Automation — 215
     - 9.2.9 Ninth Level: Nonrepeatable Production — 217
     - 9.2.10 Tenth Level: Global Production — 219
   - 9.3 Plurality of Articulations — 220

10. Sign Systems and Social Reproduction — 233
    - 10.1 Social Reproduction as the Principle of All Things — 233
      - 10.1.1 Social Reproduction, Social Practice, and History — 233
      - 10.1.2 The Idea of a Catalogue of Social Reproduction — 235
      - 10.1.3 Social Reproduction as the Matrix of All Possible Categories — 236
    - 10.2 The Articulations of Social Reproduction — 238
      - 10.2.1 Production, Exchange, and Consumption — 239
      - 10.2.2 Structure and Superstructure — 240

	10.2.3 Modes of Production, Sign Systems, and Ideological Institutions	242
10.3	Sign Systems in Social Reproduction	244
	10.3.1 The Presence of Nonverbal Sign Systems	244
	10.3.2 The Influence of the Nonverbal upon the Verbal	245
	10.3.3 The Position of Language in the Structure-superstructure Circle	247
	10.3.4 Planning at Three Levels of All Behavior	249
	10.3.5 Sign Systems and the Production of Consensus	249
Notes		251
References		251

11. Ideas for the Study of Linguistic Alienation 253

    11.1 Introduction 253
    11.2 Linguistic Capital, Constant 256
    11.3 Linguistic Capital, Variable 258
    11.4 Total Linguistic Capital 259
    11.5 Linguistic Exploitation 262
    11.6 Linguistic Consumerism 264
    Notes 265
    References 266

IV. Signs and Material Reality

12. Signs and Bodies 271
    Notes 276

13. Ideas for a Manifesto of Materialistic Semiotics 277

14. Toward a Theory of Sign Residues 281

    14.1 Introduction: Sign Systems and Social Reproduction 281
    14.2 The Typology of Signs as a Function of Social Reproduction 284
    14.3 The Totality "Sign," and "Sign Residues" 285
        14.3.1 Residues on the Side of Signantia 289
        14.3.2 Residues on the Side of the Signata 294
    14.4 Signs as Mediating between the Material and the Social 298
    References 299

Writings by Ferruccio Rossi-Landi 301

Index Auctorum 311

Index Rerum 317

Introduction*

1. The type of cultural organization required by capitalism in its present phase is intimately linked to the development of the capitalist system itself: indeed they identify with each other. From this it ensues that, firstly, it is difficult to separate ideological interests from the objective, material interests of the development of capital; not only is ideology a constituent part of production but, more than this, it produces profit. Secondly, given that culture is made of signs and that without signs ideologies cannot be conveyed, indeed cannot even be produced, this interrelation between cultural organization and capitalist system concerns both verbal and nonverbal signs, which play a determining role in the current phase of social reproduction. Today, the expression 'cultural capital' is no longer a mere metaphor, but a reality. Work operations and forms of behavior of the most disparate types produce and develop cultural capital and, as in all capital producing processes, such cultural capital is in turn augmented through surplus value and therefore through surplus work. Not only does all this come about without the subject knowing what the aims of his work are, but often he is not even aware that some of his most basic activities may be defined as work.

Immediate consequences of all this are what may be referred to as the "invisibility" of ideology determined by its functionality to the development of capital, and the "imperceptibility" of exploitation determined by its dissemination throughout most of our activities. It might well be maintained that we are now experiencing one of the most difficult times ever as far as the critique of ideology and analysis of social alienation is concerned, and it is not incidental that such issues are quickly set aside by proclaiming the "crisis," or even the "end" of ideology, and by judging expressions like "alienation," "class interest," and "social exploitation" as outdated. On the contrary, for an adequate critique of the present-day cultural system we must study the mechanisms that regulate the reproduction of cultural capital and describe the new role carried out by ideology, and therefore by the signs that form ideology and culture in general.

The increased involvement of signs and ideology in the reproduction process of capital has caused the individual to take on a new role in that process; consequently his role as a subject must now be re-examined. The notion of "alienated subject" does not fully describe the situation of unconscious integration in a process in which the goals are unknown to the individuals involved. The expression 'alienated subject' takes the very concept of subject for granted, whilst it should be questioned given its specific ideological character. The subject is overlooked not only in the case of "visible alienation," which society denounces and relegates as abnormality, pathology, or, "mental alienation," and which results in a lack of functionality to the system, but also in the case of "invisible alienation," alienation in the Marxian sense, which no longer only concerns life in the factory but extends to most if not all spaces of the social and, unlike "visible alienation," is functional to the system.[1]

The Italian philosopher Ferruccio Rossi-Landi (1921-1985) conducted pioneering work in semiotics and the philosophy of language from the 1950s to the second half of the 1980s. One of the main aspects of his research is his critique of language and subsequently of ideology in relation to sign-production processes, considered, in turn, in relation to the overall process of social reproduction. Present-day social reality confirms Rossi-Landi's updated definition of the ruling class as the class that controls communication channels together with the rules governing the formulation and interpretation of messages, as well as his theory of the sign-mediated character of the relationship between so-called structure and so-called superstructure.

The above-mentioned years covering Rossi-Landi's intellectual production coincide with the formation of a new phase in the social reproduction process, as well as with a period in which the fundamental role of signs and of verbal and nonverbal communication programs in the production process of capital was accentuated.[2] It would not have been possible to study the unconscious programs underlying verbal and nonverbal behavior before the assertion of neocapitalism, just as the demystification of bourgeois economy would not have been possible, with its consequent unveiling of man's exploitation and oppression within the production process, before the full development of capitalism and, therefore, before the progressive weakening of the organic structure of capital and of the value of workers in favor of that part of capital which remains constant. As Rossi-Landi writes (1972b: 18-42):

> Man acts according to programs in any socio-economic situation whatever and certainly not in the neocapitalist one alone. [But] that such program-

ming has emerged is the result or at least has been favored by the neocapitalist alteration of the organic structure of capital.[3]

We have now reached such a highly advanced stage in this type of social reproduction that programming processes and the role of subjects in these processes have become difficult to perceive to the very point that, as mentioned, the end of ideology has been proclaimed, and the critique of alienation and of the exploitation of man described as anachronistic. The overall impression is that this system cannot be set aside; it appears as the natural result of human history so that all theory and criticism and all forms of revolutionary praxis are considered as devoid of realism, as mere utopian fantasies.

This could be another reason for returning to such concepts as Rossi-Landi's "linguistic work," "linguistic capital," "homology between material production and linguistic production," which are of particular interest today. Such notions put Rossi-Landi in a position to interpret merchandise as messages and messages as merchandise in his project for the constitution of a general semiotics which is historical and materialistic in orientation. According to Rossi-Landi, production systems, sign systems and ideologies require and complete one another and impose unitary developments. The demystification of ideologies and of the very notion of the subject is only possible through a critique of signs that keeps account of the specific social context in which such signs are produced and circulate.

Of special interest for the study of the mechanisms through which subjects are constructed is an essay by Rossi-Landi,[4] "Criteri per lo studio ideologico di un autore" (Criteria for the Ideological Study of an Author) (1976c: 5-32), in which he delineates two different approaches. On the one hand, he overcomes a fetishistic vision of the subject, in this case the author, by beginning with an analysis of the author only to end by reinstating him in the communicative situation in which he has, in fact, developed:

> The expressed contents are social; the instruments used to express them are also very much so; and even expression (including also the material activity of writing) develops according to rules elaborated collectively. We are only able to use our own verbal sign system thanks to the non-verbal sign systems within which we operate. At the most, the author may be viewed as an instrument used by a social group to express itself (on this point Lucien Goldmann's research, corrected and integrated by his successors, is still useful). (Rossi-Landi 1985a: 187)

On the other hand, he takes the socio-historical context of the subject as his starting point, and examines the author's ability to free himself from his immediate context. Rossi-Landi distinguishes between factors that condition the author and an excess that characterizes him. This excess can only lie in the new values that the author exerts himself to produce and through which he perceives, makes the reader perceive and in some cases even plans a different society from his own. The ideological character of the author and his work may be evaluated by reconstructing the dialectic between the subject, the social context and excess. With the concept of excess Rossi-Landi too, like Mikhail Bakhtin though independently from him,[5] works on the concept of *vnenakhodimost'*, now translated into English with the terms "outsideness" or "exotopy." Referring specifically to the literary text, Rossi-Landi (1985a: 191) observes that:

> The text may be viewed as action that takes place on stage and, therefore, refers to a setting. All texts contain a dialectic between stage and setting, or allude to it. A substantial part of our own work lies in the reconstruction of this dialectic. If the author contains an excess with respect to his own social reproduction, it is as though the stage lights extend a little toward the background setting; if he limits himself to repeating current values, it is as though the setting comes forward, surrounding and confounding the stage almost.[6]

2. In a typewritten bio-bibliographical note of 1978 requested by the publishers of his book *Ideologia* (English transl. as *Marxism and Ideology* see Rossi-Landi 1978c and 1990), Rossi-Landi signaled the following as volumes he was in the course of preparing:

– *Dall'analisi alla dialettica* (From Analysis to Dialectic), a collection of essays originally published between 1949 and 1976, with the addition of three unpublished manuscripts;
– *Between Signs and Non-signs*, a volume collecting essays in English first published between 1952 and 1976, with the addition of various unpublished manuscripts;
– *Sistemi segnici e riproduzione sociale* (Sign Systems and Social Reproduction) which included three published papers: one from 1976 in Italian, "Criteri per lo studio ideologico di un autore"; another from 1977 in English, "Introduction to Semiosis"; and a second in English from 1978, "Sign Systems and Social Reproduction."

"Introduction to Semiosis" is an ample preview description of *Sistemi segnici e riproduzione sociale* which like the two preceding volumes, however, remained unpublished. Both this paper and "Sign Systems and Social Reproduction" have now been included in the present volume. The only book that Rossi-Landi was ever to publish after 1978 (apart from new editions of some of his earlier works), and his last, given that it appeared just a few months before his death in May 1985, was *Metodica filosofica e scienza dei segni* (Philosophical Methodics and the Science of Signs). This also includes "Criteri per uno studio ideologico di un autore" which, as mentioned above, was originally scheduled to appear in *Sistemi segnici e riproduzione sociale*.

In the bibliography of his introduction (see Rossi-Landi 1979d) to the second edition of *Significato, comunicazione e parlare comune* (Meaning, Communication and Common Speech), Rossi-Landi only mentions the first two books of the three listed above: *Dall'analisi alla dialettica* and *Between Signs and Non-signs*. Furthermore, he explains that while plans for the first volume remained unaltered and included the essays originally envisaged, those included in the second had been extended to 1978.

The volume we are now presenting is an attempt at bringing a project that was originally Rossi-Landi's to a happy conclusion. As Rossi-Landi did not actually assemble the material himself, we have not been able to trace some of the unpublished manuscripts. On the other hand, however, the period originally planned by the author has been extended to include papers published after 1978: the most recent, "A Fragment in the History of Italian Semiotics" (Chapter 2), was presented at the Congress of the International Association for Semiotic Studies in Palermo in 1984 (published in 1988). The essays added to the present edition are closely related to the topics covered in the original plan and were also written directly in English. Organized in this way, *Between Signs and Non-signs* spans the period from 1952 to 1984 (or from 1953 to 1988 if we prefer to keep publishing dates in mind), and consequently offers an interesting if not exhaustive overview of Rossi-Landi's lifelong research. For the reader unfamiliar with Rossi-Landi, this volume is a synthesis of all the main aspects of his work, for the specialist it is a useful guide in perusing the highly problematic and labyrinthine multiplicity of his intellectual itineraries (as developed in the numerous books and essays besides this volume), with the effect of showing the thread that unites them.[7]

3. *Between Signs and Non-signs* is a collection of fourteen essays all closely interrelated not only on the level of theme, but also in research perspective. The volume is divided into four Parts with the addition, at the beginning, of a brief self-presentation by Rossi-Landi entitled "Sidelights" (written in 1984).

The essays included in Part One entitled "Signs and Masters in Semiotic History," deal with some contemporary figures – in particular Giovanni Vailati,[8] Ludwig Wittgenstein, and Charles Morris[9] – and with given periods in the history of the philosophy of language and the science of signs. Specific references are also made to certain phases in the history of Italian semiotics as well as to more recent developments on the semiotic scene in general after Morris. As Rossi-Landi specifies in the first paper in this section, he was concerned with such thinkers as well as others (such as Eugenio Colorni,[10] Francis Herbert Bradley, Hugo Dingler, Edmund Husserl,[11] Gilbert Ryle, etc.) not as a professional historian of ideas, but as a theoretician interested in discussing problems. Such is the approach adopted in the monograph *Charles Morris* (see Rossi-Landi 1953a and 1975d).

Rossi-Landi's intellectual formation was heavily influenced by his critical confrontation with Morris (among other things he translated Morris's important 1938 book, *Foundations of the Theory of Signs*, see Rossi-Landi 1954d), with American pragmatism, operationalism, English analytical philosophy and especially the studies of Ryle (Rossi-Landi 1955a is a free translation of Ryle's *The Concept of Mind*), and with Wittgenstein. Furthermore, Rossi-Landi also revived the minor Italian tradition, which boasts such significant figures as Giuseppe Peano, Giovanni Vailati, Mario Calderoni, Federigo Enriques, and the same Eugenio Colorni, with respect to dominating idealism, symbolized at the time by Benedetto Croce and Giovanni Gentile.

Rossi-Landi was soon dissatisfied with the notion of *ordinary language* as it had been elaborated by the English analytical philosophers (the object of his studies while at Oxford between 1951 and 1953). In particular, he questioned the notion of *linguistic use* which, all things considered, was no more than the study of the characteristics of a given historical language, in this case English, mistakenly thought to represent ordinary language in general (an error involving such a renowned linguist as Chomsky even[12]). On his part, Rossi-Landi was intent upon identifying the general conditions of language-thought at the basis of linguistic use and which as such are valid beyond the scope of a given historical language. This project led Rossi-Landi to his 1961 book, *Significato, comunicazione e parlare comune*, in which he developed his theory of *common speech* with the aim of *constructing a general model for the explanation of linguistic use, a model of speaking* as Rossi-Landi called it, by identifying those elements that are common to and constant in the different single languages. The notion of *common speech* refers to the fundamental techniques underlying speech, operative in all languages; it refers to the whole set of general conditions which make such operations as signifying and communication *possible*. In this context "possible" is intended in the Kantian sense, so that Rossi-Landi's research unfolds as the study of the *a priori* in language in his effort to identify the operations inevitably accomplished when we speak (see Ponzio 1986a).[13]

The notion of common speech was subsequently developed in terms of Rossi-Landi's notion of *linguistic work* (the original result of his studies on G.W.F. Hegel, Karl Marx, and Classical Political Economy). Indeed, *Significato, comunicazione e parlare comune*, which intends to *explain* rather than just simply describe linguistic use, marks the beginning of a research itinerary that Rossi-Landi was to continue in his fundamental book of 1968, *Linguaggio come lavoro e come mercato* (English transl. 1983b), in which the Wittgensteinian notion of linguistic use is overtly criticized. This critique is put forward in Marxian terms with the consequence that Rossi-Landi maintains that the limit of Wittgenstein's theory of linguistic use is the absence of the notion of labor-value:

> that is, of the value of a given object, in this case a linguistic object, as the product of a given linguistic piece of work. From the linguistic object, he [Wittgenstein] moves only forward and never backwards. (Rossi-Landi 1968h; English transl. 1983b: 31)

Wittgenstein too was often at the center of Rossi-Landi's attention, playing a fundamental role in his intellectual formation. Rossi-Landi himself drew our attention to this when, for example, he shifted the chapter on Wittgenstein (significantly entitled "Towards a Marxian Use of Wittgenstein") in his 1968 book to the beginning of the volume in the new Italian edition of 1973. To use the words of the title of one of the books listed above, *Dall'analisi alla dialettica*, this change may be interpreted as a sign of the determining influence exerted by Wittgenstein on Rossi-Landi in his transition "from analysis to dialectic." The paper included in the present volume, "Wittgenstein, Old and New" (1981a), is a development of this earlier study by Rossi-Landi in the light of his subsequent theoretical production and of the current debate on the problem of signs.

Part Two in the present volume entitled, "Signs as Cognitive and Evaluative Instruments," includes three papers the first of which (written in 1952), "Toward an Analysis of Appraisive Signs in Esthetics," appeared in the journal *Methodos* in 1953.

Methodos, subtitled *A Quarterly Review of Methodology and Language Analysis*, was founded in Italy (Milan) in 1949. The main languages for publication were Italian and English though other languages were not excluded. This was rather exceptional at the time in Italy, a real effort to eliminate residues of cultural provincialism. In addition to his collaboration with *Methodos*, Rossi-Landi was constantly involved in editorial work for various other journals, which he often directed. He belonged to the editorial committees of the journals *Occidente* (1955-1956), *Nuova corrente* (1966-1968), and *Dialectical Anthropology* (1975-1985); he founded the two journals *Ideologie* (1967-1974) and *Scienze umane* (1979-1981);[14] he also founded and directed the small publishing house "Edizioni di ideologie" (Rome); and together with Tomás Maldonado, Luis Prieto, and Adam Schaff, he directed the book series "Semiotica e pratica sociale" (Feltrinelli-Bocca).

In addition to Rossi-Landi's own contribution, the same issue of *Methodos* (vol. 5, no. 18, 1953) includes Morris's important paper of 1952, "Significance, Signification and Painting" in the English original. Rossi-Landi's paper is substantially a study of Morris's esthetic theory, the subject of yet another study of 1967 entitled, "Sul modo in cui è stata fraintesa la semiotica estetica di Charles Morris" (On how Charles Morris's Esthetic Semiotics Has Been Misunderstood). This was subsequently included in his 1972 book *Semiotica e ideologia* (Semiotics and Ideology) though it originally appeared as the introduction to the Italian edition of three papers by Morris published in *Nuova corrente* (42-43, 1967): "Esthetics and the Theory of Signs" (1939); "Aesthetics, Signs and Icons," written in collaboration with D.J. Hamilton (1965); and a "Foreword" presented by Morris especially for the occasion. As in the case of Wittgenstein, then, Rossi-Landi often returned to Morris throughout his lifelong studies thus continuing the work begun with his monograph of 1953; in fact, though their research itineraries were different, they frequently intersected.

Morris and Rossi-Landi both dealt with the problem of values: Morris was particularly interested in esthetic and ethical value, Rossi-Landi in linguistic and economic value. Their regular correspondence, which lasted for more than twenty-five years – from approximately 1950 to 1976 – testifies to the influence exercised by Rossi-Landi over Morris in the latter's studies on the relation between signs and values and, therefore, between semiotics and axiology, which were to find maximum theoretical expression in his 1964 book, *Significance and Signification*.[15]

"On Absurdity," the second essay in Part Two of the present volume, also belongs to the initial phase of Rossi-Landi's research: this phase, which he described as the analytical, spans the years from the early 1950s to 1961 when his book, *Significato, comunicazione e parlare comune* was published. "On Absurdity" (the slightly modified English version of Chapter Five of his 1961 book) was published in English in the journal *Semiotica*, in 1976, with the addition of a Head Note written in 1975 (this text appeared directly in English and has no Italian equivalent). In the Head Note Rossi-Landi explains the differences between his position in 1975 and that at the time of writing this particular paper, in 1963.

Here we only wish to underline the essential continuity linking these two phases, the analytical and the dialectical, of which perhaps not even Rossi-Landi was fully aware. Not only does such continuity concern the fact that many of the ideas marking the subsequent period, and formulated in books like *Language as Work and Trade* (1968), *Semiotica e ideologia* (1972), *Linguistics and Economics* (1975 [1974]), *Metodica filosofica e scienza dei segni* (1985) "were already present, if only in an embryonic form," as Rossi-Landi says, "in the 1961 book" (1968h; English transl. 1983b: xi), but even more significantly, it concerns his *research method*. As observed by Augusto Ponzio (1988a: 51) in his monograph on Rossi-Landi, it is not incidental that the latter should have proposed a "*methodics* of common speaking" in 1961 and that the title of his 1985 book (the last to have appeared before his death) includes the expression "philosophical methodics." In truth, Rossi-Landi's whole theoretical itinerary, as it developed from the early 1950s to 1985, may be viewed in terms of a transition from the methodics of common speaking to the methodics of common semiosis (Ponzio 1988a: 92-98; see also Biancofiore and Ponzio 1987: 25-46).

Rossi-Landi called the method he was concerned with the "homological method," which he theorized in "Omologia della riproduzione sociale" (Homology of Social Reproduction). (This paper was originally published in 1972 in the journal *Ideologie* and subsequently developed in both *Linguistics and Economics* and *Metodica filosofica*). The homological method pushes beyond the mere identification of analogies or similarities by integrating structural and dynamic analyses. As such it was already operative in Rossi-Landi's 1961 book, *Significato, comunicazione e parlare comune*, in which he constructed his common speech model on the basis of the identification of homologies between different languages. Beginning with the research flowing into *Language as Work and Trade*, Rossi-Landi investigated homological relations connecting the production, exchange and consumption of material goods with the production, exchange and consumption of signs: in this framework he examined both verbal and nonverbal language in terms of work. Such an approach amounted to the search for a homology between *homo faber* and *homo loquens*, which led Rossi-Landi to formulating his theory of the homology of production in general, that is, of both sign and non-sign production.

"On the Overlapping of Categories in the Social Sciences" (published in 1978 though written in 1972) contains numerous references to *Significato, comunicazione e parlare comune*. In this essay, Rossi-Landi studies some pairs of categories which can only function and be explained in relation to each other: communication and behavior, language and thought, production and consumption. The terms forming these pairs are not identical and in any case they cannot be reduced to each other. In addition to these, another fundamental pair of categories in Rossi-Landi's research is work and activity.

Rossi-Landi deals explicitly with these two concepts in Chapter One of *Metodica filosofica*. With respect to his 1968 book, Rossi-Landi now goes a step further by developing the concept of language in terms of work rather than activity. Activity is not programmed and is an end in itself; on the contrary, work mediates the relation between needs and the satisfaction of those needs, and to this end employs the specific instruments and materials of given models and programs with their specific goals. Moreover, the distinction between work and activity also concerns that between signs and non-signs. The footprints impressed upon the sand as the result of the activity of walking are not signs and persist in their non-sign status until they become the object of interpretive work.

But if the distinction between work and activity lies in the fact that work is planned, intentional and part of a program while activity is not, at the same time, however, work is not necessarily conscious of its objectives and programs. In fact, work can be "alienated" work as demonstrated by the Marxian analysis of capitalist society; or like Freud we may speak of "oneiric work," which implies that even the production of dreams is work. The unconscious is a social product and dreams are the result of work just as their translation into the discourse that narrates and analyzes them is the result of work, of interpretive work. That work may be realized without conscious programs provides "a special contact zone," says Rossi-Landi, "for the Marxian use of Freud or the Freudian use of Marx" (1985a: 7).

Part Three in this volume, "Signs, Linguistic Alienation and Social Reproduction," includes papers from one of Rossi-Landi's most innovative periods: he proposes a global approach to the study of signs by examining not only the rules that govern message exchange, but also those that regulate their production. In other words, Rossi-Landi reconducts the sign values underlying exchange to the social relations of sign production.

The 1960s mark a break in Rossi-Landi's career, especially in relation to the Italian academic world. In 1962 he abandoned his Chair of Philosophy at the University of Padua owing to the incompatibility between the novelty of his ideas and an academic world that was intolerant of him. Consequently, Rossi-Landi left for the United States. He acted as visiting professor at Ann Arbor University in Michigan between 1962 and 1963 and at the University of Texas at Austin in 1963. He also taught at various European and American Universities between 1964 and 1965 and, furthermore, held courses in philosophy and semiotics at the Universities of Havana and Santiago (Cuba).

Publications by Rossi-Landi from this period include: *Ideologies of Linguistic Relativity* of 1973 (the English re-edition of the Italian original published in the journal *Ideologie* in 1968); his 1974 essay "Linguistics and Economics" (published in book form in 1975); "Signs about a Master of Signs," an essay first published in English in 1975 in the American journal *Semiotica* and subsequently in Italian in the second enlarged 1975 edition of his monograph on Morris, *Charles Morris e la semiotica novecentesca* (1st edition 1953).

Rossi-Landi returned to Italy in the mid 1970s initially as Full Professor of Philosophy of History at the University of Lecce, and subsequently as Full Professor of Theoretical Philosophy at the University of Trieste. At the time he was concentrating particularly on the issue of linguistic alienation and on the link between language and ideology. His important 1978 book, *Ideologia,* which he subsequently developed into a second enlarged edition of 1980, also belongs to the same period.

As the papers in the present volume show, Rossi-Landi founded the notions of ideology and linguistic alienation on the homology between linguistic production on the one hand, and material production on the other. His studies on the plural articulations of linguistic and nonlinguistic artefacts

(Rossi-Landi 1968h includes a critique of Martinet's theory of double articulation), and on the notion of linguistic money (which may be traced back to his early book of 1961) work in the same direction.

However, as will soon become obvious on perusing this third section, the concept dominating Rossi-Landi's research of the 1970s is *social reproduction*. Rather playfully echoing an expression from the origins of ancient Greek philosophy, Rossi-Landi maintained that social reproduction is the principle of all things. It is to social reproduction that the communicative process, verbal and nonverbal, must be attributed. Following Marx, Rossi-Landi divided social reproduction into three closely interrelated phases:

1. *non-sign material production* in which bodies are produced and not signs, but in which signs too come into play;
2. *exchange* which simultaneously covers sign and non-sign material exchange or communication. Sign exchange includes:
   a) sign production;
   b) sign exchange;
   c) sign consumption;
3. *non-sign material consumption* in which bodies are consumed and not signs, and in which signs do not come into play.

The meaning of the title, *Between Signs and Non-signs* (established by Rossi-Landi himself), should now be clear. The reference is not only to the epistemological question of the relation between signs and things, though of course Rossi-Landi did not ignore this problem; indeed it is central to the essays collected in Part Four. Beyond this, however, the expression 'between signs and non-signs' recalls the fundamental fact that the relation between signs and things cannot be viewed separately from the global process of social reproduction. For Rossi-Landi, the relation between signs and non-signs is the relation that constitutes social reality. All the social develops between signs and non-signs.

The relation between signs and non-signs throws light upon yet another major issue concerning the social system and its transformations; the relation, that is, between so-called structure and so-called superstructure, or between socio-economic reality and ideology. This is possible thanks to the introduction of a mediating element between modes of production and ideology (productive forces and relations of production); our reference is to sign systems, to sign systems in their entirety, verbal and nonverbal, and, therefore, to that important phase in social reproduction listed above as phase 2 – the combination of sign production, sign exchange, and sign consumption.

The importance attributed to the notion of social reproduction by Rossi-Landi is confirmed by the two successive plans (dated, respectively, May 1981 and August 1984) of a book entitled *Introduction to the Study of Signs*. He sent both plans to Augusto Ponzio whom he wished to involve at the time as co-author though subsequently decided to proceed alone; as he explained in a letter to Ponzio of January 28, 1985, he was motivated by an invitation to hold a course of twelve lessons in São Paulo (Brazil) in September 1985 (which never took place because of his sudden death in May of that same year). The first chapter in both planned versions of this book (which was never published) is dedicated to *social reproduction* and covers the following topics: social reproduction as the principle of all things; a catalogue of social reproduction; models of social reproduction; material reproduction and symbolic reproduction; structures, sign systems and superstructures. After dealing with such issues as the transmission of sign systems, the verbal and nonverbal, the homology of production, the sign totality and its residues, the second plan closes on a section dedicated to sign alienation, which in turn concludes with a chapter on language and ideology.

Rossi-Landi continued his research on the same topics during the 1980s working along the same lines as in the 1970s. His main concern was to perfect and clarify his intuitions regarding the homology of production and the mechanism of social reproduction.[16]

As briefly mentioned above, the three essays forming Part Four of the present volume, "Signs and Material Reality," concentrate on the materiality of signs and on "the bodily residue of nonverbal messages" (see Petrilli 1986 and 1988b): notions that were fundamental in Rossi-Landi's work as early as the 1960s (and already systematically treated in his 1968 book). In addition to the concepts mentioned so far, Part Four presents still others including the concept of *material* (and therefore of *materiality*), which is related to the concept of *residue* (sign and non-sign residue or bodily residue), and both are inevitably reconducted to the principle of social reproduction.

Rossi-Landi proposes the following five propositions (first presented in this form in 1974; see his 1979 paper "Signs and Bodies," now in this volume):

(A) All signs are bodies
(B) Not all bodies are signs

(C) All bodies can be signs
(D) Signs are not bodies
(E) All bodies are signs

A, B, and C characterize the materialistic model of semiotics; D and E the idealistic model.

Rossi-Landi isolated the sign totality or "cell," as he called it, described as a unit consisting of a *signans* and a *signatum* (he introduced this Augustinian terminology with the intention, apart from anything else, of avoiding the mentalistic ambiguity of the Saussurian *signifié*), and on this basis he elaborated the concept of sign *residue*. Irreducible residues of a bodily and of a social material order are present both on the side of the *signans* and of the *signatum*. On the side of the *signans*, bodies, either natural bodies or artefacts – but in any case social – act as sign vehicles. On the side of the *signatum*, *social residues* are classifiable as interpretants in Peirce's sense intended both as intension, sense, *lekton*, and as extension, referent or *designatum*. In other words, the sign is characterized by a double materiality, physical and socio-historical, which determines the specificity of semiotic materiality.

Though Rossi-Landi distinguished between signs and non-signs, it was not his intention to establish two different modes of existence: things that are signs and things that are not signs, as though signs are signs of their own accord, by nature and independently of communication and interpretation processes, of socio-historical relations among human beings. It is common knowledge that not all things are signs, which does not exclude the fact that there is nothing that cannot become a sign once it has been caught up within the web of semiosic processes. The point for Rossi-Landi was not to distinguish *tout court* between signs and non-signs, but rather to study the ongoing transformation processes from the status of sign to the status of non-sign and vice versa, and of explaining the conditions that make such operations possible – something which further clarifies his choice of the word 'between' in the title of the present volume. Against trends colored by a sort of semiotic panlogism and according to which the world is uniquely populated by signs, against sign fetishism, and against arbitrary separations imposed by recourse to abstract categories, Rossi-Landi worked on notions that not only provided common ground for an adequate analysis of signs and non-signs, but were also able to account for the mechanisms underlying the very production – and reproduction – of signs and their multiple diversity.

INTRODUCTION

xxiii

I wish to thank Iris Zavala for having read this introduction and given advice for its improvement. I also thank her and Myriam Díaz-Diocaretz for having accepted my proposal to publish this collection of essays by Ferruccio Rossi-Landi (made in the Summer of 1989 during the seminars held annually at the Centro Internazionale di Linguistica e Semiotica, Urbino), and for having welcomed it into their book series. A special thanks must also go to Professor Augusto Ponzio. He has made this volume possible thanks to the information so generously supplied and to his advice in the far from simple reconstruction of the theoretical itinerary it proposes. Such assistance was also fundamental in writing the present introduction.

Susan Petrilli
Bari, January 1991

For bibliographical references relative to the writings of Rossi-Landi, see the general bibliography at the end of this volume:

PART I	contains: R.-L. 1988;	R.-L. 1975c;	R.-L. 1978e;	R.-L. 1981a.
PART II	contains: R.-L. 1953b;	R.-L. 1976a;	R.-L. 1978d.	
PART III	contains: R.-L. 1977;	R.-L. 1974e;	R.-L. 1978b;	R.-L. 1979i.
PART IV	contains: R.-L. 1979b;	R.-L. 1979g;	R.-L. 1979c.	

Notes

* All information in square brackets throughout this volume has been inserted by myself.

References to the writings of Ferruccio Rossi-Landi have all been included in an updated and revised bibliography at the end of the volume.

Notes and reference sections have been placed at the end of each respective paper. This criterion has been used so as to enable the reader to ascertain information as originally given by the author relative to the time of writing.

Chapters Two and Three are both dedicated to the work of Charles Morris; as such both refer to the general bibliography of his writings, edited by Rossi-Landi (and revised by myself), in the final section of Chapter Two, where it was originally placed by the author.

In conformity with editorial requirements as established by the publishers, the spelling has been systematically Americanized; and words formed with prefixes have been written without a hyphen wherever possible. – S.P.

1. On the relation between social alienation, language and madness with particular reference to literature, see Iris M. Zavala *et al.* eds., 1987.

2. The development of a theoretical-ideological movement at an international level, and perhaps especially in France (M. Foucault, L. Althusser, P. Bourdieu, etc), during the 1960s and 1970s was not incidental. This movement was described by Raymond Boudon with critical overtones in terms of "*neo*-Marxism" (see Boudon 1986). It would seem that the accusation of "superficial functionalism" characterizing this movement with respect to the problematic character of Marxian analysis (which led to its description as "*neo*-Marxism"), is especially suitable in the case of Bourdieu (cf. the pages dedicated to him by Boudon 1986, Chapter 8). However that may be, Bourdieu has the merit of having turned his attention to the social-ideological function of certain institutions (e.g. the education system) as well as to language and culture in general (cf. Bourdieu 1979, 1982; Bourdieu and Passeron 1964, 1970). A degree of hyperbolic functionalism is evident in the identification of a direct relation between culture, education, and language on the one hand, and reproduction of the ruling class – through unconscious, invisible *habitus* mechanisms – on the other. Furthermore, this operation is carried out on the basis of a definition that falls into the vicious circle of explaining the function of cultural institutions in terms of the ruling class. Rossi-Landi's study of the mediating function of signs, and therefore his dialectic conception of the social programming of behavior, offers a possible alternative to such a mechanistic orientation. For further details see the following note. Another important volume from the same period (mid 1970s) is the monographic issue of *Langages* entitled *Analyse du discours: Langue et idéologie*, see Pêcheux *et al.*, 1975.

3. As mentioned in the note above, Bourdieu defines the *habitus* as the mechanism through which social behavior and cultural institutions are unconsciously and invisibly rendered functional to the reproduction of the ruling class (cf. Bourdieu 1974: 16-17). The notion of *habitus* may be developed dialectically with Rossi-Landi's concepts of "program" and "programming." Indeed, the same Bourdieu defined "*habitus*" in terms of "types of programs (in the sense of informatics)" (see Bourdieu 1985: 110). For the notion of social program, see Rossi-Landi 1968i: 304-319, now in Rossi-Landi 1972i; see also Part III, this volume.

4. As observed in a footnote to the second edition (in Rossi-Landi 1985a), this essay is part of Rossi-Landi's general research on social reproduction. See also Rossi-Landi 1977 (written in 1974), and Rossi-Landi 1978b (written in 1976). Both essays are now included in the present volume.

5. See, for example, the essays collected in Bakhtin 1984.

6. Rossi-Landi returns to the concept of excess in a paper entitled, "The Author between Social Reproduction and Discontinuity," held at a seminar at the Institute of Philosophy of Language, Bari University, April 19, 1985 (see Rossi-Landi 1985b). The problematic of the ideological interpretation of the author in Rossi-Landi is further examined in an essay by Biancofiore and Ponzio entitled "Autore e ideologia" (in Ponzio 1988a:189-223).

7. For an exhaustive and critical study of Rossi-Landi's research, see Ponzio 1988a. Some of Ponzio's work on specific aspects of Rossi-Landi's theoretical production is also

available in English, see Ponzio 1986a and 1986b, now in Ponzio 1990b. The latter also includes an essay by myself, "On the Materiality of Signs" (see also Petrilli 1986). To the thought of Rossi-Landi has also been devoted a monographic issue of the journal *Il Protagora* (see Petrilli 1987a) with contributions from Umberto Eco, Paolo Facchi, János Kelemen, Romano Luperini, Roland Posner, Thomas A. Sebeok, Giuseppe Semerari, Tatiana Slama-Cazacu, Tullio Tentori, and an unpublished paper by Rossi-Landi, "La 'non-filosofia'" (pp. 191-195).

8. Giovanni Vailati (1863-1909) was one of the first Italians to have understood the importance not only of Charles S. Peirce's (1839-1914) semiotics, but also of his *pragmaticism*. Vailati was also in contact with the English scholar Victoria Lady Welby (1837-1912) at a time when her theory of meaning, or *Significs*, was generally ignored. Welby's work is only just now claiming attention in its own right (despite her intellectual exchanges with Peirce and her influence upon such authors as C.K. Ogden and I.A. Richards), thanks also to the recent re-editions of her works, see Welby 1983 and 1985a. A collection of her writings has also appeared in Italian translation, see Welby 1985b. For studies on Welby, see Schmitz 1990 and Heijerman-Schmitz 1991.

As to the relation between Vailati and Welby, and Vailati and Rossi-Landi, see Ponzio 1988b, 1989, and 1990a; see also Petrilli 1989.

9. On the relation between Rossi-Landi and Morris, see Petrilli 1987b and 1992.

10. Rossi-Landi edited a collection of published and unpublished papers by Eugenio Colorni with an introduction by Norberto Bobbio (see Rossi-Landi 1975a). As pointed out by Rossi-Landi himself, though this material was published in 1975 he actually worked on it as early as the years between 1964 and 1966.

11. The first edition of *Significato, comunicazione e parlare comune* (Rossi-Landi 1961d) includes a long analytical appendix on Edmund Husserl. This was eliminated from the second (1980) edition of the same book given that it was scheduled to appear in the volume, *Dall'analisi alla dialettica*. On this aspect of Rossi-Landi's work, see Ponzio 1988c.

12. For a critical appreciation of Noam Chomsky's linguistic theory in the light of considerations made by Rossi-Landi as well, see Ponzio 1973 and 1991.

13. For a discussion of this particular phase in Rossi-Landi's work, see Eco 1987 (now in Ponzio 1988a: 291-308) which also takes into consideration Rossi-Landi's introduction to the second (1973) edition of his 1968 book *Linguaggio come lavoro e come mercato*; see also Caputo 1988; Mininni 1988 and 1990.

14. On the important theoretical work carried out by Rossi-Landi in relation to *Ideologie* (his essays and editorial notes have all been collected in Rossi-Landi 1972d) and, between 1979 and 1981, to *Scienze umane*, see Ponzio 1991: 203-291.

15. The correspondence between Rossi-Landi and Morris in English is now available as a monographic issue of the journal *Semiotica*. Morris's 1964 book has recently been published in Italian with a collection of some of his other papers, see Morris 1988. A discussion of the relation between Morris and Rossi-Landi is available in the introductions to both volumes.

16. Literature on Rossi-Landi's work has been appearing since the end of the 1960s. The following is a version, updated by Ponzio and myself, of a list of references which had originally been prepared by Rossi-Landi and sent to Ponzio (other writings on Rossi-Landi have already been mentioned throughout this introduction): Bernard 1991: 17-39; Bernard, Hanl, and Withalm 1985: 94-127; Bernard and Withalm 1985: 3-9; 1986a: 329-366; 1986b: 173-202; 1986c: 1-200; 1991: 367-390; Calabrese and Mucci 1975, *passim*; Casetti 1977, *passim*; Chatterjee 1991; Gak 1975; Kelemen 1975: 592-598; Miceli 1982; Mininni 1977; Miscevič 1981; Mondadori 1968-1969, vol. 3, 48-58; Petrilli forthcoming; Ponzio 1972: 378-389; 1973, *passim*; 1974, passim; 1976, passim; 1986a: 136-166; 1986b: 207-221; 1988a; 1988c: 107-120; 1989; 1990b, *passim*; 1991 *passim*; Senofonte 1982, cf. para. 3.4 and *passim*; Steinbacher 1972; Williams 1969: 97-115.

References

Bakhtin, Mikhail. 1984. *The Dialogic Imagination*. Ed. by M. Holquist. English transl. by C. Emerson and M. Holquist. Austin: University of Texas Press.

Bernard, Jeff. 1991. "Die Sozialphilosophie und Sozio-semiotik Rossi-Landis." In *Philosophie und Semiotik. Sektionsakten – Zweiter Kongreß der Österreichischen Gessellschaft für Philosophie – Universität Wien, März 1990*. Ed. by L. Nagt, E. List, J. Bernard, and G. Withalm, 17-39. Vienna: ÖGS/ISSS.

Bernard, Jeff, Ilse Hanl and Gloria Withalm. 1985. "Ferruccio Rossi-Landi. *Metodica filosofica e scienza dei segni*. Milan: Bompiani. (Appendix: Provisorische bibliografische Übersicht – Ferruccio Rossi-Landi)." *Semiotische Berischte* 9, 1/2: 94-127 (Appendix, 122-127).

Bernard, Jeff and Gloria Withalm. 1985. "In Memoriam Ferruccio Rossi-Landi." *Semiotische Berichte* 9, 1/2: 3-9.

———. 1986a. "Ferruccio Rossi-Landis dialektisch-materialistische Zeichentheorie. Einordnung – Überblick – Diagrammatik." In *Geschichte und Geschichtsschreibung der Semiotik. Fallstudien. Akten der 8. Arbeitstagung des Münsteraner Arbeitskreises für Semiotik, Münster 2-3, 10, 1985*. Ed. by K.D. Dutz and P. Schmitter, 329-366. Munich: MAKS Publikationen.

———. 1986b. "Materie Dialektik Arbeit/Gesellschaft Geschichte Vermittlung. Ortende Bemerkungen zu Rossi-Landis sozio-prozessualer Zeichentheorie." In *Die Zeichen der Historie. Beiträge zu einer semiologischen Geschichtswissenschaft* (= Materialien zur historischen Sozialwissenschaft, 5). Ed. by G. Schmid, 173-202. Vienna-Cologne: Böhlau.

———. 1986c. "Zeichen und soziale Realität." In *ÖGS-Projektteam. Zeichentheorie und Zeichenpraxis. Forschungsprojekt – Endbericht*. Vienna: unpubl. typescript, 1-200.

——. 1991. "Ein Schlüssel zur Welt (des Denkens, der Zeichen und der Dinge). Ferruccio Rossi-Landi: Marxism and Ideology." *S – European Journal for Semiotic Studies. Dialectics, Semiotics, Materialism. In Memoriam Ferruccio Rossi-Landi* 3, 1/2: 367-390.
Biancofiore, Angela and Augusto Ponzio. 1987. "Il metodo omologico: Rossi-Landi e Gramsci." *Il Protagora. Per Ferruccio Rossi-Landi* 11/12: 25-46.
Boudon, Raymond. 1986. *L'ideologie: L'origine des idées reçues*. Paris: Fayard.
Bourdieu, P. 1979. *La distinction*. Paris: Minuit.
——. 1974. "La causalité du probable." *Revue française du sociologie* 15.
——. 1982. *Ce que parler veut dire*. Paris: Fayard.
——. 1985. *Entretiens avec "Le Monde": La société*. Paris: La Découverte-Le Monde.
Bourdieu, P. and G.C. Passeron. 1964. *Les héritiers: Les étudiants et la culture*. Paris: Minuit.
——. 1970. *La reproduction: Éléments pour une théorie d'une système d'enseignements*. Paris: Minuit.
Calabrese, Omar and Egidio Mucci. 1975. *Guida alla semiotica*. Florence: Sansone.
Caputo, Cosimo. 1988. "Sulla semiotizzazione dell'*a priori*: Rossi-Landi e Hjelmslev." *Il Protagora* 13/16: 121-134.
Casetti, Francesco. 1977. *Semiotica*. Milan: Accademia.
Chatterjee, Ranjit. 1991. "Rossi-Landi's Wittgenstein: 'A Philosopher's Meaning Is His Use in Culture'." *Semiotica* 84, 3/4: 275-283.
Eco, Umberto. 1987. "Whatever Lola Wants. Rilettura di una rilettura." *Il Protagora. Per Ferruccio Rossi-Landi* 11/12: 13-23; now also in Ponzio 1988a: 291-308.
Gak, V.G. 1975. "Language, Implement and Commodity." *Linguistics. An International Review* 143: 17-32.
Heijerman, Erik and H. Walter Schmitz (eds.). 1991. *Significs, Mathematics and Semiotics. The Signific Movement in the Netherlands. Proceedings of the International Conference*. Bonn, 19-21 Nov. 1986. Munich: Nodus Publikationen.
Kelemen, János. 1975. "Visszavezethetok-e a nyev kategoriai gazdasagi kategoriakra?" *Magyar filozofiai szemle* 5: 592-598.
Miceli, Silvana. 1982. *In nome del segno*. Palermo: Sellerio.
Mininni, Giuseppe. 1977. *Fondamenti della significazione*. Bari: Dedalo.
——. 1988. "Il parlare come lume storico della riproduzione sociale." *Il Protagora* 13/16: 135-147.
——. 1990. "Common Speech as a Pragmatic Form of Social Reproduction." *Journal of Pragmatics* 14: 125-135.
Miscevič, Nenad. 1981. *Filozofija jazika*. Zagreb: Naprijed.
Mondadori, Fabrizio. 1968-1969. "Language and Logic in Italy in the Past Ten Years." In *La philosophie contemporaine*, 3 vols. Ed. by R. Klibansky, vol. 3, 48-58. Florence: La Nuova Italia.
Morris, Charles. 1938. *Foundations of the Theory of Signs*. In *International Encyclopedia of Unified Science* 1/2. Chicago: University of Chicago Press.

———. 1939a. "Esthetics and the Theory of Signs." *Journal of Unified Science* 8: 131-150.
———. 1939b. "Science, Art and Technology." *Kenyon Review* 1: 409-433.
———. 1952. "Significance, Signification and Painting." Paper presented at the *Thirteenth Conference on Science, Philosophy and Religion*. New York, 1952. *Methodos* V, 18, 1953: 87-102; now in *The Language of Value*, ed. by R. Lepley, 58-76. New York: Columbia University Press, 1957.
———. 1964. *Signification and Significance: A Study of the Relations of Signs and Values*. Cambridge, MA: MIT Press.
———. 1967. "Premessa" written for the Italian edition of Morris 1939a and Morris and Hamilton 1965. *Nuova corrente* 42/43: 113-119.
———. 1988. *Segni e valori. Scritti di semiotica, etica ed estetica*. Italian transl., introd. and ed. by S. Petrilli. Bari: Adriatica.
Morris, Charles and Daniel J. Hamilton. 1965. "Aesthetics, Signs and Icons." *Philosophy and Phenomenological Research* 25, 3: 356-364.
Morris, Charles and Frank Sciadini. (1966). "Paintings, Ways to Live and Values." In *Sign, Image, and Symbol*. Ed. by G. Kepes, 144-149. New York: Braziller, 1966.
Pêcheux, M. *et al.* (eds.). 1975. *Analyse du discours: Langue et idéologie. Langages* 37.
Petrilli, Susan. 1986. "On the Materiality of Signs." *Semiotica* 62, 3/4: 223-245; now in Ponzio 1990b.
———. (ed.). 1987a. *Il Protagora. Per Ferruccio Rossi-Landi* 11/12.
———. 1987b. "Il contributo di Rossi-Landi allo studio di Charles Morris." *Il Protagora. Per Ferruccio Rossi-Landi* 11/12: 105-114.
———. 1988a. *Significs, semiotica e significazione*. Bari: Adriatica.
———. 1988b. "Ferruccio Rossi-Landi and the Science of Signs." In Petrilli 1988a: 219-223.
———. 1989. "La critica del linguaggio in Giovanni Vailati e Victoria Welby." In *Giovanni Vailati nella cultura del '900*. Ed. by M. Quaranta, 87-102. Sala Bolognese: Forni.
———. 1992. (introd. and ed.). "Social Practice, Semiotics and the Sciences of Man. The Correspondence between Charles Morris and Ferruccio Rossi-Landi." *Semiotica* 88, 1/2.
———. forthcoming. "Italian Semiotics in the 1970s and 1980s." Paper presented at the Convention on *Refractions: Literary Criticism. Philosophy and the Human Sciences in Contemporary Italy*. Carleton University, Ottawa, September 27-29, 1990.
Ponzio, Augusto. 1972. "On Language as Work and Trade." *Semiotica* VI, 4: 378-389.
———. 1973. *Produzione linguistica e ideologia sociale*. Bari: De Donato.
———. 1974. *Filosofia del linguaggio e prassi sociale*. Lecce: Milella.
———. 1976. *La semiotica in Italia*. Bari: Dedalo.

———. 1986a. "On the Methodics of Common Speech." *Differentia* 1: 136-166.
———. 1986b. "On the Signs of Rossi-Landi's Work." *Semiotica* 62, 3/4: 207-221.
———. 1988a. *Rossi-Landi e la filosofia del linguaggio*. Bari: Adriatica.
———. 1988b. "L'eredità di Giovanni Vailati nel pensiero di Rossi-Landi." In Ponzio 1988a: 183-198.
———. 1988c. "Sull'epoché di Husserl in F. Rossi-Landi." *Il Protagora* 13/16: 107-120.
———. 1989. "L'eredità di Giovanni Vailati nel pensiero di Rossi-Landi." In *Giovanni Vailati nella cultura del '900*. Ed. by M. Quaranta, 103-118. Sala Bolognese: Forni.
———. 1990a. "Significs and Semantics: Victoria Welby and Giovanni Vailati." In *Essays on Significs*. Ed. by W.H. Schmitz, 165-178. Amsterdam-Philadelphia: Benjamins.
———. 1990b. *Man as a Sign. Studies in the Philosophy of Language*. Introd. English transl. and ed. by S. Petrilli. The Hague: Mouton.
———. 1991. *Filosofia del linguaggio 2. Saggi sul segno, ideologia, dialogo*. Bari: Adriatica.
———. forthcoming. "Ideology." In *Semiotics: A Handbook on the Sign-Theoretic Foundations of Nature and Culture*. Ed. by R. Posner, K. Robering, and T.A. Sebeok. Berlin: de Gruyter.
Rossi-Landi, Ferruccio. [See his general bibliography at the end of the present volume.]
Schmitz, Walter H. (ed.). 1990. *Essays on Significs*. Amsterdam-Philadelphia: Benjamins.
Senofonte, Ciro. 1982. *Sociologia e filosofia del linguaggio*. Naples: Liguori.
Steinbacher, Karl. 1972. "Nachwort." In Rossi-Landi 1972j.
Welby, Victoria. 1983. *What is Meaning? Studies in the Development of Significance*. Ed. by A. Eschbach. 1st ed. 1903. Amsterdam-Philadelphia: Benjamins.
———. 1985a. *Significs and Language. The Articulate Form of Our Expressive and Interpretative Resources*. Ed. by H.W. Schmitz. 1st ed. 1911. Amsterdam-Philadelphia: Benjamins.
———. 1985b. *Significato, metafora, interpretazione*. Italian transl. introd. and ed. by S. Petrilli. Bari: Adriatica.
Williams, Roy. 1969. "Dialettica dei sistemi sociali." *Scienze umane* 3: 97-115.
Zavala, Iris M. *et al.* (eds.). 1987. *Approaches to Discourse, Poetics and Psychiatry. Critical Theory*. Amsterdam-New York: Benjamins.

Sidelights

Perhaps the main feature of my intellectual formation is that it was culturally twofold. I absorbed contemporarily or alternatively views, ideas and intellectual instruments both from the European Continental and the British-American traditions. This did not amount only to reading books in various languages (I am, or was in different periods of my life, sufficiently fluent in Italian, English, French, German, and Spanish, not to speak of some knowledge of other languages and of a long though forgotten training in Latin and Greek); it also amounted to existential experiences which I had by living many years in countries other than Italy, especially in England and the United States, and by marrying (this time not contemporarily) two non-Italian women with whom I had five bilingual or plurilingual daughters. On the other hand, my mother was a bilingual (Italian and German) Austrian subject who became Italian after World War I. Thus it happened that I felt, and still partially feel, that I belonged not only to the Italian tradition, but also, to an important extent, to the cultural traditions of Austria and Germany, England, and the United States.

In fact, after a degree in French literature soon after the Second World War, in 1951 I earned another degree ("dottorato" in Italian terminology) in philosophy, and the subject was American semiotics. In 1953 I published a monograph on Charles Morris as the refounder of semiotics (the founder, of course, was Charles Sanders Peirce whose work I had been studying since the early 1950s). As far as my knowledge goes, it was one of the first books in semiotics as the general theory of signs which ever appeared in Italy and possibly also in Europe. But the time was not ripe for it. I had made the mistake of presenting to one cultural tradition something that belonged to another. I repeated this mistake several times, and in various directions.

In the early 1950s I also spent two years in Oxford doing research work in analytical and linguistic philosophy; one of the results of this sojourn was that I rewrote in Italian, with the author's agreement, Gilbert Ryle's linguistic analyses. I am referring to his book *The Concept of Mind* which appeared in Italy under the title *Lo spirito come comportamento* [cf. R.-L. 1955a].

Another consequence was my book *Significato, comunicazione e parlare comune* (1961, new edition 1980) (Meaning, Communication, and Common Speech) [R.L. 1961d] in which – to quote from its 1961 Foreword – I was making an attempt at "grafting some logico-linguistic techniques on the trunk of Continental historicism." The book introduced the notion of *common speech* as the set of techniques used to communicate and taught from generation to generation as a relevant or indeed central part of *social practice*. The notion was completely different from that of "ordinary language" as well as from the *parole* discussed by Ferdinand de Saussure.

In the early 1960s I was a visiting professor in the United States which I then re-visited several times. But before, after, and some times even during my British and American sojourns I mainly studied Continental historicism, especially theories developed in German-speaking countries, and of course also a number of Italian philosophers and methodologists. My favorite authors were, and in the main still are, Hegel, Marx, and some of their German and Italian followers down to this postwar period. The books and articles that I listed above all come from this combination of interests and experiences. Most of them were written in Italian and then often translated; but quite a few were written directly in English – with the help, more often than not, of native speakers. Thus I find myself to be a twofold author even linguistically.

The double formation I have been describing was a good thing for me personally, but it was also a drawback to the diffusion of my ideas. In spite of many translations into various languages, in Italy I was known only for what appeared in Italian, and in the English-speaking world only for what appeared in English. Moreover, on the European Continent people thought that I was a semiotician, or a linguistic or analytical philosopher who did not give sufficient importance to history and society; while in the English-speaking countries people thought I was a historicist and not an analyst, or that I was *only* Hegelian, or *only* Marxist, and so on. I can report that when I was traveling between England and Italy in the 1950s I really had the impression of entering into a different world each time, and that communication between the two worlds was impossible or at least extremely difficult, or that the times were not ready for working contemporarily in the two of them. This impression lasted partially also in the 1960s and even in the 1970s, during my American trips.

From my double or perhaps manifold formation also came my various interests and – I admit it – my rather complicated production. As can be grasped even from the titles of many of my books and articles, I have been dealing with general semiotics, linguistic philosophy and the philosophy of language and other sign systems, the theory of language viewed as a sector of society, Marxist theory (not to the delight of the orthodox), the theory of ideology especially as an object of semiotic enquiry, the theory of social reproduction and the position of sign systems within it, and various problems in the "production, circulation, and alienation of linguistic and other communicative goods and commodities." The literature I used also came from various sources: it was mainly philosophical and semiotical, but also to some extent anthropological, economical, linguistic, and psychological. I was trying to solve, or at least to raise interdisciplinary problems, or problems that in my opinion did not receive adequate treatment by any given discipline and were usually disregarded by specialists.

Thus in *Language as Work and Trade* [cf. R.-L. 1968h; English transl. 1983b] I used conceptual instruments derived from economics, linguistics, and semiotics, and developed a theory of linguistic production and circulation that was already present but not fully expressed in my 1961 book on *Significato, comunicazione e parlare comune*. One central feature of the book is what I call "the homology of production" – in a few words the possibility of comparing "linguistic" with "material" artefacts; another, the beginnings of a theory of "linguistic alienation" which I then applied in other books, especially in *Semiotica e ideologia* (Semiotics and Ideology) [R.-L. 1972i]. Although in this latter book there are ideas that are not present in *Language as Work and Trade*, the two books go together in that the older one provides a theory which finds some applications in the more recent. *Semiotica e ideologia* also develops the idea that sign systems and ideologies are to be studied together because they are joined in reality and no separate approach would do.

Linguistics and Economics [R.-L. 1975b], which appeared directly in English, is a more systematic treatment of some (but not all) the basic ideas contained in the two books I just described. It contains some new developments, especially a much fuller analysis of the homology of production and the first hints at a topic which later became central in my teaching and in several articles: social reproduction. To conclude this very short survey, *Ideologia* [R.-L. 1978c; transl. as *Marxism and Ideology*, 1990] is a book-size development of ideas already partially contained in an essay of 1967 which was then collected in *Language as Work and Trade*, together, as it happens, with new ideas and within the framework of social reproduction. Although the tone of *Ideologia* is very theoretical, there are several long exemplifications, and there is also what I believe to be the first attempt at an interdisciplinary bibliography of alienation (I am still grateful to the two young graduate students who helped me in scrutinizing more than two thousand titles belonging to different fields of enquiry). One of the main tenets of *Ideologia* is that ideology cannot be approached by itself but has to be dealt with together with false consciousness and false praxis within the wider notion of alienation which contains them all.

I do not know whether I have succeeded in conveying something of my production through such a short presentation. But perhaps this is clear, that my main two subjects have been communication (especially, but by no means only, linguistic) and ideology, and that I have dealt with them either alternatively or jointly. This is also true of my forthcoming book *Metodica filosofica e scienza dei segni. Nuovi saggi sul linguaggio e sull'ideologia* (Philosophical Methodics and the Science of Signs. New Essays on Language and Ideology) [R.-L. 1985a], as the title shows, but which contains mainly materials of a methodological kind which were not used in any of my previous books.

If I were now to choose myself some sort of a general formula for describing the bulk of my production, I would say that in the main it is a synthesis of historical materialism on the one hand and analytical philosophy and semiotics on the other: the framework is historico-materialistic, the mentality and the techniques are, at least partially, analytical and semiotical. A synthesis, I said; and quite a few critics would agree. But perhaps it is only a mixture. Paraphrasing a famous saying by Wittgenstein, this is for the public to decide.

My two main hobbies are classical music and sailing, and this is not for the public to decide.

Ferruccio Rossi-Landi
Trieste, March 1984

I

SIGNS AND MASTERS IN SEMIOTIC HISTORY

1. A Fragment in the History of Italian Semiotics

Premise

Although I published in 1953 a full monograph on Charles Morris as the founder of twentieth-century semiotics, came back to him more than once, and also wrote something about Vailati, Wittgenstein, Ryle, and other contemporary thinkers, I cannot consider myself a professional historian of ideas. Even in the aforementioned writings my main interest was theoretical. I have only written books and articles about problems.

On the other hand, I have been laboring in semiotics and related fields for so many years, that I thought the readers of these *Proceedings* [cf. R.-L. 1988] may be interested in a report in which I can offer flour from my own mill; and a report is always something historical.

The paper is divided into two sections. In the first I make some general remarks on communication in the history of ideas, in the second I describe a couple of episodes in the recent history of semiotics of which I was the direct witness. The period considered goes from the early fifties to the early sixties. The remarks come from the episodes, but because of my theoretical bias I am placing them first.

1.1 Communication in the History of Ideas

The complexities of the communicative situation are all present in the history of ideas. There must be a sender, the author of a text, who transmits a message, his or her ideas, to receivers who are his or her contemporary or later readers. The author may also be writing for himself or herself, but as we find the text we can label him or her a sender who is entering a full communicative situation. Both author and readers are "dated" – it would make no sense to assume that there is a message whatsoever independent of the historical situation. Context, circumstances, channels, noise, disturbance are all highly complicated and extremely determined. And so are the codes and subcodes which are being used. An historian of ideas is a scholar presumably specialized in unraveling all these complexities to the effect of discovering what an author really meant and in explaining what his or her messages can possibly mean to us. The very phrase 'really meant' is a big problem in its own right.

But again, both sender and receiver are something much more complicated than mere individuals. They represent social groups, and are subject to determinations which are not only technical or theoretical but also, in a variety of senses, eminently practical. We shall revert to this point.

Meanwhile, let us continue to apply to the case in hand the jargon of information theory that seems to offer clarification even when it is misused. If a text is published, there is a channel at the end of which, in principle, it can be received. But what about noise and disturbance? I think we could say that the noise to which a cultural message is subjected when circulating may consist in such factors as the sheer lack of an *appropriate* journal or publishing firm, while the disturbance may be positive in the form of misrepresenting a given text, or even negative in the form of a lack of presentation of a text in places where it should be. In all these cases we can say that nothing similar to the original message has gone through, and it is difficult to distinguish between theoretical and practical dimensions as well as between various aspects of noise and disturbance. Also, the threshold beyond which disturbance becomes conscious and deliberate can be detected only sometimes, and only in individual cases. There is no general theory about it – so we have to cling to a number of theories concerning human nature. What I mean is that a receiver can "ignore" a cultural message for a variety of reasons: because the message, although it could reach him or her in principle, in fact does not; or because he or she does not understand it, at least or not fully, or understands it in a way which is removed from the intentions of the author; or because he or she sincerely considers it irrelevant; or, in some cases, because he or she is genuinely afraid of it and does whatever is possible to prevent its diffusion.

Difficulties in translating are of course always involved. They do not only concern the passage from one natural language into another. They also concern the common background of general ideas and even the existential situation of sender and receiver, and they are therefore also felt when communication takes place between a sender and a receiver who speak the same natural language, as happens with different schools of thought and different ideologies, or when we read something that was written in our own language years or centuries ago. Of this I shall give a couple of very simple examples.

Although an Italian-English dictionary rightly tells us that *esperienza* means 'experience,' at a cultural level the two words, in spite of the common root, do not have the same impact on an Italian or even Continental as on an English-speaking audience. Because of the British tradition from Francis Bacon through Locke, Berkeley and Hume, Bentham and John Stuart Mill, to modern times, there seems to be in 'experience' more rationality than in the Italian *esperienza* (I think the same obtains with the German *Erfahrung*, leaving alone the additional complication that in German you also have *Erlebnis*). The slicing of the cake 'experience-and-reason' is not the same. Thus, in many cases, a literal rendering of *esperienza* by 'experience,' or vice versa, simply would not do. The road is blocked by just one basic term.

My second example concerns the Italian philosopher and semiotician Giovanni Vailati (of whom more below). At the beginning of the century he was using such terms as 'psychology or 'anthropology' in a way so different from what we may understand by their use nowadays, that in order to fully construe his terminology we have to explain the state of those arts at his times; or alternatively, to understand his ideas we have to change the terminology. For instance, Vailati would speak about the "psychology of a word" while at the same time opposing psychologism in logic; it turns out that he had in mind something very similar to what was later to be called "the *logic* of a word."

The main factors are perhaps two. The first is that codes and subcodes are common to sender (author) and receiver (reader) only to a certain extent. Some times all they have in common is an understanding of the surface meanings of the words making up a text. The second factor is that the process of interpretation goes always much beyond the mere decoding of the received message. In fact, this is where code-and-message semiotics shows its enormous inadequacy. The circumstances of coding and decoding vary incessantly, and we know they are a mixture of theoretical and practical factors. Purely mythical is the idea of a channel exempt from noise and disturbance. Thus the cultural message, even when it does go through, is transformed by all those forces, and only an intense redundancy can, sometimes, make it overcome all the difficulties it encounters. One can see almost at a glance how all this applies to the history of ideas, especially when new ideas are introduced – and here it is almost irrelevant whether the ideas are "new" because they have been invented by an author, or simply because they are being transplanted from one cultural milieu into another. Notice that this transplantation can take place synchronically or diachronically: that is, it can consist in the contemporary presentation of the same ideas in two different cultural milieus; or in the re-presentation of some ideas at a successive stage of the very cultural milieu in which they originated, namely in a geographically identical or similar but historically diverse milieu. The case, instead, of the presentation of certain ideas both in another country and in a later period does not necessarily fall into any of the two above cases, for it well may be that a new milieu can accept the same ideas in a better way than the way they were received in the original milieu in a previous period. Plato did not like Democritus, but Galileo, Condillac and Marx certainly did.

How much the vicissitudes of ideas in general and of their cultural transmission are determined by a number of contingent factors can be briefly illustrated by an analysis of our own situation right here at an international conference. Many of us have given a paper, and we are all familiar with the fact that whether or not our ideas "go through" will depend on such varying factors as the following:

i. The level of organization we have reached in our own ideas and the amount of selective work we have put into the paper as such;

ii. Our command of the language in which we are giving the paper and the command of the same language in the audience;

iii. Whether we are reading a written text or just speaking, and at what speed, with what phonetic clarity or lack of clarity – in other words, our personal training in orally addressing an audience (let me add here, in an exhortative mood, that there are people who propound their paper in a mumbling way, possibly understandable only within a small group accustomed to their personal phonetic idiolects; they assume that there must be some sort of pasilalic dimension according to which their message must and will go through in spite of the complete lack of oral communicative techniques: it will go through, they seem to believe, by some sort of empathy, because of the very fact that they did write a text and they are sort of repeating it to themselves);

iv. The time we are allotted, and our use of it. Some lecturers are simply unable to *reduce* their exposition: they must stick to what they *have written*;

v. Our own personal conditions – physiological, psychological, social – both in general and at the moment when we are giving the paper;

vi. The mood of the audience, a situation which can in its turn be very diverse according to contingent factors such as time, weather, temperature, the disposition of chairs and seats in the hall, the success or failure of previous papers and the anticipation of later papers in the same section, etc;

vii. Last but not least, the existence of common interests and comparable intellectual preparation within the totality composed by speaker and audience.

And so on. Too contingent, someone could say. A written and published text is something different. This brings me to the fragment of Italian semiotics which gives the title to this paper.

1.2 Flour from My Own Mill

When, in 1953, I published my 1951 doctoral dissertation as a monograph on Charles Morris, I had some reasons for thinking that it might be accepted as a contribution to semiotics or at least to the philosophy of language. Such reasons were founded on the existence of a local, i.e. Italian tradition.

Apart from Medieval, Humanistic, and Renaissance approaches to questions of language, poetics, and rhetorics, it suffices here to recall two precedents, Vico and the so-called Italian pragmatists. When we come to Giambattista Vico (1668-1744) we face one of the greatest innovators of all times: an innovator, I mean, in the theory of language and cultural communication, and one who is proving, surprisingly, a contemporary of ours. This side to Vico's work was rediscovered by Isaiah Berlin as early as 1960; and owing to the excellent translations of his *Autobiography* and of *The New Science* made by Thomas G. Bergin and Max H. Fisch, and then to the Vichian work of Giorgio Tagliacozzo, Leon Pompa, Hayden V. White, Donald Ph. Verene, and many others, there is now an incredible Vico revival in the English-speaking world, especially in the United States. In 1953, however, my point was that most Italian philosophers had *always* considered Vico as an essential part of their formation. You cannot be a philosopher in Italy without dealing in one way or another with his ideas, and the same is true for many human scientists. Thus my reasoning, perhaps naive *but perhaps not*, was that *new* ideas in the philosophy of language and communication, and the foundation of a *new science* – semiotics – especially dedicated to sign systems of all description, *had* to appeal to the students of Vico's work and, in general, to Italian philosophical culture.

Moreover, as I said, there had been the Italian pragmatists. In the middle of the nineteenth century, Carlo Cattaneo (1801-1869), who was well acquainted with Vico, had already given an impulse toward something like semiotics or the philosophy of language. But it was with Giovanni Vailati (1863-1909) and Mario Calderoni (1879-1914) that attention to language became prominent in dealing with philosophical and related problems and a comparative, if not a global, approach to different sign systems began to form. Unfortunately, very little by Vailati and nothing by Calderoni, or nothing that I know of, was ever translated into English. The new edition of Peirce's *Writings* in chronological order and the *Complete Works* of Vailati [cf. Vailati, forthcoming; now 1987] will of course throw much new light on Italian pragmatists, on their relation to Peirce, and on the history of Italian semiotics since the beginning of our century.

Vailati and Calderoni were creative followers of Peirce whose importance and originality they immediately detected, carefully distinguishing his approach from that of William James. They were internationally known and corresponded with such scholars as Peirce himself, James, Mach, Frege, Lady Welby, and many others. But the whole school disappeared in the twenties. One of the reasons is connected to the early deaths of Vailati (at the age of 46) and Calderoni (34). Giovanni Gentile and Benedetto Croce, whom Vailati respected and who reciprocated his esteem, were ready to become the most influential Italian thinkers of that time. Then there was the war, then Fascism. Between the two World Wars there was little room for semiotics in Europe; on the other hand, one should not forget that Charles Morris's seminal *Foundations of the Theory of Signs* and *Signs, Language, and Behavior* only appeared in 1938 and 1946 respectively and were certainly not welcomed by American philosophers. In that period Federigo Enriques (1871-1946) continued to work, and Eugenio Colorni (1909-1944) left important manuscripts (cf. References). In the fifties, however, there began in Italy a revival of interests in the philosophy of science, analytical or linguistic philosophy, and thus also, at least potentially, in semiotics. I can name here Silvio Ceccato and Giuseppe Vaccarino with their individualistic operational theory of linguistic production; Nicola Abbagnano, Enzo Paci and Paolo Filiasi-Carcano for their enquiries into non-Italian contemporary ideas; the analytical philosophers of law Norberto Bobbio and Uberto Scarpelli; the historians of ideas Francesco Barone and Emanuele Riverso; and especially the philosopher of science Ludovico Geymonat, and Giulio Preti who shrewdly dealt with a number of problems in empiricism, phenomenology, and the philosophy of language. All these people gave a more or less direct contribution to preparing the ground for a rebirth of Italian semiotics, and it is a little surprising that contemporary

Italian semioticians seem to ignore how much they owe to them (some of their writings are listed in Rossi-Landi 1953[a], 1961[d], and 1978[e, this volume, Ch. 3]). The process described was still very slow, and it took years; but as I said it was not unreasonable to hope that a book on Morris and semiotics, while diverging from the main currents of Italian thought and in advance of them if measured against what did happen later on, could at least be welcomed by a number of scholars.

Nothing like that happened. My monograph was simply dismissed, or ignored. I had to reconcile myself with the fact that in that period Morris was still seen on the European Continent *only* as an analytical or linguistic philosopher of a neopositivist or neopragmatist description. Most of the discussion about him consisted in locating his ideas in this or that trend of contemporary American philosophy and in comparing his position with that of other philosophers of similar description. His originality was quickly perceived by a very few scholars, so much so that already in 1949 Ceccato produced a translation of *Signs, Language, and Behavior*; but, in spite of the Italian tradition I have briefly discussed above, a new idea of semiotics as a general science of signs could not yet form. The codes of sender and receiver were too different among philosophers, nor did linguists and other human scientists pay any heed to semiotics. (Incidentally, Morris's semiotics had formed outside of the human sciences, and Saussure's name is absent from his whole work. That he had never even *heard of* Saussure, was confirmed to me by Morris himself in July 1973.)

But the situation was different in 1961. Something like a philosophy of language had begun forming. A few linguists and other scholars were beginning to show some curiosity for a general theory of signs. Moreover, large selections of Antonio Gramsci's notebooks had been published in which he criticized Croce, highly praised Vailati, and showed a sustained interest in the philosophy of language. A translation of Morris's *Foundations* with commentary had appeared in 1954 [cf. R.-L. 1954d] and a selection of Vailati's papers in 1957 [cf. R.-L. 1957e, 1958c]. Thus when I published *Significato, comunicazione e parlare comune* (Meaning, Communication, and Common Speech) [R.-L. 1961d], I thought I could entertain the hope that it would not share the fate of the 1953 monograph. To quote from its Foreword (April 1961), the book was an attempt at "grafting some logico-linguistic techniques on the trunk of Continental historicism." The techniques were derived from Wittgenstein and analytical philosophy, semiotics, operationalism, and the Italian tradition centering on Vailati; the historicism taken account of was of the non-idealistic variety. My aim was to study the "meaningful conditions within common speech": a study that "had nothing to do with the cult of so-called everyday language or with other such philologizing or mathematizing mawkishness which ... had hindered the ability and the desire to think by problems." In fact, the book contained a full-winged critical discussion of some of the notions which were central in analytical and linguistic philosophy, and made a move toward a socially oriented theory of signs by introducing the notion of *common speech* as the set of techniques used to communicate and taught from generation to generation as a relevant or indeed central part of *social practice*. This involved the overcoming of the Saussurian dichotomy of *langue* and *parole* and the dismissing of the code-and-message approach, which presupposes previously formed individuals, in favor of a semiotics of interpretation where interpretation itself is a main factor in the forming of individuals. Many of my later ideas were already present, some times in an embryonic form, in the 1961 book. [In the References to this paper R.-L. lists 1968h, 1972i, 1974f, 1975d, 1978c, and 1978e, see the general bibliography of his writings at the end of this volume.]

But again, at the time, the book was viciously viewed solely as a contribution to analytical philosophy, and this in spite of the fact that its general framework derived from Vico, Kant, Hegel, Marx, and Peirce – not to speak of Bradley, the skeptic. The "trunk" was ignored, and so were the grafting operations; only the shoots were considered. It was a typically conservative reaction: had the grafting operations been considered, then the presence of the trunk had to be acknowledged too, and this involved the danger of preventing the idle iteration of commentary about the trunk in its isolation. In other words, my receivers were still dealing with traditional ideas of a presemiotic kind (the trunk); because of the changes that have intervened since 1953, some semiotic ideas could now be accepted; but what was completely denied was that such ideas might be accommodated *within* the Continental tradition.

I think these two examples – the flour from my own mill – well illustrate the theoretical remarks I made at the beginning on the communicative situation in the history of ideas. Cultural messages only go through if they are not too different from the messages usually exchanged in a given milieu. The majority tends to "kill" the minority. You cannot address an English audience in Chinese, or the other way around. For cultural communication to obtain, the codes and subcodes must be sufficiently similar *already*; and noise and disturbance must be relatively low. Alternatively, an enormous redundancy is required. To make clearer what I mean: if one wants to be properly understood, one has to repeat the same things in a high number of different occasions, through a high number of different channels. Cultural communication must become a sort of propaganda. Each author is then compelled to choose between concentrating on the production of ideas and waging a sort of warfare for conquering an audience. Here, again, we can see how inextricably fortuitous the tangle of theoretical and practical factors can be. And, as Caesar put it, "multum cum in omnibus rebus, tum in re militari potest fortuna."

References

Berlin, Isaiah. 1960. "The Philosophical Ideas of Giambattista Vico." In *Art and Ideas in Eighteenth-Century Italy*, 156-233. Rome: Edizioni di storia e letteratura.
———. 1976. *Vico and Herder*. London: Hogarth. Contains a considerably expanded version of Berlin 1960.
Calderoni, Mario. 1924. *Scritti*, 2 vols. Ed. by O. Campa. Florence: "La Voce."
Cattaneo, Carlo. 1960. *Scritti filosofici*, 3 vols. Ed. by N. Bobbio. Florence: Le Monnier.
Colorni, Eugenio. 1975. *Scritti*. Ed. by F. Rossi-Landi and N. Bobbio. Florence: La Nuova Italia.
Enriques, Federigo. 1958. *Natura, ragione e storia*. Ed. by L. Lombardo-Radice. Turin: Einaudi.
Gramsci, Antonio. 1975. *Quaderni dal carcere*. Critical edition in 4 vols. Ed. by V. Gerratana. Turin: Einaudi.
Morris, Charles. 1938. *Foundations of the Theory of Signs*. Chicago: University of Chicago Press. Italian transl. as *Lineamenti di una teoria dei segni*, with commentary by F. Rossi-Landi. Turin: Paravia, 1954, 1963(2).
———. 1946. *Signs, Language, and Behavior*. New York: Prentice-Hall. Italian transl. as *Segni, linguaggio e comportamento*, by S. Ceccato. Milan: Longanesi, 1949.
Peirce, Charles S. 1982. *Writings of Charles S. Peirce*. A chronological edition in twenty volumes. Ed. by M.A. Fisch, C.J.W. Kloesel, *et al.* Bloomington: Indiana University Press. [Vol. 1, 1982; vol. 2, 1984; vol. 3, 1986; vol. 4, 1986.]
Pompa, Leon. 1975. *Vico: A Study of the "New Science."* Cambridge: Cambridge University Press.
Rivista critica di storia della filosofia. 1963. Special issue on Giovanni Vailati, by various authors, 275-523.
Rossi-Landi, Ferruccio. [See the general bibliography of his writings at the end of this volume.]
Tagliacozzo, Giorgio. Cf. Vico, Giambattista.

Vailati, Giovanni. 1911. *Scritti*. Ed. by M. Calderoni, U. Ricci, and G. Vacca. Florence-Leipzig: Seeber-Barth.
——. 1957. *Il metodo della filosofia*. A selection of 11 writings. Ed. by F. Rossi-Landi. Bari: Laterza, 1967(2).
——. 1971. *Epistolario*. (1891-1909). Ed. by G. Lanaro. Turin: Einaudi.
——. 1972. *Scritti filosofici*. Ed. by G. Lanaro. Naples: Fulvio Rossi.
——. forthcoming. *Opere complete*, 4 volumes. Ed. by M. Quaranta. Bologna: Forni. [Published as *Scritti*. Ed. by M. Quaranta. Bologna: Forni, 1987.]
Various authors on Vico. Cf. Vico, Giambattista.
Verene, Donald Ph. 1981. *Vico's Science of Imagination*. Ithaca and New York: Cornell University Press.
Vico, Giambattista. 1969. *Giambattista Vico*. An international symposium. Ed. by G. Tagliacozzo and H.V. White. Baltimore: Hopkins.
——. 1975. *The Autobiography*. English transl. by T.G. Bergin and M.H. Fisch. Ithaca and London: Cornell University Press.
——. 1976a. *The New Science*. English transl. by T.G. Bergin and M.H. Fisch. Ithaca and London: Cornell University Press. First appeared in 1948.
——. 1976b. *Giambattista Vico's Science of Humanity*. Ed. by G. Tagliacozzo and D.Ph. Verene. Baltimore-London: Hopkins.
——. 1979. *Vico and Contemporary Thought*. Ed. by G. Tagliacozzo, M.J. Mooney, and D.Ph. Verene. Atlantic Highlands, N.J.: Humanities Press.
——. 1983. *Vico and Marx*. Ed. by G. Tagliacozzo. Atlantic Highlands, N.J.: Humanities Press.
White, Hayden, V. 1978. *Tropics of Discourse. Essays in Cultural Criticism*. Baltimore: Hopkins.

2. Signs about a Master of Signs

2.1 A Personal Premise

In preparing some remarks about the writings of Charles Morris which are reprinted in this volume [cf. Morris 1971b],[1] I have encountered a particular difficulty, in addition to those common to this sort of enterprise. Since its consequences are going to creep up anyhow in these pages, I may as well declare what the difficulty is at the beginning, even though this may have a personal ring which is usually better excluded from scientific discourse. Morris is one of the authors I have studied most. In 1951-1952 I wrote a monograph examining all of his publications up to that date (Rossi-Landi 1953[a]). At that time a monograph-length study may possibly have seemed excessive; it does not any longer, now that Morris's place as the most important representative of twentieth century semiotics has been generally recognized, and now that semiotics itself, in the fifties still considered an appendix of philosophy or a biological science, has acquired an independent status of its own as a social science[2] and is practiced by hundreds of scholars in all countries, overcoming the very distinctions between "Western" and "Oriental" culture, or those between individual-centered and society-centered communities.[3] I returned repeatedly to Morris ([R.-L.] 1953[b], 1954[d], 1958[a]); but from around 1955 I began to try to bring together, as I expressed it at the time, elements of the theory of Marxism with elements of "analytical" philosophy, so to say grafting "logico-linguistic" techniques onto the trunk of integral historicism (1961[d]). During that period, Morris, like many of his English-speaking colleagues, was still seen on the Continent as an "analytical" or "linguistic philosopher." Much time has passed. Semiotics has become established, and all of us who were paleo-semioticians have followed our own paths. My present tendency is to locate semiotics in a study of the relations between "structure" and "superstructure" (1968[h], 1972[i], and work in progress [now 1975b]). I will come back to this at the end of the article. Well, this is the difficulty: having begun to deal with Morris a quarter of a century ago, and having then followed a different path, it has now been arduous for me to deal with the same author with objectivity, making sure that I was not falling into any generational abuse. Twenty-five years is a long time, even for a great love.

2.2 Remarks about This Selection

Writings on the General Theory of Signs (= *WGTS*) contains Morris's two most important works in the field of general semiotics: *Foundations of the Theory of Signs* (= *FTS*), which appeared in 1938 as vol. I number 2 of the *International Encyclopedia of Unified Science*; and *Signs, Language, and Behavior* (= *SLB*) (1946), a book which has often been reprinted and is universally translated (to my knowledge, the first translation was by Silvio Ceccato into Italian, appearing in Milan in 1949). *FTS* is Part One of *WGTS*; *SLB* is Part Two; Part Three is entitled "Five Semiotical Studies" and includes "Signs and the Act" (Chapter I of *Signification and Significance*, 1964), "Esthetics and the Theory of Signs" of 1939, "Signs about Signs about Signs" of 1948, "Mysticism and Its Language" of 1957, and "Man-Cosmos Symbols" of 1956.

Unfortunately, the volume lacks not only a Bibliography of writings *on* Morris but indeed even a Bibliography of the writings *of* Morris. In order to identify the origin of the writings selected, one must consult and compare the "Acknowledgements" on p. 5, Morris's "Foreword" (pp. 7-8), the note to the title of *FTS* on p. 13, the note to the title of *SLB* on p. 73, and, finally, the "Pagination Concordance" on pp. 481-486. In the "Pagination Concordance," however, the places where the writings originally appeared are not given, so that one has to go back and forth every time. A bibliography of Morris's writings would have presented these data, and it would have been even better to bring together all relevant information in a unitary table at the beginning or at the end of *WGTS*. Certainly, in the excellent bibliography added by Morris to *SLB* (here [*WGTS*] on pp. 369-397, for Morris himself see p. 387) there is also a selection of his writings from 1927 to 1942 (thirteen, to be exact). But the reader must do all the work of fitting the pieces together by himself, up to the point of discovering and consulting a bibliography which is internal to one of the volumes reproduced, and what is more, incomplete. In *WGTS* there is an Index of Names (pp. 467-472) and a Subject Index (pp. 473-480). The latter is insufficient, because it contains only references regarding *SLB* (including, however, references to the Glossary added by Morris to that book, here [WGTS] on pp. 359-368), which prevents one from grasping the continuity of terms and concepts before and after 1946.

The reasoning of author, editor, and publisher in making the present selection is comprehensible. Their intention was to unite in one ample but not excessive volume the two principal writings of Morris on the theory of signs (Parts One and Two) and to then offer some examples of application (Part Three). This intention has been realized. I propose, however, a possible alternative: four separate volumes could be published for a total number of pages which, after all, would not be too much greater than the present number, as follows: Volume I, a selection of writings prior to *FTS* (for their importance, see Section 2.3 below); Volume II, *FTS*; Volume III, *SLB*; Volume IV, a much more ample selection of the applicative or lateral writings which appeared both before and after *SLB*, but in any case post-*FTS*. In the two collections of essays of Volumes I and IV, for reasons which we will be discussing presently, writings on values should also appear. Above all, each one of these large or small volumes should be placed historically by means of an ample preface, prepared by some student of Morris from the United States, and should be equipped with all the necessary bibliographical material: just as Morris himself did for his own master, George Herbert Mead.

In its present form, *WGTS* has little to say to one who is already acquainted with Morris's thought, and, given its size, it is not a substitute for the original volumes, which are handier to consult and less expensive. At the same time, it catches unawares scholars not directly acquainted with Morris, especially those young students of semiotics and related disciplines who, though they must have heard about him, have never happened to see his texts in their entirety. The rest of this review article serves to clarify these statements. It is useful, however, to advance one preliminary explanation. Each of the writings reproduced in *WGTS* was published in a particular American and international philosophical situation, at a moment which can be well identified, and which Morris studied accurately, in the development of the human sciences which were, or which he believed to be, closest to semiotics. They appeared at a given level of the discussion preparatory to the affirmation of twentieth century semiotics. Morris had to take all this into account, and seriously (it is sufficient to look at the diligence and integrity of his "replies to the philosophers" in "Signs about Signs about Signs" of 1948). Each of the writings reprinted here, therefore, has had the significance of a step forward in semiotics at a given moment of its history, or, if we like, of its prehistory. So much so that in Morris's thought on semiotics there are at least two different fundamental approaches, that of *FTS* and that of *SLB* (see below, Sections 2.4 and 2.5). But since in *WGTS* the various works are not placed and commented upon historically, the reader finds himself facing pages which, already uneven in themselves to some extent, seem to be even more uneven than they actually were when they first appeared because the necessary equipment for properly understanding and assessing them is lacking. As it is, the volume presumes that a reader of the seventies should be automatically able to furnish by himself the historical placement of writings of the thirties and forties. Instead, this is just what ought to have been supplied to the new reader.

With this insistence on the "reproductive" *and therefore* "a-historical" character of *WGTS*, I certainly intend to plead the cause for the history of ideas, or better, for the historical dimension in general, which I consider of decisive importance also for semiotics. However, I do no intend in the least to substitute an interest in the history of ideas for an interest in theoretical semiotics. Ideas come and go, and the theory of signs is still a long way from having received a unitary, universally accepted foundation. Its relations with philosophy – whether this is a mother-science, or a sister-science, or perhaps a nonscience – for example, are far from final clarification. The same can be said of its relations with biology. Ideas go and come, and the discussions Morris held with philosophers and biologists in the thirties and forties retain much value precisely as instruments for the clarification of basic theoretical questions. To the criticism he received, Morris in those years sometimes gave explicit replies, sometimes replies included in the solutions he proposed to problems (often real working instruments). Today, there is a tendency to raise those replies and solutions above their respective situations, I believe with the intention of throwing light on their residual theoretical vitality. But this procedure risks instead making them into objects which are *only* historical, and transforming then into documents of semiotic archeology. Thus a result is obtained which is the opposite of the one desired.

2.3 Semiotics and Philosophy

WGTS begins with *FTS* of 1938. In Morris's Bibliography, before *FTS* there are 35 titles: 23 books and articles (1927-1938) and 12 reviews (1927-1936). It is from this material that a selection should be made for the first volume of the *Works* of Morris. Here we find the important volume *Six Theories of Mind* (1932[a]), which leads to the identification of the mind with the symbolic process, and numerous analyses of those of the principal currents of American and European thought that appeared best adapted to flow into a general semiotics. The reader can glimpse all this well enough by running through the titles of Section 2.10.

The problem of the sign, which had been faced in openly behavioristic terms in an article of 1927, "The Concept of the Symbol," is taken up again by Morris some ten years later, when in his mind a synthetic – one would almost say syncretistic – attitude had formed. It was only then that his approach to the problems of signs took the form of a general theory. In the article "Philosophy of Science and Science of Philosophy" (1935[a]), Morris analyzed some of the conceptions of philosophy which were current in those years; such analysis is to be found again in later writings, up to and including *FTS*. The conceptions analyzed are *philosophy as logic of science*, connected especially with the name of Carnap; *philosophy as clarification of meaning*, present in American pragmatism and in one wing of the Vienna Circle (the first Wittgenstein, Schlick, Waismann; the second Wittgenstein, Moore and their advocates in Great Britain – it is remarkable how these different philosophers appear to be unified by one of their basic interests when we view them in perspective); and, finally, *philosophy as empirical axiology*, as found in Schlick and especially in Dewey. If we accept these three conceptions together, Morris said, we have philosophy as a "language of languages" or a general theory of symbolism. Various aspects of this idea were investigated – to quote only some main articles – in "The Concept of Meaning in Pragmatism and Logical Positivism" (1936[b]), "Pragmatism and Metaphysics" (1934), "The Relation of the Formal and Empirical Sciences with[in] Scientific Empiricism" (1935[b]), "The Relation of Formal to Instrumental Logic" (1929[b]). The relations of a theory of symbolism with pragmatism were analyzed in "Peirce, Mead, and Pragmatism" (1938[b]), in the introductions to Mead's works (1934[b], 1938[d]) and, later, also in "William James Today" (1942 [c]). *Scientific empiricism* was thus developed. The relationships between the above-mentioned trends and the dimensions of semiotics had been sketched out as early as 1935 in the article "Semiotic and Scientific Empiricism." When we examine the meaning of an expression from the point of view of its relations with other expressions (syntactic dimension), with the things meant (semantic dimension) and with those who make use of it (pragmatic dimension), said Morris, we open the path to its full determination. In traditional empiricism three principal defects could be found: the insufficient justice accorded to formal sciences, the inability to connect an empirical theory of meaning to a naturalistic cosmology, and the tendency to subjectivism. A scientific empiricism which has been transformed into a semiotics permits an understanding of each one of these three defects as arising from the neglect of one of the three dimensions of signs.

Of particular importance is the small volume *Logical Positivism, Pragmatism, and Scientific Empiricism* (1937), in which five of the above writings (cf. Section 2.10) are brought together. For an appropriate philosophical and genetical comprehension of Morris's semiotics, this volume, at least, should be reprinted today. The article "Scientific Empiricism" (1938[a]) is a reworking of the volume's contents for the *Encyclopedia of Unified Science*, the program of which had been developed at the "Congress of Philosophical Science" of 1935; in fact *FTS* appeared in the *Encyclopedia*. It is important, Morris insisted, to embrace an empiricism which is radical, a rationalism which is a study of method, and a pragmatism which is critical. These are the three components that correspond to the *three dimensions of semiotics*. Radical empiricism is *semantic* investigation, methodological rationalism is *syntactic* investigation, critical pragmatism is *pragmatic* investigation. The unity of science thus results from the unity of its linguistic structure, from the semantic relationships which it succeeds in establishing, and from the practical effects it produces. Notice that in this way even the three traditional fields of philosophy – logic, metaphysics, and the theory of values – were indirectly re-presented in semiotic terms.

All this may seem surprising to anyone coming to semiotics without a taste of philosophico-historical culture, and accepting the tripartition of semiotics as a mere result of objective investigation carried out on signs. Instead, such "objective" investigation would not have been possible without the described confluence of different currents of thought. Objectivity is always a complex result, even if afterwards it may present itself to us as simple. Humanity came to the construction of its first objective techniques at a relatively late stage of prehistory, and every child begins to practice objective methods at a relatively late stage in his life. *Generalized* scientific objectivity was only achieved for the first time in the seventeenth century. Objectivity can appear to us afterwards as simple precisely because its structure, as a sum of positive choices, refers back negatively to a myriad of *other* choices, in this way bearing within itself the indirect solution to numerous other problems.

As already mentioned, there are at least two main conceptions of semiotics running through Morris's works: semiotics as the heir of philosophy and the organ of the sciences – expressed especially in the preparatory writings indicated above and then in *FTS*; and semiotics as a basically biological science, or better, as a science which is behavioral in a biological sense – expressed especially in *SLB*. In the first case, philosophical discourse, provided it keeps itself up to date with regard to the development of both formal and empirical sciences, becomes semiotic discourse; in the second case, instead, philosophical discourse is considered on a plane with other possible discourses, subject to semiotic investigation. Both of these positions have been superseded and contain contingent elements together with valid elements, and both are well worthy of discussion and integration. I have already dealt with them at some length in other writings of mine, to which I refer the reader, even if I consider them obviously out-of-date (Rossi-Landi 1953[a], 1953[b], 1954[d], 1958[a]). As for the disquieting problems of the relationships between semiotics – as it has developed in the last thirty years and prospers today – and whatever may still be understood as philosophy, they cannot be faced within a review article like this.[4]

In what follows, through the discussion of some specific Morrisian problems, several elements will emerge for the examination of the two principal solutions he offered. Another aspect of Morris's production, however, will remain outside our discussion, that of the relations between signs and values; so it would be well, before going ahead, to give it at least a brief look.

A glance at the bibliography in Section 2.10 below makes it apparent, even to readers unacquainted with Morris's work, that he dealt with values as much or even more than he dealt with signs. The main titles are: *Paths of Life: Preface to a World Religion* (1942[b]); *The Open Self* (1948[c]); *Varieties of Human Value* (1956[b]); *Signification and Significance. A Study of the Relations of Signs and Values* (1964[a]); and there are many essays in addition to these volumes. In *WGTS* only the first chapter, "Signs and the Act," of *Signification and Significance* is reproduced (pp. 401-414), and it does not deal with values but with signs. We cannot introduce here for discussion ideas taken from any of Morris's writings on values. In *WGTS*, however, "Esthetics and the Theory of Signs" (1939[b]) is also included. By common judgment, this is perhaps the single essay which has most contributed to the formation of an esthetic semiotics in the proper sense, now universally diffuse and indispensable. It is also one of the places where Morris dealt expressly with signs and values in the course of the same discussion. In order briefly to indicate the way in which values are connected to signs in Morris's production, let us therefore take advantage of the presence of this essay in *WGTS*.

What Morris always proposed was not an esthetics which is semiotic, or even more narrowly, only semantic; but rather a semiotics with its three dimensions, which is esthetic insofar as it applies to the field of art. The difference between an "esthetic semiotics" and a "semiotic esthetics" is that the former is a particular application of the science of signs, and as such is a bridge between art and all that goes into the foundations of the science of signs. The latter, instead, may even be a Speculative Esthetics as a sector of some Philosophical Superscience; it may content itself with the use, some use, of some semiotical instruments.

Now the field of esthetic criticism in a wide sense, according to Morris, comprehends both esthetic analysis and esthetic judgment (the latter being esthetic criticism in the narrow sense). Both disciplines are metalinguistic because they deal with signs. The signs they deal with are the signs of which a word of art consists. According to the well-known definition of the esthetic sign "as an iconic sign whose *designatum* is a value" ([WGTS] p. 421), signs and values are thus both present. But while esthetic analysis as a sector of semiotic analysis belongs to scientific discourse, esthetic criticism belongs to "technological" discourse. Any discourse in which evaluations have taken place is 'technological': a point which becomes clearer when one knows that in the years of "Esthetics and the Theory of Signs" Morris considered as principal three types of discourse: scientific, esthetic, and technological (especially in "Science, Art, and Technology" [1939c]). In "Empiricism, Religion, and Democracy," of 1942, the types of discourse become four. This was the beginning of the process which brought Morris to the classification of Types of Discourse in *SLB* (Chapter V, pp. 203-232). If judgment belonged to technological discourse, esthetic criticism required not only a theory of signs (sufficient for esthetic analysis); it also required a theory of values (cf. Section 3 and 12 of "Esthetics and the Theory of Signs," [WGTS], pp. 418-419 and 431-433). In this way esthetic criticism involved values at two levels: at the level of esthetic analysis, because of the value bearing character of esthetic signs; and at the level of esthetic judgment, because of the necessity of a theory of values.

Known chiefly, at least internationally, as a student of signs from the beginning of his scientific career, Morris was thus placing values beside signs, and he always opposed the idea that the mere study of signs could give any right to judge about values. Right or wrong as he may have been in those years, present-day discussions on the relations between systems of signs and systems of values and ideologies (cf. again Kristeva, Rossi-Landi, and Schaff;

as well as Rastier and Verón) make it clear that not even Morris's own semiotics can be completely understood and properly assessed unless his theory of values is also taken into account.

2.4 At the Threshold of "Social Practice" in *FTS*

One thing that strikes readers of *FTS* a third of a century after it was written is the breadth of the approach. I dealt with this in "Universo del discorso e lingua ideale in filosofia" (1958), where I attempted an interpretation of the two principal phases of Morris's semiotics both in terms of the "special" (or "technical," or "ideal") languages purposely constructed to talk about signs in general, and in terms of the universes of discourse into which the special languages themselves could be included. Here I only want to stress again that the breadth of the approach in *FTS* can be seen in the following directions:

i. Morris presented a global situation in which the terms he introduced as fundamental – 'sign,' 'designatum,' 'interpretant', and 'interpreter' – "involve one another, since they are simply ways of referring to aspects of the process of semiosis" (*WGTS*, p. 19).

> The properties of being a sign, a designatum, an interpreter, or an interpretant are relational *properties which things take on* by participating in the functional process of semiosis. Semiotic, then, is not concerned with the study of a particular kind of object, but with ordinary objects in *so far (and only in so far)* as they participate in semiosis. ([*WGTS*], p. 20; [my italics, R.-L.])

Sign properties, then, are not "objective" properties like color, form, or weight; but neither are they "subjective" properties like taste, pleasure, pain. They are *nonobjective properties which any object can acquire in given circumstances*. The circumstances are those forming the global situation of semiosis. Given an approach of this kind, various remarks can be made regarding in particular the classes and systems of objects *purposely produced* for use as signs. The specific character of a large part of sign production seems to be an argument against Morris's approach. It can be maintained, in fact, that sign objects, once produced, exist in reality within their systems, and that therefore it is not true that they are nonobjective properties. But to this one can answer that the objects produced must be, in fact, *produced*, and then *used*, that is, that human operation always enters into the question; and this seems to be an argument in favor of Morris's approach. The above objection stresses in its way the separation between the products and the process of production and reproduction; the answer stresses the tie between products, on the one hand, and production, reproduction, and use, on the other. Both have their validity, and perhaps the contrast may be resolved by avoiding to confuse the nonobjective character of signs as such with the objective character of the *use of* signs. The use of signs organized in systems is a social reality, and as such is objective at least in the sense that no individual or group of individuals can change it at will. But it does not follow from the objective character of the behavioral habits of any human community or of society as a whole that the signs thus used are themselves objective instruments. If they were, demystification would never be possible. That any piece of demystification is always arduous precisely because of the objective character of social habits, is another aspect of the problem. The fact remains, however, that for Morris in *FTS*, *any object can become a sign*, provided some qualifications are made as to the use of 'object'; this is undoubtedly true, and it is the broadest approach that can be given to general semiotics.

ii. "Nothing is intrinsically a sign or a sign-vehicle," Morris later stated, "but becomes such only in so far as it permits something to take account of something through its mediation." This holds true also for meaning – for all meanings of 'meaning':

> Meanings are not to be located as existences at any place in the process of semiosis but are to be characterized in terms of this process as a whole. 'Meaning' is a semiotical term and not a term in the thing-language; to say that there are meanings in nature is not to affirm that there is a class of entities on a par with trees, rocks, organisms, and colors, but that such objects and properties function within processes of semiosis. ([*WGTS*], p. 57)

Meaning is thus extended to the whole situation of semiosis. We will come back to this point in Section 2.8 below.

iii. The fundamental terms introduced to describe the global situation of semiosis were traced back, at least hypothetically, to a single term, the 'mediated-taking-account-of' ([*WGTS*], pp. 19-21, 45, and *passim*). This primitive term was then in its turn to be traced back, especially in *SLB* ([*WGTS*], p. 108, note I), to behavioral biopsychology. In *FTS* it was introduced *alongside* the notion of "habits of behavior" in the use of a language (and thus also, necessarily, in the use of any verbal or nonverbal sign system whatsoever), and indeed ended up by becoming identified with it (*FTS*, [*WGTS*], pp. 37, 41-42, 59). Morris was explicit: "the interpretant of a sign is the habit ...," etc. (p. 47). The notion of habit is not completely clarified, nor could it have been in such a brief investigation as *FTS*; moreover, much water has flowed under the innumerable bridges of philosophy and science in these decades. From what one derives from rereading *FTS*, the notion of "behavioral habit in the use of signs" can be referred to: (a) personal characteristics of those who use a sign system; (b) biopsychological processes common to all the individuals who have that habit, when the individuals are considered in their psycho-physical materiality; (c) social facts and processes, with reference to the community to which the individuals belong and of which they are the products, or with reference to sections of such communities (the position, for example, of the exploited or of the exploiters); (d) social facts and processes with reference to general features of human society as such; (e) the specific operations, which may be formally extrapolated and described, carried out by those who are practicing that habit, that is, the techniques that anyone who uses a sign system has learned, possesses, and applies in a way which is common to other speakers and listeners (such in a proper or in a metaphorical sense) and which he can apply in a way which is more or less correct.

Clearly, the notion of habit is to be viewed in terms of disciplines which contemporary research considers as interconnected in varying degrees. Morris insists on the type of behaviorism he prefers: not a strictly biological behaviorism of the Watsonian sort, which in terms of the history of ideas is mechanistic materialism, but rather – through the broader behaviorism of Tolman and Hull – a declaredly social behaviorism like Mead's. To conclude, it seems to me legitimate to advance the interpretation most favorable to Morris: he had abandoned the narrow paths of *behaviorism* and had ventured onto the terrain of a *behavioristics* (he uses this term himself) which may end up by becoming identified with the study of praxis or human action in general. Since man is man only socially, human action could have been understood by Morris himself as *social practice*.

With the notion of social practice, there comes a pretty big leap outside the tradition of thought to which Morris belongs. Social practice, in fact, is the central pillar of the dialectico-materialistic and historico-materialistic conception of the world. In a material world, existing in reality, some animals that exist in reality started to *work*, that is, they developed a social practice which was new and different from that of all other animals. In this way man arose with his new *sign systems*, based fundamentally on *work* and on *exchange*. Historical evolution superimposed itself on biological evolution. Social practice has continued to develop in its three principal forms: the struggle for production, i.e. the appropriation and transformation of natural resources; class struggle in a wide sense, both within every community and among different communities; and scientific research. It has thus also produced the myths, the illusions, the moral techniques and the techniques of control that it needed as it went along – *including wildly different conceptions of reality*. The main point here is that the very conception of reality prevailing at any given moment is an expression of the dominant social practice, and not the other way around (cf. my paper on Mao Tse-tung, forthcoming [now 1973e]). To believe instead that social practice founded itself on a given conception of reality amounts to making a colossal inversion. This, however, does not mean that conceptions of reality are deprived of the possibility of retro-acting on social practice.

To found all knowledge on social practice means that one must have happened to follow, or have preferred to follow after due consideration, the current of thought which, through Kant and Hegel, reaches Marx, and then continues to the modern masters of Marxism. It is a fundamental theoretical and existential choice, different from the fundamental theoretical and existential choices that lead one to embrace any of the forms of idealism and, likewise, any of the forms of empiricism. It does not follow upon this choice at all that discoveries and methods of thought elaborated within various idealistic currents, much less those elaborated within the more scientifically minded empiricistic currents, must be refused. Actually, what is happening under our eyes in the seventies is a cross-fertilization of currents and approaches whose roots can be found in philosophically divided quarters. Semiotics itself is both result and agent of such cross-fertilization.

But this is not the place to continue the discussion of social practice; nor do we want to weigh down the References with many entries which would be substantially extraneous to the scope of this simple review article. In describing the breadth of interests and the profundity of views reached by Morris at the end of the thirties, we must notice the fact that his "philosophical synthesis leading to semiotics" was so vivacious that it succeeded in expressing itself even in concepts which were absent from his own tradition of thought, or just barely touched upon there, and instead considered fundamental elsewhere. Semiotics was born from truly magnanimous loins.

2.5 Semiotics as a Biological Science in *SLB*

According to a strictly behavioristic interpretation, the basic term of semiotics, the interpretant or 'mediated-taking-account-of,' is not only *accompanied by* other terms or *identified with* one of them (as, in several passages of *FTS*, with 'habit'); rather, it is *reduced to* a term which belongs to a specific field of inquiry and which brings with it a different conceptual framework. Let us look at this a little more closely. In *SLB*, the 'mediated-taking-account-of' was a response of a special type to what is called a preparatory stimulus. An organism responded to something through the mediation of something else. One could continue to consider the 'mediated-taking-account-of' as *the* fundamental term only if one saw it within the biological science of behavior. In fact, as already mentioned, Morris pointed out explicitly that his analysis "resolves this primitive term into the stimulus, response, and organic state terminology of behavioristics" ([*WGTS*], p. 108, note I). This meant neither more nor less than that the science of signs was biologically founded; it was, to be exact, a slice of behavioristic biopsychology. The fundamental terms, now, were actually those of that science. The special language of semiotics was built on them; its universe of discourse, strictly speaking, could contain only what they already contained, or what could be put into them. Having discarded such ambiguous terms as 'thought,' 'consciousness,' or 'concept,' and in general the whole apparatus of so-called 'mentalistic' tradition, Morris insisted on Peirce's interpretant and its interpretability as a differential response. In *FTS* there had been only a hint of a different position; now Morris's whole position became stronger while becoming narrower. This happened through two important innovations. The first is that the theory of signs was now considered not just as philosophy or as an organ of philosophy, but as a science in its own right; the second, that any ambiguity about the interpretation of the 'taking-account-of' was eliminated. These were two able and intelligent innovations, certainly the fruit of much thought. The separation of semiotics from philosophy broke up the biology-philosophy connection, eliminating the risk of a comical thesis like that of the direct interpretability of philosophical problems in biological terms. The definitive behavioristic choice strengthened the biology-behaviorism-semiotics relationship. Semiotics, when it tried to establish what philosophy might mean from its point of view, looked for and found in philosophy only a particular aspect of linguistic behavior. In so doing it reproduced in its own way a basic approach of the analytic philosophy of language: the reduction of philosophical problems to logico-linguistic problems.

Now the fact is that the way semiotics has developed has shown that it is necessarily a social discipline, or at least a discipline which is predominantly social. Signs-systems develop in societies. A society *is* a set of sign systems taken as an organized whole, even if it is not *only* this. Animal sign systems, so-called natural signs interpreted by men or by other animals, and the genetic code are usually brought up as exceptions. But the first two are not really exceptions. Animal sign systems, in fact, are *also* social, though in a reduced sense; this has become apparent since the beginning of a study of animal societies which has renounced all Cartesian dualism regarding men and thus also all dualism regarding men and animals, and by the consequent discovery of animal teaching. The continuity between men and other animals has thus been accentuated. "Natural" signs, like all other signs, are such only for an interpreter; they too are therefore *also* social. We call them 'natural' because their vehicles or "bodies" exist in nature instead of being produced by men or other animals.[5] As for the genetic code, it does not belong certainly to the level of behavioristic biopsychology, but to that of matter that organizes itself in order to reproduce given structures (cf. Jakobson's discussion on this, 1973: 50-55; and Masters 1970). Its extraordinary similarities to the verbal code do not constitute an argument for the biological explanation of other facts which are social. There is perhaps some tendency to metaphor in talking about the genetic code in terms of codes and messages. By means of the genetic code an *obligatory reproduction based on servo-mechanisms* takes place. 'Interpreters,' in Peirce and Morris's sense, who (voluntarily or not) exchange messages after having (voluntarily or not) codified them, and who in principle can also avoid the obligatory character of the message, do not exist here. At any rate, the fact that semiotics is a predominantly social science does not require it to be exclusively social. If we find biological confirmations of our discipline, and confirmations in the direction of dialectical materialism, so much the better. The problem remains open.

2.6 Sign-behavior vs. Behavior-as-communication

The construction of *SLB* rested in great measure on the identification and definition of the sign and sign-behavior. The field was immediately narrowed down by taking into consideration only goal-seeking behavior, or certain types of goal-seeking behavior. "Goal-seeking behavior in which signs exercise control," said Morris, "may be called *sign-behavior*" ([*WGTS*], p. 85). It was with much caution, and by successive approximations, that he came to his well-known and still seminal definition of 'sign':

> *If anything, A, is a preparatory stimulus which in the absence of stimulus-objects initiating response-sequences of a certain behavior-family causes a disposition in some organism to respond under certain conditions by response-sequences of this behavior family, then A is a sign.* ([*WGTS*], p. 87; italics in the text)

In my 1953 monograph on Morris, I had subjected this definition to criticism which – right or wrong as it may have been – was intended to get to the root of Morris's thought. My view consisted particularly in this: that it was not really possible to distinguish between sign-behavior and non-sign-behavior *by means of behavioristic biopsychology*. This implied that the distinction was, however, possible through other means. I willingly abandon such criticism to readers who know Italian and are interested in tracing the spread of logical positivism, and of the other currents of thought which flowed into Morris's semiotics, along with semiotics itself in its initial phase, in a very restive cultural environment like that in Italy in the early fifties.

In this section I should like to advance a few remarks of a different type, even if in some ways recalling the criticism of twenty years ago. It is not possible to distinguish between sign-behavior *tout court* and non-sign-behavior *tout court*, I now maintain, for the good reason that *all* behavior *is* sign-behavior. Here we are discussing not only Morris's thought, but the thing itself. The thesis is that any behavior communicates something and that, conversely, nothing can be communicated if not by means of some piece of behavior. Let us rapidly examine these statements.

Given the two very general categories, communication and behavior, we want to know their relationships of co-presence and of exclusion. There are four possibilities: neither behavior nor communication, communication and behavior, behavior without communication, communication without behavior. The first just takes away any object for inquiry. The second is obvious: there is nothing to object to the fact that behavior and communication *accompany each other*. For example, one makes a gesture or a series of gestures and thus communicates something; and another communicates by emitting articulated sounds constructed into meaningful sentences, that is, by means of verbal linguistic behavior. There remain the other two possibilities. Can there be behavior without communication? Can there be communication without behavior? The answer to both is "no."

There can be no *behavior without communication* because one cannot conceive that a human or nonhuman animal that behaves in some way, carries out some activity, in short, *does* something, is communicating nothing at all. This is true (i) in the sense that no animal can ever live *without* codes and *without* "social programmings" of his individual behavior (cf. Rossi-Landi 1972[i], Chapter XVII [2nd. ed. 1979, Chapter XV]; "Linguistics and Economics" [1974f], 1.4 and 7.5; and the references given there); and (ii), in the sense that by observing what the animal is doing or *is not doing* information can always be gained. It is only when we reduce the totality of communication to some of its sectors – for example, to those which are usually defined as conscious and/or intentional and/or finalistic – that we can then differentiate between some behavior which is sign and therefore communicative behavior, and other behavior. This 'other behavior' is declared to be non-sign, non-communicative, because it falls outside a preselected zone. The reduction, already present in the premise, emerges again in the conclusion. But really we have only distinguished between two different types of sign-behavior, between two different types of communication.

It does not take much to show that there is unconscious and/or unintentional and/or nonfinalistic (spontaneous, free, casual) behavior (and it neither proves nor disproves the doctrine of the finalism of life in general). If I speak to you, I usually *intend* to communicate something to you and am usually *conscious* of it. But certainly, if you know me and you observe me closely while I am talking to you, I also communicate other things to you which can escape even my own attention. If I keep quiet, but I scratch my head without realizing it, or I sigh or make a gesture which I do not heed, I communicate information to you about myself all the same. I do it without knowing it or wanting to, without having the intention, without any aim; and it often happens that what I communicate in these ways is indeed in contrast with an aim I do have.[6] In short, the fact is that the types of behavior "excluded" from the preselected zone are also, so to speak, "full of signs"; they cannot be otherwise because they are founded in any case on codes, are programmed, and therefore lend themselves to interpretation. A man who walks along the road without in the least paying attention to what he is doing is never a mere body moving in space and time: he is a man dressed in a certain way, who is walking in a certain way along a certain road, and so forth. With all the specifications he bears and which surround him, he cannot avoid communicating to an observer a large amount of information about himself and about the social group to which he belongs. We do not want to deny that, for certain very precise purposes, the behavior of the walker can be isolated from everything else, or considered only from the point of view of what he knows about himself in that moment, or compared to previously prepared paradigms of what a piece of behavior has to be in order to be described as sign-behavior. As a result of all this, in given circumstances it is appropriate to call it non-sign-behavior. Similarly, we do not want to deny that the behavior (examined by Morris) of the dog who interprets the buzzer as a sign for food is a typical, clear, and accessible case of sign-behavior, where the inception of a new sign, which had been expected and hoped for, and the consequences which derive from it in the behavior of the dog, are particularly evident. But the fact is that the walker is following codes and programs even if he does not know it, and is thus communicating; and the dog does the same even when he does *not* receive signals for food (for example he may give signs of hunger by moving about in an agitated way or by acting languid or droopy). So much so that we interpret very well both the sign-behavior of the walker and the sign-behavior of the hungry dog.

It would seem that just these conclusions could be used to maintain that, anyhow, there can be *communication without behavior.* Just as the man who walks along the road communicates something even if he does not know it and even if he does not want to, and likewise for the dog, so – one could argue – a man who "doesn't behave at all" also communicates something. But what does 'not behaving at all' mean? I can think of only two cases: immobility and death.

The immobility of a living being can only be partial and transitory. Partial, because its organism continues to move internally, and it is only because we restrict our point of view that we do not take account of this. It is with regard to this restriction that we call behavior only the macroscopic behavior of a whole organism, or of one of its parts which is easily visible from the outside. Even so, immobility will still always be a momentary case of non-behavior which, by a determined negation, returns under the category of behavior itself. It is precisely because life is continuous behavior that even a momentary cessation of behavior, of all behavior, communicates something. In this way, for example, somebody who instead of replying to a question remains silent, is communicating something, for instance, embarrassment. There is even the popular saying "no news is good news." But nobody would say that keeping silent or not writing letters are not ways of behaving, or are something extraneous to behavior in general.

With similar arguments one can deny even the exception of the dead man, about whom one can maintain that with his dead body itself he is communicating something. A dead man certainly no longer does anything, he does not behave in any way; but this is nothing other than the conclusion of everything that that organism has done up to the moment of its death. His immobility, this time not transitory, contrasts with the mobility of his whole life. A corpse continues to communicate something because we recognize in it what remains of a man or of an animal; in these remains we are still discovering the signs of its life. When, as the poet says, "God forgets about his face," then on that face there will no longer be signs of past life. Still, even in a skeleton disinterred after millennia the signs of socialization are found: and where these no longer exist, still a dimension of biological signs remains, interpretable by men. Death, in short, is the cessation of all behavior; it too, from this point of view, can be included in the general category of behavior. *Death exists only for life*. Having rejected even the extreme case of death, we conclude that we cannot say that there ever exists communication without behavior.

Now, since there is no communication without signs, the pair of negative conclusions we have reached can be immediately translated back into our initial statement that it is not possible to distinguish sign-behavior from non-sign-behavior *in general*. Instead, it is possible, and obviously of the greatest importance, to distinguish and classify various types of sign-behavior, at various levels, and with every possible superimposition, concomitance, or exclusion: verbal and nonverbal, conscious and unconscious, intentional and unintentional, finalistic and spontaneous (or free, or casual), founded on simple codes or on complex codes, of a digital type or of an analogical type, and so on (recall note 6). The search for sign-behavior *per se*, we must repeat, is really the search for a particular type of sign-behavior, even if this type may have much characterizing power and be perhaps necessary within a given realm of research.

When we say today that all behavior *is* communication, or vice versa, we say it from the vantage point of the gigantic developments in semiotics in the last thirty years. Nonverbal codes have in part emerged and more are emerging to the attention of scholars; and today we know that all behavior is always programmed – that is, based on codes. Should we conclude, then, that these developments, encouraged and set in motion by Morris, diminish the value and credibility of his basic insights? I would say no; indeed, I would say the contrary. It was Morris who joined in such an intimate way, and for the first time systematically, the general notion of behavior with the general notion of the sign. Let us say, rather, that he started off in a direction which was *even more fruitful* than he himself imagined or was able to foresee. The joining of the two notions contained enormous potential. Circumstances had only to permit the very first developments – and the whole panorama of the human and life sciences began to change. Morris's limits must be seen historically: they were "only" those of his environment – of the academic discussion in the United States, and of North American culture in general, in the period when he was most active. It is often said that every nation has the government it deserves. One cannot certainly say that every original thinker has the type of academy and society that he deserves. Morris surpassed the environment in which he happened to live; he was ahead of his time. Precisely because of this he was so much attacked and disturbed in his work – especially by philosophers, who by their ontological nature are quarrelsome, intolerant, and above all always terrified by new and creative ideas.

2.7 Sign-vehicles, *Signifiants*, and Signs

In *FTS*, Morris introduced his discussion of the nature of the sign with the following words: "The process in which something functions as a sign may be called semiosis" ([*WGTS*], p. 19). In this way the distinction between the sign and what functions as a sign was immediately brought in, and rightly so. No doubt about it for the Morris of *FTS*: "the sign-vehicle ([is] a sign in virtue of its functioning)" (*ibid*). In *SLB* the formulation was more complex: "A particular physical event – such as a given sound or mark or movement – which is a sign will be called a *sign-vehicle*" ([*WGTS*], p. 96). Up to this point the distinction made in *FTS* was confirmed: existence as a sign-vehicle, a bearer of semiosis, is a property which comes to the event or physical object by virtue of its functioning as a sign. Morris continued: "A set of similar sign-vehicles which for a given interpreter have the same *significata* will be called a *sign-family*" (*ibid.*). This was an ambiguous specification. As Morris confirmed in Note J (here [*WGTS*], on p. 108), the distinction between sign-vehicle and sign-family ought to correspond to Peirce's distinction between token and type.[7] Now if a sign-vehicle is a member of a type, understood as a class, then the distinction between sign-vehicle *as a vehicle* and sign in the full sense seems to disappear. Every member must have all the properties that make it belong to its class: the sign-vehicle must already be a sign in order to belong to a sign-family, just as the token must be a token in order to belong to a type.

The event or object that *functions* as a vehicle, instead, belongs only to the class of all the events or objects which are potentially capable of assuming that same function. But this concerns such events or objects, *not signs*.

Here there are many subtle difficulties. To touch upon some of them at least, let us examine more closely what a sign in the full sense is, and examine it in Morris's own terms. For those who have a copy of *WGTS*, the diagram in "Esthetics and the Theory of Signs" (p. 417) allows one to catch the situation of semiosis at a glance, even if he is not familiar with the terminology. A sign exists for Morris in a triadic network of relationships: (i) with other signs, (ii) with its *designatum* or significatum, and possibly with its *denotatum*,[8] (iii) with an *interpreter* who "has" or "unfolds" an *interpretant* (the interpreter responds to the stimulus of the vehicle in a certain way, applies a given rule, and so on). A dimension of semiosis corresponds to each of these three groups of relationships. When speaking of the sign, one cannot avoid referring at least implicitly to the whole situation just described. When all the elements indicated by the terms referred are present simultaneously, then and only then something – anything whatsoever – *functions* as a sign.

What may lead us astray both in the diagram and in its exposition is that Morris put the sign-vehicle at the center of the situation represented, i.e. of semiosis. I think this was due to the need for an initial intersubjective reference. The entire approach we are discussing concerned signs and what accompanies them: it did not consider some other element, for example human or animal organisms seen as something through which to arrive at signs. It was therefore necessary to begin with something that corresponded to what was most commonly meant by 'sign.' The vehicle, as a physical object or event observable by anybody, seemed to be the best guarantee of objectivity. To find at the center of a description of semiosis the sign-vehicle – which is what it is only insofar as it functions as a sign – creates, however, an asymmetry in the mind of the student. First the vehicle is taken as a sign; then, when one has understood that it is a sign only when the whole situation is present at the same time, so to say one goes back, and setting the rest aside, grasps it as vehicle alone, that is as a mere event or physical object. Once this twofold character of the sign-vehicle has been accepted, every time one goes back to examine its nature, that mental movement comes up again in the form of a persistent ambiguity. We can indicate this ambiguity by the graphic trick of putting the part of the syntagm 'sign-vehicle' on which we are concentrating our attention in italics. Then we can write: the notion of 'sign-vehicle' can be understood as either 'sign-*vehicle*' or '*sign*-vehicle.' The difference is this:

the 'sign-*vehicle*' is any event or object about which we know that, given certain conditions, it functions as a sign because it belongs to a family of events or objects capable of carrying out such a function. Here, however, we are considering it in its character as a mere *bearer* of a sign, that is, just as an event or object. The '*sign*-vehicle' instead, is that same event or object considered no longer and not only in its materiality for the physical properties of its body, but rather only in regard to its functioning as a sign. If it is functioning in this way, the vehicle is a *sign*-vehicle, with all that follows from this in the realm of semiosis. We will say then that every single occurrence of the *sign*-vehicle is a member of the class constituted of a given family *of signs* (in Peirce's terms, "the token ... is an *instance* of the type," [CP] 4.537). If it is not functioning as a sign, instead, it is a mere vehicle, an event or an object *whatsoever*. Here 'whatsoever' means 'unimportant from the point of view of semiosis and therefore also of semiotic inquiry.' Since we are talking about semiosis, however, it is clear that even when we speak of an event or object which is *not* functioning as a sign, what we have in mind is the possibility that it may: we are distinguishing an event or object that does *not* function as a sign from another event or object, or from the same event or object, that *does* function as a sign. To be semiotically thorough, we can then say that that very event or object can be "pre-sign," when it precedes a case of semiosis which we will have to examine; or "post-sign", when it comes after a case of semiosis which we have examined; or simply "non-sign" for us, that is, unimportant for the semiosic object of the inquiry we are making; or even "a-sign," that is, extraneous to semiosis in general.[9]

It may perhaps be valuable to bring in a different terminological framework, at least briefly: Saussure's *signifiant* and *signifié*. Much caution is necessary every time one asks what Saussure really meant (cf. Koerner 1972). Still it seems clear enough that the *signifiants* are verbal subspecies of sign-vehicles: classes of events or objects, in the case of phonetic or graphic items, destined to function as signs. This function will take place and the sign will arise when the *signifiant* are regularly coupled with *signifiés*. To begin with, one could say that as the sum of a *signifiant* and a *signifié* gives us a *signe*, so the sum of a vehicle (as a class of events or material objects) and a constant "sign portion" gives us the sign-vehicle understood as a full sign. Here, according to the graphic trick introduced above, we should write '*sign-vehicle*,' that is, accentuate both members of the syntagm. In this interpretation, the syntagm 'verbal sign-vehicle' would be thus equivalent to the term '*signe*' in Saussure; and it would be as if Saussure had always written *signifiant-*

signifié instead of writing *signe*. The very fact that he continued to speak in terms of *vehicles* which are *sign-vehicles* shows that Morris had reached on his own an awareness of the Saussurian type with regard to the internal duality of the sign. This is all the more remarkable, since Saussure's name is absent from the body of Morris's work. The sign is an event or physical object which forms a *sum* with something else. The notion of sum should not be understood arithmetically, as the mere addition of one object to another object. Certainly Morris never indulged in the conception, which both Saussure and later Wittgenstein had also fully overcome, of language as nomenclature. We would have such a conception of language only if what is added to the vehicle to make it a sign were a *significatum* or possibly a *denotatum*. Now this is precisely what Morris wanted to avoid, and did avoid, by dealing with the sign in terms of the whole semiosic situation.

To equate *verbal sign-vehicle* to *signe*, however, is certainly not sufficient. While it is true that Saussure fully admitted the existence of nonverbal *signes* and the possibility of studying them, it is also true that he concentrated on verbal *signes*. Morris instead began from definitions of the sign that can regard both verbal and nonverbal signs indifferently. His own basic examples were nonverbal more often than verbal. It is no accident that Morris rather than Saussure was the founder of twentieth century semiotics as it did in fact develop (the semioticians who use Saussurian techniques originating in the study of verbal sign-systems typically call their research *sémiologie*). But there is still more. While the *signifiant* referred back only or principally to its own *signifié*, Morris's sign-vehicle referred back to the whole situation described. Notice that we are talking about the basic definition of 'sign,' not about further developments in either author. Saussure warns us against sliding from the *signe* to the *signifiant*, but he sometimes slides himself ("le lien de l'idée et du signe s'est relâché," *Cours* [1915], p. 109, cf. the critical edition by Engler [cf. Saussure 1967], p. 167). Morris, as we shall see in the next section, warns us against sliding from the whole situation of semiosis to one of its parts capable of being arbitrarily isolated from the totality to which it belongs. The 'sign portion' of the sign-vehicle is in fact the network of semiosic relationships: in order for a sign to exist, the vehicle must be used by an interpreter, it must be in relationship with other vehicles which are in turn usable as signs, and must have a *significatum* and possibly a *denotatum*. If the *signifiant* corresponds to the sign-*vehicle* with the descriptive limitation that it is a *verbal* sign-vehicle, the *signifié* corresponds to only a part of the situation of semiosis, but leaving aside the matter of its being verbal or nonverbal semiosis. At a first glance, one might think that the *signifié* is the *significatum*. But closer inspection shows beyond any doubt that the *signifié* is, if anything, the interpretant. Where Morris, in part following Peirce, proposed the disposition to respond and habit as the explanation of the interpretant, Saussure proposed the concept, not otherwise analyzed, as the explanation of the *signifié*.[10] Thus, interpreting Saussure in Morris's terms, the *signe* as the sum of *signifiant* and *signifié* lies within the pragmatic dimension of semiosis, that is, it concerns the relationship between sign-vehicle and interpretant. But once a concept, always a concept. When he makes the *signifiant* carry the burden of the *signifié-as-concept*, Saussure reminds me of Vailati's peasant who, having to cross a river with an enormous stone, thought that he could avoid overloading his very small boat by carrying the stone on his back during the whole crossing.

The ambiguity in the notion of the sign-vehicle may be resolved, in my opinion, by decisively severing the mere vehicle, as an event or object, from *all* the rest. The operation has a Saussurian flavor but it has to do with a situation which is more complex than the one examined by Saussure (we are still at the level of initial definitions). We repeat that Morris himself refers to it by bringing up an ambiguous notion. Let us be satisfied with saying instead that *when* an event or object whatsoever happens to be in the triadic network of the relationships of semiosis, *then* it becomes a sign – it becomes a sign because it functions as a sign. The syntagm 'sign-vehicle' serves only to anticipate the function that the vehicle will have, or to recall the function that it has had, or to call attention to the fact that even when we are dealing with events or physical objects "whatsoever," our aim remains a semiotic one – those objects or events interest us principally because they have been, or can become, signs. Outside of cases like these which are legitimate, insisting too much on the sign-vehicle could even lead to the hair-raising belief that the very substance of the sign is contained within the vehicle as such.

2.8 Meaning and the Three Dimensions

In Section 2.4 under (ii) we mentioned that for Morris meaning extended to the whole situation of semiosis.

> 'Meaning' signifies any and all phases of sign-processes (the status of being a sign, the interpretant, the fact of denoting, the significatum)

> ([*WGTS*], p. 95) ... For the major purposes which the everyday languages serve it has not been necessary to denote with precision the various factors in semiosis – the process is merely referred to in a vague way by the term 'meaning.' ([*ibid.*], p. 56)

Morris preferred not to use the term because it was too vague (*FTS* [*WGTS*], pp. 55-59; *SLB* [*WGTS*], p. 95). But he examined it, and it is a good thing that he did. It has continued to be used in various ways by innumerable philosophers, linguists, semioticians, psychiatrists, anthropologists, and other scientists and *dilettanti*. It is precisely because 'meaning' is a quasi-synonym of 'semiosis' that no one succeeds in erasing it, we do not say from everyday language, but even from scientific discourse. Recognition of these facts leads us toward an interpretation of the three dimensions of semiosis which turns out to be pretty different from some rather widely spread views.

We know that the semantic dimension of semiosis refers to the relationships of signs with their *significata* and their possible *denotata*; the pragmatic dimension refers to the relationships of signs with their interpreters and interpretants; the syntactic dimension refers to the relationships among signs. The three subdisciplines of semiotics which correspond to the three dimensions each concentrate on the respective dimension, leaving the other two aside to some extent. It was with much prudence that Morris came back to his tripartition in *SLB* ([*WGTS*], pp. 301-303). The main point was – and is – that one must not believe that *there are* semantic, syntactic, or pragmatic signs: this would be silly because every sign is all three things by definition – we do not have a sign if we do not have semiosis, that is, the *simultaneous presence* of the three dimensions. It is therefore always with signs that the three subdisciplines of semiotics deal. Signs, complete signs were what was dealt with by the various currents of thought which flowed into scientific empiricism, which in its turn became identified with a general theory of symbolism, that is, with semiotics (Section 2.3 above).

What would happen, in fact, if we took away semiosis and tried to analyze what was left over? What would there be to analyze? One could think of various orders of things: (i) All physical (material, corporal) things that exist in the world, leaving aside how they are put together and used in the complex ways which produce semiosis (cf. note 9). (ii) Pieces of behavior, prevalently those carried out by human and animal organisms (cf. note 11), purposely isolated as non-sign actions, that is, as movements of bodies in space and time. (iii) Processes taking place within human or animal organisms, or within machines, examined by disciplines like physiology or electronics respectively, here too purposely excluding all of their functions which are in one way or another sign-functions. (iv) Nonphysical entities postulated by thought, whether they are recognized as products of thought itself or held to be objects of special "apperceptions" (the existence of non-sign thought remains to be demonstrated). Separately, according to the three dimensions and having taken away semiosis: the syntactic dimension becomes the study of geometric, or acoustic, or other physical relationships among vehicles which were (or will be) sign-vehicles; the semantic dimension becomes the study of the relationships among platonic objects which were (or will be) *significata*, as well as among objects whatsoever (physical or nonphysical, pieces of behavior, and also other signs or other non-signs) which were (or will be) *denotata*; the pragmatic dimension, finally, becomes the study of the *non*social relationships among organisms[11] which were (or will be) interpreters and among their pieces of behavior or modifications which were (or will be) interpretants. There is on all this in *FTS* a passage which it would be well to cite fully:

> [M]en in general find it difficult to think clearly about complex functional and relational processes, a situation reflected in the prevalence of certain linguistic forms. Action centers around handling things with properties, and the fact that these things and properties appear only in complex contexts is a much later and more difficult realization. Hence the naturalness of what Whitehead has called the fallacy of simple location. In the present case this takes the form of looking for meanings as one would look for marbles: a meaning is considered as one thing among other things, a definite something definitely located somewhere. This may be sought for in the designatum [here and below = *significatum*: cf. note 8, R.-L.], which thus becomes transformed in certain varieties of "realism" into a special kind of object – a "Platonic idea" inhabiting the "realm of subsistence," perhaps grasped by a special faculty for intuiting "essences"; or it may be sought for in the interpretant, which then becomes transformed in conceptualism into a concept or idea inhabiting a special domain of mental entities whose relation to be "psychical states" of individual interpreters becomes very difficult to state; or in desperation caused by contemplation of the previous alternatives it may be sought in the sign-vehicle – though historically few if any "nominalists" have held this position. As a matter of fact, none of these positions has proved satisfactory and none of them is demanded. As semiotical terms, neither 'sign-vehicle,' 'designatum,' nor 'interpretant' can be defined without reference to one another; hence they do not stand for isolated existences but for things or properties of things in certain specifiable functional relations to other things or properties. ([*WGTS*], p. 56)

Now we know that meaning concerns all the phases and aspects of semiosis. Saying 'sign,' 'semiosis,' or 'meaning' is saying *almost* the same thing – almost, because using one of the three terms can serve to accentuate this or that aspect of the situation. In other words, the three terms overlap almost completely (cf. Rossi-Landi on categories, forthcoming [cf. 1978d; this volume, Chapter 7]). It is from this point of view that we must judge the three 'reductions' that have generally dominated the field: the reduction of meaning to the semantic dimension alone, the reduction of the organic (or of the mental, or of the social) to the pragmatic dimension alone, and the reduction of the formal to the syntactic dimension alone.

As against these three reductions, the thesis I believe one must defend remains, basically, the thesis advanced by Morris in the thirties. If a *semiotically constitutive* property belongs to one of the three dimensions, then it belongs necessarily also to the other two. The dimensions are ways of abstracting, of leaving aside something, of concentrating on something. The totality from which one has partially abstracted continues to be present. The formal relationships do not regard only signs as sign-vehicles; they also regard *significata, denotata*, interpreters, interpretants. When we deal with a plurality of interpreters, for example, of necessity we also deal with formal relationships. *Significata* are also arranged in zones and in systems. Meaning is concerned not only with *significata* and *denotata*, but also with the relationships among sign-vehicles and, moreover, among interpretants and interpreters. Signs reciprocally delimit each other's meanings, and interpreters 'live' meanings. Without meanings in pragmatics, for example, psychology and psychiatry would not have an object. Pragmatic relationships, finally, concern not only interpreters and interpretants, but also sign-vehicles and *significata* and *denotata*. Here the alternative would consist, and has consisted, in imagining that the world of syntactic relationships and the world of *significata* and *denotata* are extra-social worlds. Thus one begins to imagine that the language (*langue*) is a mere formal machine which is brought to life with meanings by being put into relationship with a world which is independent from it but preexisting and completely preformed. And who brings it to life? The interpreters, that is who, with their network of social relationships – interpreters who supposedly intervene when things are already finished, *as if* they had not already produced those very things themselves, and as if they were not in their turn produced by them.

In short, one cannot – after having arrived at the synthesis called semiotics – simply fall back and 'force' the formal into syntactics alone, meaning into semantics alone, and the biological (or mental or social) into pragmatics alone. A full comprehension of the structure of semiosis lies precisely in this: semiosis is a network of relationships of various kinds – formal, meaningful, biological, social relationships. The whole structure of semiosis, once articulated, *is* that whole structure; all of its pieces *are* all of its pieces. These statements may well have an odd ring; however, there is in them a basic indication of how to proceed in our endeavor. Maybe the price to pay will be discontinuing not only the use of the terms 'syntactics,' 'semantics,' and 'pragmatics,' but also any attempt at *doing* syntactics, or semantics, or pragmatics as independent disciplines. I submit that now that in the seventies we are reaching the fruits of the tree of semiotics, we may well ourselves cut off the very branches over which we have been scrambling during the past decades.

2.9 Summary and Conclusions

After acknowledging that *WGTS* reproduces the best of what Morris has written in the field of semiotics but complaining that it neglects both the philosophical formation of semiotics and Morris's parallel research in the field of values (Sections 2.2 and 2.3), we have examined some highlights of Morris's semiotics as it is presented in his two main theoretical works, *FTS* and *SLB*. On the whole, we see that the position maintained in the early and rapidly written *FTS* is more vulnerable but more ample and acceptable than that maintained in the more mature and accurate *SLB*. It is almost a paradox: at a distance of so many years, one has the impression that there is now more of a link between us and Morris's line of reasoning in *FTS* than in *SLB*. In no case, in fact, can semiotics, a science which is eminently social, be founded on the categories of behavioral biopsychology (Sections 2.4 and 2.5). This can be well understood precisely with regard to the prime foundation of *SLB*, the behavioral definition of 'sign.' Trying to single out behavior which is *sign*-behavior means admitting that non-sign-behavior must also exist. An examination of the situation convinces us instead that all behavior is, in different ways, sign-behavior; so that what Morris was really trying to do was to individuate *a particular type* of sign-behavior. Later semiotic research, enlarged up to the point of identifying behavior with communication, has fully confirmed this theoretical diagnosis (Section 2.6). A little dialectical probing of the term 'sign-vehicle' reveals an ambiguity which may be overcome by making a clear-cut distinction between the event or object which serves as a vehicle and everything else (Section 2.7). Finally, we mentioned that the terms 'sign,' 'meaning,' and 'semiosis' overlap almost completely. From this it follows that it does not make sense to restrict meaning to the semantic dimension, or to limit formal relationships to the syntactic dimension, or to reduce social relationships among organisms to the pragmatic dimension alone (Section 2.8). In the course of these brief discussions, one thing has become quite clear, and this is the breadth of Morris's approach, breadth in the sense of a constant reference to the totalities with which he deals. Here Morris's merit is really sizeable. In fact, it is much more difficult to *think* in terms of a totality, bearing it in mind as such while at the same time examining its internal structures, than it is to isolate one of these structures and examine it in its isolation, even if this is done with the greatest analytic rigor.

When taking into account the confluence of behavior and communication we have seen that the developments of twentieth century semiotics have on the whole followed this part of Morris's teaching. These developments have often been tumultuous and separate, and at times difficult to reconcile, but they have succeeded in bringing out the sign-nature of every human and animal aggregate and even of life itself. If we want to continue further in the direction Morris has so largely contributed to indicate, we must, in my opinion, proceed toward new conjunctions of interests, move still further toward a unitary approach to the totalities which interest us. It is not so much a matter of grasping the *sign-part* of, for example, the language of gestures, or the economic market, or the production of the objects of everyday use, or kinship systems, and so on. What we want is not semiotics as a discipline superimposed in a neutral way upon other disciplines. Instead, what we want is to see, beyond the old academic and specialistic distinctions, those portions of human life which are describable as the language of gestures, economic market, production of useful objects, kinship systems, and so on, as made up entirely of signs, so as to be able *then* to distinguish their *non-sign residue* which is the object of study for other disciplines or other interests (cf. note 9 above). More specifically, the economic market, for example, is obviously both sign and non-sign. Commodities are messages, but they are also produced, exchanged, and consumed for non-sign aims. A semiotic examination of commodities should not be seen as a *superimposition* of the semiosic dimension over the economic dimension (or over the dimension relative to the study of commodities as such [*merceologia*], or relative to the technological dimensions of the production of the objects destined to become commodities, or over the physiological and psychological dimensions of their consumption, etc.). The semiotic examination of commodities should instead be seen as the *penetration* of semiotics into the field of commodities, into the nature of commodities, and therefore also, in an interdisciplinary way, as the *intermingling* of semiotics and economics (and, as far as necessary, of semiotics and various other disciplines). This is the kind of procedure that has already led semiotics to deal systematically with signs in fields that were previously entrusted to other disciplines which did not comprehend the sign-dimension of their objects of study, or underrated it, or did not possess the instruments for dealing with it. But these objects of study are depreciated by a treatment which is *only* semiotic, if semiotics itself is in its turn understood as a separate science.

Along the lines described, semiotics appears to me as a necessary complement to a theory of the relationships between "structure" and "superstructure." Very briefly: what we have here is the working hypothesis that the difficulties always encountered in the study of the relationships between structure and superstructure depend on the absence of a mediating element. Just as the relationships between means of production and ideology emerged in the study of nineteenth century capitalism and of the first industrial revolution, so, according to this hypothesis, the new mediating element could begin to emerge only in the study of a *new* reality, the reality of *neo*capitalism and the second industrial revolution. The mediating element consists in the totality of sign-systems, both verbal and nonverbal, which are present in every community; these "constitute" the social from primordial times and join the human to the prehuman. If this hypothesis is correct, the "pieces of the game" are three, not two: *sign-systems* must be added to *means of production* and *ideologies*. Human behavior is programmed at three levels. The difficulties so often encountered in the study of the relationships between means of production and ideologies, between the programming of human social behavior at the structural level and at the superstructural level, are difficulties which derive from an attempt to explain a triadic situation in a binary way, or to explain in a static way, by means of a juxtaposition of planes, a situation which is fluid and in which there is a continuous movement from one plane to another. It would seem that in this way the enormous contribution of twentieth century semiotics, linguistics, and communication theory can become a part of a Marxist theory of society in general (in the sense of the more comprehensive Marx of the *Grundrisse* even more than in the sense of the Marx of *Kapital*). Here the field is open for the discussion of the ways in which means of production, ideologies, and sign-systems variously interact, assuming different dialectical positions in different moments. The mediating element is mediated in its turn. But the place for this discussion is elsewhere.

2.10 Writings by Charles Morris

a. Volumes and Articles, 1927-1971

1927a. "The Total-situation Theory in Ethics." *International Journal of Ethics* XXXVII: 258-268.

1927b. "The Concept of the Symbol." *Journal of Philosophy* XXIV: 253-262, 281-291.

1928a. "The Prediction Theory of Truth." *Monist* XXXVIII: 387-401.

1928b. "Neo-pragmatism and the Ways of Knowing." *Monist* XXXVIII: 494-501.

1929a. "Has Russell Passed the Tortoise?" *Journal of Philosophy* XXVI: 449-459.

1929b. "The Relation of Formal to Instrumental Logic." In *Essays in Philosophy*. Ed. by T.V. Smith and W.K. Wright, 253-268. Chicago: The Open Court Publishing Co.

1929c. "The Nature of Mind" (= Rice Institute Pamphlet, XVI): 153-244. (In 1932a).

1931. "Mind in Process and Reality." *Journal of Philosophy* XXVIII: 113-127. (In 1932a).

1932a. *Six Theories of Mind*. Chicago: University of Chicago Press. (Comprises 1929c and 1931).

1932b. "Truth, Action, and Verification." *Monist* XLII: 321-329.

1934a. *Pragmatism and the Crisis of Democracy* (= Public Policy Pamphlet, 12). Chicago: University of Chicago Press.

1934b. Introduction. In George H. Mead, *Mind, Self, and Society*. Ed. by C. Morris. Chicago: University of Chicago Press.

1934c. "Pragmatism and Metaphysics." *Philosophical Review* XLIII: 549-564. (In 1937).

1935a. "Philosophy of Science and Science of Philosophy." *Philosophy of Science* II: 271-286. (In 1937).

1935b. "The Relation of the Formal and Empirical Sciences within Scientific Empiricism." *Erkenntnis* V: 6-14. (In 1937).

1935c. "Some Aspects of Recent American Scientific Philosophy." *Erkenntnis*. 142-149. (In 1937 and 1938a).

1936a. "Semiotic and Scientific Empiricism." *Actes du congrès international de philosophie scientifique, 1935*. Part I: 1-16. Paris: Hermann. (In 1937).

1936b. "The Concept of Meaning in Pragmatism and Logical Positivism." *Actes du huitième congrès international de philosophie, 1934*. Prague. (In 1937).

1936c. "Remarks on the Proposed Encyclopedia." *Actes du congrès international de philosophie scientifique, 1935*. Part II: 71-74. Paris: Hermann. (In 1937 and 1938a).

1936d. "Professor Schiller and Pragmatism." *The Personalist* XVII: 294-300.

1937. *Logical Positivism, Pragmatism, and Scientific Empiricism* (= Actualités scientifiques et industrielles, 449). Paris: Hermann. (Includes 1934c and 1936b).

1938a. "Scientific Empiricism." In *Encyclopedia and Unified Science* (= International Encyclopedia of Unified Science, I: 1), 63-75. Chicago: University of Chicago Press.

1938b. "Peirce, Mead, and Pragmatism." *Philosophical Review* XLVII: 109-127.
1938c. *Foundations of the Theory of Signs* (= International Encyclopedia of Unified Science, I: 2). Chicago: University of Chicago Press.
1938d. Introduction. In George H. Mead, *The Philosophy of the Act*, in collaboration with J.M. Brewster, A.M. Dunham, and D.L. Miller. Chicago: University of Chicago Press.
1938e. "The Unity of Science Movement and the United States." *Synthèse*, 25-29. (In 1946b).
1939a. "General Education and the Unity of Science Movement." In *John Dewey and the Promise of America* (= Progressive Education Booklet, 14). Columbus, OH: American Education Press.
1939b. "Esthetics and the Theory of Signs." *Journal of Unified Science* (following *Erkenntnis*) VIII: 131-150.
1939c. "Science, Art, and Technology." *Kenyon Review* I: 409-423.
1939d. "Semiotic, the Socio-humanistic Sciences, and the Unity of Science." *Journal of Unified Science*. Paper presented at the Fifth International Congress for the Unity of Science, Harvard University, September 1939. (In 1946b).
1940a. "Knowledge and Social Practice." *Frontiers of Democracy* VI: 150-152.
1940b. "The Mechanism of Freedom." In *Freedom, Its Meaning*. Ed. by R. Anshen, 579-589. New York: Harcourt Brace.
1941. "The Search for a Life of Significance: The Work of Raymond Jonson, American Painter." *Tomorrow* I: 16-21.
1942a. "Empiricism, Religion, and Democracy." In *Science, Philosophy, and Religion*. Second Symposium. Ed. by L. Bryson, 213-236 plus 5 pp. of discussion. New York: Columbia University Press.
1942b. *Paths of Life: Preface to a World Religion*. New York: Harper. (New printing at the University of Chicago Press, 1973.)
1942c. "William James Today." In *In Commemoration of William James*. Ed. by H.M. Kallen, 178-187. New York: Columbia University Press.
1943a. "Freedom or Frustration?" *Fortune* XXVIII: 148 ff.
1943b. "Comments on a Paper by A. Kaplan." *Philosophy of Science* 10: 247-249.
1944. "The Social Assimilation of Cultural Relativity." In *Approaches to World Peace*. Ed. by L. Bryson, L. Finkelstein, and R.M. MacIver, 619-626, plus 17 pp. of discussion. New York: Harper.
1945. "Nietzsche, an Evaluation." *Journal of the History of Ideas* VI: 285-293.
1946a. *Signs, Language, and Behavior*. New York: Prentice-Hall. (2nd printing August 1947, 3rd April 1949, 4th August 1950. Italian edition, *Segni, linguaggio e comportamento*, transl. by S. Ceccato. Milan: Longanesi, 1949.
1946b. "The Significance of the Unity of Science Movement." *Philosophy and Phenomenological Research* VI: 508-515. (Comprises 1938e and 1939d).
1947a. "Philosophy as Symbolic Synthesis of Belief." Sixth Conference on Science, Philosophy, and Religion, 1945. In *Approaches to Group Understanding*. Ed. by L. Bryson, L. Finkelstein, and R.M. MacIver, 626-631. New York: Harper. (In 1946a: VIII: 6).

1947b. "Multiple Self and Multiple Society." In *Freedom and Experience: Essays Presented to Horace M. Kallen.* Ed. by S. Hook and M.R. Konvitz. Ithaca, NY: Cornell University Press. (In 1948c).
1948a. "Recent Studies in Meaning and Communication." *Sigma* II: 454-458.
1948b. "Individual Differences and Cultural Patterns." In *Personality in Nature, Society, and Culture.* Ed. by C. Kluckhohn and H.A. Murray, 131-143. New York and London: Jonathan Cape.
1948c. *The Open Self.* New York: Prentice-Hall. (Includes 1947b).
1948d. "Signs about Signs about Signs." *Philosophy and Phenomenological Research* IX: 115-133.
1949. "Axiology as the Science of Preferential Behavior." In *Value: A Cooperative Inquiry.* Ed. by R. Lepley, 211-222. New York: Columbia University Press. (Criticisms and additions: 388-395, 428-433, 437-439).
1951a. "Comparative Strength of Life-ideals in Eastern and Western Cultures." The East-West Philosopher's Conference, Honolulu, 1949. In *Essays in East-West Philosophy.* Ed. by C.A. Moore, 353-370. Honolulu: University of Hawaii Press.
1951b. "The Science of Man and Unified Science." In *Contribution to the Analysis and Synthesis of Knowledge* (= Proceedings of the American Academy of Arts and Sciences, LXXX: I), 37-44; *Aut Aut* I: 2 (1951), 121-129 (in Italian).
1951c. "Similarity of Constitutional Factors in Psychotic Behavior in India, China, and the United States." *American Journal of Psychiatry* CVIII, 2: 143-144.
1951d. "Comments on Mysticism and Its Language." *ETC: A Review of General Semantics* IX, 1: 3-8.
1952. "Significance, Signification, and Painting." Paper presented as the Thirteenth Conference on *Science, Philosophy, and Religion,* New York, 1952. *Methodos* V:18 (1953), 87-102.
1955. "Value Scales and Dimensions" (with Lyle V. Jones). *The Journal of Abnormal and Social Psychology* LI, 3: 523-535.
1956a. "Varieties of Human Value." *The Humanist* XVI: 153-161.
1956b. *Varieties of Human Value.* Chicago: University of Chicago Press.
1956c. "Relations of Temperament to the Choice of Values" (with Lyle V. Jones). *The Journal of Abnormal and Social Psychology* LIII, 3: 345-349.
1956d. "Man-Cosmos Symbols." In *The New Landscape.* Ed. by G. Kepes, 98-99. Chicago: Paul Theobald.
1957a. "Significance, Signification and Painting." In *The Language of Value.* Ed. by R. Lepley, 58-76. New York: Columbia University Press.
1957b. "Mysticism and Its Language." In *Language: An Inquiry into Its Meaning and Function.* Ed. by R.N. Anshen, 179-187. New York: Harper.
1957c. "Philosophy and Behavioral Sciences in the United States." *Contemporary Philosophy and Social Sciences* I, 4: 1-8.
1958a. "Prospects for a New Synthesis: Science and the Humanities as Complementary Activities." In *Science and the Modern Mind.* Ed. by G. Holton, 92-99. Boston: Beacon Press.

1958b. "Words without Meaning." *Contemporary Psychology* III: 212-214. (Review Skinner, *Verbal Behavior*).
1959. "Philosophy, Psychiatry, Mental Illness and Health." *Philosophy and Phenomenological Research* XX, 1: 47-55.
1960a. "The Buddhist Personality Ideal as Expressed in the Works of Daisetz Teitaro Suzuki." In *Buddhism and Culture*, dedicated to Dr. Daisetz Suzuki in commemoration of his ninetieth birthday. Ed. by S. Yamaguchi, 9-14. Kyoto: Nakano Press.
1960b. "Values of Psychiatric Patients" (with Berenice T. Eiduson and Denis O'Donovan). *Behavioral Science* V, 4: 297-312.
1960c. "On the History of the International Encyclopedia of Unified Science." *Synthèse* XII: 517-521.
1961a. "Analysis of the Connotative Meanings of a Variety of Human Values as Expressed by American College Students" (with Charles E. Osgood, and Edward E. Ware). *Journal of Abnormal and Social Psychology* LXII, 1: 62-73.
1961b. "Values, Problematic and Unproblematic, and Science." *The Journal of Communication* XI, 4: 205-210.
1963. "Pragmatism and Logical Empiricism." In *The Philosophy of Rudolf Carnap*. Ed. by P.A. Schilpp, 87-98. La Salle, IL: The Open Court Publishing Co.
1964a. *Signification and Significance: A Study of the Relations of Signs and Values*. Cambridge, MA: M.I.T. Press. [Italian edition in *Segni e valori. Significazione e significatività e altri scritti di semiotica, etica ed estetica*, introd. and transl. by S. Petrilli (ed.). Bari: Adriatica, 1988].
1964b. "Otto Neurath and the Unity of Science Movement" (= Mimeographed monograph 5 of the Association for Unification and Automation in Science. General Editor: D.L. Skékeley). Jerusalem.
1965a. "George H. Mead: A Pragmatist's Philosophy of Science." In *Scientific Psychology*. Ed. by B.B. Wolman and E. Nagel, 402-408. New York: Basic Books.
1965b. "Aesthetics, Signs, and Icons" (with Daniel J. Hamilton). *Philosophy and Phenomenological Research* XXV, 3: 356-364.
1965c. "On the Unity of the Pragmatic Movement." *Rice University Studies* LI, 4: 109-119.
1965d. "Alfred Adler and George H. Mead." *Journal of Individual Psychology* XXI: 199-200.
1965e. "Technique and Human Value." For the Symposium on the Technological Society, the Center for the Study of Democratic Institutions, Santa Barbara, California, 19-23 December 1965 (mimeographed, unpublished).
1966a. *Festival*. New York: George Braziller.
1966b. "Paintings, Ways to Live, and Values" (with Frank Sciadini). In *Sign, Image, and Symbol*. Ed. by G. Kepes, 144-149. New York: George Braziller.
1966c. "Comment on 'Counseling without Assuming Free Will'" (with Phyllis Meek). *The Personnel and Guidance Journal* XLV: 217-218.

1967a. Foreword to the Italian translation of "Esthetics and the Theory of Signs" (1939b) and "Aesthetics, Signs, and Icons" (1965b). *Nuova corrente* XLII/XLIII: 113-119.
1967b. "A Tribute to Daisetz Teitaro Suzuki." *The Eastern Buddhist* (new series) II: 128-129.
1967c. "Religion and the Empirical Study of Human Values." *Religious Humanism* I: 74-75.
1968. "Thirteen Ways to Live – A Report on Reactions of Readers of *Religious Humanism*." *Religious Humanism* II: 85-86.
1970a: "The Symbol Maitreya." *Maitreya* I: 4-6.
1970b. *The Pragmatic Movement in American Philosophy*. New York: George Braziller.
1970-1971. *Foundations of the Unity of Science: Toward an International Encyclopedia of Unified Science*. 2 vols. Ed. by C. Morris, O. Neurath and R. Carnap. Chicago: University of Chicago Press.
1971a. "Changes in Conceptions of the Good Life by American Students from 1950 to 1970" (with Linwood Small). *Journal of Personality and Social Psychology* XX: 254-260.
1971b. *Writings of the General Theory of Signs*. Ed. by T.A. Sebeok. The Hague-Paris: Mouton. (Comprises 1938c, 1946a, Chapter 1 of 1964a, 1939b, 1948d, 1957b, and 1956d).
1976. *Image*. New York: Vantage Press.

b. Selected Book-reviews, 1927-1951

1927. Georges Lanuë-Villène. *Le livre des symbols: Dictionnaire de symbolique et de mythologie* (Paris: Bossard, 1927, I vol.). *Journal of Philosophy* XXIV: 581-583.
1929a. Albert Spaier. 1929a. *La pensée concrète: Essai sur le symbolisme intellectuel* (Paris: Alcan, 1927). *Philosophical Review* XXXVIII: 407-410.
1929b. Grace Andrus de Laguna. *Speech, Its Function and Development*. (New Haven: Yale University Press, 1927); John F. Markey. *The Symbolic Process and Its Integration in Children: A Study in Social Psychology*. (New York: Harcourt Brace, 1928). *Philosophical Review* XXXVIII: 612-615.
1929c. *The Problem of Truth*. Lectures delivered before the Philosophical Union, University of California, 1927-1928. (Berkeley: University of California Press, 1928). *Journal of Philosophy* XXVI: 356-360.
1930a. *Studies in the Nature of Truth*. Lectures delivered before the Philosophical Union, University of California. (Berkeley: University of California Press, 1929.) *Journal of Philosophy* XXVII: 210-215.
1930b. Hugo Dingler. *Metaphysik als Wissenschaft vom Letzten*. (Munich: Reinhardt, 1929). *Philosophical Review* XXXIX: 508-513.

1931. Charles A. Strong. *Essays on the Natural Origin of the Mind.* (London: Macmillan, 1930). *Philosophical Review* XL: 590-592.
1932a. Joseph A. Dewe. *Les deux ordres, psychique et matériel.* (Paris: Vrin, 1929). *Philosophical Review* XLI: 87-88.
1932b. G.F. Stout. *Mind and Matter.* (New York: Macmillan). *Philosophical Review* XLI: 410-413.
1933. Jean Wahl. *Vers le concret: Études d'histoire de la philosophie contemporaine.* (Paris: Vrin, 1932). *Journal of Philosophy* XXX: 714-716.
1934. Roy Wood Sellars. *The Philosophy of Physical Realism.* (New York: Macmillan, 1932). *Philosophical Review* XLIII: 205-208.
1936. Otto Neurath. *Le développement du cercle de Vienne et l'avenir de l'empirisme logique.* (Paris: Hermann, 1935). *Philosophy of Science* II: 542-543.
1951. Kenneth Burke. *A Rhetoric of Motives.* (New York: Prentice-Hall, 1950). *Review of Metaphysics* IV: 439-443.

Rome, March 1973

Notes

1. [For all references to Morris's writings in both this and the subsequent article, see his general bibliography in Section 2.10, this Chapter.]

2. Or prevailingly so. What is left undecided here is whether the various schools of semiotics now thriving recognize in the subjects studied (i.e. in signs and sign systems of any description) a merely, or a prevailingly, social nature, or tend instead to stress also their biological aspects. Any simple opposition such as the opposition between verbal sign systems "as social" and the genetic code "as biological" would not do, for obviously verbal sign systems are *also* biological and the genetic code is an object of discovery and interpretation by highly socialized people. The issue is taken up again in the text at the end of Section 2.5.

3. Contributions to semiotics from the Soviet Union and other countries of Eastern Europe are well known; and the more we Westerners learn about them, the better. There has been recently an awakening of interest in semiotics in Cuba also, where I had the opportunity of delivering fifteen lectures on general semiotics in various Institutes of the Academia Cubana de Ciencias and then again at the Universidad de Oriente in Santiago. Parts of my lectures were printed, together with the translation of some other European texts, in the journals *Casa de las Américas* (La Habana) and *Santiago* (Revista de la Universidad de Oriente, Santiago de Cuba) in 1972. Cf. in the References: Kristeva, Lézine, Lotman, Marcus, Mukařovský, Retamar, Rossi-Landi, Uspensky, and Young. Also the publications of translations from Tynianov, Jakobson, and others, and of original studies by Navarro and others, in the *Gaceta de Cuba* 1972, can be viewed as an opening on the semiotic field, although the stress of the *Gaceta* is more on literary

criticism than on general semiotics. Owing to the novelty of the thing, I thought it useful to list semiotical articles written or translated in Cuba in the three named journals in the first months of 1972. Charles Morris is by now pretty well known on the island.

4. As can be seen by inspecting *Semiotica*, the relation between semiotics and philosophy is not one of the favored topics of contemporary semioticians. Books and articles by Schaff (1962, 1967, etc.), Kristeva (1969), Ruesch (1972) and Eco (1968, 1972) are welcome exceptions. General ideas about semiotics, however, are also discussed by Revzina (1972), Verón (1971), and Žinkin (1971); see also Mulder and Hervey (1971, 1972) and Pelc (1969) on meaning. Reference can be made to my own writings of 1961[d], 1968[h], and 1972[i].

5. This is the very first step toward a classification of signs according to the *manner of production* of their "bodies" or "vehicles." The latter may "exist in nature," or be "produced for other aims," or "produced for the purpose of bearing signs": examples are, respectively, Morris's black cloud which is a sign of rain, a car which is produced to ride in but signifies in various ways, and a phoneme. Cf. below the discussion of Morris's "sign-vehicle" in Section 2.7 together with note 9, and Section 2.4.2 in "Linguistics and Economics" (forthcoming [now R.-L. 1974f]).

6. There are, of course, many other distinctions which cannot be touched upon there. Suffice it to think of the existence of recognized codes vs. codes which (according to theory) must exist but are not yet studied, or are even still unnoticed. The very distinction drawn above between "speaking in order to communicate consciously" and "communicating something without being aware of it by means of involuntary bodily signs" is far from simple, if only because there are several layers of consciousness, awareness, paying heed, voluntariness, and related conditions. Much work has been done here by Husserl and by Wittgenstein and his school (especially Ryle 1949), which should be taken account of in further classifications of sign-processes: I give some main titles in the References.

7. For Peirce's distinction between *type* and *token*, cf. *Collected Papers* 4.537; for the distinction between *sinsign* and *legisign*, *CP* 2.245-246. The latter is possibly better known than the former, but whether the two distinctions are identical or only analogous is a question of Peircean scholarship and cannot be gone into here. It is my opinion, however, that Peirce's *loci* fully support the interpretation given in the text above. This is the place to call the semioticians' attention to the painstaking and subtle analyses of many such distinctions among signs, or among stages of the sign-process, contained in a book which has not yet received the attention it deserves, H.H. Price's *Thinking and Experience* (1953).

8. In later publications Morris substitutes *significatum* for *designatum* in order to be able to use the latter term for one only of several modes of signifying. Cf. in *WGTS, SLB*, pp. 93-96 for the use of *significatum* and Chapter III, "Modes of Signifying," especially Sections 2 and 7 (pp. 142-144 and 154-157). The crossing of four main modes of signifying with four primary sign-usages makes up a table of sixteen major types of discourse (p. 205). For simplicity's sake, we shall use hereafter *significatum* (in quotes from *FTS*, however, we shall put it in square brackets after *designatum*).

As for the *denotatum*, in *FTS* it is what "actually exists as referred to," and in *SLB* it becomes "anything that would permit the completion of the response-sequences to which an interpreter is disposed because of a sign" ([*WGTS*]: 361). The notion of the "real existence" of *denotata* as opposed to some other sort of existence of significata ("semantic" existence?) is, of course, highly problematic – one may well have to begin with Aristotle's criticism of Plato's theory of ideas (for instance in *Metaphysics* I, 5, 990 b: what types of ideal species exist?). Cf. Rossi-Landi, 1954[d]: 16, note 12, and *passim*.

9. These last words concerning events or objects *extraneous to semiosis in general* are certainly not to be taken for granted. Let us call it an hypothesis, and as such, one floating on a sea of problems concerning the very foundations of semiotics. What indeed *must* be extraneous to semiosis in general? What can, in principle, *refuse to perform* the task of functioning as a sign? If we say – nothing, i.e. if we affirm that everything is sign, then we find it difficult to set limits to the field of semiotics. In my opinion, the procedure apt to take us out of such an impasse must begin with the step of distinguishing between the study of signs and the study of the *various kinds of bodies capable of functioning as signs*, together with the study of the various "manners of production" which bring about the various kinds of bodies (a hint at this was given in note 5 above). We *start with signs and then discard* the sign function from the body, in this way facing something which I have labeled "the bodily residue of signs" (*Language as Work and Trade*, chapter on verbal and nonverbal language. [Cf. R.-L. 1968h; English transl. 1983b]; "Linguistics and Economics," *passim* in Chapters II, III, and IV. [Cf. R.-L. 1974f].

10. "Nous appelons *signe* la combinaison du concept et de l'image acoustique" (Saussure 1967: 150); "nous proposons ... de remplacer *concept et image acoustique* respectivement par *signifié* et *signifiant*" (*ibid.*: 151).

11. In talking of organisms while talking of pragmatics, I follow Morris's terminological preferences, something appropriate in a review article dedicated to his work. See, for instance, in *SLB*: "Any organism for which something is a sign will be called an *interpreter*" (*WGTS*: 93). Under this aspect too, the terminology of *FTS*, while less precise, is a little less committal. – There is general agreement that both human pragmatics and zoopragmatics deal with interpreters that are animal organisms within communities. Whether or not a phytosemiotics dealing with codes and messages in the vegetable kingdom is also possible, is for future research to decide. Apparently, plants do feel the presence of men and other animals. Of many man-built machines – as simple as sundials or as complicated as computers – it can be said that they "interpret" signs of various description, but it should be added that their "interpretation" is in its turn the object of *human* interpretation. This granted, some points made in the text about organisms also apply without major variations to machines. If there is a remaining uneasiness when talking of organisms, it comes from the always impending danger of falling into some form of biologism – the reduction of social behavior to merely biological behavior, or the explanation of the former by means of the latter, or the overlooking of some basic differences between the two. To free myself of such a spell, in the text I added the qualifications "mental" and/or "social" to such phrases as "relationships among organisms," and I called "*non*-social" the relationships which remain there when semiosis is *not* taken into account. The terms 'social' and 'mental' are to be construed only as hints at two dimensions of semiotic research.

References

Chaple, Sergio. 1972. "Apuntes sobre la ciencia literaria checa." *La Gaceta de Cuba* 100: 15-17.
Eco, Umberto. 1968. *La struttura assente*. Milan: Bompiani.
———. 1972. *Le forme del contenuto*. Milan: Bompiani.
Husserl, Edmund. 1949. *Cartesianische Meditationem und Pariser Vorträge* (= Husserliana, vol. I). The Hague: Nijhoff, 2nd 1963. *Méditations Cartésiennes*. Introduction à la phénoménologie. Transl. by G. Peiffer and E. Lévinas. Paris: Vrin, 1966. *Cartesian Meditations*. An Introduction to Phenomenology. Transl. by D. Cairns. The Hague: Nijhoff, 1960.
———. 1950. *Ideen zu einer reinen Phänomenologie und phänomenologischen Philosophie*. Book 1 (1913-1930) (= Husserliana, vol. III). The Hague: Nijhoff. Book 2: *Phänomenologische Untersuchungen zur Konstitution* (= Husserliana, vol. IV). Ed. by M. Biemel. The Hague: Nijhoff, 1952. Book 3: *Die Phänomenologie und die Fundamente der Wissenschaft* (= Husserliana, vol. V). Ed. by M. Biemel. The Hague: Nijhoff, 1952.
———. 1953. *Die Krisis der Europäischen Wissenschaften und die transzendentale Phänomenologie* (= Husserliana, vol. VI). The Hague: Nijhoff, 2nd 1962.
———. 1966a. *Zur Phänomenologie des inneren Zeitbewusstseins* (1893-1917) (= Husserliana, vol. X). Ed. by R. Boehm. The Hague: Nijhoff. *The Phenomenology of Internal Time, Consciousness*. Ed. by M. Heidegger. Transl. by J.S. Churchill. Introduction by C.O. Schrag. The Hague: Nijhoff, 1964.
———. 1966b. *Analysen zur passiven Synthesis*. Aus Vorlesungs- und Forschungsmanuskripten, 1918-1926. (= Husserliana, vol. XI). Ed. by M. Fleischer. The Hague: Nijhoff.
———. 1968. *Logische Untersuchungen*. Tübingen: Niemeyer. (Reprint of the 1913 edition). Vol. I; vol. II, part I, part II. *Logical Investigations*. Transl. by J.N. Findlay from the second German edition (1913, 1921). London: Routledge & Kegan Paul, 1970, 2 vols.
Jakobson, Roman. 1973. "Relations entre la science du langage et les autres sciences." Chapter 1 (pp. 9-76) of *Essais de linguistique générale*, tome 2: *Rapports internes et externes du langage*. Paris: Minuit.
Jakobson, Roman and Yury Tynianov. 1972. "Los problemas de los estudios literarios y lingüísticos." *La Gaceta de Cuba* 100: 22.
Koerner, E.F.K. 1972. *Contribution au débat post-saussurien sur le signe linguistique* (= Approaches to Semiotics, Paperback Series, 2). The Hague-Paris: Mouton.
Kristeva, Julia. 1969a. Σημειωτική. *Recherches pour une sémanalyse*. Paris: Seuil.
———. 1969b. "La sémiologie comme science des idéologies." *Semiotica* I, 2: 196-204.
———. 1972. "La semiótica, ciencia crítica y/o crítica de la ciencia." *Casa de las Américas* 71: 36-42.

Kristeva, Julia, Josette Rey-Debove, and Donna Jean Umiker (eds.). 1971. *Essays in Semiotics* (= Approaches to Semiotics, 4). The Hague: Mouton.

Lézine, Irène. 1972. "Los inicios de la función semiótica en el niño." *Santiago*. Revista de la Universidad de Oriente 6: 44-61.

Lotman, Yury M. 1972a. "Introducción a las lecciones de poética estructural." From the volume *Lessons in Structural Poetics*, 1970, *La Gaceta de Cuba* 105: 30-32.

———. 1972b. "El problema de una tipología de la cultura." *Casa de las Américas* 71: 43-48.

Marcus, Solomon. 1972a. "Poética y matemática." *Santiago*. Revista de la Universidad de Oriente 6: 73-79.

———. 1972b. "La poética matemática." *La Gaceta de Cuba* 103: 27-30.

Masters, Roger D. 1970. "Genes, Language, and Evolution." *Semiotica* II, 4: 295-320.

Mead, George Herbert. 1934. *Mind, Self and Society from the Standpoint of a Social Behaviorist*. Ed. and introd. by C. Morris. Chicago: University of Chicago Press, 5th ed. 1964.

Meletinsky, Elizar and Dimitri Segal. 1972. "Estructuralismo y semiótica en la URSS." *La Gaceta de Cuba* 100: 11-14.

Morris, Charles. [See the general bibliography of his writings. This Chapter, Section 2.10].

Mukařovský, Jan. 1972a. "En torno al estructuralismo." *La Gaceta de Cuba* 100: 7-10.

———. 1972b. "El arte como hecho semiológico" (Document, 1937). *Casa de las Américas* 71: 51-54.

Mulder, Jan W.F. and Sándor G.J Hervey. 1971. "Index and signum." *Semiotica* IV, 4: 324-338.

———. 1972. *Theory of the Linguistic Sign* (= Janua Linguarum, Series Minor, 136). The Hague-Paris: Mouton.

Navarro, Desiderio. 1972. "Coordenadas actuales de la crítica." *La Gaceta de Cuba* 100: 3-6.

Papastamatín, Basilia. 1972. "El trabajo estructral en Francia." *La Gaceta de Cuba* 100: 18-21.

Peirce, Charles Sanders. 1931-1958. *Collected Papers*. Vols. I-VI ed. by C. Hartshorne and P. Weiss; vols. VII and VIII ed. by A.W. Burks. Cambridge, MA: Harvard University Press.

Pelc, Jerzy. 1969. "Meaning as an Instrument." *Semiotica* I, 1: 26-48.

Price, H.H. 1953. *Thinking and Experience*. London: Hutchinson.

Rastier, François. 1972. *Idéologie et théorie des signes*. Analyse structurale des *Éléments d'idéologie* d'Antoine-Louis-Claude Destutt de Tracy. (= Approaches to Semiotics, 17). The Hague-Paris: Mouton.

Retamar, Roberto Fernández. 1972. "Nota." *Casa de las Américas* 71: 3-4.

Revzina, Olga G. 1972. "The Fourth Summer School on Secondary Modeling Systems (Tartu, 17-24 August 1970)." *Semiotica* VI, 3: 222-243.

Rossi-Landi, Ferruccio. [See the general bibliography of his writings at the end of this volume].
Ruesch, Jurgen. 1972. *Semiotic Approaches to Human Relations* (= Approaches to Semiotics, 257). The Hague-Paris: Mouton.
Ryle, Gilbert. 1949. *The Concept of Mind.* London: Hutchinson. Italian edition as *Lo spirito come comportamento*, by F. Rossi-Landi. Turin: Einaudi, 1955.
———. 1957. "The Theory of Meaning." In *British Philosophy in the Mid-Century.* Ed. by C.A. Mace, 239-264. London: Allen & Unwin. Reprinted in *Collected Papers*, vol. II (*Collected Essays 1929-1968*), 350-372. London: Hutchinson, 1971.
———. 1961. "Use, Usage and Meaning." *Proceedings* of the Aristotelian Society. Supplementary vol. XXXV: 223-230. Reprinted in *Collected Papers*, vol. II (*Collected Essays 1929-1968*), 407-414. London: Hutchinson, 1971.
Saussure, Ferdinand de. 1915. *Cours de linguistique générale.* Ed. by C. Bally, A. Sechehaye with the assistance of A. Riedlinger. Paris: Payot. 3rd ed. 1931, 5th ed. 1955, reprint 1964. *Course in General Linguistics*, English transl. introd. and notes by W. Baskin. New York-Toronto-London: McGraw-Hill Book Company, 1966.
———. 1967. *Cours de linguistique générale.* Critical edition by R. Engler. Wiesbaden: Harrassowitz.
Schaff, Adam. 1962. *Introduction to Semantics.* English transl. of *Wstęp do semantyki*, 1960, by O. Wojtasiewicz. Oxford: Pergamon Press.
———. 1964. *Język a poznanie.* Warsaw: Państwowe Wydawnictwo Naukowe. *Sprache und Erkenntnis.* German transl. by von E.M. Szarota. Vienna-Frankfurt-Zurich: Europa-Verlag, 1967. *Language et connaissance.* With the addition of six *Essais sur la philosophie du langage.* Translated from Polish by C. Brendel. Paris: Anthropos, 1967.
———. 1965. *Marxismus und das menschliche Individuum.* Vienna: Europa-Verlag.
———. 1967. "À propos de l'intégration des sciences de l'homme." *Actes* du Sixième Congrès mondial de sociologie, Evian, 4-11 September 1966. Vol. II, 85-99. Geneva: Association Internationale de Sociologie.
———. 1968a. *Essays über die Philosophie der Sprache.* Translated from Polish by E.M. Szarota. Vienna-Frankfurt-Zurich: Europa-Verlag.
———. 1968b. "Sprache, Denken, Handeln." *Proceedings* of the XIVth International Congress of Philosophy, Vienna, 2-9 September, 1968. Vol. I, 306-321. Vienna: Herder Verlag.
Sebeok, Thomas A. (ed.). 1964. *Animal Communication: Techniques of Study and Results of Research.* Bloomington: Indiana University Press.
Segal, Dimitri. Cf. Meletinsky, Elizar.
Tynianov, Yuri. 1972. "De la evolución literaria. La correlación de la literatura con la serie social." *La Gaceta de Cuba* 100: 23-26.
———. Cf. Jakobson, Roman.
Uspensky, Boris A. 1972. "Sobre la semiótica del arte." *Casa de la Américas* 71: 49-50.

Vailati, Giovanni. 1911. *Scritti*. Ed. by M. Calderoni, U. Ricci, and G. Vacca, with a Biography by O. Premoli. Florence-Leipzig: Seeber-Barth.
――――. 1967. *Il metodo della filosofia*. Saggi di critica del linguaggio. Ed. by F. Rossi-Landi. Bari: Laterza, 1st ed. 1957.
Verón, Eliseo. 1971. "Ideology and Social Sciences: A Communicational Approach." *Semiotica* III, 1: 59-76.
Vodicka, Félix. 1972. "La historia de la repercusión de las obras literarias." *La Gaceta de Cuba* 100: 27-31.
Wittgenstein, Ludwig. 1953. *Philosophische Untersuchungen* (1945). Oxford: Blackwell. Text and English transl. by G.E.M. Anscombe; 2nd ed. 1958, reprint 1967.
――――. 1956. *Bemerkungen über die Grundlagen der Mathematik* (1937-1944). Oxford: Blackwell. Text and English transl. by G.E.M. Anscombe; 2nd ed. 1958, reprint 1967.
――――. 1960. *Schriften*. Frankfurt-on-Main: Suhrkamp Verlag. Comprises *Tractatus, Philosophische Untersuchungen* and minor writings.
――――. 1964. *Philosophische Bemerkungen* (1930). Afterword and ed. by von R. Rhees. Oxford: Blackwell.
Young, Kate. 1972. "Los antropólogos y las estructuras de la comprensión." *Santiago*. Revista de la Universidad de Oriente 6: 62-72.
Žinkin, N.I. 1971. "Semiotic Aspects of Communication in Animal and Man." Review-article of *Animal communication*. [cf. Sebeok 1964]. *Semiotica* IV, 1: 75-93.

3. On some Post-Morrisian Problems*

3.1 Introduction

Since this paper is a dialogue between my old friend and master Charles Morris and myself (a real dialogue to the extent to which we did exchange views during several visits), I had better give some information about my interest for Morris's ideas before I start discussing some of them. In 1951-1952 I wrote a monograph examining all of Morris's publications up to that date. When it appeared in 1953, such a monograph possibly seemed excessive. This is no longer the case, now that Morris's place as the most important representative of twentieth century semiotics has been generally recognized. Semiotics itself, which in the fifties was still considered an appendix of philosophy or a biological science, has now acquired an independent scientific status of its own as a mainly (though by no means exclusively) *social science*, is practiced by thousands of scholars in all countries and has celebrated in 1974 its first very well attended international congress. I came back repeatedly to Morris in the years from 1953 to 1958. Since around 1955, however, I began trying to bring together, as I expressed it at the time, elements of the theory of Marxism with elements of "analytical" or "linguistic philosophy" (Rossi-Landi 1961[d], 1968[h]). In that period Morris, like many of his colleagues in the United States, was still seen on the European Continent as an "analytical" or "linguistic philosopher" and duly charged with the meta-

---

* About two thirds of this paper [cf. R.-L. 1978e] is a much abridged, entirely rearranged and rewritten version of the review article "Signs about a Master of Signs" [R.-L. 1975c; this volume Chapter 2], which originated with the publication in 1971 of Charles Morris's *Writings on the General Theory of Signs* (hereafter *WGTS*) and appeared in *Semiotica* XIII, 2, 1975: 155-197. The remaining third is new. In 1974 the review article was translated into Italian and partially rewritten as the second part of *Charles Morris e la semiotica novecentesca* (Charles Morris and Twenty-Century Semiotics), 1975, the first part of which is a reproduction of my 1951-1952 monograph on Morris (1953[a], and out of print for twenty years). In the following, page references are to Morris's 1971 volume. Part of this version was read and discussed at the University of Indiana, Bloomington, and at Texas Tech University, Lubbock, in March 1975, receiving healthy criticism in both places.

physical sin of "biologism." Also, most of the discussion about him consisted in locating him in this or that trend of analytical or linguistic philosophy and in comparing his position with the position of other philosophers of a similar description. His originality, however, was quickly perceived, especially in Italy where a translation of *Signs, Language, and Behavior* was produced by Silvio Ceccato in 1949. A number of papers, sections of books, and book reviews were at that time dedicated to his "linguistic" enquiries and are still worth reading from the point of view of the relations of general semiotics to philosophy (to limit myself to the initial period, cf. Ceccato 1948, 1949, 1951; Vaccarino 1949; Paci 1950; Filiasi-Carcano 1953, 1957; Scarpelli 1950, 1955; Barone 1953; Rossi-Landi 1953[a] and [b], 1954[d], 1958[a]; Geymonat 1956 now in 1960; I believe that an anthology in English of these first reactions "from another world," which in their own way were both candid and sophisticated, would be of great interest for semioticians today). The Italian concern for Morris was favored by a local tradition, the main representatives of which are Cattaneo, Peano, Vailati, Calderoni, Enriques, and Colorni, most of whom are now available in new editions listed in the References; and it certainly contributed to the early formation of the Italian Semiotic School.

Much time has passed. Semiotics has become very diversified. It now ranges from literary and other criticism to the study of animal communication, from enquiries into all sorts of human nonverbal sign systems to new approaches to the relationship between language and economy and to those between languages and other sign systems, on the one hand, and systems of values and ideologies, on the other. My own main interest lies in human semiotics and my present tendency is to *locate* human semiosis in social reproduction. Social reproduction (*gesellschaftliche Reproduktion*) is an originally Hegelo-Marxian notion concerning man *as distinguished from other animals*. The continuity between man and other animals is preserved or indeed materialistically asserted, but the attention is focused on their differences (see Section 3.4, below). Social reproduction is the reproduction of human societies. From this point of view, 'society' is properly or at least more pregnantly used for man only and tends to be a synonym of 'human society.'

The location of human semiosis within social reproduction is an intricate business. Two main approaches consist in studying from a semiotic point of view (i) the relations between "economic base" ("structure," "modes of production") and "superstructures" ("institutions," "ideologies"), and (ii) the relations between production, exchange, and consumption. This does not involve in the least that every study of such relations should necessarily be semiotical; nor is anybody claiming that nonhuman factors do not enter into social reproduction, too. Rather, the idea is that human sign systems and messages – the proper subject of human semiotics – are to be found and studied not only at the level of the economic base and at the level of superstructures where they certainly operate all the time, but also at a third relatively independent level intermediate between the economic base and the superstructures; and moreover, that they are to be found and studied all along the circle of production, exchange, and consumption. Now we know that human behavior is socially programmed. That it is also biologically programmed is obvious in a number of different ways which are currently investigated by natural scientists and which – given our notion of social reproduction as a limit-setting notion – concern more what men and other animals have in common than the ways in which they differ. From the point of view of *social* reproduction, then, human behavior is programmed at the three levels of the economic base, the sign systems, and the superstructures; and it is also programmed all along the circle production-exchange-consumption. This is an attempt at introducing semiotics into the historical-materialistic theory of social reproduction while at the same time, so to say, circumscribing human semiosis by paying heed to all the other factors which operate within social reproduction. I have dealt with some of the problems involved in this approach since the middle sixties; in English cf. *Linguistics and Economics* (1974[f]; as an independent volume 1975[b]). Other writings on the issue have appeared in the last few years or are in preparation.

3.2 Semiotics and Philosophy

In order properly to introduce some post-Morrisian problems, let us begin with some Morrisian ones. To start with, I want to say something about one of the ways in which contemporary semiotics arose out of contemporary philosophy and biology. Notice that the human or social sciences, especially linguistics, gave a relatively secondary contribution to the formation of contemporary semiotics. The important name of Ferdinand de Saussure, for instance, is absent from Morris's works.

Let us consider some of Morris's early writings. The problem of the sign, which had been faced by Morris in openly behavioristic terms as early as

1927 in the article "The Concept of the Symbol," was taken up again by him some ten years later, when in his mind a synthetic attitude had formed. In his important volume *Six Theories of Mind* of 1932, he had already arrived at the identification of the mind with the symbolic process. It was only in 1935, however, that Morris's approach to the problems of signs took the form of a general theory. In the article "Philosophy of Science and Science of Philosophy," Morris [1935a] analyzed some of the conceptions of philosophy which were current in those years; such analysis is to be found again in later writings, up to and including *Foundations of the Theory of Signs* (hereafter *FTS*) of 1938. The first conception analyzed was *philosophy as logic of science*, connected especially with the name of Carnap. The second conception was *philosophy as clarification of meaning*, present in American pragmatism and in one wing of the Vienna Circle (the first Wittgenstein, Schlick, Waismann; the second Wittgenstein, Moore, and their advocates in Great Britain). And finally, the third conception was *philosophy as empirical axiology*, as found in Schlick and especially in Dewey. If we accept these three conceptions together, Morris said, we have philosophy as a "language of languages" or a general theory of symbolism. Various aspects of this idea were investigated – to name only some main articles whose titles already give some indication of their content – in "The Concept of Meaning in Pragmatism and Logical Positivism" of 1934 (published in 1936), "Pragmatism and Metaphysics" of the same year, "The Relation of the Formal and Empirical Sciences within Scientific Empiricism" of 1935, "The Relation of Formal to Instrumental Logic" of 1929. The relations of a theory of symbolism with pragmatism were analyzed in "Peirce, Mead, and Pragmatism" of 1938, in the introductions to Mead's works *Mind, Self, and Society* (1934[b]), and *The Philosophy of the Act* (1938[d]); later, also in "William James Today" of 1942, and again in a book on the pragmatic movement in American philosophy (1970[b]).

A philosophical synthesis called *scientific empiricism* was thus developed. When we examine the meaning of an expression from the point of view of its relations with other expressions, with the things meant, and with those who make use of that expression – said Morris – we open the path to its full determination. In traditional empiricism three principal defects could be found: the scarce justice rendered to formal sciences, the inability to connect an empirical theory of meaning to a naturalistic cosmology, and the tendency to subjectivism. A scientific empiricism which has been transformed into a semiotics permits an understanding of each one of these three defects as arising from the neglect of one of the three main dimensions of signs.

In the small volume *Logical Positivism, Pragmatism, and Scientific Empiricism* (1937), five of the above writings are brought together. I suggest that beginners in semiotics should consider it a must. The article "Scientific Empiricism" (1938[a]) is a reworking of the volume's content for the *Encyclopedia of Unified Science*, the program of which had been developed at the "Congress of Philosophical Science" of 1935; in fact, *FTS* appeared in the *Encyclopedia*. It is important, Morris insisted, to embrace an empiricism which is radical, a rationalism which is a study of method, and a pragmatism which is critical. These are the three components that correspond to the *three dimensions of semiotics*. Radical empiricism is *semantic* investigation, methodological rationalism is *syntactic* investigation, critical pragmatism is *pragmatic* investigation. The unity of science thus results from the unity of its linguistic structure, from the semantic relationships which it succeeds in establishing, and from the practical effects it produces. Notice that in this way even the three traditional fields of philosophy – logic, metaphysics, and the theory of values – were indirectly re-presented in semiotic terms.

All this may seem surprising to anyone coming to semiotics without a taste of philosophico-historical culture. For instance, one could nowadays accept, or refuse, the tripartition of semiotics as a mere result of objective investigation carried out on signs. Instead, such "objective" investigation would not have been possible without the described confluence of different currents of thought. The ideological bias of each of them was too strong.

There are two main conceptions of semiotics running through Morris's works: semiotics as the heir of philosophy and the organ of the sciences – expressed especially in the preparatory writings indicated above and then in *FTS*; and semiotics as a basically biological science, or better, as a science which is behavioral in a biological sense – expressed especially in *Signs, Language, and Behavior* (hereafter *SLB*) of 1946. In the first case, philosophical discourse, provided it keeps itself up to date with regard to both formal and empirical sciences, becomes semiotic discourse; in the second case, instead, philosophical discourse is considered on a plane with other possible types of discourse, subject to semiotic investigation. Both of these positions contain outworn and contingent elements together with valid elements, and both are well worthy of discussion and integration. In the fifties I dealt with them at some length in a number of writings which are now out of date (Rossi-Landi 1953[a and b], 1954[d], 1958[a]). As for the disquieting problems of the relationships between current semiotic research and whatever may still be understood as philosophy, they cannot be faced here. At any rate, I do not know of anyone who is completely clear about them. What I do know is that there is a conspicuous lack of philosophical depth in a majority of linguists, literary critics, and semioticians, when they happen to use such historically laden terms as, for instance, 'material,' 'ideal,' 'natural,' 'social,' 'individual,' and a good many others; they use them as if they were liable to commonsensical interpretation, and this *is* nonsensical.

3.3 Signs and Values

A glance at Morris's bibliography makes it apparent that he dealt with values at least as much as he dealt with signs. The main titles are: *Paths of Life: Preface to a World Religion* (1942[b]); *The Open Self* (1948[c]); *Varieties of Human Value* (1956[b]); *Signification and Significance. A Study of the Relations of Signs and Values* (1964[a]); and there are many essays in addition to these volumes.

We can use one of his essays as an example of this dual interest. "Esthetics and the Theory of Signs" (1939[b]) is perhaps, by common consent, the single text which has most contributed to the formation of an esthetic semiotics in the proper sense. It is also one of the works where Morris dealt expressly with signs and values in the course of the same discussion. What Morris proposed was not a semiotic esthetics, or even more narrowly an only semantic esthetics, but rather a semiotics with three dimensions, which is esthetic insofar as it applies to the field of art. The difference between an "esthetic semiotics" and a "semiotic esthetics" is that the former is a particular application of the science of signs, and as such is a bridge between art and all that goes into the foundations of the science of signs. A "semiotic esthetics," instead, may even be a Speculative Esthetics as a sector of some Philosophical Superscience; it may be content with the use, some use, of some semiotical instruments.

According to Morris, the field of esthetic criticism in a wide sense was comprehensive of both esthetic analysis and esthetic judgment, the latter being esthetic criticism in the narrow sense. Both disciplines were metalinguistic because they dealt with signs. The signs they dealt with were the signs of which a work of art consists. According to the well-known, though still embryonic, definition of the esthetic sign "as an iconic sign whose *designa-*

tum is a value," signs and values were thus both present. But while esthetic analysis as a sector of semiotic analysis belonged to scientific discourse, esthetic criticism belonged to "technological" discourse. In those years, Morris described any discourse in which evaluations have taken place as "technological," a point which becomes clearer when one knows that he considered then as principal three types of discourse: scientific, esthetic, and technological (especially in "Science, Art, and Technology" [1939c]). In "Empiricism, Religion, and Democracy" (1942[a]), the types of discourse became four, according to four main functions of signs. This was the beginning of the process which brought Morris to the still important and seminal classification of Types of Discourse in Chapter 5 of *SLB*.

If judgment, however, belonged to technological discourse, esthetic criticism required not only a theory of signs (sufficient for esthetic analysis), but also a theory of values (cf. Sections 3 and 12 of "Esthetics and the Theory of Signs"). In this way, esthetic criticism involved values at two levels: at the level of esthetic analysis, because of the value bearing character of esthetic signs; and at the level of esthetic judgment, because of the necessity of a theory of values. Morris was thus placing values beside signs and opposing the idea that the mere study of signs could give any right to judge about values. Presentday discussions on the limits of structuralism, on the differences between analysis and evaluation, and on the relations between systems of signs and systems of values or ideologies tend to indicate that no semiotic system, and the more so no text, can be completely understood and properly assessed unless the values it necessarily springs from, and conveys, are also taken into account (to give a few examples, cf. the works of Corti, Eco, Kristeva, Rastier, Rossi-Landi, Segre, Verón, and Bakhtin-Voloshinov).

3.4 Charles Morris and Social Practice

One thing that strikes readers of *FTS* a third of a century after it was written is the breadth of its approach. I dealt with this in an essay of 1958, where I attempted an interpretation of the two principal phases of Morris's semiotics both in terms of the "special" (or "technical," or "ideal") languages purposely constructed to talk about signs in general, and in terms of the universes of discourse into which the special languages themselves could be included. Here I only want to stress that the breadth of the approach in *FTS* can be seen in several directions. I shall comment on three of them: habits in the use of signs as social practice in this Section, semiosis and meaning, in Section 3.5.

In *FTS* the fundamental terms introduced to describe the global situation of semiosis were traced back, at least hypothetically, to a single term, the 'mediated-taking-account-of' ([*WGTS*], pp. 19-21, 45, and *passim*). This primitive term was then in its turn to be traced back, especially in *SLB* (note I [*WGTS*], p. 108), to behavioral biopsychology. In *FTS*, however, it was introduced *alongside* the notion of "habits of behavior" in the use of a language (as of any nonverbal sign system), and indeed ended up by becoming identified with it (*FTS* [*WGTS*], pp. 37, 41-42, 59). Morris was explicit: "the interpretant of a sign is the habit ...," etc. (p. 47).

The notion of habit was not completely clarified by Morris, nor could it have been in such a brief investigation as *FTS*. Much water has passed under the innumerable bridges of philosophy and science in these decades, so that the notion of habit must now be viewed in terms of disciplines which contemporary research considers as interconnected to varying degrees. From what one derives rereading *FTS*, the notion of "behavioral habit in the use of signs" can be referred to: (a) personal characteristics of those who use a sign system; (b) biopsychological processes common to all the individuals who have that habit, when the individuals are considered in their psycho-physical materiality; (c) social facts and processes, with reference to the community to which the individuals belong and of which (according to the doctrine that individuals are "produced" by their community) they are products, or with reference to sections of such communities (social classes and other divisions and oppositions within a given society); (d) social facts and processes with reference to general features of human society at large; (e) the specific operations, which may be formally extrapolated and described, carried out by those who are practicing that habit, that is, the techniques that anyone using a sign system has learned, possesses, applies, and transmits to younger generations in a way which is common to other speakers and listeners, and which can be applied in a more or less correct manner.

Morris insisted on the type of behaviorism he preferred: not a strictly biological behaviorism of the Watsonian sort, which in terms of the history of ideas is mechanistic materialism, but rather – through the broader behaviorism of Tolman and Hull – a declaredly social behaviorism like Mead's. It seems legitimate to me, therefore, to advance the interpretation most favorable to Morris: he had abandoned the narrow paths of *behaviorism* and had ventured onto the terrain of a *behavioristics* (he uses this term himself) which may end up by becoming identified with the study of practice or human action in general. Since man is man only socially, human action could have been understood by Morris himself as *social practice*. He even used this expression in the title of a short article in 1940; and in our conversations he accepted this interpretation of his "behaviorism" as substantially more correct than any other he could think of.

There is, of course, a tradition in the use of the syntagm 'social praxis' within the United States. To give a relatively remote example, John Dewey's Presidential Address to the American Psychological Association in 1899 was entitled "Psychology and Social Practice," and we find it reprinted in 1963 in a collection of Dewey's earlier papers, edited by J. Ratner under the title *Philosophy, Psychology, and Social Practice*. By introducing the notion of social practice at this point, however, we are making a jump outside the tradition of thought to which Morris, or even Dewey, belongs. The generalized notion of social practice is the active side to social reproduction and in some contexts almost becomes a synonym of it. As such it is the central pillar of the historico-materialistic conception of the world. According to this conception, some animals started *to work together* on this planet, that is, they began developing a quasi-social practice which was new and different from the practices of all other animals. Attention is focused here on what was and remained new and different, not on what was left unchanged or fell back to the original level. Historical evolution in a wide sense began to superimpose itself on biological evolution also *insofar as* the animal destined to become man was using new, more and more species-specific and species-universal sign systems based fundamentally on *work* and *exchange*. Other animals do use complex systems of communication (Sebeok 1972); there is no main kind of sign which is exclusively human (Sebeok 1976: 117-142); and the field is possibly open to extraordinary discoveries. But again, what interests us here is the measure in which the new sign systems were in fact developed until they did become basically species-specific and species-universal, not the measure in which there remained in them something shared by other animals, or that in which they developed differently in various human tribes.

Moreover, what one does find at a certain point in historical evolution is the exclusive, species-specific and species-universal *co-presence of various factors*, whether or not any one of them is also present in this or that non-human species. Quantitative accumulation gave rise to *qualitative leaps*. Even the notion of territory which is basic for the study of all animals undergoes a radical change when we use it for the human world (Vaughan's unpublished manuscripts); and so do the notions of aggression, hierarchy, and many others. There is no more direct connection to the animal world when we state that what comes to be known by scientific enquiry is also due to the transformation of nature operated by man, *and* vice versa (cf. on this the long-overdue English translation of Kosík 1963 in the *Boston Studies in the Philosophy of Science*, 1976). The disconnection is even deeper when we add that both scientific enquiry and the transformation of nature are strictly intertwined with the production of consensus by political power within what Gramsci labeled "civil society" (cf. the magnificent analytical index at the end of the critical edition of his *Quaderni del carcere*, 1975). As Hegel put it, "paradise is a garden where only animals can remain" (*Philosophie der Geschichte*, IX: 391; Italian transl. III: 241).

Successive generations were *taught* to build and use new sign systems in better and better ways through social practice, the common activity of the people. What is essential in this process is that *new results were continuously used as new materials and new instruments*. In fact, the most constructive side to social practice is work, and work is basic in the formation of the most elementary units of so-called material production. Flints already required pretty complicated operations which of course had to be taught by experts (cf. Leakey 1954: 128-139). As I have tried to show since 1965, work is also basic in the formation of such elementary units as phonemes (Rossi-Landi 1965, now in 1968h, 2nd ed. 1973: 61-68, 181-221; 1972[c]: 65-70; 1974[f], now in 1975b, 2nd ed. 1977: 32-54, 78-108; and cf. Prieto's contribution to the issue, 1975: 53-56, 124-127, and *passim*). If we considered phonemes either as natural or as mental entities, we would be subtracting them from human work, i.e. from the core of the common activity of the people. Odd problems would then arise. For instance, if such entities are only either natural or mental, or (by re-joining the two severed pieces) only natural-and-mental, why is it that they are different from one language to another, from one place to another, from one period to another, from one human group to another? The obvious answer is that they are instead the product of social practice; and social practice, while having common features everywhere, can vary endlessly *in its manifestations*. What matters here is that in a given community the same operations are performed and taught to the new-born. Within the community people understand each other as a result of having learned the same social practice, and not the other way around. To assume instead that people can learn the same social practice *because* they understand each other would amount to putting the Cartesian cart of a preformed self before the horse which is responsible for pulling it. The different ways in which the social practice of the various communities is distributed among different aims give us an opening on such problems as the complication of primitive languages as distinguished from the relative simplicity of languages of highly developed communities.

Social practice continued to develop in its three principal forms: the struggle for production, that is, the appropriation and transformation of natural resources; class struggle in the wide sense of group distinctions, oppositions, and exploitation within every community and among different communities; and scientific research allowing for new technological developments in their turn furthering the struggle for production. Complementary layers of communicative systems, both verbal and nonverbal, were developed within these three forms. Social practice also produced the myths, the illusions, the moral techniques and the techniques of control for the formation of the consensus that it needed as it went along – *including different conceptions of reality*. The main point here is that the very conception of reality prevailing at any given moment is an expression of the dominant social practice, and not the other way around. To believe instead that social practice founded itself on a given conception of reality amounts to making a colossal inversion. This, however, does not mean that conceptions of reality are deprived of the possibility of retro-acting on social practice. In fact, they do retro-act by means of sign systems, in this way shaping *future* social practice – much as it is in terms and by means of sign systems that the various conceptions of reality are expressed. While this is not the place to continue the discussion of social practice, the point must be made that Morris's "philosophical synthesis leading to semiotics," was so vigorous that it succeeded in expressing itself even in notions which were used only in a restricted sense or occasionally within his own tradition of thought, so to say enlarging these notions from the inside. Those very notions, however, had been generalized, and are still considered fundamental, elsewhere.

3.5 Semiosis and Meaning

Morris had the merit of presenting semiosis as a *global situation* in which the terms introduced as fundamental – 'sign,' 'designatum,' 'interpretant,' and 'interpreter' – "involve one another, since they are simply ways of referring to aspects of the process" (*WGTS*, p. 19).

> The properties of being a sign, a *designatum* [later called *significatum* by Morris himself, R.-L.], an interpreter, or an interpretant are relational properties which things take on by participating in the functional process of semiosis. Semiotic [later called semiotics, but apparently only because of a mistake made by a typist some time in the thirties, R.-L.], then, is not concerned with the study of a particular kind of object, but with ordinary objects *in so far (and only in so far)* as they participate in semiosis. (*ibid.*, p. 20 [my italics, R.-L.])

Sign properties are not "objective" properties like color, form, or weight; but neither are they "subjective" properties like taste, pleasure, pain (things are not this simple; but the dichotomy objective-subjective is still useful). They are *nonobjective properties which any object can acquire in given circumstances.* The circumstances are those forming the global situation of semiosis. Given an approach of this kind, various remarks can be made regarding in particular the classes and systems of objects *purposely produced* for use as signs.

The specific character of a large part of sign production seems to be an argument against Morris's approach. In fact, we could maintain that sign objects, once produced, exist in reality within their systems, and that therefore it is not true that they are nonobjective properties. But to this one can answer that the objects produced must be, in fact, *produced*, and then *used*, that is, that human operation always enters into the question; and this seems to be an argument in favor of Morris's approach. The above objection stresses in its way the separation between the products and the process of production and reproduction; the answer stresses the tie between products, on the one hand, and production, reproduction, and use, on the other. Both have their validity; and perhaps the contrast may be resolved by avoiding the confusion between

A. the *nonobjective character of signs as such*, and
B. the *objective character of the use of signs*.

B. the use of signs organized in systems is a social reality; as such, it is objective at least in the sense that no individual or group of individuals can change it at will.

But it does not follow from the objective character of the behavioral habits of any human community or of society as a whole (B) that the signs thus used are themselves objective instruments (A). If they were, demystification would never be possible. That any piece of demystification is always arduous precisely because of the objective character of social habits, is another aspect of the problem.

To put it in a different way, the property of being a sign is a *social property* which has nothing to do with the properties of either *signans*, or *signatum*, or thing signified, especially if we consider each of them by itself, before it enters the semiosic synthesis. The property of being a sign is the direct result of a given piece of the social practice that I call "linguistic production" and "linguistic work." This result is used as an instrument whose properties are not objective. Every instance of social practice – unless for some purpose it is viewed itself as the result of a previous or of a higher-order social practice – is instead what it is; you cannot change it, and when you think that you are discarding it, all you are doing in most cases is just proceeding to *another* instance of social practice. This is the sense in which social habits do have an objective character and it is so difficult really to undo them. A rudimentary example is that you cannot use *perro* for a cat in a Spanish speaking community; you cannot interfere with the social practice in the sense of undoing it. But you can of course go over to another community, in this way "changing" the instance of social practice by mere substitution and find, for example, that in a Hungarian speaking community one has to use *kutya* for a dog, and cannot use it for a cat anymore than one could use *perro*. There is nothing objective in the linguistic signs *dog, perro*, or *kutya*. But the behavioral habits, i.e. the instance of social practice which put them into effect by using those *signantia* as they are used, are objective. Notice that if you go to a Spaniard and tell him that Hungarians describe cats as *kutyák*, you are using the objective character of his linguistic production both if you succeed in cheating him and if you do not.

The fact remains that for Morris in *FTS* any object can in principle *become* a sign, provided some qualifications are made as to the use of 'object.' This is undoubtedly true. Actually, it is the broadest approach that can be given to general semiotics without falling into the idealistic fallacy of asserting that everything *is, and cannot help being*, a sign (I have examined some other features of these problems in "Signs and Bodies," forthcoming [cf. 1979b; this volume Chapter 12]).

Another aspect of the breadth of Morris's approach is his conception of meaning. "Nothing is intrinsically a sign or a sign-vehicle," Morris stated, "but *becomes* such only *in so far as* it permits something to take account of something through its mediation" ([*WGTS*], p. 57; my own italics). This holds true also for meaning – for all meanings of 'meaning':

> Meanings are not to be located as existences at any place in the process of semiosis but are to be characterized in terms of this process as a whole. 'Meaning' is a semiotical term and not a term in the thing-language; to say that there are meanings in nature is not to affirm that there is a class of entities on a par with trees, rocks, organisms, and colors, but that such objects and properties function within processes of semiosis. (*ibid.*)

Meaning is thus extended to the whole situation of semiosis; it is a semiotical, not merely a semantic term.

> 'Meaning' signifies any and all phases of sign-processes (the status of being a sign, the interpretant, the fact of denoting, the significatum) ([*WGTS*], p. 95) ... For the major purposes which the everyday languages serve it has not been necessary to denote with precision the various factors in semiosis – the process is merely referred to in a vague way by the term 'meaning'. ([*ibid.*], p. 56)

Morris preferred not to use the term because he felt it was too vague (*FTS* [*WGTS*], pp. 55-59; *SLB* [*WGTS*], p. 95). But he examined it, and it is good that he did so. The term has continued to be used in various ways by innumerable semioticians, linguists, logicians, philosophers, anthropologists, sociologists, psychologists, psychiatrists, and other scientists (leaving alone picturesque hosts of *dilettanti*). It is precisely because 'meaning' is a quasi-synonym of 'semiosis' that no one succeeds in erasing it not only from everyday language, but even from scientific discourse.

In Morrisian terminology, the semantic dimension of semiosis regards the relationships of signs with their *significata* and their possible *denotata*; the pragmatic dimension concerns the relationships of signs with their interpreters and interpretants; the syntactic dimension involves the relationships among signs. Each of the three subdisciplines of semiotics, which corresponds to the three dimensions, concentrates on the respective dimension, leaving aside to some extent the other two. It was with much prudence that Morris came back to his tripartition in *SLB* ([*WGTS*], pp. 301-303). The main point was – and is – that one must not believe that *there are* semantic, syntactic, or pragmatic signs; this would be absurd because every sign is all three things by definition – we do not have a sign if we do not have semiosis, that is, the *simultaneous presence* of the three dimensions. It is therefore always with signs that the three subdisciplines of semiotics are dealing. Signs, complete signs were what was dealt with by the various currents of thought flowing into scientific empiricism which, in its turn, became identified with a general theory of symbolism, that is, with semiotics.

What would happen, in fact, if we took away semiosis and tried to analyze what remained? What would there be to analyze? One could think of various orders of things: (i) All physical, corporal, or material (in an inclusive sense of this term – the sense in which electric and other waves are obviously material too) "things" that exist in the world. What is left aside here is *how* such "things" can be put together and used in the complex ways which produce semiosis. (ii) Actions, prevalently those carried out by human and animal organisms. These actions are purposely isolated as non-sign actions, that is, as sheer movements of bodies in space and time (cf. Sections 3.6 and 3.7 below). (iii) Processes taking place within human or animal organisms, or within machines, examined by disciplines like physiology or electronics, respectively. Here, too, all the functions which are in one way or another sign functions are purposely left aside. (iv) Nonphysical entities postulated by thought, whether they are recognized as products of thought itself or held to be objects of special "apperceptions." (The existence of non-sign thought is, of course, a problem on its own; even more so is the independent existence of nonphysical entities.)

Separately, according to the three dimensions and having taken away semiosis: the syntactic dimension would become the study of geometric, or acoustic, or other physical relationships among vehicles which were (or will be) sign-vehicles; the semantic dimension would become the study of the relationships among platonic objects which were (or will be) *significata*, as well as among objects whatsoever (physical or nonphysical, actions, and also other signs or other non-signs) which were (or will be) *denotata*; the pragmatic dimension, finally, would become the study of the *non*-social relationships among organisms which were (or will be) interpreters and among their actions, or internal modifications, which were (or will be) interpretants. There are, on all this, several passages in *FTS* which I would advise any reader to examine carefully (cf., for example, page 56 in *WGTS*).

It would seem to follow from the above discussion that saying 'sign,' 'semiosis,' or 'meaning' is saying *almost* the same thing – almost, because using one of the three terms can serve to accentuate this or that aspect of the situation. In other words, the three terms tend to *overlap*. It is from this point of view that we must judge the three "reductions" that have generally dominated the field: the reduction of meaning to the semantic dimension alone; the reduction of the organic (or of the mental, or of the social) to the pragmatic dimension alone; and the reduction of the formal to the syntactic dimension alone.

As against these three reductions, the thesis I believe one must defend remains, basically, the thesis advanced by Morris in the thirties. If a *semiotically constitutive* property belongs to one of the three dimensions, then it belongs necessarily also to the other two. The dimensions are manners of abstracting, of leaving aside something in order to concentrate on something else. The totality from which one has partially abstracted continues to be present, just as the parts from which one is provisionally prescinding are present. Abstraction of one part from the rest of the totality it belongs to is a stage in social practice posterior to the stage in which the totality was produced. One cannot – after having arrived at the synthesis which is called semiotics – simply fall back and "force" the formal into syntactics alone, meaning into semantics alone, and the biological (or mental or social) into pragmatics alone. A full comprehension of the structure of semiosis lies precisely in this: semiosis is a network of relationships of various kinds – formal, meaningful, biological, *social* relationships. The whole structure of semiosis, once articulated, *is* that whole structure; all of its pieces *are* all of its pieces. Morris's anti-separatistic stance was very clearly stated in his own work. And, as we said, in spite of the terminology he had to use at that time, his approach almost coincided with an approach based on social practice, i.e. on the common activity performed by men as members of a given historical community.

3.6 Behavior and Communication

The construction of *SLB* pivoted in great measure on the identification and definition of the sign and of sign-behavior. The field was immediately narrowed down by taking into consideration only goal-seeking behavior, or certain types of goal-seeking behavior. "Goal-seeking behavior in which signs exercise control," said Morris, "may be called *sign-behavior*" ([*WGTS*], p. 85). It was with much caution, and by successive approximations, that he came to his well-known and still seminal definition of 'sign':

> *If anything, A, is a preparatory stimulus which in the absence of stimulus-objects initiating response-sequences of a certain behavior-family causes a disposition in some organism to respond under certain conditions by response-sequences of this behavior-family, then A is a sign.* ([ibid.], p. 87; italics in the text)

In my 1953 monograph on Morris, I had subjected this definition to criticism which – right or wrong as it may have been – was intended to get down to the root of Morris's thought. My view consisted particularly in this: that it was not really possible to distinguish between sign-behavior and non-sign-behavior *by means of behavioristic biopsychology*. This implied, however, that the distinction might have been possible through other means.

I would now like to advance a few remarks of a different type, even if in some ways recalling the criticism of twenty-five years ago. It is not possible to distinguish between sign-behavior *tout court* and non-sign-behavior *tout court*, I now maintain, for the good reason that *all* behavior *is* sign-behavior; otherwise it is something to be called 'moving about,' or perhaps only 'physiological process.' We shall return to this point in Section 3.7. Here we are discussing not only Morris's thought, but "the thing itself" (I take the liberty of uttering these sacred words only after a trip to Königsberg, now Kalinengrad, and not without paying proper attention to Euler's problem of the seven bridges). The thesis is that any piece of behavior – in the central sense of this term – communicates something and that, conversely, nothing can be communicated if not by means of some piece of behavior. Let us examine these statements.

Given the two very general categories, communication and behavior, we want to know their relationship of co-presence and of exclusion. There are four possibilities: neither behavior nor communication, communication and behavior, behavior without communication, communication without behavior. The first eliminates any object for inquiry. The second is obvious: there is nothing to object to the fact that behavior and communication *accompany each other*. There remain the other two possibilities. Can there be behavior without communication? Can there be communication without behavior? The answer to both is "no."

There can be no *behavior without communication* because one cannot conceive that a human, or also a nonhuman, animal that behaves in some way, carries out some activity, in short, *does* something, communicates nothing at all. This is true in two senses: that no animal can ever survive in his community without codes and without some sort of social or at least collective programming of his individual behavior; and that, in any case, by observing what the animal is doing or *is not doing*, information can always be gained. If we reduce the totality of communication to some of its sectors – for example, to those which are usually defined as conscious and/or intentional and/or finalistic – we can then believe that we are differentiating between some behavior which is sign and therefore communicative behavior, and other behavior. This "other behavior" is declared to be non-sign, noncommunicative, because it falls outside a preselected zone. The reduction, already present in the premise, emerges again in the conclusion. But really we have only distinguished between two different types of sign-behavior, between two different types of communication.

It does not take much to show that there is unconscious and/or unintentional and/or nonfinalistic (spontaneous, free, casual) behavior (and it neither proves nor disproves the doctrine of the finalism of life in general). If I speak to you, I usually *intend* to communicate something to you and am usually *conscious* of it. But certainly, if you observe me closely while I am talking, I also communicate other things which can escape even my own attention. If then I keep quiet, but I scratch my head without realizing it, or I sigh or make a gesture which I do not heed, I communicate information about myself all the same. I do it without knowing it or wanting to, without having the intention, without any aim; and it often happens that what I communicate in such ways is indeed in contrast with an aim I do have. In short, the fact is that the types of behavior "excluded" from the preselected zone are also so to say "full of signs"; they cannot be otherwise because they are founded in any case on codes, are programmed. They must have been learned, if only by unconscious imitation, and therefore lend themselves to interpretation. A man who walks along the road without in the least paying attention to what he is doing is never a mere body moving in space and time: he is a man dressed in a certain way, who is walking in a certain way along a certain road, and so forth. None of these things come from (mere) nature. With all the specifications the man bears and which surround him, he cannot avoid communicating to an observer a large amount of information about himself and about the social group to which he belongs.

We do not want do deny that for certain very precise purposes the behavior of the walker can be isolated from everything else, or considered only from the point of view of what he knows about himself in that moment, or compared to previously prepared paradigms of what a piece of behavior has to be in order to be described as sign-behavior. Thus, as a result of all this, in given circumstances it may appear to be appropriate, within that special context, to call it non-sign-behavior. Similarly, we do not want to deny that the behavior (examined by Morris) of the dog who interprets the buzzer as a sign for food is a typical, clear, and accessible case of sign-behavior, where the inception of a new sign, which had been expected and hoped for, and the consequences which derive from it in the behavior of the dog, are particularly evident. But the fact is that the walker is following codes and programs even if he does not know it, and is thus communicating; and the dog does the same even when he does *not* receive signals for food (for example, he may give signs of hunger by moving about in an agitated way or by acting languid and droopy). So much so that we interpret very well both the sign-behavior of the walker and the sign-behavior of the hungry dog.

It would seem that just these conclusions could be used to maintain that, anyhow, there can be *communication without behavior*. Just as the man who walks along the road communicates something even if he does not know it and even if he does not want to, and likewise for the dog, so – one could argue – a man who "doesn't behave at all" also communicates something. But what does 'not behaving at all' mean? I can think of only two instances: immobility and death.

The immobility of a living being can only be partial and transitory. Partial, because its organism continues to move internally, and it is only by restricting our point of view that we do not take account of this. It is with regard to this restriction that we call behavior only the macroscopic behavior of a whole organism, or of one of its parts which is easily visible from the outside. Even so, immobility will still always be a momentary case of non-behavior isolated as a *determined* negation and thereby returning under the category of behavior itself. It is precisely because life is continuous behavior that even a momentary cessation of behavior, of all behavior, communicates something. In this way, for example, somebody who instead of replying to a question remains silent, is communicating something, for instance, embarrassment. There is even the popular saying "no news is good news." But nobody would say that keeping silent or not answering letters are extraneous to behavior in general.

With similar arguments one can deny even the exception of the dead man, about whom one can maintain that with his dead body itself he is communicating something. A dead man certainly no longer does anything, he does not behave in any way; but this is nothing other than the conclusion of everything that that organism has done up to the moment of its death. His immobility, this time not transitory, contrasts with the mobility of his whole life. A corpse continues to communicate something because we recognize in it what remains of a man or of an animal; in these remains we are still discovering the signs of its life. When, as the poet says, "God forgets about his face," then on that face there will no longer be signs of past life. Still, even in a skeleton disinterred after millennia the signs of socialization are found; and where these no longer exist, still a dimension of biological signs remains, interpretable by men. Being the cessation of *all* behavior, death is a negation fully determined by behavior itself and must be included in the general category of behavior. This amounts to saying that *death exists only for life*. Having rejected even the extreme case of death, we conclude that we cannot say that communication ever exists without behavior.

Now, since there is no communication without signs, the doubly negative conclusion we have reached can be immediately translated into the initial statement that it is not possible to distinguish sign-behavior from non-sign-behavior *in general*. It is instead possible, and obviously of the greatest importance, to distinguish and classify various types of sign-behavior, at various levels, and with every possible superimposition, concomitance, or exclusion. The following are some of the main distinctions: verbal and non-verbal, conscious and unconscious, intentional and unintentional, finalistic and spontaneous (or free, or casual), founded on complex codes or on simple codes, of a digital type or of an analogical type, from the point of view of the sender or from that of the receiver, as isolated as possible and taken by itself or instead projected on the background of concentric or excentric contexts of various sizes, for its immediate signification or for the consequences that derive from it; and so on, one might almost say, endlessly. The distinction between signification and communication, of which some linguists seem to make so much, appears to be a pile of some of the above distinctions. Apart from some cases of separatistic make-believe, what one usually finds here is a stipulatory definition of 'human communication' as a field of enquiry, the basic terms of which are 'intention of the transmitter,' 'awareness of the receiver,' 'common possession of the complex code of verbal language,' and the like. This being the legitimate interest of the stipulator, all the rest recedes in the background as "mere signification" – sometimes it is an illegitimate recession.

It bears repetition that Morris himself had systematically begun (often very acutely and always in a balanced manner) distinctions and classifications of the various kinds of sign-behavior and of their contexts (in Chapters IV and V of my 1953 [now 1975d] monograph on Morris, many important passages from *SLB* and other texts on such issues were systematically anthologized). The fact remains that the search for a sign-behavior is actually the search for a particular type of sign-behavior, even if, within a given range, this may be a very characteristic and even a necessary one. To imagine that one sign-behavior is more sign than the others would recall Orwell's famous fable of the community of equals in which some equals were more equal than others.

3.7 Behaving and "Moving About"

I would like to observe, at least in passing, that the assimilation of behavior and communication does not at all exclude, and in fact requires, that there be in the world "non-sign things"; behavior and communication, and thus behavior and signs, join hands so that *together they may distinguish themselves from all the rest*. What lies in the background of this approach is an interpretation of behavior, and therefore also a definition or proposal for the use of the term 'behavior,' that I think particularly useful for the purposes of semiotics. If there is no behavior without communication, that is, if all behavior *is* sign-behavior, semiotics can – with its own instruments, from its own point of view, and within its own limits – investigate every type and occurrence of behavior. And if there are neither signs nor communication without behavior, the investigation will have at least this anchor to something men can deal with in common. This last formulation, while bringing us back to the notion of social practice, still retains a certain Morrisian flavor. And why shouldn't it? Morris had already tried to pass from a mechanistic behaviorism to a social behaviorism. We have hinted above in this paper at the nearness of the two notions of social behavior and social practice. *An operational foundation* of the human sciences in social practice is not only possible, but urgently needed, even in our field. We want to dispel scientific myths founded on the assumption that the *principles* of things can be located somewhere outside of social practice, so that their consequences could be transferred by some sort of privileged deduction from that anonymous zone into social practice itself. The principles of things, instead, are always high-level social products and thus themselves belong to highly developed social practice.

On the other hand, behavior is always accompanied by something else which is not behavior since, in an animal which behaves-and-communicates, other processes are going on as well. Not everything in the world is behavior. This means that semiotics, starting from the methodological identification of behavior and communication, can perhaps work out its own limits with precision, cutting off at the root the risk of some sort of "semiotic panlogism" – a risk which is anything but an imaginary one, and which may seem inconspicuous only to those who are unable to muster the historical dimension within their own work.

According to the terminology and categories I have adopted in Section 3.6, it is difficult to accept that an animal *does something* in a completely non-sign manner. One would rather say that some kinds of sign-behavior are privileged and that as a consequence of this operation it seems that there must be at least one other kind of behavior to which the label 'non-sign' would be applicable. By assuming that the animal does act in a non-sign manner, I would be forced to say that he is not really *behaving*, but simply "moving about," or that the process he is going through is "only physiological." The point which counters the assumption is that, even in these cases, what the animal is doing can be interpreted in several ways. The issue, however, does have a terminological aspect that cannot be ignored. My provisional distinction between "behavior" and "moving about" seems to correspond in part to the ethological distinction between "social behavior" and "mere behavior" (for a specifically ethological analysis of "social behavior" in the animal world, I refer particularly to Tinbergen's classic work of 1953). Or, at least, this correspondence seems to hold within the zones of reality which general semiotics and ethology may have in common. If ethologists like to assimilate *social* behavior into *sign* behavior, and call social only behavior in which signs occur, this is their own terminological business. It is also their business to explain what are the signs by the study of which they can come systematically to decide that there are no signs at all. A social scientist would probably tend to say that the ethologist's "social behavior" is "social" in a sense which is both very stretched and very restricted, and that such usage, useful as it may be within the ethological field, raises additional and unnecessary problems in other fields.

Beneath the terminology there is of course the issue of the *first inception* of something with a sign character. To begin with, there arises here the ethological problem of the formation of animal rituals, of the "passage" of an animal from the "moving about" as a purely chance (random, casual, only physiological) activity (= "mere behavior") to behavior proper (= "social behavior"), that is, to an action governed by some sort of codification and interpretable as a sign. One has here to be careful not to confound a socially induced ritual with a phylogenetically induced one – a difficulty that even Konrad Lorenz was not always able to avoid (cf. Lorenz 1963, English transl. 1966). Now, the observable piece of behavior interpretable as a sign must be a *signans* of something else which is happening or will happen in the animal itself or in the environment around him (the *signatum* of that *signans*) and which is either unobservable in principle (as is a relation as such), or not directly observable, or just not observed or not observable at the moment. There are here many subtle questions connected with the distinction between "transaction" (as proposed especially by Dewey and Bentley in 1949) and "interaction" (as emerging from the discovery of ecosystems in ecology); that is, questions concerning the measure and manners in which an animal forms a unity with its environment or is, instead, something discrete in front of it. In the one case behavior emerges *within* a transaction, or *is* such a transaction; while in the other the animal behaves *in front of* the environment, interacting with it (for a painstaking analysis of the whole issue, cf. De Crescenzo 1975). Now both *signans* and *signatum* must belong to the animal, or the environment, or both. It follows that the way in which we shall approach the first inception of anything significant, i.e. the way we draw our most rudimentary distinction between sign and non-sign, is strictly determined by our assuming a transactional, or an interactional, or a compound stance.

Elementary decisions where methodological consequences invest whole fields of research, however, must be left to the various specialists: in our case, to ecologists, ethologists, geneticists, child psychologists, psychiatrists, paleoethnologists, and evolutionists. Basic theoretical choices and difficulties exist in every field. When they regard signs, semioticians cannot just ignore them. But it would be well if semioticians also kept themselves as removed as possible from the foolish pretension of the paladins of some philosophical superscience: the pretension of making laws in other peoples' houses. Such a pretension was, and still is, doubtless tied to a hegemonic and thus to a "class" attitude: "I am the one who decides even if you are the one who works." This has little to do with what was rightly called the "internal democracy" of the scientific method. A philosophical superscience not only has nothing to do with the historical-materialistic interpretation of scientific work itself, as a group of socially determined and socially determining processes founded on social practice, but it constitutes, indeed, its precise contrary.

3.8 Conclusion

When we say today that all behavior is communication, or vice versa, we say it from the vantage point of the developments in semiotics in the last thirty years. Nonverbal codes have in part emerged and more are emerging to the attention of scholars; verbal codes have been studied in all their aspects, including those which could not even appear before the notion of *non*verbal codes was formed. In short, today we know that all behavior is always programmed, that is, based on codes. Should we conclude then that these developments, encouraged and set in motion by Morris, diminish the value and credibility of his basic insights? I would say quite the contrary. It was Morris who joined in such an intimate way, and for the first time systematically, the general notion of behavior with the general notion of the sign. Moreover, he was already advancing, in a way which was completely explicit and not without articulations, a conception of culture as a set of sign systems. He did not put positive limits to his own work in the sense of wanting to defend it; but rather he himself invoked the necessity of new and different research. Neither did he put negative limits to what could be, and in fact later were, the extraordinary developments of the approach he had inaugurated. Getting back in touch with his work today means finding in it numberless cues for investigations which were later carried out in many countries by scholars of the most varied provenience, whether or not they turn out to have been directly inspired by his teaching.

Let us say, rather, that Morris had started in a direction which was *even more fruitful* than he himself imagined or was able to foresee. The joining of the notions of behavior and sign contained enormous potential. Circumstances had only to permit the very first developments, and the whole panorama of human and life sciences began to change. Morris's limits must be seen historically: they were "only" those of his environment, of the academic discussion in the United States, and of North American culture in general, in the period when he was most active.

Anyone who has lived long enough in the world of culture, trying to introduce new ideas (even just *new for that culture*), knows very well that one has to fight not only the lack of reactions and collaboration, but also reactions and sometimes even collaboration that have nothing to do with the ideas introduced. Most of one's energies are absorbed in the attempt to explain things which after some years or decades – if the whole operation is successful – will be considered obvious. Morris surpassed the environment in which he happened to live. He was ahead of his own cultural situation. Even if his writings do necessarily reflect that situation in various ways, it can be safely said that they are dated much more in the letter than in the spirit.

References

Bakhtin, Mikhail. Cf. Voloshinov, V.N.
Barone, Francesco. 1953. *Il neopositivismo logico*. Turin: Edizioni di Filosofia.
Calderoni, Mario. 1924. *Scritti*. 2 vols. Ed. by O. Campa, with a preface by G. Papini. Florence: S.A.E. "La Voce."
Cattaneo, Carlo. 1960. *Scritti filosofici*. 3 vols. Ed. and introd. by N. Bobbio. Florence: Le Monnier.
Ceccato, Silvio. 1948. Review of *Signs, Language, and Behavior* by Charles Morris. *Sigma* II: 547-548.
———. 1949. "Il linguaggio." *Methodos* I, 3: 235-239.
———. 1951. *Il linguaggio con la Tabella di Ceccatieff*. Paris: Hermann.
Colorni, Eugenio. 1975. *Scritti*. Ed. by F. Rossi-Landi and N. Bobbio, introd. by N. Bobbio. Florence: La Nuova Italia.
Corti, Maria. 1976. *Principi della comunicazione letteraria*. Milan: Bompiani.
De Crescenzo, Giovanni. 1975. *L'etologia e l'uomo*. Florence: La Nuova Italia.
Dewey, John. 1900. "Psychology and Social Practice." Address of the President before the American Psychological Association (New Haven 1899). *The Psychological Review*, March: 105-124; reprinted in Dewey 1963.
———. 1963(1). *Philosophy, Psychology and Social Practice*. Essays selected and edited by J. Ratner. New York: Capricorn Books, 1965; cf. pp. 295-315.
Dewey, John and Arthur F. Bentley. 1949. *Knowing and the Known*. Boston: Beacon Press.
Eco, Umberto. 1975. *Trattato di semiotica generale*. Milan: Bompiani.
Enriques, Federigo. 1958. *Natura, ragione e storia*. Introd. and ed. by L. Lombardo-Radice. Turin: Einaudi. (One of Enriques's main books, *Problemi della scienza*, was translated into English by K. Royce and appeared in Chicago in 1914 with a Preface by Josiah Royce.)
Filiasi-Carcano, Paolo. 1953. *Problematica della filosofia odierna*. Rome-Milan: Bocca.
———. 1957. *La metodologia nel rinnovarsi del pensiero contemporaneo*. Naples: Libreria scientifica editrice.
Hegel, G.W.F. 1832. *Vorlesungen über die Philosophie der Geschichte*. Vol. 9 in *Vollständige Ausgabe durch einem Verein von Freunden des Verewigten*. Berlin. Italian transl. by G. Calogero and C. Fatta of the text edited by G. Lasson for Meiner's Philosophisce Bibliothek, *Lezioni sulla filosofia della storia*. 4 vols. Florence: La Nuova Italia, 1941-1963.
Geymonat, Ludovico. 1960. "Il linguaggio e la conoscenza scientifica" (1956). Now Appendix I, 161-180 in *Filosofia e filosofia della scienza*. Milan: Feltrinelli.
Gramsci, Antonio. 1975. *Quaderni del carcere*. Critical edition of the Istituto Gramsci directed by V. Gerratana. 4 vols. Turin: Einaudi.
Kosík, Karel. 1963. *Dialektika konkrétního. Studie o problematice člověka a světa*. Prague. English transl. by K. Kovanda and J. Schmidt. *Dialectics of the*

Concrete. A Study on Problems of Man and World. Boston Studies in the Philosophy of Science, vol. III. Dordrecht: Reidel, 1976.

Kristeva, Julia. 1969. "La sémiologie comme science des idéologies." *Semiotica* I, 2: 196-204.

Leakey, L.S.B. 1954. "Working Stone, Bone, and Wood." *A History of Technology*, vol. I: 128-143. Oxford: Clarendon.

Lorenz, Konrad. 1963(1) *Das sogenannte Böse. Zur Naturgeschichte der Aggression.* Vienna: Borotha-Schoeler. English transl. by M. Latzke, with a Foreword by J. Huxley as *On Aggression*. London: Methuen, 1966.

Morris, Charles. [See the general bibliography of his writings in Section 2.10; this volume Chapter 2.]

Paci, Enzo. 1950. "Linguaggio, comportamento e filosofia." Offprint of 15 pages from the volume *Filosofia e linguaggio*. Padua: Liviana.

Peano, Giuseppe. 1957-1959. *Opere scelte*. Ed. by U. Cassina. Rome: Cremonese. Three volumes containing 130 writings on various logical, mathematical, and linguistic topics.

Prieto, Luis J. 1975. *Pertinence et pratique. Essay de sémiologie*. Paris: Minuit. Italian transl. by D. Gambarara, revised by the author. Milan: Feltrinelli-Bocca, 1976.

Rastier, François. 1972. *Idéologie et théorie des signes*. Analyse structurale des *Éléments d'idéologie* d'Antoine-Louis-Claude Destutt de Tracy. The Hague: Mouton.

Rossi-Landi, Ferruccio. [See the general bibliography of his writings at the end of this volume.]

Scarpelli, Uberto. 1950. "L'unità della scienza nella *International Encyclopedia of Unified Science.*" *Rivista di filosofia* XLI, 3: 280-297.

———. 1955. "Osservazioni sul concetto di segno nel pensiero di Charles Morris." *Rivista di filosofia* XLVI, 1: 64-74.

Schaff, Adam. 1960. *Wstęp to semantyki*. Warsaw: PWN; English transl. as *Introduction to Semantics*, by O. Wojtasiewicz. Oxford: Pergamon Press, 1962.

———. 1964(1). *Język a poznanie*. Warsaw: PWN, 1967(2).

———. 1967. *Szkice z filozofii języka*. Warsaw: Książda i Wiedza. French transl. as *Langage et connaissance*, by C. Brendel. With the addition of six *Essais sur la philosophie du langage*. Paris: Anthropos, 1967.

Sebeok, Thomas A. 1972. *Perspectives in Zoosemiotics*. The Hague: Mouton.

———. 1976. *Contributions to the Doctrine of Signs*. Lisse: Peter de Ridder Press.

Segre, Cesare. 1969. *I segni e la critica. Fra strutturalismo e semiologia*. Turin: Einaudi. English transl. as *Semiotics and Literary Criticism*, by John Meddemmen. The Hague: Mouton, 1973.

Tinbergen, Niko. 1953(1). *Social Behaviour in Animals: With Special Reference to Vertebrates*. London: Methuen; Science Paperbacks, 1965.

Vaccarino, Giuseppe. 1949. Review of the Italian edition of *Signs, Language, and Behavior*, by Charles Morris. *Methodos* I, 4: 370-372.

Vailati, Giovanni. 1911. *Scritti*. Ed. by M. Calderoni, U. Ricci, and G. Vacca, with a Biography by O. Premoli. Florence-Leipzig: Seeber-Barth.
——. 1971. *Epistolario 1891-1909*. Ed. by G. Lanaro, with an Introduction by M. Dal Pra and a "Memoir" by L. Einaudi. Turin: Einaudi.
——. 1972. *Scritti filosofici*. Ed. by G. Lanaro. Naples: Fulvio Rossi.
Vaughan, Genevieve. *Unpublished Manuscripts* on "Human Territoriality" and other topics in the philosophy of language and general semiotics.
Verón, Eliseo. 1971. "Ideology and Social Sciences: A Communicational Approach." *Semiotica* III, 1: 59-76.
Vološinov, Valentin Nikolaevič and Mikhail Bakhtin. 1929. *Marksizm i filosofija jazyka: osnovnye problemy sociologičeskogo metoda v nauke o jasyke*. Leningrad. English transl. as *Marxism and the Philosophy of Language*, by L. Matejka and I.R. Titunik. New York-London: Seminar Press, 1973, with a "Translators' Introduction" and two Appendixes.

4. Wittgenstein, Old and New*

4.1 Foreword

A lecture like this ought to be based on nuances, innuendoes, and unsaid things, things capable of emerging by themselves and filling up the communicative atmosphere. But since, unavoidably, I was asked to speak a language which I learned as a grown-up and which is, much as I like it, foreign to me and also to part of the audience, I am afraid that it will not be possible for nuances, innuendoes, and unsaid things to play their subtle role here.

But *why* should this lecture try to grasp more things than it can actually say? I shall try to answer this question with a few rather cavalier propositions. To begin with, Wittgenstein was not a semiotician, yet he made a great though indirect contribution to the foundation of twentieth-century semiotics and to the development of some of its branches. Another point is that there are several Wittgensteins depending on which of his books the various scholars in different countries think is more important. Moreover, Wittgenstein is an iceberg, by which I mean that there is an emergent portion of his work which is known already, but also a submerged and bigger portion which – whether recently published or still unpublished – has begun to be explored only in the last decade or so. And finally, there is what Wittgenstein *says* in either the emergent or the submerged portion, and then there is what he *shows*, and what he *points to*, and what he *stands for* or (some times very symbolically) *represents* as against the background *finis Austriae*, the background of the Viennese heritage but also of the great changes which have intervened in our way of life and our cultures during the span of Wittgenstein's life and since his death.

On the other hand – let us be clear about this – I am not a Wittgensteinian scholar, even if now and then I happen to find myself reported as one. Apart

---

* This is a revised and expanded version of a paper read in Vienna at the 2nd Congress of the International Association for Semiotic Studies in the series "The Viennese Heritage" (1979 [cf. R.-L. 1981a]). The style and tone of an oral address to a general public have been retained.

from a number of scattered references to his work, especially to the *Untersuchungen* (the appearance of which I witnessed at Blackwell's in Oxford on May 1st, 1953), and apart from some systematic use that I tried to make of some of his seminal ideas in a book on meaning that I published in 1961, there have only been two truly Wittgensteinian episodes in my life. The first was a long exchange of views that I had with Piero Sraffa in his Cambridge rooms in November 1960. I was trying to elicit some information about his famous influence on Wittgenstein's transition from the world of the *Tractatus* to that of the *Untersuchungen* (as Wittgenstein's intermediate researches were then unknown, this was the way in which his development was phrased at the time). I had imagined and perhaps secretly hoped that Sraffa's stimulus (*Ansporn*, as Wittgenstein puts it in the *Vorwort*) had taken place in the sacred entrances and corridors of Trinity College. But what I did elicit was only a dusty reply: it had been a question of some strolls on the banks of the Cam.

My second Wittgensteinian episode was at the beginning of 1966, when I published an essay entitled "For a Marxian use of Wittgenstein" [cf. R.-L. 1966b and 1968h]. The title was a faithful one: I was trying to approach the Austrian philosopher within a Marxian framework and with Marxian intellectual tools, in this way pointing to some connections between emerged and submerged portions. Notice that in Italian we distinguish between *marxiano* (Marxian) and *marxista* (Marxist). In an oversimplified, and indeed blunt manner, the distinction is the following: *marxiano* refers to the use of Marx's philosophical and methodological apparatus as it can be derived directly from his writings, insofar as they are studied within the tradition or traditions of thought they belong to; *marxista* refers to the ideological and political developments which have occurred since his death, under the banner of his name. Thus, in principle, someone could be to some extent a Marxian without being a Marxist, or (more easily) a Marxist without really being a Marxian. Whether or not it sounds Byzantine to your ears, I am reporting this distinction to make it clear that my Marxian approach to Wittgenstein was respectful and reconstructive and had nothing to do with the (to say the very least) very oversimplified things that nobody less than Lukács György deemed useful to say in his *Zerstörung der Vernunft* about Wittgenstein as a mere representative, or almost as a victim, of a general irrationalistic trend which originated with Schelling and culminated in Adolf Hitler. There is no point in objecting here – as somebody did – that Lukács is dead and therefore incapacitated to answer our queries. If we accepted such a point of view, we would have to admit that Plato and Aristotle are even more dead than Lukács. With the greatest respect for Lukács's constructive work, including the initial chapters of the *Zerstörung*, one cannot help feeling that the final portion of the same book was based on scanty information and is perhaps the lowest level he ever reached (or unreached, much as was the case with Humpty-Dumpty's "unbirthday presents").

There are other directions of approach. The complete text of Marx and Engels's *Die deutsche Ideologie* appeared for the first time in 1932 and certainly reached Cambridge, where there was a thriving Marxian, and perhaps also a Marxist, Economic School. It is difficult to imagine that Wittgenstein, the friend of Sraffa who was Gramsci's friend, remained unaware of the provocative and very well-written text that two young German refugees had concocted in high good humor in Brussels in 1845-1846. In fact, a comparative examination of *Die deutsche Ideologie* and the *Philosophische Untersuchungen* convinced me that in the latter several ideas of the former were taken up again and sometimes expressed in a surprisingly similar language. I have come to believe that a thorough examination of Marx's influence on the best of Wittgenstein and on the best of Lukács – an examination which would make it possible to place both of them in the proper historical perspective, as against the background of *finis Austriae* and the advent of socialism in Eastern countries – would bring to light a number of common assumptions and basic ideas in the Austrian and Hungarian philosophers.

In what follows I shall only be able to take up, or better, only to *name* some general issues. Thus, for instance, I will say that Freudian therapy *consists of* linguistic interpretation, or that linguistic alienation *is* false thought. I am well aware that in such cases I am using tags which cover whole fields of far-from-settled discussion. But much as one should avoid the silly belief that general statements are important just because they are general, one should also avoid confining oneself to meticulously detailed arguments for fear of seeming unprofessional to a next-door colleague. There *are*, fortunately, many levels of communication. If all this is clear, let me anticipate that I shall deal successively with the following topics: Wittgenstein's iceberg; Wittgenstein and semiotics; Wittgenstein, Marx, and Freud; Wittgenstein and alienation.

4.2 Wittgenstein's Iceberg

I shall begin, then, with some remarks on the iceberg metaphor. Every thinker is an iceberg; or indeed, every person is. It is interesting here how individual and cultural dimensions overlap: the metaphor applies both to the relations between the conscious and the unconscious mind within any individual and to the relations between our present knowledge of a thinker and what he really meant to say in the totality of his work. The latter is typically Wittgenstein's case. Within the so-called Anglo-Saxon world, up to ten or at most fifteen years ago his work was only approached from points of view which bear the labels of 'logico-formal,' or 'neopositivistic,' or 'analytical philosophy,' or 'the philosophy of language' as separate disciplines. This amounts to saying that only the emergent portion of Wittgenstein's iceberg was taken account of.

I want to state emphatically that such an interpretation of Wittgenstein was legitimate as far as it went, and that it expressed itself in a vast and important series of books and articles aiming at the illustration and application of a central portion of Wittgenstein's thought. According to this interpretation, he was the builder of subtle models, the master of prudence and rigor, the professed enemy of spurious generalization, and an excellent example of rationality. It is a good thing that such an approach should continue to be developed, and that it should be handed down to new generations of scholars. Notice, however, that the then emerged portion of Wittgenstein's iceberg fitted certain central features of British and Northern American mentality particularly well, it became them, if only at a cultural level. Ideological problems were avoided, and philosophy was reduced to a clarifying technique or to a therapeutic activity. Individuals were theoretically privileged; and even when the functions of their interpersonal relationships were studied, these were precisely relations among preformed individuals. In other words, a proper approach to the social dimension in the Continental sense was barred: the notion that individuals are themselves social products did not come to the fore. It was, perhaps, implicit; but the lenses through which the emerged texts were read prevented the reader from making it explicit.

But just as with an iceberg, the submerged portion of Wittgenstein's production and personality is much bigger than the emergent one. What is involved here is the whole world in which Wittgenstein grew up as a person and as a scholar. In fact, recent investigations concerned with the submerged portion deal with Austromarxism, the various schools of depth psychology, Brentano and Meinong, Mach's empiriocriticism, twelve-tone music, Kraus and Musil, Loos and Kokoschka, and so on. This is already a wide cultural network; and yet, it is not sufficient. Various important trends in German speaking culture are beginning to be investigated with regard to Wittgenstein, especially those which go back to Schopenhauer, Marx, and Nietzsche. The *Proceedings* of the yearly Wittgenstein Symposia at Kirchberg offer good evidence for all this.

Further evidence can be gained from a number of journals in various countries. Let me name here the special issue dedicated by *Nuova corrente* to Negation in Freud (nos. 61-62, 1973), Nietzsche (nos. 68-69, 1975-1976), Wittgenstein himself (nos. 72-73, 1977), and to *Finis Austriae* (nos. 79-80, 1979). Edited by Mario Boselli and the late Giovanni Sechi with the advice of a board comprehending some of the most advanced young Italian scholars in the field, *Nuova corrente* also shows the quasi-paradoxical truth that Italy is the most important "Wittgensteinian country" because it is the only country in which Wittgenstein's ideas have always been and continue to be systematically examined both in the Anglo-Saxon and in the Austro-Hungarian fashion, both as ideas in the philosophy of language and as ideas concerning wider problems of contemporary civilization. Not for nothing the first non-neopositivistic discussion of the whole production of Wittgenstein which had appeared at the time is Emanuele Riverso's (1964, new edition 1970). Or, take Massimo Cacciari's *Krisis*, an essay on the development of "negative thought" from Nietzsche to Wittgenstein. It is a difficult, abstruse, irritating book, and still in its way an enthralling one. I am naming it here as a perfect example of an attitude to Wittgenstein which would have been utterly incomprehensible to the Oxford and Cambridge dons of the fifties.

Thus the submerged portion of Wittgenstein's iceberg has begun to come to light. We are facing immense possibilities of historical and conceptual excavation, and are aware that we are going to deal with problems that concern the destiny of man. That these things can be felt and said about Wittgenstein, is a remarkable revolution in cultural approach. But in another sense, it is also a restitution. In the early fifties, many Continental scholars including myself were feeling that Wittgenstein had been so to speak lifted out of reality, as if there were no historical dimension which could affect his intellectual techniques. These techniques were applied atemporally, as something handed down from the Heavens. But not even Wittgenstein was an angel. His philosophical production was historically determined as all production, whether intellectual or not, always is. The same is even more true of the interpretations a philosopher can receive. This is what I meant when I used as a motto for my 1966 essay a paraphrase of one of Wittgenstein's most famous sayings – "Do not seek a philosopher's meaning, seek his use: a philosopher's meaning is his use in the culture." It is rewarding to learn from his last published writings that Wittgenstein himself was perfectly aware of all this, as Georg Henrik von Wright pointed out in a recent paper of his.

Let us now try to make the distinction between emergent and submerged portions a little more operative, and we will have finished with this Section. The 'emergent (or emerged) portion' comprehends in any given moment all the writings of Wittgenstein which have been published and taken account of together with all the information that we can muster about him. When the *Untersuchungen* appeared in 1953, the emergent portion was of course much smaller than it is now. That was perhaps the moment in which the iceberg metaphor was most suitable. At that time scholars used to say that there were "two Wittgensteins," and reference to the submerged portion was either never made or ineffective. The notion of the submerged portion is more difficult by itself and it is also getting more and more complicated. Its final destiny, or so we hope, is that it will thin out entirely. We have here to take account of a number of factors:

i. The still unpublished material. According to the Budapest philosopher Nyíri Cristof, who is certainly not a Tractarian but rather an Untersuchungarian, there are still some ten thousand pages to be edited and printed. Much more correspondence is also to be located and edited, and will certainly add to our knowledge;

ii. Whatever is still to be known about Wittgenstein's life, education, travels, contacts, and activities other than the literary;

iii. The ways in which Wittgenstein does represent or symbolize the *finis Austriae* and the cultural and political developments which prepared, accompanied, and followed it;

iv. New interpretations of the above phenomena from the point of view of what Wittgenstein can teach us. This point is complementary to the previous one: the more we learn about Wittgenstein, the more we shall learn about *finis Austriae*, and reciprocally so;

v. Wittgenstein's published materials should be revisted in the light of all the points listed above. This must of course extend to all published writings, whether they appeared before or after the beginning of the emergence of the previously submerged portion of the iceberg. It is for instance completely clear that the *Tractatus* read when only the *tractatus* "existed" cannot be the same *Tractatus* which is now being reread against the background of Wittgenstein's formation and in the light of all his subsequent writings. A specialized scholar like Brian McGuinness has repeatedly explained this point.

In short, what we badly need is a complete critical edition in which everything Wittgenstein ever wrote is reprinted in *strict chronological order*, and no arbitrary selection by some devoted or devout editor is allowed. It would be easy to be polemical about much that has been done so far. From the point of view of current Continental scholarship, it is in fact unbearable that somebody took the liberty of going through "scraps" written by Wittgenstein over a period of twenty or thirty years and proceeded to select them according to his own taste and to arrange them "according to topics," while simply ignoring all the rest of the *Nachlaß* and the very different historical circumstances, in which the various "scraps" had been written. In an allegedly atemporal world where all "different topics" could be, once and for all, dogmatically detected, the reflections of one of the keenest minds of the century were in that way *used for contingent ideological aims*. The users, to say the least, grossly underrated the motivating power of such aims within themselves.

4.3 Wittgenstein and Semiotics

Contemporary semiotic literature does not seem to be very concerned with Wittgenstein. Negative evidence is no evidence, of course. If you want to find out whether or not there are red-haired people in the village, one red-haired person is already positive evidence that there are, while a list of black- or fair-haired people is no evidence against somebody else being red-haired. In the scientific field, however, we can also proceed by crucial examples. Thus it seems significant to me that so little use of Wittgenstein is made in *Semiotica*, the official journal of the International Association for Semiotic Studies; or that Wittgenstein is never even named in Thomas A. Sebeok's important book *Contributions to the Doctrine of Signs*; or that he is named only twice in Umberto Eco's *Trattato di semiotica generale* which appeared contemporarily in English under the less impressive title *A Theory of Semiotics*. Owing to the systematic character of his book, Eco's case is particularly relevant. He refers to Wittgenstein in passing and merely for the purpose of illustration rather than for scientific concerns. The first reference is to Wittgenstein's reaction to Sraffa's famous Neapolitan gesture; the second is to the *Untersu-*

chungen, §§ 29-30 on the procedure of ostension. Only the *Tractatus* and the *Untersuchungen* are named in the Bibliography. And that is all.

On the other hand, as hinted at the beginning, Wittgenstein was no semiotician. This statement too is subject to confirmation, for I am certainly not maintaining that Wittgenstein never named and discussed semioticians or never used some piece of semiotic terminology somewhere in his works. The existence of so many unpublished manuscripts would make such a claim even less warranted. Of course, the statement that Wittgenstein was no semiotician only acquires its meaning if we know what semiotics is. Unfortunately, we do not. Having spent so many years in the field, I have come to learn that no simple definition will do. Thus I shall content myself with repeating here the few words that a freshman attending an elementary course is likely to hear on his first day: "Semiotics is the general science or doctrine or theory of all signs and sign systems, whether verbal or nonverbal, conscious or unconscious, animal or human, and so on." These few words already refer directly or indirectly to a series of problems which then have to be dealt with in the elementary course: what a sign is and how it is compounded, how many kinds of signs there are, what sign systems are and what the relations are among different sign systems, how to classify signs, and so on. It is clear that, however elementary the course, some difficulties of a general kind are also present, difficulties that the lecturer can choose to face or perhaps, instead, to avoid for the sake of clarity in what he does say: suffice it to think of the opposition conscious-unconscious.

To the question, "But did not Wittgenstein himself labor on those problems from beginning to end?" a first answer could be – "Yes, but in an asystematic manner which does not seem to belong to the spirit of semiotic studies." The very idea of a *general* science, or doctrine, or theory of *all* signs and sign systems would have probably appeared aberrant, if not abhorrent, to his mind.

There are, or so it seems to me, two ways out of this apparently stalemate situation. One is the piecemeal comparison between Wittgenstein's treatment of a number of individual problems and the treatment the same problems receive in current semiotic literature. This work is in process, but I have the impression that it is done more by Wittgensteinians than by semioticians, more by philosophers than by linguists and other human scientists. I think that even a cursory inspection of some of the main philosophical journals in various countries and of the *Proceedings* of philosophical conferences will easily prove the point. No detailed example can be given here, as this would require a whole talk by itself which would be a talk about the problem selected and not about Wittgenstein. Let us try, however, to convey an idea of what such a comparison could be.

Beginning perhaps with the *Untersuchungen*, and then more and more in the later years of his life, Wittgenstein developed a conception of human conduct and intelligence which could be labeled 'the automaton conception of human life.' If I am not wrong, such a conception is to be found especially in *Zettel* and in *Über Gewißheit*, and it could be that the unpublished manuscripts will give us additional material on the subject. According to the automaton conception, all we are able to do is governed by rules that we have learned, and we have learned them because they have been taught to us. This is true even for the recognition of an elementary shape or a color, and it becomes more and more evident with the increasing difficulty of the performance and consequently with the amount of teaching that is required.

There is here a striking resemblance with what is maintained by a number of semioticians. The style and even the jargon are different; and semioticians, bad Wittgensteinians as they are, tend to build theories or at least to organize what they think into certain patterns. It took Wittgenstein's talent to do only aphoristic work and still reach such a depth of thought. Still, the resemblance is there; and I think it can be presented under the two labels 'programs of communication' and 'social programming of all behavior.' Franz Boas had seen very well that communication is the central process of every culture. George Herbert Mead approached the mind as a system for communication, which made it advisable to describe the mind in terms of signs rather than trying to explain signs by means of some notion of the mind. In more recent times, Jurij M. Lotman has conceived of culture as information, and of its transmission as conservation of sign systems suitable for *controlling the behavior of individuals*. Let us add that experience takes place in an environment already shaped by man, so that every individual, when he is born and develops, in a certain sense finds *everything ready-made*. The very behavior of the individual is anchored to something that precedes and guides it, that is, it is programmed. Sign systems include programs of behavior; communication itself is always programmed. There are "behavioral units" which, when executed according to programs, refer us back to past human work. Thus, also according to a general trend within semiotics, we are automata in a number of ways, just as the later Wittgenstein was saying.

The automaton conception of human life has much greater consequences than are perhaps seen at first sight. According to the character of this lecture, let me try to hint at some of them by the simple procedure of a brief discussion of an elementary example. I have been taught to say that something is red when I see a red object, and I do. Traditionally, this gave rise to the insoluble problem of *how* I *correctly say* that something is *red* when something *is* red. An *intermediate world* had been constructed within which "red" was supposed to exist as a preformed object of knowledge, and men as knowers had to go through a special process of cognition in order to detect it accurately and properly name it. But let us assume instead that there is no intermediate world, i.e. let us refute the construction of an artificial intermediate world. My own self is then continuous with the rest of the world. There is no ontological break either within myself or between myself and the rest. *Pulvis sum et in pulvim revertar.* That I correctly say that something is red is a linguistic act describing the occurrence of the same phenomenon by two different pieces of matter, in two different places in the world. It is not, of course, *pulvis* itself: it is the transmission of habits in society through acculturation and education which requires the use of energy as a form of matter. In this way the overwhelming importance of society in the formation of individuals is extolled; but so are the material nature and limitation which become human beings. To be a human means to be a piece of matter-and-energy at a high level of organization which has received the rules for all "it" does from the community to which "it" belongs from birth. I, the 'this-is-red-sayer,' am what natural and historical evolution have made me, *and nothing else*. This is perhaps harsh to the ear. But if we consider that it took two million years for man to emerge, that mammals had been existing for fifty million years, and that life originated on the planet Earth more than two billion years ago – then we should be proud: we are, in fact, the supreme offspring of it all.

There are of course plenty of problems here – all the problems traditionally connected with being a human, if you like, plus some new problems which have come to the surface in recent decades. But no mysterious, insoluble problem is involved; or at least, a decisive step has been made toward expelling insoluble and mysterious problems from our discussions on fundamentals. To use the terminology introduced by Silvio Ceccato (an original student of Dingler and Bridgman) since the forties, and also by Dewey and Bentley in their famous book of 1949, the *duplication* of knower and known is abolished. There is, in a sense, nothing to be *known*, and there is no knower in the traditional sense. There is instead a natural process by which men, as other animals, can detect the difference between red and other colors and react to it because they are reacting to the emergence of a differentiation within themselves as parts of the same natural world; and there is an historico-educational process by which, with important differences with respect to other animals, men are taught to *name* colors as they do (that higher animals also *indicate* colors by nonverbal means, as is especially the case with the "new monkeys" in the American labs, is a fascinating topic we cannot even begin entering here).

Ignorance or refusal of the necessity of natural evolution, of the total arbitrariness of historical evolution, and of the compulsive influence of both, had produced in all the main cultures (in Europe since the Greeks) an impossible science called 'the theory of knowledge' which was based on that nonexistent duplication – the intermediate world. But, to leave aside other examples, already in 1941 Arthur F. Bentley proposed that *epistemology* (in the American sense of the term) be relegated to the realm of prescientific enquiry together with alchemy and astrology.

In addition to recent semiotic enquiry, I have named three approaches which have something essential in common: the transactional approach of Dewey and Bentley, the operational approach of Dingler, Bridgman, and Ceccato, and Wittgenstein's. The last one used to be labeled an 'analysis of everyday language and common speech.' This is clearly inadequate. Much more is involved in the direction of a final crumbling of myths in the theory of knowledge and of an extension of criticism to the social situations in which languages are taught. One can see the gap here between the interpretation of Wittgenstein as an explorer of language and as a researcher into man's total situation in nature and history.

The other attempt at overcoming the juxtaposition of Wittgenstein and semiotics consists in reexamining some central features regarding the origins of semiotics itself. This requires a short historical excursus.

In the mid-thirties the late American philosopher Charles Morris, whom I consider to be the founder, or the main founder, of contemporary semiotics, wrote a number of papers in which the formation of the semiotic approach can be followed step by step. The bulk of these papers was a comparative examination of some of the main conceptions of philosophy which were current in European and American countries in those years. The first conception analyzed was philosophy as logic of science, connected especially with the name of Carnap. The second conception was philosophy as clarification of meaning, present in American pragmatism and in one wing of the Vienna Circle (the first Wittgenstein, Schlick, Waismann). The third conception was philosophy as empirical axiology, as found in Schlick and especially in

Dewey. If we accept these three conceptions together, Morris said, we have philosophy as a "language of languages" or a general theory of symbolism. And when we examine the meaning of an expression from the point of view of its relations with other expressions, with the things meant, and with those who make use of it, we open the path to its full determination. *Traditional* empiricism was impaired by the scant justice rendered to formal sciences, the inability to connect an empirical theory of meaning to a naturalistic cosmology, and the tendency to subjectivism. It is now important, as Morris insisted, to embrace an empiricism which is radical, a rationalism which is a study of method, and a pragmatism which is critical. That these were presented as the three components of a *new* empiricism may be of little interest nowadays; what is striking is that they corresponded to the three dimensions of semiotics. Each one of the aforementioned defects of traditional empiricism, said Morris, arose from the neglect of one of the three main dimensions of signs. Within the new empiricism, the radical side to empiricism itself is *semantic* investigation, while methodological rationalism takes care of *syntactic* investigation, and critical pragmatism of *pragmatic* investigation. The unity of science – a great philosophical aim in those years – would then result from the unity of its linguistic structures, from the semantic relationships which it succeeds in establishing, and from the practical effects it produces. Notice that in this way even the three traditional fields of philosophy – logic, metaphysics, and the theory of values – were represented in semiotic terms: logic was seen as the ancestor of syntactics, metaphysics of semantics, and the theory of values as the ancestor of pragmatics.

What you have just heard is a passage of bad prose bristling with big words, precisely of the kind Wittgenstein, but some of his British followers more than he, so much disliked. On the other hand, the big words stand for real moments in the history of thought, they are a sort of intellectual shorthand for referring to whole arrays of publications which were seminal at their time and still retain their importance. Even from the very reduced information that I have conveyed to you by compressing into a few propositions some ten years of Morris's original research, a couple of interconnected consequences can be drawn.

To begin with, the philosophical origins of semiotics may seem surprising to anyone coming to semiotic studies without a taste for philosophic-historical culture. For instance, one could nowadays accept, or refuse, the tripartition of semiotics as merely the result of objective investigation carried out on signs. But such "objective" investigation would not have been possible without the described confluence of different currents of thought. The ideological bias of each of them accepted separately was too strong. It was Morris's merit to have perceived what those currents of thought had in common, in spite of the ways in which they diverged, and to have stressed and coordinated their symbolic dimensions. The so-called objectivity of semiotics was a result, not a point of departure. Objectivity is always a complex result, even if afterwards it may present itself to us as simple.

The second consequence is that the objectivity reached by semiotics in the thirties is not satisfactory any longer because it was provisional when it first emerged, and it was provisional because it was dated. Although he had himself, as a man and as a scholar, many other interests, the framework of ideas of Morris as a philosopher-semiotician was empirical and pragmatic with a biological bias. Now empiricism and pragmatism are extremely important movements of thought, and long life to biology; but there is much else that contributes to the formation of human feelings, practice, and thought. It is not without reason, then, that discussion has never subsided about the very foundations of semiotics, its basic features, its relations with philosophy and the human sciences, its significance for human life, its social bearing, and a number of related problems. And still, in spite of so much discussion, very few semioticians now consider it rewarding to go back to the original debates which presided over the very birth of their discipline.

This is the moment in the script where Wittgenstein reenters. Morris acknowledged that he was one of the founding fathers of the semantic dimension. Could he have known in the late thirties what Wittgenstein was then writing, he would have made this statement even more strongly. That Wittgenstein also contributed to the syntactic dimension has only been too obvious since the appearance of the *Tractatus*. But the point of major interest is yet another one; it is Wittgenstein's progression from syntactics to semantics and then to pragmatics. If I do not read him incorrectly, it was especially with pragmatic questions that his later writings were concerned. In this he anticipated a trend which can be found operating within semiotics itself. My conclusion is the following: once the philosophical origins of the semiotic endeavor are acknowledged, Wittgenstein's teachings and methods ought to be applied to current discussion about the foundations of semiotics and about particular semiotic problems as well. In other words, the game is not over, especially now that the whole range of Wittgenstein's research and his proper historical collocation have at long last begun to be discerned and properly assessed. To put it almost in the terms of a pun: however small the historical connections between Wittgenstein's *Nachlaß* and semiotic studies, as they have in fact developed during the last forty years or so, there certainly is a deep relation between Wittgenstein and *semiosis*, the process by which something functions as a sign. Now, there would be no semiotic studies without semiosis. There's the semiosic, and semiotic, rub.

4.4 Ideas for a Common Approach to Marx, Freud, and Wittgenstein

If we try to approach Karl Marx, Sigmund Freud, and Ludwig Wittgenstein in terms of what they have in common, we can begin by saying the following. Marx wanted the change from a social condition of exploitation to a condition in which exploitation would subside, or at least be substantially reduced. Freud wanted the change from an individual situation in some ways sick, or unsatisfactory, to a situation in some ways healthy or at least more satisfactory. And Wittgenstein – to use three famous metaphors of his own – wanted the fly to get out of the bottle, language to cease being idle, and mental cramps to be resolved. This means that the three of them necessarily resorted to:

i. A philosophical anthropology, that is, a theory of human nature. As a prerequisite, human nature had to be conceived of as "in movement," because an immobile human nature would simply refuse any intervention aimed at changing it in the course of time;

ii. A criteriology for distinguishing, each of them in his own field, "false" situations from "true" situations: each of them felt he was capable of spotting a "false" situation and envisaging its substitution by a "true" situation. The logic of "true" vs. "false" in these statements is, of course, a complex one. I have dealt with it in other recent publications, and here I have to content myself with saying that it has little to do with the simple opposition of 'true' and 'false' in everyday language or in formal logic. "False" is the disease or discomfort, whether individual or social, on which each of the three thinkers started operating in order to overcome it;

iii. An instrumental apparatus with which to bring the change about. Such an apparatus obviously had to be intellectual, but not only intellectual. It also had to include moral features and it had to be fit for the real situations in which it had to be used;

iv. The will to operate the change. This is an especially intriguing point. In order to "have" that will, to be aware of it, and to practice it, one needs an additional set of criteria for distinguishing what is good from what is evil, and also principles by means of which the "true" can be considered good, and evil "false." Moreover, the criteria and principles must be such that, by taking them into account, we are, so to speak, compelled to prefer the good-as-true to the evil-as-false.

The towering stature of the three thinkers we are talking about should not prevent us from acknowledging that they were aware of the four groups of elements we have just listed to a very different extent. We now have the vantage point of accumulated criticism (*gigantium humeris insidentes*). Thus, for instance, we can now venture to say that human nature appeared easier to modify to Marx than to Wittgenstein, or to Wittgenstein than to Freud. But it is obvious in all three cases that changes must occur in it, both in the direction of deterioration and in the direction of recovery. If at this point somebody remarked that perhaps the changes are nothing but deviations from a central common standard and returns to it, the discussion would be opened not only on the differences between the three thinkers, but on human nature itself.

Or, consider the question of the extent to which each of the three really *wanted* to change things. What does 'wanted' mean in contexts as intricate as these? Is it that Marx *wanted* to change things more than Wittgenstein, or rather that the former *believed* more than the latter in the possibility of such a change? It is difficult to answer these questions in a scientific fashion, for one always has the impression that one is reporting facts about the author's individuality rather than examining his ideas at a *Gattungswesen* level.

What seems essential to me is that the three thinkers – each one within the realm of problems on which he was concentrating – had in common a declared preference for what is "true" because it is good, for the "true-as-good." Each of them was a healer in the direction of change and offered his instruments for achieving the change envisaged. Theory was not enough for them. They also started a new practice. This operational and constructive aspect of their thought does not deserve underrating, even if we are bound to juxtapose Freud's pessimism or Wittgenstein's conservatism to Marx's revolutionary optimism, or Marx's social practice and Freud's personal therapeutic praxis to Wittgenstein's operating only on a few pupils or on the readers of his books (which on the other hand was also done by the other two).

There is a rapidly increasing literature on these relationships, especially on those between Marx and Freud. As for some similarities in the demystifying activity of Marx and Wittgenstein, I take the liberty of referring to the essay named at the beginning (1966 [cf. R.-L. 1966b and 1968h]). I would also like to report that by studying in a parallel manner some founding steps of Marxian and Freudian theory I seemed to recognize a very similar use of distinctions and operations at the most elementary level (1978[a] and [c]). The main point is perhaps that the three basic properties of things in their relation to men, as described by Marx in the analysis of commodities and elsewhere, are also used by Freud in his interpretation of neurosis and perversion. There are, in fact:

i. "Natural" properties that things carry independent of human intervention, like weight or color (there is of course human intervention in *describing* these properties as natural; before the emergence of men they were not described at all and therefore, *in a sense*, they didn't exist; but we need not take up this difficult but partially verbal discussion for our present aims);

ii. "Socio-natural" properties (*gesellschaftliche Natureigenschaften*) that things may appear to be carrying themselves, but which are instead the result of an interaction between things and man, like the capacity to satisfy a need (use-value);

iii. Social properties which things simply neither have nor contribute to the formation of, because they are the results of interactions between men, like exchange-values or prices (things of course often *carry* such properties in the sense in which the material body of a *signans* carries the *signatum* to the extent that the whole thing becomes a sign: but being a sign or a commodity is certainly not a property of bodies as such).

As a rule, troubles begin when different properties are confused, or when a property takes up a role which is not its own. According to Marx this is what happens, for instance, when a commodity seems to come back to us as the bearer of a natural property of its own when, in reality, that property is acquired as a consequence of a relation among men. According to Freud, something very similar happens, for instance, in the case of fetishism. The fetish acts upon the man who has created it as if such action came from properties inherent in the fetish itself.

Having dealt at some length with these problems elsewhere, I have formed the opinion that they can be clarified, and that the clarification follows much the same path, whether you are dealing with Marx, or Freud, or Wittgenstein. This brings me directly to my last topic which is, as you will remember, Wittgenstein and alienation.

4.5 Wittgenstein and Alienation

To my mind, there is little doubt that Wittgenstein dealt with linguistic alienation from beginning to end. In this I disagree with Wittgensteinians who still find it strange to connect Wittgenstein's name with any problem of alienation, let alone the intellectual rearguard of those who still delude themselves into believing that nothing like linguistic alienation exists.

My theory (as I have developed it especially in my 1978 book on ideology) is that we can have alienation at the level of preverbal or nonverbal consciousness, or at the level of verbalized thought. I am resorting here to a fundamental distinction introduced by Hegel, especially in the *Enzyclopädie*, between consciousness and thought. The evolution from consciousness to thought requires the intervention of language which forms in its turn with the advent of memory, while mere signs are precedent to memory. Thus, if there is fully developed and expressed thought, there must be, or must have been, language. From this it does *not* follow that thought cannot express itself through channels other than verbal language. Consciousness is thought upon which language has not yet intervened, or does not intervene any longer. Thought is consciousness developed through language and is usually also expressed linguistically. Now, if anything goes wrong at the level of consciousness, we have false consciousness in the complex sense of 'false' hinted at above; and the same with thought. False consciousness and false thought, together with various kinds of false praxis, are parts of the wider notion of alienation.

False thought is *linguistic* alienation, and that Wittgenstein dealt with false thought is obvious. But certainly he also dealt with false consciousness, and this in several manners. He distinguished false consciousness negatively from false thought and he examined mental conditions which are not verbally expressed but which can be perceived by studying nonverbal behavior. Moreover, he could not help dealing with false praxis as well, namely with human action accompanying or not accompanying consciousness and thought when these are false. It is a commonplace to recall here his unswerving attention for the real situations in which the various language games operate as "forms of life."

It could be objected that according to Wittgenstein, or at least to some Oxonian interpretations of his teaching, communication can break down but can also be restored by returning to the appropriate linguistic rule in the right language game. When this happens, the disease or trouble which has caused the break is removed. If we talk in terms of generalized linguistic alienation, it would appear instead that we are alienated just when we respect the rules which have been taught to us. In other words, a Wittgensteinian linguistic therapist is able to single out real cases of disturbed communication and finds in the respect for the various language games a therapy for it. The notion of generalized linguistic alienation would instead seem to exclude the very possibility of finding an appropriate therapy.

I cannot here enter a discussion on the tangle of problems raised by such an objection. I shall simply limit myself to making a few remarks which will also bring me to the end of this lecture.

Before Wittgenstein's time, Marx, Nietzsche, and Freud had given to common sense and ordinary language much more importance than is usually acknowledged. Suffice it here to recall the criticism of philosophical jargon as something detached from reality and operating through verbal devices, in *Die deutsche Ideologie*; Nietzsche's demystification of philosophical activity as the expression of the personal life of the philosopher; and Freud's resorting to common sense and everyday language in the *Psychopathologie* of 1901 and in the essay on *Witz* of 1905. And still, Marx, Nietzsche, and Freud did also advance a generalized theory of alienation, of a condition common to all human beings which could perhaps be healed if something substantial were changed. The alienation dealt with by Freud is constitutionally linguistic: the unconscious is itself a form of language or symbolic system, and therapy consists mostly of linguistic expression, analysis, interpretation, and reformulation. Nietzsche went so far as to anticipate a number of problems of contemporary sociolinguistics, for instance, the problems centering on the notion of linguistic relativity. Marx dealt with communicative alienation of the non-verbal kind throughout his analysis of the commodity, money, and the market. And Wittgenstein? Would it really make sense to say that nothing like that is present in his vast work – in the portion already emerged, and possibly even more in the still submerged one?

I believe that Wittgenstein's concern for the birth and death of languages, for the influence that linguistic structures receive from the outside, for the historically limited character of our troubles, for the "obscurity of the times" which could be overcome only by some radical change in our ways of living, and so on, allows us to conclude that he did possess a generalized theory of linguistic alienation that can escape attention only if we limit our approach to his thought to the commonsensical and everyday language interpretation that was dominant twenty years ago.

There is no contradiction in granting that Wittgenstein's generalized theory of alienation, linguistic and otherwise, comprehended as a special though very common case, provisional and remediable breakdowns in communication. I would put it like this: given a certain historical situation and a certain way of living, there are, within them, commonly accepted linguistic games the transgression of which causes a break in "normal" communication. What is here in question is the meaning and scope we feel entitled to confer on the syntagm 'normal communication.' Is the communication we are trying to assess normal only for individuals who have received a certain education, or also for all individuals of any given community? Is it normal for all social groups and classes within a given community and society, or also for individuals coming from different communities and societies? And in the case in which individuals of different descent and extraction fail to communicate, are we going to say that this is one more case of breakdown which can be restored by resorting to the appropriate language game (in this way denying that we have to resort to additional criteria)? Is there perhaps in all human groups and societies something in common that goes so deep that, whenever we reach it, *we have normal communication among all human beings*, whatever their native language, education, class, profession, beliefs, and so on? Answering this last question in the affirmative, and the previous ones in the light of such an answer, amounts to making extremely serious assumptions about human nature and history; still, these assumptions would have to be made if we were to maintain the thesis of a generalized "normality" as against the thesis of generalized communicative and especially linguistic alienation.

To my mind, these assumptions were never made by Wittgenstein himself; they were, of course, made – more often implicitly than explicitly – by some of his followers, and this is possibly one of the reasons why he always felt that his teachings were deeply misunderstood. Wittgenstein, on the contrary, was well aware that the total communication of any way of living or any historical situation is itself abnormal in another and much more encompassing sense because it produces tension, discomfort, anxiety, unhappiness. In fact, he said, communication as a whole as we live it must sooner or later be replaced by different kinds of communication belonging to different ways of living and different historical situations.

To conclude, if I have succeeded in conveying to the audience the feeling that much new work must be done on Wittgenstein, and that it can only be done by first reordering and reassessing both historically and structurally the whole of his published and unpublished manuscripts against the background he belonged to, then the main and perhaps only aim of a lecture like this has been achieved.

Whereupon, *verehrtes Publikum*, I have prepared two *finali*. The first is that in case somebody feels that I have not being talking Wittgenstein "proper," that the Wittgenstein I was referring to is not the real Wittgenstein, I shall try to protect myself by paraphrasing a famous saying by him: whether this is a Wittgenstein or not, is for the public to decide.

But – second *finale* – whenever we talk of Wittgenstein, we should not forget the total dedication and integrity of his thinking. To use a phrase he wrote two days before his dying, *his* dream was actually "connected with the noise of rain" – *mit dem Geräusch des Regens zusammenhängt*. Except that he was not dreaming: he was, in his own highly personal and original way, reflecting and interpreting the tragedy of our age.

References

Boas, Franz. 1966. *Race, Language and Culture* (1940). New York: Free Press.
Bentley, Arthur F. 1941. "The Human Skin: Philosophy's Last Line of Defense." *Philosophy of Science* VIII: 1-9.
———. 1949. *Knowing and the Known*. Cf. Dewey, John.
Cacciari, Massimo. 1976. *Krisis. Saggio sulla crisi del pensiero negativo da Nietzsche a Wittgenstein*. Milan: Feltrinelli.
Ceccato, Silvio. 1951. *Il linguaggio con la Tabella di Ceccatieff*. Paris: Hermann. (Italian text and English transl.).
———. 1964. *Un tecnico fra i filosofi*, I: *Come filosofare* (1940-1947). Padua: Marsilio.
———. 1966. *Un tecnico fra i filosofi*, II: *Come non filosofare* (1947-1953). Padua: Marsilio.
Dewey, John and Arthur F. Bentley. 1949. *Knowing and the Known*. Boston: Beacon Press.
Eco, Umberto. 1975. *Trattato di semiotica generale*. Milan: Bompiani. English transl. *A Theory of Semiotics*. Bloomington: Indiana University Press, 1975.
Engels, Friedrich. Cf. Marx, Karl.

Freud, Siegmund. 1901. *Zur Psychopathologie des Alltagslebens* (*Über Vergessen, Versprechen, Vergreifen, Aberglaube und Irrtum*). Now in *Gesammelte Werke*, vol. 4. Frankfurt: Fischer, 1941, 1969(5). *The Psychopathology of Everyday Life*. Transl. from German by A. Tyson under the general editorship of J. Strachey. London: Hogarth Press, 1960.

———. 1905. *Der Witz und seine Beziehung zum Unbewußten*. Now in *Gesammelte Werke*, vol. 6. Frankfurt: Fisher, 1940. *Jokes and Their Relation to the Unconscious*. Transl. from German by J. Strachey. London: Hogarth Press, 1960.

Lotman, Jurij M. 1965. "Rol' semiotiki v kiberneticeskom issledovanii celoveka i kollektiva." In *Logičeskaja struktura naučnogo znanija*, 75-90. Moscow. "Ruolo della semiotica nell'indagine cibernetica dell'uomo e della collettività." Transl. by R. Faccani. In *I sistemi di segni e lo strutturalismo sovietico*, 41-54. Milan: Bompiani, 1969.

———. 1967. "k probleme tipologii kul'tury." In *Trudy po znakovym sistemam*, III, 30-38. Tartu. "Il problema di una tipologia della cultura." Transl. by R. Faccani. In *I sistemi di segni e lo strutturalismo sovietico*, 309-318. Milan: Bompiani, 1969.

———. 1971. "*O semiotičeskom mechanizme kul'tury*." In *Trudy po znakovym sistemam*, 144-176. Tartu. Now in Lotman 1975.

———. 1973. *Ricerche semiotiche. Nuove tendenze delle scienze umane nell'URSS*. In collab. with Boris A. Uspensky. Ed. by C. Strada Janovič. Turin: Einaudi.

———. 1975. *Tipologia della cultura* (1973). In collab. with Boris A. Uspensky. Ed. by R. Faccani and M. Marzaduri. Milan, 1962.

Lukács, György. 1952. *Die Zerstörung der Vernunft*. Reprint, 1960. Neuwied: Luchterhand, 1962.

McGuinnes, Brian. 1978. "Il cosiddetto 'realismo' del *Tractatus* di Wittgenstein." *Lingua e stile* XIII, 2: 161-173.

Marx, Karl and Friedrich Engels. 1845-1846. *Die deutsche Ideologie*. In *Werke*. Berlin: Dietz Verlag, vol. III, 1962.

Mead, George Herbert. 1934. *Mind, Self and Society from the Standpoint of a Social Behaviorist*. Ed. with an introd. by C. Morris, 13th print. Chicago: University of Chicago Press, 1965.

———. 1938. *The Philosophy of the Act*. Ed. with an introd. by C. Morris *et al.*, 5th print. Chicago: University of Chicago Press, 1964.

Morris, Charles. 1932. *Six Theories of Mind*. Chicago: University of Chicago Press.

———. 1937. *Logical Positivism, Pragmatism, and Scientific Empiricism*. Paris: Hermann. (Comprises five previously published papers.)

———. 1938. *Foundations of the Theory of Signs* (= International Encyclopedia of Unified Science, I: 2). Chicago: University of Chicago Press.

Nietzsche, Friedrich. 1870-1889. *Werke. Kritische Gesamtausgabe*. Ed. by von G. Colli and M. Montinari. Berlin: de Gruyter, 1972.

Nyíri, Cristof. 1974. "Beim Sternenlicht der Nichtexistierenden. Zur ideologiekritischen Interpretation des platonisierenden Antipsychologismus." *Inquiry* XVII, 4: 399-443.

———. 1975. "Wittgenstein's New Traditionalism." In *Essays on Wittgenstein in Honour of G.H. von Wright. Acta philosophica fennica* XXVIII, 1-3 (1976): 503-512.

———. 1977. "Wittgensteins Geschichts- und Gesellschaftsauffassung in ihrer Bedeutung für die Gegenwart." In *Wittgenstein and His Impact on Contemporary Thought. Proceedings* of the 2nd International Wittgenstein Symposium (Kirchberg 29 August – 4 September 1977), 36-41. Vienna: Hölder-Pichler-Tempsky, 1978.

Nuova corrente. 1954- A journal founded by M. Boselli and G. Sechi. Now ed. by M. Boselli, T. Perlini, F. Rella, and G. Sertoli. Cf. special issues on Freud, Nietzsche, Wittgenstein, Heidegger, and *Finis Austriae*.

Riverso, Emanuele. 1964. *Il pensiero di Ludovico Wittgenstein*, 2nd ed. 1970. Naples: Libreria scientifica editrice.

Rossi-Landi, Ferruccio. [See the general bibliography of his writings at the end of this volume.]

Sebeok, Thomas A. 1976. *Contributions to the Doctrine of Signs*. Lisse: Peter de Ridder Press.

Semiotica. 1969- Journal of the International Association for Semiotic Studies. Ed. by T.A. Sebeok.

Uspensky, Boris A. Cf. Lotman, Jurij M.

Von Wright, Georg H. 1977. "Wittgenstein in Relation to His Times." In *Wittgenstein and His Impact on Contemporary Thought. Proceedings* of the 2nd International Wittgenstein Symposium (cf. under Nyíri).

Wittgenstein, Ludwig. 1920. *Tractatus logico-philosophicus*. Text and new transl. by D.F. Pears and B.F. McGuinness. London: Routledge & Kegan Paul, 1961.

———. 1945. *Philosophische Untersuchungen*. Text and English transl. by G.E.M. Anscombe. Oxford: Blackwell, 1953. New edition 1958.

———. 1929-1948 (!). *Zettel*. Text, transl. and ed. by G.E.M. Anscombe and G.H. von Wright. Oxford: Blackwell, 1967.

———. 1949-1951. *Über Gewißheit*. Text and transl. by D. Paul and G.E.M. Anscombe. Oxford: Blackwell, 1969.

II

SIGNS AS COGNITIVE AND EVALUATIVE INSTRUMENTS

5. Toward an Analysis of Appraisive Signs in Esthetics

The first Section of this article [cf. R.-L. 1953b] is an examination of a behavioral approach to values in general and to esthetic values in particular, as represented in Charles Morris's article "Significance, Signification, and Painting," printed in the present issue of this journal [cf. Morris 1952].[1]

This reference does not involve the claim that the same criticisms would suit all similar approaches: how far they do, should be decided case by case. The relevant trend, behaviorism, is thus referred to from a *methodological* and not from an historical point of view.

In the second Section another approach to the same problems is drafted.

5.1 Morris's Behavioral Approach

Empirical investigations may be of importance when the signification of appraisive terms is concerned: as Morris says, it is strange that so much discussion is carried on without almost ever resorting to them.[2] It is just this experimental attitude which lends to Morris's approach a simplicity rarely found in the treatment of these problems, so often characterized by the sophistications of personal taste.

To begin with, the simple distinction between preference-ratings and appraisal-ratings is a good device. Had this distinction not been made, tested people would have been liable to confound what they liked with what they considered worthy of appraisal even if they did not like it personally. In this case much self-deception would have been possible as when, for example, one imagines to have a preference simply because a certain painting corresponds to certain patterns which have been taught to be preferable.[3] Now one can ask: Does the distinction, fruitful as it may be, avoid self-deception? Can completely reliable ratings be obtained from people tested in this way? Up to what point are such ratings relevant to the problem of value?

Morris speaks of criteria used by people in giving appraisals: consideration of a painting in terms of the number of people who would like it;

whether a museum director would want the painting in his museum, etc. Self-deception is likely to arise in the use of these criteria, which are applied by the individual on the basis of what he believes to be the preferences of other people, or the decisions of museum directors, etc. Whether these beliefs are true[4] or not, can only be determined by testing all the people the tested person has in mind while giving his own answers: these would probably be people he is acquainted with, or people of whose opinions he has been informed, or people to whom he is attributing opinions, or hypothetical people whose opinions he is imagining. If the same test were applied to all these people (leaving it to the reader how to track down "hypothetical people"), the same situation would arise, and so on – the limit of this progression being an imitation of what actually takes place in a culture. The distinction between preferences and appraisals is then mainly a distinction between the tested individual's preferences and other people's preferences from his own point of view. The former are expressed without an interposed person; the latter through an interposed person, on the assumption that this person is able to represent them faithfully. If one wants to abandon such a "representation-assumption," one faces the problem of examining the way in which the tested person elaborates other people's preferences in order to use them as criteria for recognizing and assessing works of art even against his own personal tastes. This problem concerns all kinds of criteria, those also that Morris labels as "subjective," his distinction between subjective and objective criteria being far too simple and vague.

Altogether, it does not seem that fully reliable ratings can be obtained through testing. When people are proposed a scale of numbers from which they have to choose a mark, too many variables are at work, of which answers are to be a function: differences in mood, in the way reasons are given, in the criteria one happens to apply, etc., may affect and change one's judgments within a relatively wide range. It is therefore likely that what is expressed is a provisional decision reached in that very moment for the sake of the experiment. Such answers are too casual, and cannot be rated with opinions reached after careful scrutiny on a professional basis or, at least, as a result of long commerce with artistic objects. The connoisseur, given a certain set of works of art, may be able to grade them, i.e. to find some of them better than others. But even the connoisseur himself is rarely in a position to use a definite scale; so much the less does this seem possible for people who have to make up their mind on the spot and without adequate preparation. A small experiment has been made with a dozen prints from well known painters. Several people were asked Morris's questions: they turned out to be rather perplexed about which they liked the most and which was the best; or at least, they were not able to decide in such a way as to be sure it was their deep and definitive preference or appraisal they were expressing. The phrase '*deep* and *definitive* preference or appraisal' requires a qualification. It does not mean entities dwelling in some mysterious place to which the individual has (to use a phrase of Gilbert Ryle's) "privileged access"; it merely means patterns of behavior able to persist in time and to repeat themselves through changes in environment. In this sense one can say, for instance, that somebody's liking of music constitutes a real and definitive trait of his personality: there is evidence for it. The argument here is that the same is not the case in Morris's ratings, supported as they are only by the thin evidence of oral answers. One more remark on this point. We are contesting the validity of rated preferences and appraisals not in regard to the works of art, within art criticism, but in regard to the person who utters them, within that study of the signification of appraisive terms that Morris has in mind. The validity of the appraisals of (the paintings as) works of art is a much more complicated issue than that now under discussion; at the present stage, it has not yet presented itself.

One of the merits of these experimental researches is that they confirm the untenability of a position based on the absoluteness of taste. But if answers obtained in this way from people are thought to express directly their "natural" or "real" taste, the belief in the general absoluteness of taste may be replaced by a belief in the absoluteness of the personal taste of him who is answering questions. The fact that somebody reacts in a certain way would then be considered as proof of the inevitability of this reaction, as when any normal person acquainted with the use of color words is expected inevitably to recognize colors. Values are much more complicated than that, and no one-to-one relation can explain them.

At this point, the claim could be made that the answers secured are proved to be reliable by the relations found between the two sets of ratings on the one hand, and constitutional needs as expressed by physical differences, according to Sheldon's constitutional psychology, on the other. One should not deny that such relations may be found in principle.[5] Before feeling sure of such relations, however, one should be sure of both terms. An examination of whether one can rely upon the 'constitution-need' terms does not belong to this article; it has been suggested that one cannot rely upon the 'preference or appraisal' term. If this is right, the following unfortunate procedure might be involved: while the relation between preferences and needs stands, if preferences and needs are reliable, preferences are said to be reliable as a consequence of their relation with needs.

A possible line of defence could be the following: people tested say something; what they do not say cannot be checked, nor can what "took place in them" before they uttered anything be dealt with; therefore, the investigation must content itself with what they actually say. This is sound in principle, but in principle only. And indeed, I think that to place such limitations means to leave the field of values substantially unexplored once and for all.

From what has been said, it does not follow that experimental methods should be given up in the study of values. It does follow, however, that they should be confined to psychological investigations of very simple reactions to simple stimuli, leaving alone such complex things as paintings. As for the collection of evidence about people's preferences and appraisals by means of the customary historical, sociological, literary, and everyday methods, one may agree that this is an empirical enquiry: it is certainly not an experimental one.

'Good' and 'bad,' the most general terms for values, signify in a different manner from, for example, a designative word such as 'banana.' These terms can have the same signification for a number of persons even though the "objects" (in Morris's general sense) to which they apply differ with the persons: as they signify objects in some specific relation to persons, they can be used by different persons for different objects, provided the relation is the same. What is this relation then? An example of the behavioral approach is Morris's answer that it is a capacity to satisfy needs.

There is in this the intention to resort to something which takes place *in* the valuating person before any word is uttered (this metaphorical 'in' simply meaning that a person, in order to come to utter an appraisive term, must have done something *himself*). This is Morris's intention, one would say, in spite of the fact that his procedure deals only with what is said by tested people. But does such a biological explanation tell us something about values?

It is perhaps correct to say that a pear has a particular kind of value when it satisfies one's need of food. This would probably be called a "practical" (or "economic," or "instrumental") kind of value: it concerns a very small part of the field of values, and a relatively unimportant one for philosophy. Esthetic, ethical, legal, religious, "cognitive" values remain substantially untouched; to reduce them to economic values has a queer resemblance to Marxian reductions of superstructures. And indeed: to say that the appraisal of a painting, death for one's country, preference for a certain way of living, guilt feeling in regard to some actions or persons, etc. etc., are values because of their capacity to satisfy needs, does not give us any additional information about them. 'Need' is here used in such a wide sense as to loose all characterizing power. By being told that values satisfy needs, one does not improve one's capacity for producing, recognizing, and assessing values, or for selecting different kinds of values, or for keeping free from the bias of personal values or of values imposed by the community, while carrying out a scientific enquiry; and the like. To do all this, one still has to resort to other methods or criteria – the same already used in order to simply start talking precisely of values instead of something else. The very distinction between preferences and appraisals (as well as, for instance, between preferential behavior and need-reducing behavior) proves the necessity of introducing, in one way or another, something more than a mere biological explanation in terms of the satisfaction of needs.

The point is the following. A portion of man's behavior can be explained in terms of stimuli, responses, needs, and satisfaction of needs; another cannot (or not yet, or not by using those terms as they are used in behavioral psychology). Sign-behavior and value-behavior, for instance, cannot. Value-behavior (with the possible exception of practical values when the immediate satisfaction of a need can be checked through experimental methods) is based upon sign-behavior; and there is no necessary relation between sign-behavior and satisfaction of needs.[6]

Morris claims that his behavioral approach constitutes only a segment in a wider field. I also think it constitutes an arbitrary extension of some procedures to fields of enquiry other than the ones in which those procedures had been worked out and had proved satisfactory. If one contrasts that "segment" with the rest, one may see both that the rest is what really matters and that that segment does not tell us anything important about the rest, or at least anything which we did not already know from the rest. Many philosophers would agree in labeling such an extension "the philosophical sin of scientism": in the behavioral case, a form of "biologism."[7]

What then are the other methods and criteria which enable us to speak of values?

The right question to be answered seems to be "What do we *do* when we come to speak of values?" This simple question does not yet involve any presupposition whatever; or rather, it only involves the presupposition that values are something we have to come to and not something we are administered by occult powers. One should keep in mind the phrasing of this question even when, for the sake of brevity, reference is made to what values *are*.

Using an expression of Morris's, one could start by saying that values are "postlanguage symbols," interpersonal as far as they are shared by several interpreters, and personal as far as they are not shared. In order to study them, one has to accomplish a manifold task.

The processes, by means of which such postlanguage symbols are produced, are not (or not yet) observable; in any case, no necessary relation between such processes and the overt behavior of the organism which produces them can be established for the moment. Observable can be said to be the utterance of their results ("I think that painting is good") or even the manifestation of their results in some nonlinguistic manner (somebody's behavior under certain conditions which enable us to speak, e.g. of "ethical behavior"). Morris himself [cf. 1946: 84] wrote that "in self-observation the prescriptor is accompanied by a sense of obligation to act in a certain way". How does this 'sense of obligation' come to be? How are similar 'senses' realized? What happens when we say something is beautiful or ugly, moral or immoral, and the like? To try to answer these questions does not mean to resort to any of the interpretations known as "mentalistic," and which, in spite of their subtlety and comprehensiveness, do not further any intersubjective knowledge of man [cf. Morris 1946, 1: 4, 9; 11: 7; Appendix 2, 4 and 5]. One possible way of studying these nonobservable processes could be as an extension of the behavioral method, provided we turn to the current and original meaning of "behavior" (possibly better conveyed by the Italian *comportamento* and by the German *Haltung*) as opposed to the specific meaning (overt and observable performances of organisms) the term has assumed in psychology and therefrom in philosophy. However, in order to avoid misunderstandings, it is better to label this "extended behaviorism" as a new sort of *operational analysis*, which consists in tracing out the "operations" through which we come to speak of the various values, and the criteria used therewith.

5.2 Draft of an Operational Approach to Esthetic Values

> Ist dieses schon Philosophie?
> Das hängt davon ab, ob wir es
> so benennen wollen
> *Hugo Dingler*

It is not a question of measurement operations, as for instance in Bridgman's case: other kinds of operations are examined through the application of which one comes to speak of values, to attribute a value to a certain object or to a piece of behavior.[8] Consider for example the case of passing from an esthetically neutral piece of behavior (e.g. listening to a series of notes) to the same piece of behavior with either positive or negative esthetic value (listening to the same series of notes and recognizing in them a tune endowed with esthetic significance – either positive or negative, i.e. in common terms, either beautiful or ugly). We set out to study that which, added to the mere piece of behavior symbolized by "listening to a series of notes," makes it an esthetic experience, thereby making the object experienced esthetically significant.

The idea of "passing" from one piece of behavior to the same piece of behavior endowed with additional properties, and hence the idea of "adding" something to the former when the passage to the latter takes place, are not easily grasped by some readers. Consider passing from the recognition of "an animal" to that of "a horse," and then of "a mare"; and from "this is a series of notes" to "this is a tune," and then to more complicated expressions such as "I like this tune," "this tune is beautiful," "this tune is beautiful because ...". If we use as a criterion of simplicity the fact that, when we speak like that, each member in the two series requires the preceding one, we can say that 'animal' is simpler than 'horse,' and that 'this is a series of notes' is simpler than 'this is a tune,' and so on. Now, what happens when we pass from one expression to the next one? While it is easy to say that one passes from "animal" to "horse" by specifying that a horse is not only an animal, but one in the order mammalia, and moreover that it has a certain size, four legs of equal length, a tail, a mane, and so on, it is difficult to say what is added when the passage from one member to the next one in the esthetic series takes place. Each of these steps deserves careful examination; but the most important leap into a new field occurs when we pass beyond the mere recognition of an audible series of notes. It is with this particular passage that we are mainly concerned in this article.

If we set out to examine this "addition," however, we are not concerned with the question as to whether it takes place in regard to any given object: this is open to empirical investigation. Nor are we concerned with the question as to whether art critics or other specialists would suggest that it is a case of considering something as a tune and not merely as a series of notes, or as a beautiful tune and not merely as a tune: all this is linked with something we have not yet hinted at, and are not going to examine in this paper, namely the use of criteria for the recognition of works of art as distinguished from other artefacts and from objects other than artefacts, and of criteria for the assessment of works of art. We are concerned merely with the activity through which the passage takes place when it does take place. This activity will be referred to hereafter with the label of 'processes.' If we want to study these processes, we have to split them into separate repeatable pieces or steps, otherwise we would not be able to deal with them. (The same happens in all enquiries concerning human behavior, independently of the way in which the relevant processes are performed. For instance, men can infer, or draw conclusions, in an instantaneous manner, without being aware of what is going on; but if we want to make a science of these processes, namely logic, we have to split them into principles and rules.) The term 'operations' is retained to symbolize these steps; if one does not like it, it can be dropped, provided it is remembered that there are such processes and that it is possible to study them technically. What these processes are and what they are not, and what is involved in refusing to consider them, should appear more clearly below.

Such operations are laid down in the form of instructions, more or less according to that type of discourse which Morris calls 'technological'; they are articulated as much as is necessary to have them performed without misunderstanding; their results are tested by comparing them with previous results, according to the program of operational technique (this program is still being evolved, but for the sake of the present article can be put roughly in the terms of "considering the meaning or use of a linguistic expression as a result of possible operations, and tracing out what operations upon what material produce the result" – cf. note 8). Two examples of a very different kind may be helpful on this point. First example. You want to reproduce a cake but you are not acquainted with the recipe; you start making cakes until comparison shows that you have produced the same cake, i.e. you have reproduced the cake assumed as a model. Second example. You are not a believer in the Python-God and want to become one. You do not know how, but you start imitating the behavior of believers in the Python-God in order to attain their condition, until comparison permits you to say that you too are a believer in the Python-God. The tremendous difficulty of religious experience (even when it is simply a question of the Python-God) in comparison with cake-making should not blur the fact that in both cases it is a question of going through certain processes in order to attain certain results that are recognized on the basis of comparison. (No offense either to cooks or to believers in the Python-God is involved.) Of course, it may be the case that one (i) has no interest either in making cakes or in becoming a believer in the Python-God, and therefore simply does not even bother trying, or (ii) does not have the capacity, in either case, to perform the relevant operations. There are persons who will never be able to cook anything well and there are persons who will never be able to become a believer in the Python-God: we are not concerned here with these questions of typology.

Team work at the Italian Center of Methodology and Language Analysis has shown it possible to perform all kinds of operations with a certain intersubjectivity, in the sense in which intersubjective operations are performed in well-established fields, as for instance arithmetic. The difficulties encountered in trying to communicate these operations in such fields as those of signs and values, say nothing against the method; consider the long evolution that has been necessary to attain an intersubjective technique in geometry, arithmetic, and the like, and the long training which is necessary for a child to get acquainted with the use of, for instance, value-words. Such operations show that "values" can be understood in terms of certain ways of "behaving" with regard to something (provided one keeps in mind what has been said about extended behavior as opposed to behavior in the restricted sense of overt and observable performances of organisms). These ways of behaving, to be understood as symbolic processes, have to be brought to awareness (= consciousness, but the first term is preferable because of its independence from the idea of psychological consciousness). There is, then, an analogy with what takes place in psychoanalysis. There are also important differences: briefly that the aims are quite different and that no assumption is made of unconscious states of the mind, where processes are imagined as continuing by themselves, so that it would be possible to track them down through a sort of naturalistic enquiry. On the contrary: the various theories of mind – as entity, faculty, process, relation, etc. – range themselves among the most interesting "results" of alternative sets of possible operations.

We now want to sketch a process through which one can come to speak of a particular kind of significance which seems to be of fundamental importance in esthetic appreciation. This sketch is deliberately drawn in quasi-behavioral terms, in order to retain a connection with the terminology used in Morris's article. This can lead to misunderstanding, if only because such highly problematic terms and phrases as 'stimulus,' 'response,' 'actor,' 'object,' 'feeling,' 'between an actor and an object,' 'within the actor,' etc., have to be introduced uncritically. In this article, however, I prefer to run this risk rather than the risk of transplanting into English, without adequate qualifications, the new Italian terminology developed within operational analysis or technique. *In this technique the above mentioned terms and phrases are either excluded or operationally defined in their turn.*[9] The process is split here into three operations. One should remember that each operation could be considered a process to be split into further operations, and that the whole process could be summed up as one operation only: the extent of the splitting is decided on practical-pedagogical grounds: as in the case of chemical, physical, mathematical formulae and procedures, and of all sorts of recipes, rules, and instructions.[10]

Op. 1. An object acts as a stimulus producing a response in a man; within this situation, let us call the object a "stimulus-object" and the man in whom a response is elicited, an "actor." This operation takes place between a man and an object, these being distinguished for the sake of the present description by using the epidermis as a criterion (but see provision c below).

Remarks: a. There is response as there is stimulus, and vice versa; this links together actor and object within the process.
  b. "Stimulus" and "response" are used here in a rather wide and loose sense as referring to the two poles of one unitary process (to be described elsewhere as, for instance, "perception" or "observation"); no reference to physical energy on the side of the stimulus or to nerve activity on the side of the response is required.
  c. The stimulus may well come from within the actor, for instance in the form of imagining something. This means that the process described here could start without any object being perceived by the actor. As we intend eventually to speak of works of art, which are physical objects, we shall however limit ourselves here to the case of interaction between actor and stimulus-object.
  d. No awareness of the operation is necessarily involved: the actor can be unaware of responding to an object, or even of the object itself. But usually there is awareness of the presence of the object. (General remark c below deals with the "aware or unaware" behavior throughout the three operations.)

e. We speak of a man, but nothing in principle would prevent us from supposing the same kind of reaction, say, in a primate.

Op. 2. As a consequence of, or together with, his response, the actor reacts on his own toward operation 1. This operation takes place "within" the actor, in the sense that no interaction between him and anything else is necessary for its realization. We can call this: "feeling something" about the stimulus-object.

Remarks: a. It is not the object which is now being reacted to, but the actor's relation with the object, i.e. the original stimulus-response situation.
b. A distinction between outer response, inner response, and feeling something is involved, but this need not affect the present step in the process: we are not concerned here in how a feeling may originate out of a mere response, and the like, but merely with the fact that men are liable to feel something as a response, or as the consequence of a response, to some stimulus originally localizable as coming from some object.
c. The covert behavior described in operation 2 does not necessarily find expression as an overt behavior. When there is such an overt behavior, it is not necessarily a response to the original stimulus: for us to say this, the result of our enquiry should already be available to us. This is meant to exclude the possibility of approaching our problem in restricted behavioral terms.
d. Whether or not the inner response described might be checked even when it remains nonobservable by, for instance, neurological means does not concern us here.
e. No awareness of the operation is necessarily involved; nor is awareness necessarily involved of operation 1 during the performance of operation 2, whether this involves awareness or not.
f. In the case when the actor is aware of both his feeling and the object, and the process does not go any further afield, the actor can say at this moment that "he likes" the object.

Op. 3. The actor attributes the result of operation 2, i.e. in a sense that which he has felt, to the stimulus-object. This operation is still going on "within" the actor. But while at the stage of operation 2 the object was no longer involved and might have disappeared without affecting it, by operation 3 the object is somehow involved again.

Remarks: a. The object is involved again at least in the awareness of the actor, otherwise no attribution of property to it would be possible.
b. The object is involved again also in the sense of physical presence if further description of it has to be possible.
c. No awareness of the operation is necessarily involved; nor is awareness necessarily involved of either operation 1 or operation 2, or both,

or neither, during the performance of operation 3, whether this involves awareness or not.

d. As the process is not necessarily spoken, not even in its result, we are not concerned with a change, if any, in linguistic usage, which may (or, *a posteriori* and from the point of view of grammar, should) accompany operation 3. If it were spoken, one could pass for instance from a phrase like 'a feeling of pleasure' to a phrase like 'a pleasant object.'

Result: As a consequence of the process split above into operations 1, 2, 3, the stimulus-object acquires the property of being significant to the actor, of having a value for him.

General remarks

a. The process described is not "in time" in any recognized sense of the phrase. It may take time for somebody to attribute significance to a certain object; in other cases, the significance can be attributed in an instantaneous-like way: this belongs to the psychology of the individual concerned, and has no bearing on our enquiry. Reference can be made to the field traditionally called logic when it is said that formulae are out of time. Time-words, such as 'before,' 'after,' 'during,' 'while,' used in regard to operations, then, refer to the way operations are laid down, and not to something which can be measured with a clock. How long it takes for a psychological subject to perform a certain process is for experimental psychology to decide.

b. For similar reasons, the process described is not "in space" either. But as we are aiming at esthetic judgment, and this concerns above all men and objects to be labeled "artistic," reference has been made to a man as an actor and to an object as a stimulus-object.

c. (See remarks 1, d; 2, e; 3, c.) The process described is not necessarily aware (conscious); on the contrary, the relevant operations are so common in everyday life that one usually carries them out without being aware of them at all. As the operations are three, we have a net of two awareness-unawareness cases at the stage of operation 1, of four at the stage of operation 2, and of eight at the stage of operation 3. Moreover, at the stage of operations 2 and 3 there may still be awareness of the antecedent operation or operations, or they may have been forgotten. While leaving to the reader the amusement of tracing out all possible relationships between aware and unaware operations throughout the process, we point out here the following two particular cases:

(i) If, at the stage of operation 3, the actor, while being aware of the presence of the object, is not aware of operations 2 and 3, the object may appear to him as endowed in itself (*sua virtute*) with the property projected upon it. This would correspond to an ontological theory of values as properties carried by objects in the world.

(ii) If, at the stage of operation 3, the actor is aware of attributing a feeling of his own to an object but has forgotten operations 1 and 2, the quality he is projecting may appear to him as a creation of his own. This would correspond to an idealistic theory of values as a result of the activity of the mind.

Traditional philosophical theories seem to correspond to various kinds of unawareness at one stage or another of the process. New philosophical theories can be traced out by resorting to yet unexploited kinds of unawareness.

d. As a matter of course, when one sets out to study such processes, one has to lay them down in some manageable form; so they have to be fully brought to awareness. Among all possible combinations of aware and unaware operations, the operational treatment corresponds therefore to the case where (i) all three operations involve awareness, (ii) awareness of both operations 1 and 2 is maintained up to the stage of operation 3, (iii) the result is considered as the result of the three operations.

e. One may ask what meaning can be attributed to the refusal of these operations, i.e. to the refusal of bringing them to awareness. Does the refusal mean that the operations do not take place for the person who does not recognize them? This point, and some of its implications, can be clarified by a series of remarks:

(i) Hemoglobin is transformed by oxygen into oxyhemoglobin even when we are not aware of this, and even among primitive tribes. There is something going on; chemistry is one way of explaining what and how. If one prefers so, one is free to refuse to get acquainted with chemistry and to keep on thinking either nothing or, for example, that men live under the auspices of the *archeus*'s working upon *sulphur, mercurius*, and *sal*.

(ii) Not differently, somebody may prefer not to get acquainted with reasons which could prevent him from believing, for instance, in some political ideology such as racism, or in the "self-development" of the "universal spirit," or in the Cartesian theory of mind, or in language as a copy of reality, or in a strictly behavioral approach to signs and values, etc. etc.

(iii) Not differently, one can refuse to get acquainted with the operations for significance, and keep on thinking that the property of being significant belongs to the nature of things or is produced by some mysterious and indescribable faculty of the Spirit (possibly contenting himself with distinguishing this faculty from others in order then to connect its particular activity with some linguistic usage, which is either a tautology or an arbitrary conjunction).

f. The property of significance remains, so to say, "sticks," to the stimulus-object only insofar as the process *is being performed*: it is not a property *of* the object, and it is not a property created by the actor either. This does justice to both the objective and the subjective theories of significance. The object does not undergo any transformation because of its having or not having the property of being significant as a result of the process described.

g. However, one can recall that an object is significant without actually performing the process, and one can tell another person that an object is significant without making this person perform the relevant operations. *One can use the result without the operations.*

h. If a tree performed the operations described in regard to a pebble, the pebble would acquire the property of being significant to the tree. We are not measuring the operations against the world, but the world by the operations.

i. So far, we have vaguely spoken of significance following Morris's distinction between signification (that which is signified by a sign, i.e. "the properties something must have for the sign to apply to it") and significance. This term is used as a first reference to the field of values, which is thus approached prior to the distinction between positive and negative significance: the *genus* significance is being looked for, and not one of its two *species* signified by such general terms as 'good' and 'bad.' This is meant to avoid the traditional mistake of searching for what is good as distinguished from what is bad, a mistake resting on the unawareness of the criteria used to make the distinction, and which usually leads to a surreptitious introduction of the value searched for into its definiens, and so to vicious circles.

j. If we keep in mind that we have to approach the *genus* significance as such, we can then proceed to distinguish several kinds of significance, i.e. several different values (practical, esthetic, legal, cognitive, ethical, etc.), each of them either positive or negative. Only one particular kind of significance, i.e. only one particular value, has been traced back here to its generating process. It is not a practical value: a pear has practical value because it satisfies somebody's hunger, or is expected to do so: it acquires such value by being somehow used by the actor, or by being recognized as liable to be used. On the contrary, the value attained by the object through the process described above does not imply any use of it by the actor. It seems clear that our value is not ethical, or religious, or cognitive, or legal. It is a property of something *as if* the property was independent of the actor, *as if* it belonged to the object considered as detached from him; and at the same time, it is always in relation to an actor that an object is described as having such a property.

k. Similarly to all properties in a value-situation, the former is liable to be described by the general terms 'good' and 'bad'; but it is better conveyed by such adjectives as 'beautiful' and 'ugly,' and so corresponds to "esthetic" significance or value. This usage is *decided* on the basis of available evidence from common experience and relevant criticism, with the following in mind: to purge linguistic usage of the hopeless ambiguities of everyday talk while trying to retain as much as possible of such usage. One has started with a reference to a portion of common speech, but one has tried to link this portion to something which comes before common speech. Moreover, one has tried to get hold of the branch before the leaves, or of the trunk before the branches. No claim is made that this is how that particular kind of significance necessarily comes into being, or that no other way could be traced out. The claim is only made that the process described does clarify an important section of our linguistic usage of terms for esthetic significance, so to say, from inside the process which leads us to utter them.

l. *The usage proposed does not involve that an object spoken of as esthetically significant* (or as endowed with esthetic value) *is thereby a work of art.* And indeed, we also describe as beautiful or ugly artefacts extraneous to any recognizable field of art, objects other than artefacts, as well as human behavior and all sorts of situations, occurrences, and events. This shows that the process described can take place on all sorts of occasions, independent of piecemeal everyday habits; it also shows the necessity of resorting to something that precedes language in order to get hold of those processes the results of which are represented by language in all its indefinite variety of nuances. (The following, thus, can be said about values in general: they are already represented in the structure of our common language; the point is to trace out *how* this structure was produced. Reference to common language is necessary; but it should be understood as the using of a rule of prudence, and not as the making of a search for truth: otherwise, either the ontological-realistic approach would simply be transferred into language without being overcome, or the analyst would limit himself to a dictionary-making task.)

m. One more example may help the reader to avoid certain misinterpretations of the process described. Suppose a new tool is proposed in carpentry. As a result of its application, new ways of working may arise, pieces of furniture somehow different from the customary ones may be produced, the behavior of carpenters may undergo some changes, etc. This granted, consider the following questions: How much of the new ways of working, pieces of furniture, and habits and procedures of carpenters, are represented in (conveyed by, anticipated in the structure of, ...) the new tool? What can we tell of the consequences of the applications of the new tool without having yet applied it? What are the relations between the new tool and all the possible objects produced by using it?

In drawing some conclusions we shall now also try to suggest a bridge to further enquiry.

The process traced corresponds to what is usually meant by "valuation" only up to a point. It does not tell us how valuations are actually arrived at, but merely presents us with some patterns of behavior (in the extended sense) following which one comes to a valuation: the process is not yet any particular valuation either positive or negative. To say what the process is, is not to answer such questions as "What is this esthetic value?" or "Is this an esthetic value?," and the like; it is to answer the question "What is it for an esthetic value to be an esthetic value?," or – as hinted at above – "What do we do when we come to speak of esthetic value?" It follows that, in order to come to an actual judgment of value (e.g. "This painting as a work of art is good, or bad") not only must we perform the relevant operations which enable us to pass from an esthetically neutral to an esthetically significant piece of behavior, and thereby to consider a certain artefact as esthetically significant, etc.: but we must also do something else. This leads us to another field which remains substantially unexplored in a behavioral approach (while it is more or less directly examined by trends based on the analysis of linguistic uses): what are the criteria by means of which we come to recognize and to assess works of art? and how do we use them? Morris's hints at such criteria seem to be only the very first reference to this wide field of enquiry, which could be called "criteriology".[11] It will be a question of finding out, among other things: (i) how we come to recognize in an artefact a work of art, either esthetically significant or not; (ii) in the case we have considered it esthetically significant, what reasons are we able to give for its assessment? The various stages of this process are not meant to be necessarily independent of one another, nor must they necessarily overlap. In considering them critically, however, they have to be distinguished as much as it is necessary to get well acquainted with each of them: as in the case of operations, they have to be kept out of time. What then is the relation between this way of dealing with them and what happens when somebody actually makes a criticism (either professionally or in everyday life: in any case "in reality," as some people would put it)? I think it is a relation of a kind similar to the relation between recipes to produce cakes and the description of how one cake in one kitchen in the world is produced by one cook. Operations and criteria, moreover, are to be seen as "pure cases": recipes as opposed, this time, to the description of how all possible cakes are produced in all possible kitchens in the world by all possible cooks. One deals with the recipes, not with cook-behavior. Of course a recipe to produce cakes has a bearing on the behavior of cooks. The point is to grasp what sort of bearing.

New College, Oxford
(Received on December 15, 1952)

Notes

1. Here is for the reader's convenience, a short outline of Morris's article. An empirical study of the signification of "value terms" or "appraisive signs," such as 'good' and

'bad,' is carried out by testing people's reactions to a set of paintings, here used merely as a convenient way of eliciting a sign-behavior of an appraisive kind. Such reactions are *preferences* when the tested person indicates, according to a proposed scale, how much he likes each picture (hence one has preference ratings), and *appraisals* when he assesses each picture as a work of art (appraisal ratings). The aim is not to propose a definition of 'good,' and 'bad,' but to trace out what these terms actually mean when commonly used – such an enquiry being a segment of a vast domain that can be characterized as an approach to human values through the study of human action. Morris comes to the following conclusions:

    1. Appraisals involve, or are a "function of," both objects and persons, and of neither alone; this *objective-relativist* position excludes the positions known as *objectivist* (reference only to the object reacted to) and *subjectivist* or *relativist* (reference only to the actor).

    2. There are some relations between (i) preferences, appraisals, and relations between preferences and appraisals, and (ii) somatotype classes into which the tested persons had been previously classified according to Sheldon's constitutional psychology.

    3. Appraisive signs signify objects in their capacity to satisfy needs, according to the objective-relativist position.

2. In *Signs, Language, and Behavior* (Morris 1946, VIII, 5), we read for instance that "even a small draft of experimental material would act as a cleansing wind" in contemporary discussion on the "theory of value" (p. 232).

3. The term 'self-deception' is used here to refer to all those cases in which a person, in spite of goodwill, does not express himself in a way satisfactory to the investigator, i.e. thinks he has and appears to have answered the question he was put, but actually has not. It is assumed that a more careful examination of the case might enable this fact to be detected, even though a *prima facie* examination had raised no doubt. What 'a more careful examination' is, will depend on the position of the examiner. – No question of bad faith is involved.

4. Here and below the term 'true' is used according to Morris's own semantical concept of truth. Cf. Morris 1946, IV: 7; and Tarski 1944.

5. In *The Open Self* and in several articles [see the bibliography of his writings; this volume, Chapter 2, Section 2.10], Morris himself has shown both that this is possible and the benefit we can obtain from it for the study of man.

6. This last point cannot be dealt with here. The reader may refer to my study on Charles Morris [R.-L. 1953a, 2nd ed. 1975d] as representing an attempt at extending behavioral methods to the study of signs and of values. Morris's behavioral theory of signs and language is criticized there at some length, and an alternative approach to signs is drafted.

7. In his article "The Science of Man and Unified Science," Morris gives a diagram representing the science of man as based upon physical and biological sciences, through the science of values and the science of signs. Particularly decisive criticisms of various forms of "biologism," "psychologism," and the like, are to be found in the contemporary British school of analytical philosophy developed out of Wittgenstein's oral

teaching in Cambridge, as well as, but from a quite different point of view, in all the more important works of Hugo Dingler.

8. For operationalism as developed by the Italian operational group into a new sort of operational analysis labeled "operational technique," I refer the reader to previous issues of this journal, as well as to Ceccato's first formulation in *Language and the Table of Ceccatieff*. Let us remember here simply that the operational method was first shown to be fruitful by Percy W. Bridgman in the field of physics and by Hugo Dingler in physics as well as in arithmetic, geometry, and logic. While Bridgman's operationalism is well known and has received many criticisms, Dingler's *Methodik* is so far relatively unknown (it is a claim of the editors of this journal [R.-L. is here referring to *Methodos* in which the present article originally appeared in 1953; for further information see my introduction to the present volume], that they have contributed to the diffusion of Dingler's work). Reference can be also made to Jean Piaget's *psychologie opératoire*.

9. Alternative terminologies connected with different traditions could be used to approach the same operations, and in each of them some terms and phrases would have to be introduced uncritically. For instance, one could refer to Gentile's "actualistic idealism": starting with his idea of "pure activity" and splitting it into repeatable pieces; but then one should also become aware of the processes by which one comes to speak of that activity, and in so doing one would abandon actualistic idealism. Another example: one could start with the analysis of linguistic uses as represented in common language; but then one should go beyond common language in order to dig out those processes which cannot be represented in it because they underlay it: to begin with, the very process by which one comes to speak of language (or, more generally, of signs); and in so doing one would abandon the analysis of linguistic uses.

10. I owe the basic structure of these operations to Silvio Ceccato: cf. 1951: 45, 47, 49, 238-240. No necessary relation between his treatment and mine is involved, however. I use smaller print below in the text in expounding operations, in order to allow for a more comprehensive glance.

11. In his *New Bearings in Esthetics and Art Criticism*, B.C. Heyl does (or relates to) some work in this direction.

References

Bridgman, Percy W. 1927. *The Logic of Modern Physics*. New York: Macmillan.
Ceccato, Silvio. 1951. *Language and the Table of Ceccatief*. Paris: Hermann.
Dingler, Hugo. 1938. *Die Methode der Physik*. Munich: Reinhardt Verlag.
Heyl, Bernard C. 1943. *New Bearings in Esthetics and Art Criticism*. A Study in Semantics and Evaluation. New Haven: Yale University Press.
Morris, Charles. 1946. *Signs, Language, and Behavior*. New York: Prentice-Hall.
———. 1948. *The Open Self*. New York: Prentice-Hall.

———. 1951. "The Science of Man and Unified Science." In *Contributions to the Analysis and Synthesis of Knowledge. Proceedings of the American Academy of Arts and Sciences* 80 (1, July, 1951): 37-44. *Aut-Aut* 1 (2): 121-129 (in Italian).

———. 1952. "Significance, Signification, and Painting." Paper presented at the Thirteenth Conference on Science, Philosophy and Religion, New York, 1952. *Methodos* 8 (1953): 87-102.

Piaget, Jean. 1950. *Introduction à l'Épistémologie génétique*. Paris: Presses Universitaires de France. Tome I: *La pensée mathématique*; Tome II: *La pensée physique*.

Rossi-Landi, Ferruccio. [See the general bibliography of his writings at the end of this volume.]

Sheldon, William H. (with S.S. Stevens). 1942. *The Varieties of Temperament*. New York: Harper & Brothers.

Sheldon, William H. (with S.S. Stevens & W.B. Tucker). 1940. *The Variety of Human Physique*. New York: Harper & Brothers.

Tarski, A. 1944. "The Semantical Conception of Truth." *Philosophy and Phenomenological Research* IV: 341-376.

6. On Absurdity

Head Note

Apart from some stylistic corrections and from the addition of section titles, this paper "On Absurdity" is printed here [cf. R.-L. 1976a] as it was written for a staff colloquy held on May 24, 1963, in the Department of Philosophy at the University of Texas where I was visiting at the time. It belongs to a stage of my thinking concluded around 1964, a stage which preceded the development of a social approach entirely based on the dialectical method. Actually, the paper is even older than it looks, because I had transcribed it into English from my book *Significato, comunicazione e parlare comune* (Meaning, Communication, and Common Speech) which appeared in 1961 and was then intended to sum up and conclude a line of research I had been following in the fifties. There would be no point in rewriting "On Absurdity" now. Nor shall I describe it in this Head Note. The paper speaks for itself, and is particularly good in showing its own limitations while attempting to show those of the "linguistic" philosophy to which it belongs in spite of its attack on one of the main procedures of such philosophy. Rather, let us try to see if there is in these old pages any interest from the point of view of semiotics. In doing this, I shall draw especially from my recent publications *Linguistics and Economics* and "Sul denaro linguistico" (On Linguistic Money), which both appeared in 1974.

What all verbal messages have in common when their capacity to satisfy various linguistic needs is left aside, is precisely the quality of being simply messages, that is, the *mere results* of linguistic work. Ludwig Wittgenstein seems to be pointing to this when he speaks of words *in general* as compared with tools *in general* (*Philosophical Investigations*, 1953: I, 11, 12, and 13), or when he states that "the clothing of our language makes everything alike" (*ibid*. II, xi: 224). (This was perhaps anticipated in the *Tractatus* [1961]; for instance, 4.02: "we understand the sense of a propositional sign without its having been explained to us"; 4.002; "the proposition *shows [zeigt]* its sense"; and see 4.121 on the logical form "mirrored" in propositions; and *passim.*) When we observe what I have elsewhere called "the linguistic market" (cf. especially *Il linguaggio come lavoro e come mercato* [*Language as Work and Trade*, R.-L. 1968h]), we notice that everyone speaks; everyone is capable of using words and syntagms and of producing verbal messages. This is independent of the particular relationship which each word-as-product and each message-as-product must nonetheless have with the specific linguistic work which has determined its use-value. Given the existence of a language spoken by a certain human group and of its linguistic market, we have here a phenomenon which we could call "inevitability of meaning," i.e. the grasping of meaning as something natural (it is, in fact, a sort of social pseudo-naturalness). Here, too, Wittgenstein comes to our aid: "... where there is sense there must be perfect order. – So there must be perfect order even in the vaguest sentence" (1953: I, 98); "... the sentence must ... have *a* definite sense. An indefinite sense – that would really not be sense *at all*" (I, 99). These are just two of the many passages where Wittgenstein is saying, or almost saying, that no speaker can *escape* the "apprehension" of sense. It is interesting to compare these statements with some statements of *Pragmatics of Human Communication* (Watzalwick *et al.* 1967: 2.2, on "The Impossibility of Not Communicating," pp. 48-49): "Behavior has no opposite ... There is no such thing as nonbehavior or ... one cannot *not* behave. Now, if it is accepted that all behavior in an interactional situation has message value, i.e. is communicative, it follows that no matter how one may try, one cannot *not* communicate." What intrigues me here is that while Wittgenstein is stating something about the nature or structure of the message, and the authors of *Pragmatics of Human Communication* are stating something about (or from the point of view of) the sender of the message, the point I was making above concerns the receiver. Given the communicative situation, the three approaches converge, or so it seems to me; so much so, that the general formula may perhaps be advanced that "one cannot help communicating – by means of a message endowed with a definite sense – to a receiver who cannot help interpreting the message according to that sense."

This formula, however, is mainly true of an *initial portion* of the interpretation of the message. What we are really contending, is that a hearer cannot help *beginning* to interpret in some way or another an expression uttered by a speaker of his own linguistic community, whatever *further interpretation* he may then give to that same expression according to differing contexts and to his own personal previous experience and existing inclinations.

Moreover, the inevitability of meaning does not involve in the least that either the sender or the receiver is in control of the linguistic working processes with which those words and those syntagms are produced and those verbal messages are made up and transmitted. When we begin to discuss these processes in a systematic manner, in fact, we realize how immensely complicated they are, and we run into the most serious disagreement on their nature and importance and consequently also on the nature of their results. On the level of common linguistic exchange, we all know how to use, with sufficient fluency, most of the very terms over which argument amongst scientists and philosophers has been raging for thousands of years: terms like 'number,' 'cause,' 'duty,' 'part,' 'movement,' and innumerable others. Moreover, we all produce correct sentences; but only over the last few years has scientific investigation given rise to hypotheses or working models which attempt to explain how this happens. Whether they belong to post-Chomskyan (1972) generative semantics, to Ceccato's (1959, 1969, 1972) or Vaccarino's (1974) study of "mental operations," to my own approach to language in terms of "linguistic production," or to other attempts at describing what goes on in language, the danger of all such models is that they may refer only to the activity of the scholar who "reconstructs" the activity of the common speaker within his specialized jargon. Some models may pay for the "glory" of approximating a "realistic description" of what the speaker is "actually doing" with the "shame" of becoming mentalistic (cf. on Chomsky, Ponzio 1971, now in 1973; on "mental operations," see 6.5 in *Linguistics and Economics* [cf. R.-L. 1974f and 1975b]). Provisional models, however, are better than no models at all insofar as they contribute to overcoming that pseudo-natural approach to language which considers it as the "free," relatively unconditioned activity of speakers.

In *Linguistics and Economics*, I labeled the deception hidden in the idiom of linguistic uses "empirico-mercantilistic reductionism," because it sees language in action as the mere *use* of words and syntagms *which have already been produced, while ignoring their production*. This reductionism appears very clearly when we distinguish between linguistic "knowing-how" and scientific knowledge of the internal operation of language. In an important sense, knowing how to use a word is not at all the same as knowing how it functions, let alone knowing how we make it function as it does. Although we accept the general principle that within society as a whole consumption *is* production, we still consider that, in the limited sense in which we say that one consumes an object that one hasn't produced, the distinction between consumption and production is illuminating.

After 1964 I have come to think that many semiotic problems can be clarified by introducing into the study of language (as well as, of course, other sign systems) the fundamental distinction between use-values and exchange-values together with the conceptual apparatus that goes with it. Originally developed by Smith, Ricardo, and especially Marx in economic theory, this distinction has a general value for all social sciences. The ability to understand the exchange-value of words, syntagms, and verbal messages is mere "expenditure of linguistic labor-power." We are always dealing with linguistic work, but here we are considering it in its abstractness, as generic and undifferentiated productive activity. It is in relation to this type of linguistic work that linguistic *exchange-values* are determined as distinct from linguistic *use-values*, i.e. from the capacity of linguistic products to satisfy linguistic needs. An insight on this can be gained if we consider how certain people, who "speak badly," "do not know the language very well," "cannot express themselves convincingly," and so forth, are sometimes capable of handling very well this or that sector of the specific linguistic work that produces linguistic use-values. We all know of stuttering poets, logicians who make a mess of every sentence they utter, language analysts who seem to suffer from aphasia, psychoanalysts who are at a loss whenever they have to solve a practical problem, and the like.

In *Meaning, Communication, and Common Speech*, I tried to deal with some aspects of the problem of the inevitability of meaning in terms of a distinction between "initial meanings" and "additional meanings." This distinction was compared with other distinctions, such as – with regard to meanings – direct vs. indirect, immediate vs. mediated, explicit vs. implicit, literal vs. metaphorical, present vs. latent, and so on. Once the initial meaning has been grasped – which, as said before, is "inevitable" – additional meanings are either spontaneously or purposively extricated from various layers of context, and in function of various presuppositions. The initial meaning, whatever it may be, is capable of triggering further interpretation (though it does not trigger it necessarily). Since, as we said, the inevitability of initial meanings has nothing to do with any control on the productive process of the words or syntagms or sentences which carry it, *no descriptive or systematic definition of "initial meaning" holds water*. The only possible definition is rather a methodological or even a contingent one: the initial meaning is any meaning one starts with *de facto* in any given case (or class of cases) of interpretation. The consequence of this is that in many cases (or groups of cases) the meaning one does start with belongs to what would usually be described as a more complex, and not a simpler, level than the additional meanings delved out by further interpretation. In other words, we do have the temptation, but there is no possibility, of simply pairing "initial" to either "immediate," or "explicit," or "literal," or "present" meaning – though there may of course exist measures of overlapping. We may begin with something very simple and direct; but we may also begin with something very complicated. It is only *afterwards* that we can begin to grade simplicity and complication. Some messages are received and immediately interpreted, for instance, just because of their metaphorical import, while their literal sense may *or may not* be discussed at a later stage. Would we then say that the immediate meaning of these messages was metaphorical, and that we reach a literal meaning only through further interpretation? The first reaction to some other messages is such that one has to construe it as an unconscious response to a latent aspect of the message. Would we say that what was operating here was some sort of prelinguistic or sublinguistic apprehension? These and other similar difficulties make it necessary to undertake several complementary orders of enquiry. I shall list here only some of them: (i) the enquiry into the relations between meaning and context (cf. Slama-Cazacu 1961); (ii) the enquiry into universes of discourse, a notion first introduced by Augustus De Morgan in 1846 and clearly related to the current notions of semantic, or semiotic, field (cf. Rossi-Landi 1958[d], 1958[a], and 1961[d], Ch. II; also 6.3 in *Linguistics and Economics* [1974f and 1975b]); (iii) the enquiry into conscious vs. unconscious operation of the mind in the field of language; (iv) the enquiry into the formation of "unconscious knowledge" in terms of human needs, social programs, and the use of products of previous work; (v) the enquiry into the relations between verbal and nonverbal codes which are operating together in any given case of communication; (vi) the enquiry into categories or "logical types."

It is as a preliminary to enquiries like these that my 1963 paper "On Absurdity" should be read and perhaps it still does make some sense also from the point of view of general semiotics. In fact, most of its material was drawn from Chapter V of *Meaning, Communication, and Common Speech*, where different kinds or levels of nonsense or defective signification and/or absurdity were examined in order to pave the way for the methodological distinction between initial and additional meanings. If initial meanings do not exist *in re*, neither can completely *objective, context-free* distinctions between different kinds of meaning exist. All such distinctions are entirely context-bound, which amounts to saying that they are ideologically determined down to the level of individual stylistic choices. Literality, for instance, is a metaphysical myth, and so are all the oppositions which use literality as one of their two terms (including the use of absurdity as a philosophical tool, as described in the paper that follows). The defense of literality as against metaphoricity, or any similar defense, is in fact the defense of one's own ideological conditioning. Looking for literality *in general* sounds like trying to describe what objects in the world *are* "on the left" – I mean, on-the-left-by-themselves. There is nothing like a literal use of language *in se*. What there is, is the literal use of a language by *one* individual author *in a given situation*. The proper totality to be examined is always *that text in that context* as different from all other texts and/or contexts.

Once all this is understood, nothing prevents us from re-admitting into the stage, as well-disciplined actors, the very characters we had previously had to chase away. But our actors must follow a script – *commedia dell'arte* is not permitted in our field. Whereupon – juggling a little with dialectic terminology – we may even go so far as to satisfy ourselves that different kinds of meaning, unexisting as they are *in se*, have been brought, through negation and specification, to a sort of existence *per se*. Which means not only that we cannot *look for* such differences; it also means that, if we want to speak about them, we have got to construct them ourselves.

Rome, June 1975

On Absurdity (1963)

Absurdity has both a long history and an intricate logic. In this paper, which consists of excerpts from a longer study of the subject,[1] I shall mainly concentrate on the use of absurdity, within "linguistic" or analytical philosophy, as a tool for solving philosophical problems.

6.1 "Category Mistakes" and the *Reductio Ad Absurdum* According to Linguistic Philosophy

Linguistic philosophers often maintain that solving, dissolving, or clarifying a philosophical problem amounts to being able to overcome a "conceptual tangle or distortion," successfully to tackle "puzzle-generating ideas," to avoid "linguistic infelicity," to find a way out of an "intellectual cramp." All of these situations can, in principle, be reduced to category mistakes – namely, to breaches of logical rules governing the use of concepts. These category mistakes need to be identified and avoided.

According to linguistic philosophy, philosophical problems arise as a consequence of particular ways of misusing language. It follows that the rules broken by category mistakes are semantic rules governing the use of words or expressions which represent concepts. Such rules determine the category to which a word or expression belongs.

In order to avoid category mistakes and to find out what the categories are (or, as it is also said, the logical types) to which the various concepts have to be allocated, pertinent linguistic uses are submitted to a "test of absurdity," which shows how "categorial mis-allocation" produces absurd expressions. Absurdity is thus used, by applying patterns of argument describable as species of the genus *reductio ad absurdum* (hypothetical arguments of the pattern known as *ponendo tollens*), as a tool for the determination of differences between categories or logical types.

The whole procedure is considered by many authors to be proper and even "proprietary to philosophy." The claim involved is that there is something specifically philosophical within the activity of reasoning itself, so that philosophy can be structurally distinguished from other intellectual endeavors: we can "tell a philosophical problem" on the ground that it must involve a question of categorial allocation. This allocation can be achieved by resorting to the notion of absurdity. Alternative terminologies refer to what cannot be said, or, at least, not significantly, or to what does not make sense or is meaningless. This kind of reduction does not aim at proving the truth (or falsity) of any given statement, but, more radically, at proving that some expressions are in fact pseudo-expressions and that we must therefore wipe them altogether off the field of what can be significantly said.

I believe that this approach has constituted an important attempt to find out and determine what philosophy is about without resorting any longer to those vague definitions of its final aims or of its subject matter which we come across throughout the history of the discipline and which have been devouring one another almost as rapidly as they have been advanced. The linguistic approach did give some generations of philosophers a feeling that they had something important to do and that procedures were available for them to do it. This is particularly important in a period like ours, when philosophical schools differ at least as savagely as they ever did and when scientific enquiries have taken over so many problems previously considered to be specifically philosophical. Again, the procedure I am talking about has been applied in the direction of clarification and intersubjectivity. A given field of enquiry – language understood and approached in a certain way – appeared, so to speak, to have been laid open: a field within which the procedure could be applied and results could be achieved and tested by a community of people.

In the following, I shall single out one particular statement of the procedure in order to make it more precise and to avoid the impression that I am dealing with a straw-man. I shall then try to submit some points with a view to contending that the appeal to absurdity is not proprietary to philosophy; that a "single-tracked" notion of absurdity, subject to being reduced to a simple either/or situation, does not exist, and that such a notion is usually unsatisfactory and oversimplified (there are different kinds of absurdity or nonsense, or scarce signification, or lack of it); that absurdity and related notions are subject to context and, to some extent, to historical becoming and linguistic differences; and finally, that no notion of absurdity or nonsense can be used without resorting to those very categories or logical types which it would allegedly be able to distinguish, the procedure of *reductio ad absurdum* being therefore vexatiously circular and able to prove only something which had been surreptitiously assumed already.

6.2 Ryle's Procedure

Almost all the most important representatives of linguistic or analytical philosophy have dealt with this problem or have referred to it.[2] Since I find that the clearest and most exhaustive statement of the whole procedure was given by Gilbert Ryle in two mutually supporting papers which have been very influential on the whole movement, I shall take the material for a more precise statement of the case from them [Ryle 1938, 1945].[3]

It is patent that sentences contain parts. To avoid the idea that a part is an independent or self-sufficient unit, we shall call such sentence-parts "sentence-factors." A sentence-factor is any partial expression – single words as well as phrases of any degree of complexity – which can enter into sentences that are otherwise dissimilar. The word 'factor' is also intended to suggest that a sentence-part can only occur in complexes of certain sorts, and only in certain determinate ways. Not any factor is fit to be the complement of any sentence-gap (such as indicated by the dotted line in 'Socrates is ...'); but there is an indefinite range of possible factors of the same pattern which could complete any given gap.

This, however, says Ryle, is not sufficient. If I complete the gap in '... is in bed' with the noun 'Saturday,' I break no rule of grammar; yet the sentence is absurd. The complements, then, must be not only of certain *grammatical* types such as nouns or pronouns, but they must also express proposition-factors of certain *logical* types. Grammar is concerned with what can be said in English or in German and according to various stylistic criteria; logic "with something ... indifferent to these differences." Sentences and sentence-factors are grammatical items; propositions and proposition-factors logical ones. When a sentence is absurd, it is so because some of its proposition-factors belong to different and reciprocally unsuitable logical types; or, conversely, "to say that a given proposition-factor is of a certain category or type is to say that its expression could complete certain sentence-frames without absurdity." And this occurs, however, when the vocabulary of the sentence is "conventional" and its grammatical construction is "regular." To ask the question "To what type or category does so and so belong?" amounts to asking "in what sorts of non-absurd sentences and in what positions in these sentences can the expression 'so and so' enter?". The word 'absurd' is preferred to 'nonsensical' or 'meaningless' "for the reason that both the two last words are sometimes used for noises ... and ... for collocations of words having no regular grammatical construction."

Particular emphasis is given to the expediency of "talking logic in the semantic idiom." There are no absurdities in nature. Concepts and conceptions cannot be said to be or not to be absurd. It is absurd *to say* that there are absurd propositions, for what is absurd is unthinkable. Expressions and only expressions can be absurd. What we have to examine, then, is whether such and such expressions may or may not be coupled in such and such ways with other expressions.

Eventually, Ryle propounds the following rule: "Two proposition-factors are of different categories or types, if there are sentence-frames such that when the expressions for those factors are imported as alternative complements to the same gap-signs, the resultant sentences are significant in the one case and absurd in the other."

Once this approach is understood, the central importance for philosophy ascribed to *reductio ad absurdum* arguments can be readily seen. There is some agreement among philosophers that philosophical arguments are neither inductions of the kind used in natural science nor demonstrations of the Euclidean type, that is, deductions of theorems from axioms or postulates. Philosophers, when they are neither aping scientists nor indulging in the myth of some superscience, are mainly using a sort of "strong" *reductio ad absurdum* which shows how a given proposition (actually, according to the semantic idiom, the sentence or sentences expressing that proposition) is not merely false but nonsensical or absurd. This strong *reductio* has to be distinguished from the "weak" one used in Euclidean demonstrations and aimed at proving questions of truth or falsity-as-contradiction about theorems related to axioms.

Many more shrewd and important points are made by Ryle himself in these two papers and elsewhere (as well as by the other authors mentioned in note 2); but I think that I have reported at least some of the crucial ideas to which we now have to turn in a critical manner.

6.3 General Weakness of the Appeal to Absurdity

To begin with, the contention that the appeal to absurdity is proprietary to philosophy could be easily rejected even if we took for granted that there is a single-tracked notion of absurdity that is independent from context and liable to be used in order to proceed in a linear manner toward the detection of categorial differences. It would be sufficient to show how *reductiones ad absurdum* in the stronger sense are actually used by scholars in fields other than philosophy when they are dealing with general ideas. This is so obviously the case, that there is no need to waste words on it.

A line of defense, perhaps, would consist of stating that when a philosopher, as distinguished from all other scholars and indeed also from the man in the street, applies the *reductio* and turns down a sentence as absurd, this sentence is not only wiped off any given field of enquiry but is also expelled from language in general. Again, one doesn't see why this shouldn't be done by nonphilosophers. If it is contended that when nonphilosophers apply the *reductio* in determining the absurd, they are behaving philosophically, the contention is circuitous and the demarcation between philosophy and other activities is blurred rather than made more precise. As an alternative, the contention could be traced back to the old myth that philosophy should be a sort of superscience that examines on its own rights and with better results the concepts basic to all human endeavors; and it would follow that scholars specialized in various fields are inferior to philosophers looking into such fields from the outside. This would be pretty odd, for one characteristic of analytical and linguistic philosophers is that they reject at the drop of a hat the idea of philosophy as a superscience.

Moreover, it is apparent that *reductiones* in the weaker sense are also used by *both* philosophers and nonphilosophers; that philosophers use deductive and inductive arguments; and that both philosophers and other scholars use both kinds of reduction when dealing not only with general ideas (e.g. with sentences expressing propositions of a categorial kind), but also with particular ones.

The fact is that there is little sense in speaking about absurdity as if it were immediately clear what an absurd sentence is – as if (as stated above) there were a single-tracked notion of absurdity reducible to a simple either-or situation. We are told that 'Saturday is in bed' *is* absurd, but we are not told why this must be so. We are told that sentence-frames can be completed with or without absurdity, and that sentences are either absurd or nonabsurd, but no alternative to such an alternative is offered. It is taken for granted, first, that everybody immediately recognizes – as if in a flash of intuition – the presence or absence of absurdity; and, second, that such recognition is intersubjective and even intercultural in such a way that the appeal to absurdity should convey something like the definitive settlement of the issue to which it is applied.

Though absurdity is described as a property of sentences, this description does not include its belonging to any given sentence as such, which would in fact involve the existence of an English vs. a German, or a highbrow vs. a lowbrow, or a pedantic vs. a jargon, absurdity. Rather it is presented as a property of the way in which a range of "similar" sentences are constructed with unsuitable *propositional* factors. It may appear necessary to resort to propositions and their "factors" if we want to have a criterion for detecting the absurd sentences expressing them, and indeed if we want to know what sentences do express (or fail to express) the same proposition; nevertheless, it is clearly stated that propositions (ideas, concepts, conceptions, beliefs, suppositions, and the like) cannot even be said to be absurd. Alternative terms such as 'meaningless' and 'nonsensical' are disposed of with a few words about some of their usages. And finally, no reference is ever made to such vast movements as go under the tags of phenomenological and existential philosophies, in which the notion of absurdity has certainly come to play a central role.

It seems to me that the situation is extremely garbled. And all the more dangerously so, as the philosophers who are using such a vague and indiscriminate notion of absurdity are committed to a philosophical method characterized by the heed it usually pays to the most subtle differences in linguistic use and by its capacity to explain away the most delicate kinds of nonsense. Indeed, this notion of absurdity is one of the main tools (according to many, the main tool) by means of which all those subtle differences could and should be detected.

6.4 Various Types of Absurdity, from "Linguistic" to "Real"

In this section I shall submit some material and attempt an analysis of it which may help to ungarble the situation. With regard to this material we can say that (i) we usually speak of either absurdity, nonsense, lack of sense, or scarce signification, and so on; (ii) one may use each of these terms in different ways to point to different kinds of absurdity (or nonsense, and so on); (iii) it is not always clear, and sometimes it is very unclear, whether the absurdity (or nonsense) referred to belongs to the sentence, to the proposition expressed by that sentence, to the situation that proposition is about, to some features of the situation in which the proposition is being expressed, or to the manner in which we approach one of the above items. The examples will be listed and discussed in an order which goes roughly from cases which appear to be merely, or mainly, linguistic (in one sense, at least, of this most polymorphous term) to those which appear to be real, or factual, or connected with a situation. I shall try not to presuppose any particular usage of the terms 'absurd,' 'nonsensical,' and the like, as more important than others; nor shall I commit myself to any of the several distinctions which seem to have exercised such a heavily preconditioning influence toward over-simplification of the doctrine under examination.

6.4.1 Unknown Words and Their Combinations

In a sense, unknown words such as those of a language with which we have little or no acquaintance, are meaningless to us although we know that they are words and, as such, must mean something. We certainly do not say that they are absurd, or that a certain combination of them which is presented to us as a sentence is an absurd sentence. But we do use some notion of absurdity and nonsense in the process of interpretation: when confronted with a half-understood passage, we confer to the portion that is not understood some potential or possible meanings according to patterns extracted from what we have understood already, and thus possibly turn down as absurd or nonsensical certain suggestions found in a dictionary or imagined in the effort of "making sense" out of the whole. In the process, shreds of meaning attained at random in different portions of the text are "kept together" under the focus of attention, and, in this way, some gaps are determined and made more and more precise with the intention (and the hope) of eventually filling them up. The whole meaning of the fragment emerges little by little; and whatever piece of meaning is acquired casts some light on the rest, or on a given part of it. We are continuously resorting to significant matrices and molds while waiting to be able to fill them up; and we can redistribute the whole interpretative model as soon as a new and unexpected piece of significant information comes to light. This amounts to saying that we are thinking both about the fragment as a whole and about its parts, accepting and discarding pieces of interpretation according to patterns and criteria which can be very complicated indeed. In this very common experience (it is what we want students to learn to do when we ask them to find their way through a Greek or Latin passage), there is nothing like an either/or acceptance of absurd vs. non-absurd (i.e. significant) sentences. It would be very comfortable indeed if there were.

6.4.2 Odd Combinations of Words

Odd combinations of words, such as "The arm in the crystal upon the intimation of the midge equinox." There is a sense in which this string of words is utterly meaningless. Each of the words used, however, has a recognizable sense. If they were not being used at all, on a somewhat more basic level, that is, if they were sheer marks on paper, we could not even say, as we do, that they are used improperly. When we read them, our mind, as it were, starts to move in a number of directions, but then stops and doesn't arrive anywhere. Still, there is nothing vague about the way we recognize the meaning carried by each of those words; we can even go so far as to try to bring some of them together according to some recognizable pattern or piece of it. But – unless an extremely complicated context is invented – we do not succeed in pulling them together entirely in such a way as to confer upon them a complete signification. However, if we proclaim their combination to be absurd, as we certainly can and perhaps must, we neither have a sentence-frame with a gap to be filled, nor can we clearly detect the distinction between a sentential vs. a propositional level – indeed, my opinion is that, when we are *trying* to confer some signification on those words, we are operating at both levels and in a very intricate manner. Absurdity, here, seems to be a sort of pervasive property of the whole string of words. But one could also maintain that some portions of it are more, or less, absurd than others. For instance, "the arm in the ..." and "... the crystal upon ..." could be properly described as sentence-frames making some sense, or waiting for something to confer them complete sense by filling in their gaps; and one may find himself wondering what a "midge equinox" is.

6.4.3 *Difficult or Contradictory Combinations of Words*

I propose the following examples with a view to both that which they have in common and to that in which they differ. They are understandable in certain ways and make sense up to a certain point – so much so that the question can be raised as to whether language is, or is not, correctly used in them. Here are the examples: "He was at the foot and on top of the belfry at the same time"; "I saw him running just a few days after his legs had been amputated in the hospital as a consequence of the crash"; "During the whole month of July he remained in Portugal; however, this did not prevent him from paying me a visit in Paris on the 14th in order to celebrate the seizing of the Bastille."

Perhaps there will be some agreement that the belfry case can't be taken as referring, in a literal way, to a normal individual. A number of contextual specifications, however, can easily make such a reference acceptable. We may be talking about the model of a belfry in a room and about an architect standing by it. In this case, the phrase 'being at the foot and on top of the belfry at the same time' would be taken to mean "being as tall as the (model of the) belfry." We may recast the way in which this nonabsurd proposition is expressed and are able to do this by comparing two possible propositions and discarding one of them as absurd. In other words, one has to think about the two cases – the real belfry vs. the model – in order to discover that the original sentence can be interpreted as meaning something acceptable, although it is better to use another, similar sentence to avoid misunderstandings. There is nothing like a single sentence-frame to be filled. Other contexts can be imagined. In a fairy tale, we could read about a giant as tall as belfries, and this would be a case somewhat similar to, but by no means identical with, the case of the model belfry and the architect. Or, if the phrase 'at the same time' is construed as meaning an enlarged unit of time, distinguished from simultaneity, it may be, in that sense, true that someone was at the foot and on top of the belfry within that unit of time. Or he may appear to be. I remember a war story about a man who single-handedly defended a belfry and appeared to be "everywhere at the same time." The enemy were astonished when they discovered, upon seizing the position, that they had been fighting a single man (there were two machine-guns, one on top of the belfry and one at ground level; our hero – war is often a little ridiculous – went constantly up and down the stairs to fire both guns alternatively).

As for the case of the "legless running man," I think that this can make sense in at least one of the following ways: (i) As stating something miraculous. Now the logic of miracles cannot just be disposed of as being absurd; and, in any case, it would be a *factual* absurdity, the overcoming of the so-called natural order. To people who believe in miracles, the language reporting them is properly used. People who do not believe in miracles would then perhaps say that it is absurd to believe in them, locating absurdity in a belief. (ii) As reporting an unprecedented case of kine-prothesis. Once such a case is accepted, the sentence-frame, "I saw him running ..." can be completed with the rest of the example as given. It may be, however, that one has to construe "running" in an attenuated sense to be determined out of the whole context (i.e. can a man with artificial legs be *properly* described as running?). (iii) As hinting at the idea that our initial information was wrong. The man's legs had not been cut off in spite of the crash, after all; or he was not on board that plane; and now that we see him running, we have evidence that we were wrong in believing that he was crippled. What is interesting here is that in any such case a phrase like 'his legs had been amputated in the hospital' acquires a different meaning; it is used in a different way, losing, or better, displacing, its referring power. For instance, it may obliquely refer to what some people believed, or to an erroneous piece of information printed in the newspaper, or to a lie which somebody found a nasty pleasure in telling. For the whole expression to take on an acceptable sort of meaning – for its apparent contradictory or absurd or nonsensical character not to be felt any longer – it is sufficient that it be rewritten in a slightly different manner, such as with an exclamative mark at the end of it or with the addition of such a clause as 'just imagine,' or that it be uttered with a particular tone of voice and with some well-balanced stresses on the pivot words. (iv) A still different interpretation could hinge on a metaphorical use of 'running': in a cruel metaphorical manner, or instead, perhaps, with a tone of admiration, the speaker may mean that, in spite of his amputation (which, in this case, is thereby confirmed), the poor man was hurrying around much in advance of the moment we expected him to appear in public after what he had experienced.

Let us now turn to the "Portugal and Paris" example. On the literal interpretation of 'he remained in Portugal,' our character could not come to pay me a visit in Paris (I am not going to examine the logic of ubiquity and/or omnipresence). Here, too, there are some other interpretations which could be termed nonliteral or metaphorical but which, for a number of reasons, I prefer just to call different. For instance, we may construe the phrase 'he remained in Portugal' as a short way of saying that he was staying in Portugal, had a flat and most of his belongings there, had made quite a few friends, did not intend to leave soon, and was sharing in the Portuguese life. Now all this does not prevent a man from making a quick overnight round-trip flight to Paris without really breaking the normal rhythm of his local living – perhaps none of his Portuguese friends ever even noticed his absence.

In the three examples we have just been examining, something presents itself which is either contradictory or absurd or at least difficult to be construed in a direct way – unless previous linguistic material had been put forward in such a way as to command a certain interpretation, in which event we would say that such an interpretation is a direct one and that it is so on the background of what we knew about the case already. The contradiction or absurdity belongs in a system; because of the contradiction which first faces us, we have to choose one of a number of possible systems. By 'system' here I only mean a situational and linguistic set whose total meaning is recognizable with sufficient clarity. It is upon some of these different systems that I have been drawing while attempting to show some of the different ways in which the examples can be considered. Notice that the fields of application of the various linguistic units (be they sentence-factors or not in Ryle's sense) change according to the global interpretation which eventually obtains, i.e. according to the system in which they have been placed. This is similar (though not identical) to saying that their meanings vary, or that they are used in different ways. It is also interesting to note that we operate these changes – shifts in use, meaning, application – in common, eventually reaching an agreement on what context may explain the contradiction or absurdity: there is something intersubjective in the set.

6.4.4 Illegitimate, or Spurious, Combinations of Words

I place in this group combinations of words (not necessarily complete sentences) which are commonly said to be absurd or meaningless for some reason which is added to, and more decisive than, the reasons called on when ascribing absurdity or meaninglessness to the previous cases; I surmise that this additional reason (i) is somewhat closer to the very way in which words are used together within the linguistic unit under examination, and (ii) does not (characteristically or necessarily) convey the element of strangeness and whimsicality that is found in some of the previous examples. The advocates of the appeal to absurdity as a tool for categorial allocation seem to have been particularly, or exclusively, concerned with this group. We have here such well-known examples as 'pink numbers,' 'perfumed triangles,' and 'rectangular feelings'; or 'absent-minded stones,' 'choral whales,' and 'superstitious trees,' as well as Richard von Mises' 'On January 34 at 16 a.m.' and 'Justice is red' [in his *Kleines Lehrbuch*, 1939], or Ryle's own 'Saturday is in bed.'

About all these, various authors state that: they cannot be said; they don't make sense; they break the rules of grammar; they break the rules of logic; their logic is incorrect although their grammar is all right; they are not incorrect but meaningless; they do convey a meaning but this meaning is wrong; they are not sentences (or sentential factors); they are not complete sentences (or sentential factors); they are complete sentences (or sentential factors) but don't express any proposition; they do express propositions (or propositional factors) which, however, are spurious or pseudo ones; they express real propositions (or propositional factors) which, however, belong to the class of absurd propositions; they cannot even be thought; they can be thought perfectly well; they are not absurd but just false; they are false in some specific manner; and so on. *Embarras de richesse*. Since nobody has so far advanced any fully acceptable theory of sentences and propositions and since the very basic terms of the whole discussion, such as 'grammatical,' 'significant,' and 'absurdity,' are "in a completely undigested state" [cf. Alston 1962: 713], it does not seem possible to identify – let alone properly describe – the particular way in which those sentences or combinations of words are meaningless or absurd or false as distinguished from the way in which other combinations are. After stating some generalities about them, all that one can try to do is to distinguish among different subgroups. For instance, one could try to say that, in talking about 'pink numbers,' an observational property is attributed to non-observational entities while the contrary obtains in talking about 'superstitious trees.'

6.4.5 Strangeness in the Thing Reported or Spoken About

Strangeness in the thing reported or spoken about as in "My grandfather is very skillful in destroying pianos by axe-strokes." Such a combination of words can be properly described as a perfectly correct sentence and as a meaningful statement. It does by all standards express a thinkable proposition. The sentence-frame 'My grandfather is very skillful in ...' can be filled in by the rest of those words. We understand it both in the individual words used and in their being together as they are. There is nothing contradictory or illegitimate. The proposition-factors do not belong to different and reciprocally unsuitable logical types.

However, many people (and I am one of them) would say that there is something strange and perhaps absurd in such a sentence. It is not sufficient, though, to assume it unlikely that I have a grandfather who is given the opportunity of exercising a skill, which consists of dismantling pianos. There is something to it which is more specifically articulated. To begin with, the same amount of strangeness or absurdity cannot be ascribed to each sentence-factor. The idea of destroying pianos on purpose is less familiar than the idea of possessing at my age a grandfather capable of enduring such a heavy physical job as successfully handling an axe; and since pianos are useful and beautiful artefacts by which spiritual values are transmitted, there is something appalling about it. Besides, the idea of destroying pianos *by axe-strokes* is less palatable than the idea of destroying pianos *tout court*, for the former involves a particular resoluteness and indeed the acquisition of an ability. When we proceed to bring together the pianos and Grandfather, the feeling of uneasiness is destined to increase. One almost visualizes a very elderly gentleman who has spent much of his time making himself familiar with nothing but the destruction of pianos – by axe-strokes. He certainly had to practice his skill over a fairly long period of time, little by little discovering the essential strokes for a quick and really efficient performance. One wonders from what angles he hits and how many strokes are required for different types of pianos. And since it seems very unlikely that people possessing pianos would whole-heartedly welcome Grandfather when he shows up with his axe, eager to chop them into pieces, one is almost brought to infer that Grandfather has got to buy the pianos himself, in which case he must have been pretty well-off and have found that way to squander his patrimony more congenial than, say, maintaining race horse stables or entertaining friends with *grands de Bourgogne*. Such ways to squander patrimonies as the latter two are, at least in some countries, socially approved, while we do not have evidence that the piano-and-axe way is. This may bring us to imagine that Grandfather had to satisfy his leaning in a secret way; otherwise, he would have been taken to a lunatic asylum.

I hope I have done enough to convey a feeling of absurdity. I should add that the more we dig out what is involved in such a case, the more absurd we find it. Nor do I see why, either in English or in any other natural language, it must sound incorrect to describe the situation reported as *somewhat* meaningless or perhaps nonsensical. One has to insist, however, that the piece of language under consideration, according to a number of criteria, is being used in a technically perfect and adequate manner in a sense in which many philosophers would say that 'I met a purple square root,' 'Josephine got married with a surd number,' and 'Saturday was in bed while Sunday took a plane for Mexico,' aren't. Absurdity or nonsensicality, at least in such cases, therefore, has to be located somewhere other than in the use of language as such. I would tend to say, in the first instance, that it is the situation reported which is absurd; and in second instance, that the proposition about that situation, namely (according to one interpretation of what propositions are), the way in which we think that situation, is unsatisfactory. Or again, if we think the situation through, we grow overly-concerned with its credibility, not only insofar as it is one particular situation, but also when considering the situation-type – *such* situations usually don't obtain, and there is something either contradictory or at least which does not tally perfectly with the ideas connected with them.

In other cases, to the contrary, the strangeness of the reported thing is such that doubt can arise about whether the sentence (or sentences) by which we report the thing(s) is (are) legitimate or not. A careful examination of a series of sentences arranged in a progression from mere strangeness in the reported thing to strangeness (or illegitimacy) in linguistic use would show us how and at what levels the difference, or differences, can be detected. Here I shall limit myself to two more examples and to very brief comments on them. "Philip can take off and fly by flapping his arms in the air"; "Old Aunt Ceres is the real authoress of all that goes under Stravinsky's and Picasso's names: the two men have been hiring her all along under an exclusive contract and have been circulating her production as their own." I should say that the strangeness of the first example does concern linguistic use insofar as the possibility of taking off and flying by flapping one's arms does not belong to the concept of man; perhaps we are not using language in a completely correct manner when we are propounding that proposition as stating something real. The strangeness of the second example is of a more subtle character which emerges through an examination of what is involved in it. A painter like Picasso and a composer like Stravinsky are, in a important sense, "historical" products: it took not only personal talent and application, but also a number of social and cultural circumstances for each of them to be able to become what he is. To have produced what they have produced is a full lifetime business. Whatever her talents, no Aunt Ceres could have done both jobs at the same time. But then, we would have known this anyway, if only because it is impossible that a person of that brilliance would have consented to being hired and, moreover, that the two men succeeded in keeping the whole thing secret, and so on. The point is that not only is that statement obviously false (there is plenty of evidence for it), it is also partially nonsensical for it contradicts normal linguistic use. Not only is language used here to report strange and impossible things, but it is strange itself for it does violence to the contextual rule of its use.

6.4.6 Self-effacing Combinations of Words

In his paper "Every Event Has a Cause," G.J. Warnock [1953] gives an example about invisible tigers which I shall use, rephrasing and expanding it as follows: "In the zoological garden there is an invisible tiger walking in the alleys in-between the various cages." If we ask whether this invisible tiger, at least, manifests itself in some other ways, the answer is "Not at all; besides being invisible, it is also odorless; it does not roar, yelp, howl, whimper, whine or bellow; nor does it leave tracks. In no way is it possible to ascertain its presence. It never even rent anyone. It never manifested itself, but, still, *there it is*." If we insist and say "But at least, it must be possible to touch it," the answer is "No: it notices our presence and moves out of reach," or (better) "It is as untouchable as it is invisible; if you put your hand into the portion of space it occupies, you do not touch anything: your hand passes across it. *And still, there it is.*" The conversation can go on.

In such a conversation we understand every word; we ask questions and get answers. Absurdity emerges from the fact that the very requisites usually connected with the propounded propositions are being denied. In the sentences by which that proposition is communicated, the very conditions necessary for such sentences to be significant in an accomplished manner are being taken away. A tiger is a physical object, to begin with; and with regard to this physical object, of which it is stated that it exists, the constitutive characteristics of occupying a piece of space and of being visible, touchable, and so on, are denied. We imagine the tiger walking about in-between the zoo cages and thereby attribute to it properties which, at the same time, we are asked to withdraw from it. The statement that the tiger is there, while being perfectly understandable, destroys itself as a statement; it establishes a reference to a fact and to an object, but it also specifies that this reference is impossible – indeed, the modes of such impossibility are even described in some detail!

The following are other examples of variously self-effacing statements which involve some degree of absurdity: "In the Nebula of Andromeda all children of primary schools go to classes only five months a year"; "If we asked Homer which of his two poems he prefers, no doubt he would answer that it is the *Odyssey*"; "Bacteria of type x are more sensitive to Monteverdi's than to Frescobaldi's music."

6.5 Absurdity and Logical Types

If we now compare the very restricted statement about absurdity described at the beginning of this paper with the variety of the ordinary uses of 'absurd' and related terms and with the intricacy of their logic as we have seen them in this summary discussion of a simple list of strange examples, it is at least legitimate to suspect the following. In order to arrive at that restricted statement, many choices as to what criteria to use, what material to select, what procedures to consider valid, had to be done *beforehand*.

As was noted above, no reason is given to explain *why* 'Saturday is in bed' *must* be absurd. It is taken for granted that all of us *must* feel that it is. But even if we grant a sort of discomfort while entertaining that proposition (or whatever it is), it is clear that we are being asked to assume (i) that 'Saturday' is to be used in the literal sense as the name of a day of the week, and (ii) that the whole sentence is to be understood independently of any special context which may modify its interpretation. For if 'Saturday' were the nickname of a person or of a pet, then we would usually admit that there is no absurdity – that we would experience no discomfort – in saying that Saturday is in bed

(I say *usually*, for here too special contexts may bring us to say something to the contrary: for example, if the pet called Saturday died one year ago, or were an imaginary one, or if there were no bed in the room, and the like).

But again: let us concede that 'Saturday is in bed' is absurd if 'Saturday' means a day of the week and not absurd if it refers to a person or a pet. This very distinction pays heed to Ryle's contention that the two sentence- (or proposition-) factors represented here by two different uses of the (phonetically and graphically) same word belong to different categories, or logical types. Even if this is so, the question now is: *How do we come* – or better, *How have we come to distinguish the two different uses?* And the obvious answer is: by applying categorial or "logical" distinctions beforehand. In order to come to any such conclusion as to what use has to be selected, what context applied (or not applied), and the like, and before we put the words involved to a text within the framework of something like a sentence-frame with a gap to be filled, we must be acquainted with both the ordinary and special uses of all of those words and we must be capable of applying the rules which govern their being strung together in different ways. All of this appears even clearer if we consider some slightly more complicated schemes, as the following:

(1) 'Saturday is in bed.'
(2) 'John Smith is in bed.'
(3) 'Saturday comes after Friday.'
(4) 'John Smith comes after Friday.'

According to Ryle's literalism, (2) and (3) are significant; (1) is absurd; and (4), I take it, is absurd unless we construe it to mean that one Mr. Smith is not arriving before Saturday. It is only by building up an artificially simplified situation that such cases can be decided upon in such a single-minded manner.

I am not denying that, within a given context and taking such a criterion as complete literalism for granted, categories can be brought out into the open by means of contrasting such things as sentence-frames and proposition-factors. If those categories have been put into operation through the very construction of that example within that context and according to that criterion, in an important sense they are there already, and all we are doing is clarifying them. This can be important in a number of cases, but does not bring us much farther than we were.

What I am denying is that categories can be established by this method and that philosophical decisions can be made by applying it. Philosophical decisions lie deeper, at the level where categories are first used in order to build up examples within contexts, according to certain criteria and principles. Philosophical books in which the linguistic method is exemplified have received criticism which seems to confirm the above diagnosis – namely, that examples and their interpretation are put forward through a process of categorial selection which makes them what they are and that this process precedes that of squeezing from the interpretation of the examples a certain predetermined philosophical juice.

Absurdity, in order to be predicated of any sentence or proposition or situation, requires categories or logical types. We cannot assume that it is predicated in the same way within different natural languages, for there can be cases in which what sounds absurd in one language does not sound so in another ("seeing erroneously" has been said to be absurd in English while one would not say that the Italian "vedere erroneamente" is; and, of course, the question of which uses of both terms have been preselected creeps up again). Absurdity is obviously conditioned by the state reached by knowledge (the ancient held that belief in the antipodes was absurd, for men down there would have had to spend their lives upside down) and, again, by the general ideas and beliefs of those who speak of it. It does not just cut across various universes and types of discourse, for one does speak of, for instance, logical, legal, poetic, scientific, moral, absurdity. It depends to a large extent on the context and on the whole situation, and contexts and situations can sometimes be extremely broad.

In conclusion, the whole procedure claiming that the appeal to absurdity can be used for the detection of category mistakes, and thereby for the determination of categories themselves, needs to be revised from scratch. Categories or logical types – whatever may be understood by these highly problematic terms – have to be disconnected from absurdity and reapproached on their own right. They come first – though this, too, should not be taken dogmatically.

Notes

1. As stated in the Head Note, the paper is mainly a summary of Chapter Five ("Parlare comune e scarsa significazione," which I would now translate as "Common Speech and Various Levels of Meaninglessness or Absurdity"), pp. 105-131 of my 1961 book.

2. Cf. for example, Wittgenstein 1953 I: 11, 109, 123 ("Ein philosophisches Problem hat die Form: 'ich kenne mich nicht aus'"); 1961, Vorwort: 26, 4.003; Wisdom 1953, and other papers therein on the psychological side to the notion of perplexity; Austin 1961.
3. *The Concept of Mind* and the essays "Systematically Misleading Expressions," "The Theory of Meaning," and "Taking Sides in Philosophy" also clarify or exemplify Ryle's technique of the *reductio*. (All the essays mentioned are now reprinted in Ryle 1971).

References

Alston, William, P. 1962. "Philosophical Analysis and Structural Linguistics." *The Journal of Philosophy* 59, 23 (1962), 713.
Austin, John. 1961. "Performative Utterances." Now in *Philosphical Papers*. Oxford: Clarendon.
Ceccato, Silvio. 1959. *Tappe nello studio dell'uomo*. Milan: Feltrinelli.
———. 1969. *Corso di linguistica operativa*. Milan: Longanesi.
———. 1972. *La mente vista da un cibernetico* (= Nuovi quaderni, 8). Turin: ERI.
Chomsky, Noam. 1972(8). *Aspects of the Theory of Syntax*. Cambridge, MA: MIT Press, 1st ed. 1965.
Mises, Richard, von. 1939. *Kleines Lehrbuch des Positivismus*. The Hague & Chicago. Revised English transl. as *Positivism: A Study in Human Understanding*. Cambridge, MA: Harvard University Press, 1951.
Ponzio, Augusto. 1972. "Grammatica transformazionale e ideologia politica." *Ideologie* 16: 137-212. Reprinted in A. Ponzio, *Produzione linguistica e ideologia sociale. Per una teoria marxista del linguaggio e della comunicazione*. Bari: De Donato, 1973.
Rossi-Landi, Ferruccio. [See the general bibliography of his writings at the end of this volume.]
Ryle, Gilbert. 1938. "Categories." *Proceedings of the Aristotelian Society* XXXIX (1938-1939): 189-205. Now also in *Logic and Language* II. Oxford: Blackwell, 1953.
———. 1945. "Philosophical Arguments." Inaugural Lecture. London: Oxford University Press.
———. 1949. *The Concept of Mind*. London: Hutchinson.
———. 1971. *Collected Papers*. 2 vols. London: Barnes and Noble.
Slama-Cazacu, Tatiana. 1961. *Langage et contexte: Le problème du langage dans la conception de l'expression et de l'interprétation par des organisations contextuelles* (= Janua Linguarum, Series Maior, 6). The Hague: Mouton. Spanish transl. as *Lenguaje y contexto*, by C. del Solar. Barcelona-Mexico: Crijalbo, 1970.
Vaccarino, Giuseppe. 1974. *La mente vista in operazioni*. Messina-Florence: D'Anna.

Warnock, G.J. 1953. "'Every Event Has a Cause'." In *Logic and Language* II: 95-111. Oxford: Blackwell.

Watzlawick, P., J.H. Beavin, and D.D. Jackson. 1967. *Pragmatics of Human Communication: A Study of Interactional Patterns, Pathologies and Paradoxes*. New York: Norton.

Wisdom, John. 1953. "Philosophical Perplexity." Now in *Philosophical Papers*. Oxford: Clarendon.

Wittgenstein, Ludwig. 1953. *Philosophische Untersuchungen* (1945). Text and English transl. as *Philosophical Investigations*, by G.E.M. Anscombe. Oxford: Blackwell. New edition, in a revised translation and an analytical index, printed in 1958, reprinted 1967.

———. 1961 *Tractatus logico-philosophicus*. The German text of Ludwig Wittgenstein's *Logisch-philosophische Abhandlung*, in a new translation by D.F. Pears & B.F. McGuiness and introd. by B. Russell. London: Routledge & Kegan Paul.

7. On the Overlapping of Categories in the Social Sciences

A category is any very general concept used for its power to confer some order to a system, or at least to an aggregate, of other concepts of lesser generality, either in everyday life, or in scientific enquiry, or in both. As shown by Ryle (1971 [1938]: 170-184; 1949), among others, the idea that there exists a finite and very short catalogue of unconditioned categories is pure myth (Ryle 1971: 179). Moreover, categories must be understood historically. It is true that the most general categories (such as Aristotle's ten classes or Kant's fourfold division of triads, to give the main European historical examples) are endowed with a special persistency of their own, so much so that persistency may be used as a criterion for generality; however, this does not necessarily involve any reference to metaphysical, i.e. either superhistorical or hypohistorical entities. The stress should be laid on the changes that categories undergo in time and space. Not only do we find that categories differ from culture to culture, but we are also able to examine problems from different categorical angles, selecting which category must exercise its ordering power upon which others, thereby changing our own categorical system and the level of generality of the categories involved.

Categories are a reflection of reality as operated upon by men in their *social practice*, and thus they are also *human products*. Scientific enquiry is one slice of social practice, and scientific procedures and results are among the most refined human products. The idea that anything which is a human product may be exempt from change is another pure myth; on the other hand, constant features of social practice determine constant categories.

Examples of categories as they are understood here are matter, movement, space, time, connection, relation, totality, part, reciprocal action, contradiction, chance, necessity, regularity, causality, law, structure, system, essence, phenomenon, reality, appearance, and so on. At a level which may, in principle, be described as less general, we find all the basic categories of the social sciences, such as action, behavior, work, exchange, communication, code, message, production, utensil, product, distribution, consumption, money, language, speech, thought, mind, society, nature, culture, person, public, private, tradition, institution, innovation, acculturation, enculturation, education, and so on.

It should be clear that these two lists are only a very rough indication of a particularly broad use of the term 'category.' However, we may assume that categories of the first roster are necessarily common to all sciences and to all human exchange, verbal or nonverbal; while categories of the second roster, although also widespread, are mainly used in organized groups as fundamental terms of various social sciences.

There is an argument which claims that it is necessary to distinguish each category from all others on its own grounds. If we were to resort to categories other than the category under examination – so the argument runs – it would seem that we would be depriving the category under examination of its very character of being a category proper. A category described by means of another category would simply be an instance of the other category. This is a wrong approach, a leftover of the dual myth that there is a finite (and very small) number of unconditioned categories, and that they are unchangeable.

On the contrary, we maintain that (1) whenever we want to give an adequate account of any category, we do have to resort to other categories; (2) while this is readily granted in some cases (e.g. speaking and language, or tool and product), it is not in others; indeed, the habit of dealing with some categories as if they were entities more or less independent of each other is still common, especially in the social sciences, and constitutes a stumbling block to the advance of knowledge; and (3) when we accept the principle that categories overlap, and deal with two or more categories jointly, nothing like the feared collapse of one category under the rule of some other category need take place; all categories in general, and especially categories used in the social sciences, receive instead full light only if their overlapping is given complete attention.

Here we shall give a brief illustration of this approach.

7.1 Some Cases of Paired Terms

The ways in which categories are interconnected and overlap may be best introduced through an *excursus* on a relatively simple matter, paired terms. These are words (or syntagms, or even phrases) which acquire full meaning only insofar as they involve each other. There is no "right" unless there is a "left," nor is there an "over" unless there is an "under," and so on. We meet the same situation with comparatives: when we say that Charles is *more* fluent in Bulgarian, we refer at least implicitly to the so-called second term of comparison, that is, we assume the existence of someone who is *less* fluent than Charles, or we are implying that at a previous stage Charles himself was less fluent in Bulgarian, or that he is less fluent in other languages. This concerns proper, nonmetaphorical usages.

At a more complex level we meet paired terms of a higher biological, historical, or social content, such as male and female, father and son, husband and wife, king and subjects, master and servant, exploiter and exploited. According to the usage adopted in this paper, these are important categories of the social sciences. A factor of complexity here is that it is more difficult to distinguish proper usages from metaphorical usages. While it is obvious, for example, that there is no father without a son (or daughter), paternal and filial attitudes are also to be found outside of real "father-son" situations. It then remains to be seen whether calling the attitude of a person who never had any child "paternal" is to be considered a proper or a metaphorical usage.

Paired terms, of course, are also interconnected as pairs. For an offspring to exist, a father does not suffice: you also need a mother. When you speak of a son or daughter, you presuppose both parents. Thus the categorical net enlarges: we have offspring versus parents; both offspring and parents can be male or female. Or, we can distinguish males from females and then proceed to say that both males and females can be parents, and surely are offspring in their turn.

Let us give another example. There is no master without a servant, and vice versa. On the surface the situation appears as simple as that of "over" versus "under." Beyond the paired terms, however, one glimpses a much more complicated situation. 'Masterly' and 'servile' are adjectives which can also be applied independently of any precise "master-servant" relation. And whenever such a relation does exist, it certainly is not as simple as the relation between "right" and "left." To understand properly what is involved by the paired terms 'master' and 'servant,' or 'lord' and 'bondsman,' one has to examine the dialectic by which, as long as their relation continues, the master becomes more and more of a master and the servant becomes more and more of a servant, up to the final stage where the master is destroyed by the servant and the whole situation collapses (as shown by Hegel 1964 [1807]: 229-240).

One last example: the situation represented by the paired terms 'husband' and 'wife' is marriage. Now we know that the institution of marriage differs greatly in time and space: it follows that the reciprocal position of the two partners also differs. Polyandry and polygamy, the phenomenology of subordination of one partner to the other in different societies, the recent cases of "marriages" among homosexuals, various forms of cohabitation of two or more persons of the same or of different sex, so-called social sex, many instances of communitarian life, and so on, are all cases in which the properties of being husband or wife cannot be reduced to any simple definition of the pairing of two terms, or in which these properties may even disappear.

The overlapping of categories is clear already at this relatively simple level. You would be at a loss, if you tried to explain what being "husband" or "slave" is without resorting, first, to the other term of the pair and, second, to the whole situation to which the pair belongs. As noticed by Vailati (1966 [1908]: 140-141; cf. Rossi-Landi 1967[a]), it is as if words had *valences* like chemical elements, so that all valences of each word must be satisfied in order to understand it properly.

7.2 Instances of Overlapping Categories

Let us now examine in a slightly more detailed way a few more cases where the overlapping of categories assumes a more insidious character. There are cases where the categories are more general, or where their overlapping is not indicated by the terms which represent them, or where such terms are not used in pairs and do not even evoke any opposition between them. There are also cases where, at the superficial level, categories present themselves as, and are used as, reciprocally exclusive. Constellations of categories are of course important; but for reasons of space we shall have to limit ourselves here to categorical pairs.

7.2.1 Production and Consumption

Although this typical case is one of the most difficult ones, we shall begin with it for two reasons. The first reason is that it is, indeed, an extreme case. At first glance, it appears that if you are producing, you are not consuming. The activities of production and consumption are not paired in the same way that husband and wife are. Indeed, they do not even creep in from language as joined terms. The second reason is that we possess a classical analysis of the overlapping and reciprocal action of production and consumption, an analysis which can be used as a model for other such analyses. I am referring to

Marx's "Introduction of 1857," which up to some years ago used to be published as an Appendix to his *Critique of Political Economy* of 1859 but which has now been restored to its rightful place as the general introduction to the immense body of the *Grundrisse der Kritik der politischen Ökonomie* (see Marx 1953 [1857-1858]; McLellan 1971: Introduction; Nicolaus 1968).

There is of course, says Marx, a shallow conception according to which production, distribution, exchange, and consumption exist side by side, as self-contained, independent spheres. But there is also a deeper conception that sees them as belonging to an organic whole. "Not that production, distribution, exchange, and consumption are identical; but they are all members of one entity, different aspects of one unit ...; a mutual interaction takes place between the various elements, [as] is always the case with every organic body [Dies ist der Fall bei jedem organischen Ganzen]" (Marx in McLellan 1971: 33).

While Marx's analysis concerns all four of the aforementioned terms, i.e. production, distribution, exchange, and consumption, we shall limit ourselves to summarizing here what he says about the relation between production and consumption only. In addition to what has been said by economists on *productive consumption* as distinguished from consumption proper, there is also a *consumptive production*: as when in nutrition, which is a form of consumption, man produces his own body. More important than this sort of direct unity of production and consumption, however, are the ways in which consumption furthers production and production furthers consumption. Consumption furthers production "by providing for the products the individual for whom they are products," so that "the product receives its last finishing touches in consumption," or indeed it becomes a *real* product only in consumption (Marx in McLellan 1971: 24). Moreover, "consumption produces production by creating the necessity for new production": it "provides the ideal object of production, as its image, its want, its impulse and its purpose ... No needs, no production. But consumption reproduces the need" (p. 25). "Consumption is not only the concluding act through which the product becomes a product, but also the one through which the producer becomes a producer" (p. 27).

On the other hand, production (1) "furnishes consumption with its material, its object"; and (2) "it gives consumption its definite outline, its character"; indeed, "the object is not simply an object in general, but a definite object, which is consumed in a certain definite manner prescribed in its turn by production"; and "not only the object of consumption, but also the manner of consumption is produced by production," and in this sense "production creates the consumers." Furthermore, (3) "production not only supplies the want with material, but supplies the material with a want. When consumption emerges from its first stage of natural crudeness and directness ..., it is itself, as a desire, mediated by its object. The want for it which consumption experiences is created by its perception of the product" (pp. 25-26).

Must we conclude that production and consumption are simply identical, that there is no difference between them? This is by no means Marx's conclusion. Production could be said to be identical with consumption only if we committed the idealistic error of considering a nation *only* as a whole, or mankind *only in abstracto*. But "to consider society as a single subject is ... a false mode of speculative reasoning. For an individual, production and consumption appear as different aspects of one act. The important point to be emphasized here is that whether production and consumption are considered as activities of one individual or of separate individuals, they appear at any rate as aspects of one process" (p. 27).

7.2.2 Public and Private

That two categories act upon each other in a way that requires an analysis of the whole situation to which they belong is a general principle. As such, it can be applied to a number of pairs or aggregates of categories. We shall see that the way in which the above action or influence is exercised may be very different from case to case.

If we consider dialectically the opposition of public and private, for example, we will come to the conclusion that being private is a case of being public. To state the kernel of this at the beginning: the proper totality which both categories refer to *is* public. *Inside* that totality there is a zone which is private.

Although private and public apply to a number of different situations such as life, behavior, or even language, the most typical case is perhaps that of property, the private or public ownership of material goods. We maintain that the property[1] of material goods can be private only insofar as it is public. For a man abandoned on an island or isolated in a desert it is impossible to claim the property of this or that portion of the island or desert, the reason for this impossibility being that no other such claim is advanced by anybody else. Nor does it make sense for him to claim the private property of the whole island or desert, the reason for this being that nobody else *renounces* the possession of that very property. Something arises as private only insofar as it displaces something else which is also private: in other words, inside a totality which is public, at least two parts are distinguished from each other by the mark of being private. And even after this has taken place, the totality *remains* public.

Thus, for instance, I am the private owner of my car only insofar as no other member of the community I belong to is the private owner of that very car. To say that all members of a community, or a majority of them, are the private owners of one and the same car would be nonsense. On the other hand, if there are at least two cars and two citizens, a distribution can take place to the effect that citizen A is the private owner of car A while citizen B is the private owner of car B. Similarly, if there are at least two men on that island, they can claim some sort of preference and right to different sectors of the island, and this may be understood as an embryonic form of private property of those sectors.

In all these cases, and in all possible cases, however, the basic fact is that an island and a car *are* public things. Let us take the case of the automobile, of an individual automobile, more specifically, my own automobile which is my private property. Such an automobile *is* public for at least the following reasons: (1) it exists under the eyes of everybody; everybody can see it, touch it, hear the noise of its engine and sniff at the smell of its exhaust; (2) it is a *product*, and this means that it has been produced by the joint efforts of several men, according to projects which can be repeated, and using as materials previous products; there is nothing private or individual about the existence of a particular car; (3) every driver can use it; (4) even nondrivers, in another sense, use it whenever they are transported in it. If it were deprived of all of these public dimensions, my own car could not even be sold or given away as a present, i.e. it could never become somebody else's private property.

The common oppositions between private (or covert) and public (or overt) behavior in psychology, and between private and public language in philosophy (especially by the Wittgensteinians) are, I believe, to be dealt with in the same manner. There is private behavior only insofar as behavior is basically public; and the same is true of language.

To conclude, the simple opposition of the terms 'public' and 'private' does not take us very far. At a superficial level, what is private is *not* public, and vice versa. But dialectical probing shows us that what is private *is* but a case of being *public*, while being public is certainly not a case of being private.

7.2.3 Communication and Behavior

A different case is that of categories which do not present themselves as necessarily related, if only because the terms used for them do not demonstrate the same reciprocity as paired terms like 'husband-wife' or 'public-private.' An important example of this is communication versus behavior. A simple splitting of the possibilities inherent in any two-term opposition gives us the following combinations: communication with behavior, communication without behavior, behavior with communication, behavior without communication. We can at least think in terms of these four cases, positive as well as negative; we cannot, however, even conceive of the two corresponding negative cases drawn from the splitting of such pairs as "husband-wife" because the phrases "husband without wife" and "wife without husband" are simply nonsense. (We can of course speak of a husband who is without *his* wife, but this is no argument against the formation of the pair "husband-wife.") However, further analysis shows that while the cases of communication with behavior and of behavior with communication are of course all right, the case of behavior *without* communication does not exist, and the case of communication *without* behavior can be conceived of only if we confer on 'behavior' a very restricted sense. We can eliminate this latter case by means of an example: it may be said that even by being immobile and quiet, i.e. without displaying any overt behavior, one does under certain circumstances communicate something. If this were true, there would exist communication without behavior. But "being quiet and immobile" is hardly a good way of excluding behavior in general; the individual action or lack of action consisting of being quiet and immobile at a given moment is nothing but an accidental moment frozen out of its behavioral context. Even by *not* performing any act of overt behavior, one is not escaping the category of behavior. Death may appear to be the only possible exception. A dead man does not act any longer yet his corpse may communicate much information to the onlooker. Not even this exception, however, is a real one, because a dead man is a man who has performed behavior up to the moment of his death and whose corpse bears signs of it. Death is, among other things, the cessation of behavior, and in this sense the understanding of death must necessarily resort to the category of behavior. There is then no communication without behavior. As for the case of behavior without communication, it is inconceivable that if someone *does* something, i.e. performs some act of behavior, no information whatsoever can be drawn from it.

Behavior and communication always go together. Resistance to this conclusion may come from the identification of communication with *verbal*, or *conscious*, or *intentional* communication. But as soon as one realizes that man communicates with his entire behavior in several verbal *or* nonverbal, conscious *or* unconscious, intentional *or* unintentional ways, then one has to accept the idea that communication and behavior are categories which overlap almost entirely.

What is involved here is a distinction between sign-behavior and non-sign-behavior. We maintain that such a distinction is not really valid or, to put it a better way, that it has to be understood as a distinction between two different sorts of sign-behavior. It is clear that if you assume that a man strolling through a meadow on a lovely springtime morning is not communicating, then what you are actually doing is identifying the category of communication with the subcategories of verbal, or intentional, or conscious communication. But as soon as you realize that our springtime morning stroller, whether intentionally or not, is in fact communicating to the onlooker a remarkable amount of information about himself and his social group by the way he walks and is dressed and groomed, and by the very fact that he *is* strolling, then the identification of communication with either verbal or intentional or conscious communication collapses; what remains is the fact that the *only* possible identification is that of behavior with communication without any further restriction. From this it follows that communication and behavior cannot be dealt with independently of each other. You cannot really examine behavior unless you are also examining communication, and you cannot examine communication unless you are also examining behavior.

That *all* behavior *is* communication, is a major breakthrough of twentieth-century semiotics. This advance has come about by joining, not disjoining, categories, and by taking the overlapping of categories as seriously as possible. It has enriched both the category of behavior and that of communication.

7.2.4 *Language and Thought*

Quite different is the case of language versus thought. While you cannot act without communicating, you can certainly think without speaking, and in some sense you can also speak without thinking. The attempt has been made by Lenneberg (1967) and others to prove that the acquisition of language is independent of intelligence; this seems to reduce the importance of thought for language. The fact is that the two categories, speaking and thinking, overlap in very special ways of their own. If, as Marx says, "*language* is the immediate actuality [*Unmittelbare Wirklichkeit*] of thought" (Marx and Engels 1968 [1845-1846]: 503), it would seem to follow that thought is the mediated actuality of language. This means that one cannot assume thought by itself as something not mediated, as something independent from language. To say this, however, is not to say that no thinking can go on or manifest itself without resorting to language or in the absence of language. Intelligent behavior shows the presence of thinking even when it shows no presence of language. And still, it is principally in the use of language that many of the most important aspects of thought exist; we do much of our thinking through the use of language. It is impossible to imagine that thought developed in mankind as it did without linguistic communication. The two grew together, and together with them grew all the other main factors of social life.

As Wittgenstein (1953 [1945] and Ryle (1949) – who may or may not have been aware of the fact that they were expanding some principles put forward by Marx and Engels in *The German Ideology* (Rossi-Landi 1966[b]; 1968[h]: 77-126) – showed in great detail, the main mistake here lies in believing that first *there is* thought which then *manifests itself* linguistically.

The categories of language and thought, of speaking and thinking, and all similar categories, overlap to a great extent, and neither term of any such pair can be properly understood without resorting to the other. Distinguishing various aspects of language from various aspects of thought is an intricate business which itself requires continuous references to both.

7.2.5 Thought and Social Institutions

Social institutions certainly cannot be reduced to verbal activity. Intelligent nonverbal behavior contributed to bringing them into existence. The same can be said of "material" culture in its entirety: it is the product of human thought, and when we examine any one of its instances we are certainly not content with weighing or measuring it; we try instead to reconstruct the thinking that went into it, its use, its purpose, and the position it held within that culture.

Thus it could be said that while, on the one hand, thought overlaps to a remarkable extent with language, on the other, it also overlaps with social institutions and material culture. It would be impossible to fully assess the thought of any community or culture or society unless we took into account not only its language and literary production, but all the rest of it as well, everything that is *not* language in the proper sense.

This does not mean in the least that thought occupies a central position as traditional philosophers so often used to maintain. On the contrary, the overlapping of language with thought and of thought with social institutions and material culture is there to show that thought, as such, has no central position at all. Thought cannot be understood by itself. To understand it, we have to examine all the various fields in which man has exercised his productive powers.

Social institutions and material culture are nonverbal sign systems, forms of communication. This feature points to additional dimensions of the general overlapping of categories in the social sciences.

7.3 A Hint at the Dialectic of Essence and Phenomena

Categories interconnect and overlap to such an extent that the study of any one of them in isolation is impossible, and continuous references to many of them are often necessary. Within the limits of a few pairs of categories, we have seen how production and consumption further each other; how being private is but a case of being public; how behavior and communication overlap almost entirely; how language stretches, so to say, to cover a great deal of thought, and vice versa; how thought, however, also covers social institutions and material culture which are nonverbal sign systems, i.e. forms of communication. It is as if there were one common core which expressed itself by means of different phenomena in several fields.

This brings us to a dialectic which has been labeled within a certain tradition as the dialectic of essence and phenomenon; in its turn, it overlaps to a great extent with the dialectic of reality and appearance. The dialectic between mere description and scientific explanation proper may be considered a special case, or a limited application, of the dialectic between essence and phenomenon. Things vary enormously as far as phenomena are concerned, of course; and it is certainly one of the tasks of scientific research to describe all the phenomena of the various fields in the most complete and accurate manner. Underlying the various groups of phenomena, however, there is a unity which alone can account for the overlapping of categories and for the fact that it is impossible to go beyond the level of description to achieve scientific explanation as long as one remains within the limits of any isolated category.

We said that semiotics made a breakthrough when it came to "identify" behavior and communication. It was, of course, a dialectical, not a one-to-one static identity; it was an "identity" of essence, not of phenomena, and it was reached by viewing both categories as parts of a broader totality. I believe that this example can be followed in other fields as well, and have myself made an attempt to this effect to give a unitary treatment to the usually severed fields of language and material production (Rossi-Landi 1968; 1975). After all, it is with the essence of things, not their phenomena, that we as social scientists are most intensely concerned.

Rome, December 1972

Note

(1) Here and in the following discussion, 'property' must be used in place of 'ownership' because the phrase 'private property' cannot be substituted.

References

Hegel, Georg W.F. 1964 [1807]. *The Phenomenology of Mind.* Transl. by J.B. Baillie. London: Allen and Unwin. (Originally published in 1807 as *Phänomenologie des Geistes*.)

Lenneberg, Eric. 1967. *Biological Foundations of Language*. New York: Wiley.

Marx, Karl. 1953 [1857-1858]. "Einleitung von 1857." In *Grundrisse der Kritik der politischen Ökonomie*. Berlin: Dietz.

Marx, Karl and Friedrich Engels. 1968 [1845-1846]. *The German Ideology*. Moscow: Progress Publishing. (Originally published in 1845-1846 as *Die deutsche Ideologie*.)

McLellan, David. 1971. *Marx's Grundrisse*. Introduction and anthology. London: Macmillan.

Nicolaus, Martin. 1968. "The Unknown Marx." *New Left Review* 48: 41-61.

Rossi-Landi, Ferruccio. [See the general bibliography of his writings at the end of this volume.]

Ryle, Gilbert. 1949. *The Concept of Mind*. London: Hutchinson.

———. 1971 [1938]. "Categories." In *Collected Papers*, II: 170-184. London: Barnes and Noble.

Vailati, Giovanni. 1966 [1908]. "The Grammar of Algebra." *Nuova corrente* 38: 131-157.

Wittgenstein, Ludwig. 1953 [1945]. *Philosophical Investigations*. Transl. by G.E.M. Anscombe. Oxford: Blackwell.

III

SIGNS, LINGUISTIC ALIENATION AND SOCIAL REPRODUCTION

8. Introduction to *Semiosis and Social Reproduction**

8.1 Foreword and Outline

In this book I shall make some moves toward placing semiotics in the context of the social sciences. Should these moves not bring us to a satisfactory stage, I shall have to conclude that semiotics cannot have a place of its own in the context of the social sciences, the reason possibly being that it is present in each of them as one of their dimensions.

If, instead of talking in terms of disciplines, we talk in terms of subject-matters, the attempt at placing semiotics in the context of the social sciences can be transcribed as an attempt at placing sign systems in the context of social reproduction. This transcription avails itself of the customary description of semiotics as the science of signs and sign systems. I add that semiotics and the other social sciences, whether distinguishable or not, have social reproduction as their object. But what about formal and natural sciences? Don't they belong themselves to social reproduction? The answer to this query will consist in reassessing formal and natural sciences as being, in a measure and according to certain criteria, social sciences themselves.

My two main terms, or basic notions, then, are 'sign systems' and 'social reproduction.' Sign systems, the object of *semiotics*, are characterized by *semiosis*, viz. by the functioning of signs which are always organized in systems. Hence the title chosen, but we could also speak of "sign systems *and* social reproduction," or – with an important and perhaps subtle difference –

---

* This is a first draft, written in 1974 and now slightly retouched [cf. R.-L. 1977], of Chapter I, "Introduction," of a book on which I began working at that time and which I hope to finish in both an English and an Italian version by 1978. [This book was never published, see my introduction to the present volume.] The main ideas contained therein are being discussed with colleagues and students during my courses in the philosophy of history at the University of Lecce, and in semiotics at the University of Urbino. A short anticipation of part of the argument has appeared in *Quaderni latinoamericani* 2, 1976[c]: 5-32 under the title "Criteri per lo studio ideologico di un autore." Sections 3 and 4, and a longer version will appear in *Nuova corrente* possibly by 1977, under the title "Teoria della collocazione ideologica di un autore." [Unpublished.] Some information about the whole book is given in Sections 8.1 and 8.5 hereafter.

we could speak of "sign systems *in* or *within* social reproduction." By provisionally pairing 'semiosis' *and* 'social reproduction,' we avoid prejudging the independent existence of sign systems within social reproduction, or worse, outside of it.

'Sign system' is a basic term for any student of semiotics or linguistics and related disciplines. There is a vast literature about sign systems, and I have dealt with them myself, in one way or another, in most of my previous publications. 'Social reproduction' is, instead, from the point of view of current semiotic literature, a less common and perhaps even a slightly mysterious term. It will be clarified as we go on. Let us say, for the moment, that social reproduction is the totality of the processes by which any given society proceeds in time from generation to generation, keeping itself going in history (or prehistory, as the case may be) while both preserving its internal structure and administering some changes in it. These practices may be relatively simple in the case of a very primitive, prehistoric community bordering on the tribe; or immensely complicated, as is the case with contemporary societies. We shall have to deal mainly with our own situation; but, especially in Chapter 3, elementary cases will also be taken into account, if only because they offer paradigmatic tools.

Semiosis and Social Reproduction is a continuation of *Linguistics and Economics* which appeared, with typical Moutonian rapidity, in December 1974, only three and a half years after it was delivered, as part VIII of volume twelve of the *Current Trends in Linguistics* mammoth enterprise, where it lay wrapped in its cocoon until it proceeded from caterpillar into butterfly as an independent volume in the series "Janua Linguarum" (1975[b], 1977^2). In fact, *Semiosis and Social Reproduction* begins by picking up one main conclusion of the previous book, namely that sign systems can perhaps be introduced in-between economic base or structure and superstructures – with an alternative though strictly related terminology, between modes of production and ideologies. Readers acquainted with *Linguistics and Economics* will perhaps find this book more palatable. It is, however, a wholly independent book, and it is a popular book rather than a book for colleagues.

To continue to exist, a society must obviously produce and exchange goods, teach children to speak and to interpret nonverbal sign systems, build a suitable environment, organize the relations among its members, transmit some basic values, and so on. All these various processes can be grouped into vast categories according to different criteria. One usual and fruitful grouping consists in opposing the *economic base* or *structure* to the *ideological super-*

structure (a *Bau* to an *Überbau*). The economic structure comprehends all the processes required for the production of goods and can be basically described in terms of the prevailing *mode of production*. A mode of production is the sum of *productive forces* and *relations of production*. The ideological superstructure comprehends all sorts of institutions, such as legal systems, religions, or folklore, and all "cultural or intellectual life," such as philosophy, the arts, or literature. The basic feature of any given ideological superstructure, however, rests on its dominating ideology. An ideology is a *social design* of a general type, over the long term, concerning society as a whole: it is the general framework within which all the programs of the society must fit. Economic structures, or modes of production, determine to some extent ideological superstructures. Ideologies, however, retro-act on the modes of production, so that there is a circle between the two levels.

The main proposal to be made in this book is that *sign systems* must be introduced as a third vast category in-between modes of production and ideologies. What is the function of semiosis in social reproduction? And since semiosis, in its turn, is socially reproduced, what are the influences of modes of production and of ideologies upon it? Obviously, for a society to reproduce itself sign systems must also be reproduced. In the book, sign systems are going to be first introduced as mediating between modes of production and ideologies; but they will also be considered as mediated in their turn by either modes of production or ideologies. In other words, one can either start with sign systems, oppose them to ideologies, and mediate between the two in terms of modes of production, or start with modes of production, oppose them to sign systems, and mediate between the two in terms of ideologies. This dialectical terminology represents the fact that a third item has been introduced into a previous two-item totality, and expresses the author's approach to a *materialistic semiotics* as a portion of a general science of man.

8.2 Does Semiotics Exist?

But does semiotics, altogether, exist? This is not meant to be a joke, nor a merely rhetorical question. Indeed, one possible answer would be – nobody really knows! The available literature shows us that the relations between semiotics and philosophy have never been properly and definitively assessed, and that the limits and purposes of semiotics as distinguished from other scientific endeavors are far from being clear. Sometimes semiotics is presented as one scientific discipline among others; but then, since there are signs everywhere and it is very difficult to say what is *not* a sign, semiotics seems to expand to cover the whole field of human knowledge. This would bring us to the opposite conclusion that semiotics is only a sort of superimposed awareness, or a set of new methods that scholars of various fields are invited to learn in order then to apply them to their own individual pieces of research. Difficulties of this kind are felt also in the history of the subject. It is, for instance, almost impossible to decide the extent to which Peirce's semiotics is independent from his metaphysics and valid even without it; and there are two very different conceptions in Charles Morris's main books – the conception of semiotics as a psycho-biological science and the conception of semiotics as a new organon for science in general, namely of semiotics as the present stage of what used to be called philosophy, taking its twentieth-century "linguistic turn" into account.

Let us proceed again from the idiom of disciplines to the idiom of subject-matters. Our question will then be – What are the relations between sign systems and social reproduction? In one main sense of the umbrella term, 'behavior,' nonmeaningful behavior simply doesn't exist. No man can operate without consciously or unconsciously using some sign systems, and it is in fact with the whole of his social organization that man communicates. In other words, every human action, whatever else it may be, must also be sign action. This is why it is social; or perhaps, with a more conservative formulation, this is the main reason why we call it social. (Notice that "private actions" are themselves just a species of the kind "social actions"; in fact, the very opposition between "private or individual" and "public or collective or social" is a social opposition.)

Which is, then, the relation between a general theory of signs and sign systems, or semiotics, and a general theory of social reproduction? Two solutions seem to be theoretically possible; and indeed, they are dominant in the literature I am acquainted with. It can be maintained that sign systems exist *within* social reproduction. In the most obvious sense of 'within' this is certainly true. No human activity exists outside of social reproduction. Thus the statement that sign systems exist *within* social reproduction is unimportant. Or, one has to be careful. If, by stating that sign systems exist *within* social reproduction, we mean to divorce sign systems *from the rest of* social reproduction, we may lose sight of the fact that the whole of social reproduction is also, necessarily, the reproduction of sign systems; and even more so, that social reproduction could not even take place *without* sign systems. Some scholars take the opposite view that all there is to social reproduction is the reproduction of sign systems. This amounts to saying that sign systems are themselves the social reality, namely, that there is nothing more to social reality than sign systems. When this latter solution has its root and justification in the refusal of the consequences of the former, it can even be taken as a serious effort to find a way out of them. Its danger, however, is that it is easily transformed into an idealistic solution. A sort of "semiotic panlogism" is then born. Much as Hegel's "Idea devoured Reality," now the "Sign devours Society." I have dealt with these fantastic developments elsewhere. I shall say here only that, in my view, semiotic panlogism must be given the sack straight off. What we need here is preventive repression. Paraphrasing a Chinese proverb reported in Latin by the Jesuit Fathers, let us proclaim that *In semioticam aulam nefas introducere panlogismum.* Social reproduction is based on need, work, exchange, class division, exploitation: that is, on factors that brutally beset the very body of man in its psycho-physical materiality, and not just the sign systems practiced by him. Signs are immensely important; but the furniture of the world doesn't consist of signs alone, and there is something of the ideology of total control in the contention that it does.

In *Linguistic and Economics* I tried to find some mediating solution by stating that without sign systems the contents of reality, whether sign contents or not, would not be lived as social; and that one comes to grasp this fact as soon as one has given all nonverbal sign systems, as distinguished from verbal and post-verbal sign systems, the importance they deserve. The argument is fairly long and complicated, and I cannot repeat it here. I still believe that the "lived-as-social-through-sign-systems" approach is a sound one. In this book, however, I shall mainly follow a different path. I shall begin not with semiotics, or semiosis, or signs, or sign systems, or perhaps symbols, or meaning, or whatever you may find in the pockets of linguists and semioticians, but rather with social reproduction in general. It will be only after having acquired some more knowledge about social reproduction, that I shall try to locate sign systems within it. My point of view will be the point of view of social reproduction, not the point of view of sign systems. If we succeed in clarifying to any extent the location and function of sign systems in social reproduction, to that very extent we shall have learned something about semiotics as distinguished from the other social sciences and from philosophy as well.

8.3 Social Reproduction in General

As we said, social reproduction is the totality of the practices by which any tribe or community or society continues to produce itself, viz. reproduces itself, thus proceeding in time from generation to generation. I am saying tribe *or* community *or* society not to exclude any of them from consideration. I shall, however, use mainly 'society' hereafter, and the other terms only when necessary to the context. Also, I shall use as fundamental the term 'practice'; but some words on its partial synonyms are in order. 'Process,' which sounds perhaps a little less political, accentuates both the time dimension and the objective character of what is going on. There are both social and biological or physical processes, while practices are only social. By stressing the necessity of motivation or the ethicity of the societal performance, 'task' is instead a more subjective, man-centered term. There are both collective and individual tasks, while practices are only social. Now social practices *are* social processes *and* social tasks, with the differences indicated by comparing the three terms. Moreover, social practices avail themselves of, and can themselves be seen as, structures or systems which continue to exist in time and to be recognizable by successive generations although they are subject to continuous variation. When this side of social practices wins the center of our attention, we usually call them institutions. The term 'institution' (with all that, as we shall see, must go with it) stresses the structural or permanent side to social practices. Now, social reproduction preserves the internal structure of the society while at the same time administering some changes to it. The dialectic between preservation or conservation and change or revolution belongs to social reproduction and is to be found within each of the institutions. This means that institutions, while being less temporalized than social practices as such, also necessarily move in time. The same is, of course, true of social tasks and processes. According to a difficult dialectic we shall have to examine later on, it is also true of biological and physical processes. But not in the obvious sense that time is there as an unavoidable dimension; rather, in the sense that biological and physical processes are *also* subject to *social time*, to historical (or prehistorical) time. In this sense, 'social practice' is a wider term than 'process,' and this is one more good reason to use 'practice' as our fundamental term. Another term to be examined later on is 'program.' It would be scholarly easy to fill up several pages with a terminological discussion inspired by contemporary theories in such fields as political science, sociology, anthropology, ethnology, and many others. I prefer to state simply that social reproduction is the totality of social practices.

The vision of social reproduction as an all-inclusive totality may induce a number of false beliefs. One is the belief that a society is a sort of gigantic organism. If this metaphor is useful to convey some ideas, let's use it; but let's hasten to add that social reproduction is *not* the reproduction of an organism. It is the reproduction of a nonbiological system usually called society which consists of social individuals who are also animals. Another false belief is that the totality-character of social reproduction is so intense that no internal structures can be recognized in it; or, if they can be, they aren't important. This is particularly dangerous insofar as it may remove attention from such basic issues as the struggle between the classes, exploitation, and the very opposition between economic base and superstructures. We shall deal with this issue in Chapter 4.

Let us consider here, instead, a third false belief which must be disposed of if we want to proceed at all. This is the belief that everything that happens in a society is necessary to its reproduction. A more prudent and therefore more acceptable formulation would be: every social practice, in principle, is necessary to social reproduction. The kernel of truth in this proposition is that, *in principle*, there isn't anything in society that does not deserve our attention. But if we want to study social reproduction as a whole and at the same time avoid the risk of the second false belief, namely that no internal structure is recognizable or important, then we must deny that all social practices are necessary to social reproduction. Practices necessary to social reproduction must be *basic social practices*. This is, of course, a poor proposition. But there is no way of avoiding some distinction between basic and additional, primary and secondary, necessary and contingent, fundamental and accessory, universal or at least general and particular, permanent and transitory. Difference of level and importance in all that goes on in a society cannot be ignored. Basic theoretical decisions are already involved at this stage. The field of the decisions to be made is no less than the field of the various possible theories about human nature at large.

One main difficulty is that practices to be considered basic may vary very much from society to society, and thus in a number of ways different practices may be considered basic in different societies; the same practice may be very different from society to society, and have a different standard in each of them; and the way in which any set of two or more practices are interconnected may also vary very much. Thus, for instance, it can happen that practice *A* which at first glance appeared to be superficial or accessory or whatever, must be given a second thought because of its connection with practice *B* about whose basic character no doubt could arise. Are we going to call practice *A* nonbasic but functional to practice *B*, or shall we rate it as basic as well? A little reflection about intricacies of this sort would seem to bring us to the conclusion that which practices are basic and which are not is a feature to be redetermined anew for every society whose reproduction we decide to investigate. This conclusion is both right and wrong. The way in which it is right is obvious. The way in which it is wrong can be elicited from its wording: the conclusion is true only if we have decided *to investigate a given society*, i.e. one real totality as distinguished from all other real totalities existing in space and time. But this is not at all our present concern.

Our concern about social reproduction – the aspects of it we are interested in – is that we want to be able to speak about something which must be common to any society actually reproducing itself. Now every conceivable society must either reproduce itself or disappear, and if it does disappear now it must have reproduced itself in the past otherwise it wouldn't have ever existed; and if it did disappear, say, five thousand years ago, it must have been reproducing itself before disappearing. But consider the following propositions: 1. there must be some basic social practices which every society must go through; 2. a society failing to fulfill the requirements of 1. doesn't exist, or would cease to exist almost immediately. I would call these propositions hypothetical because, much as they are obvious at the level of common sense, they can become very garbled as soon as we subject them to dialectical probing. By means of what criteria, in fact, are we going to single out practices so basic, that without them no social reproduction could take place even at the most rudimentary level? If we answer that *we know* what a society is, it would seem that our procedure is circuitous, insofar as we need a notion of society to accept or discard social practices, while we are attempting just the opposite, namely to characterize society by individuating some basic social practices. Another problem is where one has to make one's cut in the process of social evolution, whether closer to the original level of the tribe, or through history at the level where societies have already reached a high degree of complexity. But above all, how shall we abstract, from the historical (or prehistorical) reality of the various practices, some social practices as universal moulds capable of accommodating the variety of facts?

The only possible answer, or so it seems to me, is that we have to resort to the deliberate construction of some artificial models which are so abstract and general that they can apply everywhere. We shouldn't feel paralyzed by this. Social reproduction does exist; we want to talk about it; we've got to begin somewhere. If models are what we need, let's invent models.

On the other hand, we cannot avoid reflecting the point of view of the societies we belong to, whether neocapitalist or socialist, in the present age of world-wide communication, overdeveloped technology, international market, contrasting ideologies, and so on. This being *our* level of complication, we must be careful not to exclude aprioristically any existing practice from the range of the practices which are basic *for us*. We must secure an interpretation which is, in principle, as complete as possible. While not actually describing the facts of the social reproduction of this or that society (for instance of Italy vs. France, or of Europe vs. the Americas), we must describe social reproduction in the widest possible terms.

These contrasting exigencies will make it necessary to approach our problems from different angles, through successive stages. Let us try, meanwhile, to give a first rough list of some basic social practices as they occur to common, prescientific reflection. This first list is extremely provisional and will be taken up and developed further in Chapter 2. I need it here both to break the ice with my readers and to use it as a target for the arrows of some remarks on the methodological relevance of social reproduction *as a category* and *a conceptual tool*. Thus, *prima facie*, to reproduce itself a society, every society, must:

1. Produce and exchange maintenance goods, beginning, of course, with food.
2. Select and use, or build, a suitable environment for its members to live in.
3. Transmit to children the social patrimony of language, nonverbal and postverbal sign systems, rituals, folklore, mores, basic values, and other codes.
4. Organize the relations among its members at all possible levels and to all possible effects.
5. Take care of groups of people in special conditions, whether these are recurrent or not: infants, pregnant women, old people and all so-called abnormal or deviant people (according to given criteria of normality and conformity, of course).
6. Further, control, or make possible, or simply tolerate the transmission and development of other social activities such as the arts, music, literature or story-telling, philosophy or *Weltanschauungen*, religions, scientific or prescientific enquiry, and the various technologies.

7. (Do a number of other things which just happened to be left out of this initial list.)

All basic social practices are so to speak "always present," whether operating or not, at any level and on any point of social reproduction. This must be true in principle, because there is no way to approach social reproduction with a pair of metaphysical scissors and slice off some portions of it. At least to a great extent, it is also true in reality; the only cases one can think of in which it isn't true are some transitory cases of emergency such as wars or floods or hurricanes, whose description, however, involves a reference to all the social practices suspended or made impossible precisely because of the emergency. In other words, no social task can be properly accomplished *in the absence* of the other social tasks, no properly social process can develop by itself alone, as it were, in a vacuum. This is apparent even in our first rough list, where, for instance, the social practices collected under point 3. are concurrent with those collected under point 6. In Chapter 2 we are going to deal in a more detailed way with this problem of the co-presence of, and continuity among, all social practices. To make the point clearer even now, consider that there would be no production and exchange of goods without some knowledge and some technology, or without some social organization of the individuals, or without some systems of communication (at least the natural language of the group). Or, it wouldn't make any sense to teach children to speak and to use and interpret nonverbal sign systems, if folklore, customs, some knowledge of the world, and some technology to operate upon it didn't exist. Or again, no suitable environment could be selected or built, unless these operations were inspired by some accepted values and unless the techniques available to the group were employed. Indeed, social reproduction is a totality of different basic social practices which are inextricably intertwined. Even the organization of consensus, which is necessary for any ruling class or group to continue to rule, can only be achieved through a continuation of all main social practices. This point is easily brought out by the remark that ruling classes or groups want to rule over living and not over dead people (although in some cases they may use the dead to impress upon the living), and that the ruled people couldn't even be ruled unless they were able to speak and work and had learned a number of basic rules of conduct.

To sum up, in order to continue to exist a society must accomplish a huge array of tasks. Moreover, it must accomplish them *together*: between any two of these tasks, once they are recognized as fundamental, there must be no major contradiction capable of preventing either or both from being accomplished. This proposition can be reversed and made into *a methodological principle for the individuation of basic social practices*: we shall say that two social practices are basic whenever there can be no major contradiction between them. This does not mean that no contradiction at all must arise; quite the contrary, contradictions are always present. But, to give an example, feeding people cannot prevent teaching children to speak; if it did, new ways to accomplish both tasks would have to be invented; and if they were not, neither the feeding nor the teaching could take place any longer – social life would simply disintegrate.

One important and perhaps difficult feature of social reproduction is that it includes biological reproduction, while biological reproduction does not include social reproduction. Once the reproduction is social, biological reproduction must be seen as a part of it, and not the other way round. Social reproduction includes, of course, (i) the biological reproduction of human individuals; but also (ii) the biological reproduction of domesticated animals, and (iii) the biological reproduction of all life relevant to the human species and to the animals it uses. This has always been true, to some extent, since the first arising of human settlements and of constructive relations between men and animals (although animals themselves, we must admit, may not always feel that such relations are constructive). In our present, ecologically threatened world, it can be said that social reproduction must take care of, and can be affected by, practically all that happens to animal and plant life at large. As soon as the most primitive, originary level of immediate appropriation of the spontaneous products of nature is abandoned, social reproduction must include much more than the mere survival of life, whether human, or animal, or vegetable. Biological and nonbiological dimensions have grown more and more interconnected. Not even the survival of life at the human level could now be assured without the continuous intervention of nonbiological processes. This is one of the senses in which the formal and natural sciences are themselves an expression and a part of social reproduction.

Each of the practices of social reproduction is itself a vast collection of activities. Each of us, as an individual, possesses some information about some of these activities and is acquainted with the general fact that there is an enormous amount of different activities going on on the planet. But this doesn't mean in the least that any one of us can practice more than one or a few activities, let alone have any structural or operative knowledge about their systems. As scholars accustomed to the amount of labour required for getting properly acquainted with the problems and methods pertaining to any given limited field of enquiry, our first reaction when confronted with this or that practice of social reproduction would be to proceed to examine its component parts and then concentrate on one of them, rather than to try to group two or more practices into some even broader category. In fact, different disciplines concentrate on this or that social practice, or on a few among the activities comprehended by any social practice, and disregard the others, which are the subject of different disciplines. But if we are to throw some light on some general features of social reproduction, our approach must be global, it must concern society as a whole. This raises again a question of method to be faced straight off, before we feel authorized to proceed at all.

Perhaps we can begin clarifying our question of method by calling attention to what some existing disciplines actually do. Ethnologists, for instance, do practice a global approach, but only with primitive societies which haven't left written records, haven't developed complicated technologies, and lend themselves to being isolated one from the other in order to make them into suitable objects of study. Cultural anthropologists concentrate instead on culture as a social patrimony comprehending knowledge, beliefs, values of all description, and techniques for action; but they tend to leave everything else outside their scope. Historians of technology often produce global descriptions of all that a given society is capable of performing in terms of transforming nature to human ends, but nobody would fault them for not taking into account, for instance, moral and other codes. Now without these codes human agents would not be human at all and it would follow that even nature as an object of human transformation would cease to exist. Sociological theories of the social systems such as the theory advanced by Talcott Parsons and E. Shils (and anticipated by Malinowski since the twenties) are still incomplete if compared with an extended catalogue of the social practices actually comprehended by social reproduction. Moreover, they usually describe the external, manifest organization of social practices, and they concentrate on consciously coded practices while disregarding those practices whose codification is unconscious, but no less rigorous or less binding.

Socially minded historians, when they have a proper tendency toward complete representation, often give us examples of a global approach to social reproduction. They couldn't present us with a fair picture of a given society unless they informed us of all or most basic social practices pertaining to it. Indeed, we say that a piece of historical writing is partial or biased particularly when it stresses only certain social practices at the expense of others. The phrases 'diplomatic, military, cultural, etc.' history send us back to histories free of the very limitations set on them by those adjectives. Except that we are not concerned here with directly recounting the history, phase after phase, of any given society. Our own overwhelming historical bias is that we live in the 1970s, in a western country characterized by a neocapitalist mode of production, in the context of the contemporary world as it is. Our exigency is to encompass a social totality much as historians sometimes do, but our methods and attitude are different. We aim at ungarbling the structure, or system, or we could say the basic logic, of the situation examined.

Thus, perhaps, this piece of research pertains to general anthropology, also called philosophical anthropology. In traditional terminology, philosophical anthropology is a sector of moral philosophy which was also labeled, significantly, the *philosophy of action* or *practice*, or *practical philosophy*.

In traditional moral thought, there were two fundamental limitations. The first was that the action or practice to be examined was an *individual* action or practice; universalism was sought, but it was the universalism of all individuals. Individuals, who had just emerged as masters of themselves insofar as they were bourgeois individuals, could not be thought of as social products. They were free agents. This was, of course, among other things, the ideology of bourgeois private property – something one had to stop in front of as if it were a natural item in the furniture of the world. One couldn't trace private property back to labour without endangering it, without questioning the whole social system. Strictly connected with this limitation of the free individual was the second main limitation of traditional moral thought, namely that only the conscious side of the mind was ever taken into account. Not only was the individual free as being his own private property, isolated before society; he was also free within himself, in the sense that no internal factor could determine his actions. But since individuals, in spite of all their freedom, or abuse thereof, did act in many wrongful ways and often tended to destroy each other, legal systems and moral philosophies had to be invented which sought for universal laws to which all individuals were expected to conform.

In this way two apparently unbreakable barriers were erected against any approach to the individual as a social product. They are well documented in the history of European philosophy especially from Locke to Kant – they are, when viewed in the proper perspective, the core and motivating force of that history. Kant's *Critique of Practical Reason* is its peak; it cannot be "improved": it can be abandoned, and very respectfully so, as being the brilliant and moving reflection of a previous stage in human relations and social organization. But now the new thing is that not only can Kant's *Critique* be substituted by new constructions reflecting the present stage in human relations and social organization, but it can also be substituted by a construction claiming to be the *ante eventum* reflection of new human relations and a new social organization which don't yet exist but which we think possible to bring into existence by revolutionary planning and action. Thus the substitution, at least in principle, can be twofold. This wouldn't have been thinkable without Hegel's grandiose epitome of whatever had been thought about man before him. Hegel was somewhat halfway between the bourgeois ideology of his immediate predecessors and the possibility of overcoming it. Or better, he still represented that ideology, and in several ways even made it worse by inventing the ultimate metaphors reflecting the advent of Capitalism: an all-encompassing Spirit as a metaphor for Capital, an ever-moving Idea as a metaphor for Money. But these were metaphors beyond which no one could proceed by theory alone. No new, still more comprehensive metaphors could be invented. All one could do was to expose *those* metaphors. In other words, the whole approach had to be changed; and the idea began emerging that the situation represented by Hegel's metaphors could be changed too. While generalizing and exaggerating the bourgeois ideology, Hegel supplied his followers and critics both with the final metaphorical framework of all possible philosophies as reflecting all possible stages in human relations and social organization, and with the instrument for overcoming that framework and destroying his own philosophical construction. This instrument is the dialectical method, and it allows the exposition of Hegel's own metaphorical framework. In this way traditional philosophical theorizing, or philosophy as a sort of constructive superscience describing nonhistorical entities, was brought to its historical end.

8.4 Social Reproduction vs. Reality

A few remarks on the philosophical and methodological bearing of the category "social reproduction," and I am almost finished with these introductory remarks. Let us perform the intellectual experiment of figuratively jumping into the middle of social reproduction and, once we are there, of looking all around. What we shall see in any direction is social reproduction itself, *and nothing else*. Social reproduction is the totality of reality in the sense that it is the totality of what we can speak about. Nothing can be said of anything supposedly existing by itself outside of social reproduction. We can, of course, speak about individual trees, or about the stars; we can also speak about a much more sophisticated thing like the geological past of the Earth before the advent of man, and even about abstract things like Nature or Matter in general. The reality of all these things is not denied by my argument; if it were denied, my argument would be an idealistic one. Instead, my argument is that the reality of things "external to man, or to his individual consciousness," is a reality belonging itself to social reproduction. Other animals don't speak about trees or stars, let alone the geological past of the Earth, because they don't possess relations of generality. It was only through nomination that generality arose and anything "natural" was objectified as opposed to the formation of human subjects, or externalized in concomitance with the construction of internal structures. Moreover, whatever concept of "external" reality we entertain, it is always the conception, or one of the conceptions, prevailing within the society we belong to as something necessary to its reproduction or at least tolerated by it. Theories of nature and attitudes regarding the relation of the subjective to the objective are typical ideological items which vary enormously from society to society and with the passing of time within any society. Even the precision and level of abstraction reached in the description of natural events and in their handling by contemporary scientific procedures cannot but correspond to equally precise and abstract operations taking place internally to man. The domination of the objective is a domination of the subjective. All these "things" don't exist themselves in nature: they are historical, social results, as such belonging entirely to social reproduction.

Social reproduction was first fully described by Karl Marx, especially in the *Grundrisse*, which is his main text and probably his masterpiece. *Capital*, with its many thousand pages, is "only" a special application of the general ideas contained in the *Grundrisse* to the case of capitalistic society as it was reproducing itself under Marx's eyes. This is why Marxist scholars limiting themselves to *Capital* and unable to accept the *Grundrisse* are so often dogmatically unable to understand the contemporary world or to make a constructive use of new scientific discoveries and intellectual techniques (which is really odd, if we consider the enormous attention dedicated by Marx and Engels to the new scientific discoveries and intellectual techniques of their time).

Social reproduction, in this view, is the widest possible totality we can conceive of; there is no structure moving in time more comprehensive than social reproduction. Therefore, social reproduction is, and must be, the basic category for all of our enquiries. It lends itself perfectly well to logico-historical reality, or better, it is *the* logico-historical reality. Or again: reality can be fully approached only in both logical and historical terms. We cannot grasp its structures unless we perceive how it develops in time, and we cannot grasp its developments unless we acquaint ourselves with its structures. The logico-historical method is the originary formulation of ideas which were later worded, and watered down, as structural-historical or synchronic-diachronic. This opposition between "logic, or structure" and "history" shouldn't be confused with the opposition between "structure as economic base" and "superstructures." Both structures as economic base and superstructures are to be studied by the logico-historical method.

8.5 Three Complementary Approaches

The bulk of this book consists of approaching social reproduction from three separate angles, always keeping in mind that we want to try to locate sign systems within it rather than, as we said, "starting with" sign systems. It is my intention that the three approaches shall be complementary, or at least mutually supporting ones; they ought to throw some light on different aspects or levels of social reproduction. Since social reproduction is the widest possible structure moving through time, the three different approaches all necessarily apply some portions of the logico-historical method.

The first approach consists of compiling a catalogue of many possible institutions. As we know, institutions are social practices seen as systems or structures. Our use of 'institution' will be a broad one, whose quasi-synonyms are 'code' and 'program.' Now a catalogue is a static list, and this means that institutions are described in abstraction from their reproduction or even from their movement through time. The logical, or structural, or synchronic side to the method is fully privileged here. The second approach, on the other hand, is a dynamic schema of social reproduction in terms of production, exchange, and consumption (a previous, much less developed version of this schema was contained in a section of Chapter 2 of *Linguistics and Economics*). This approach begins by examining the basic requirements of production at the level of survival, which means at a merely structural level, in an embryonic representation of the economic base; and proceeds to inspect the first emersion of something in its turn embryonically superstructural in terms of exchange of signs. The third approach, finally, fortifying itself with whatever clarification has been attained by the use of the first two approaches, consists in taking up again the traditional opposition of structure or economic base and superstructures as we find it within the Marxist tradition, and in trying to transform it into a three-term description by introducing sign system as a third item. This transformation was perhaps already implicit in Marx's own writings; and at any rate, times seem now to have ripened for examining it.

While the first approach is entirely static or synchronic, the second and third approaches take care of movement in terms of reciprocal influences obtaining between the various items of the totality of social reproduction. These reciprocal influences are not only simultaneous; more often than not, they require a scansion of time. The time dimension is thus necessarily present in the second and third approach. It is present, however, in the general sense in which it is present in dialectics. A *proper history* of any case of social reproduction belongs to a different field of enquiry, or at least falls entirely outside of the present research.

With this my introduction is finished and we can proceed to our first approach.

9. Articulations in Verbal and Objectual Sign Systems

Foreword

In this essay [cf. R.-L. 1974e] a theory of the articulation of verbal and objectual sign systems will be expounded. The starting point is Martinet's well-known theory of the double articulation operating within the system of a language – the articulation of *sentences* into *monemes* (also called *morphemes*), and the articulation of *monemes* into *phonemes*. This theory has been generally accepted by contemporary linguistics, and it has been pointed out that it also obtains within the genetic code. In both cases, the "aim" of the double articulations is *economy*: only some thirty phonemes – fifty for all known languages – allow us to construct many thousands of monemes; and by combining monemes we can produce an indefinite number of sentences of any complexity on any possible topic to any imaginable effect.

The theory of articulation to be expounded here is new in two respects: (i) it maintains that there are two more articulations to be taken into account with regard to any language – provided the language is not viewed as a machine in its isolation but rather as a sector of society, i.e. in its continuity with other human activities. The other two articulations are higher level articulations, pivoting on the *syllogism* and on the automated *programming* of linguistic performances. (ii) The four levels of articulation are to be found not only in the field of language, but also in the field of *material production*. The principle of economy which allowed man to construct his languages was also applied in the construction of *nonverbal sign systems of the objectual kind*, including the material bodies of such systems.

In order to bring out the four articulations in both fields, the central and longest part of the essay is dedicated to a parallel examination of ten successive levels of complication in the process of production (the "homology of production").

A previous treatment of the subject appeared under the title "Omologia della riproduzione sociale" (Homology of Social Reproduction) in *Ideologie* [cf. R.-L. 1972c]. A different version of the same essay, written in 1971, is incorporated in the monograph *Linguistics and Economics* [cf. R.-L. 1974f and 1975b]. Readers interested in a more thorough treatment are referred to the above publications, where bibliographical apparatuses will also be found. They may also consult my previous writings, where a number of related problems are examined: *Il linguaggio come lavoro e come mercato* [cf. R.-L. 1968h]; and *Semiotica e ideologia* [cf. R.-L. 1972i].

This essay is mainly a reproduction of parts of some subsections, and a summary of some other subsections, from Sections 2 and 3 of *Linguistics and Economics*.

Some hints at the terminology used hereafter, and discussed in my other publications, may be of help. 'Work' is used for productive, qualitative activity whose results are use-values. Work is distinguished from both 'labor' (quantitatively measured to assess exchange-values) and mere 'activity' which has its aim in itself, i.e. doesn't leave products. 'Production' is understood in terms of *social* reproduction: it concerns material objects, sign systems, and institutions of every description. 'Verbal' is used for languages in the proper sense; 'nonverbal' is only a provisionally negative definition of signs and sign systems based on codes composed of materials other than articulate sounds; 'objectual' refers to the sign systems of so-called material production; 'sign system' is used in an anthropological or philosophical sense rather than in a strictly linguistic one: a sign system is comprehensive of at least a code, the messages transmitted and received by using that code, and the conditions which make its operation possible.

9.1 Artefacts and Work

An *artefact* in the most general sense, from *artĕ* and *factum*, is any product of human work, that is, something that did not exist in nature and that has required man's intervention for its existence. Since dictionaries admit of both the spellings *artifact* and *artefact*, let us use the latter, although it is less common, because it brings out the Latin roots. The notion of artefact is connected to the problem of the relation-distinction between *man* and *nature* and shares its profundity. In its position between the notion of man and that of nature, it sends us back necessarily to the mediating notion of *work*. Work is what transforms nature into artefact. In every single working process, the materials from which one starts are assumed as something natural insofar as they are *given* to us; the product, that *for which* we must work, will be nonnatural.

This is true for man, too. The essential point is the following: if we don't want to admit that something *human* exists for man without the intervention of man himself, we must hold to the principle that every artefact, however understood, is the result of work which man has done and can do again. This also suits the sounds emitted by human organisms. As we know, such sounds are the stuff of the codes of verbal sign systems. For simplicity's sake, in what follows we will call them, directly, linguistic sounds. The fact, then, that any sound bears the imprint of man is enough to make us regard it as produced in some way instead of simply emitted, and we can therefore recognize in it the character of artefact. All sound objects constituting a language are the fruit of human work. Words, sentences, and discourses certainly do not exist in nature without the intervention of man; not even the individual variants of a phoneme exist in nature with the characteristics that make them suitable for the scope for which they were made. Often the emission of a single sound is enough to give immediate evidence of the possible presence of man. A very brief spoken chain, even one belonging to a completely unknown language, takes away all doubt: a man must be there. This means that the operations with which linguistic objects are produced are so specific and precise that we recognize them immediately in their products.

We sustain then the Vichian and Marxian thesis that the notion of artefact is in principle applicable to language. Sign systems, both verbal and non-verbal, are systems of artefacts. Nonverbal production exists; so does verbal production. From the semiotic point of view, the principal *systematic* difference between nonverbal and verbal artefacts is to be sought in the aims for which they are produced. While verbal artefacts are produced just and only for use as signs, and any other use of them is occasional or subsidiary, non-verbal artefacts are not used as signs *only*, and indeed, the majority of them are produced for other aims. The use-values are distributed differently. Even in the cases in which nonverbal objects are produced expressly for use as signs, like, for example, signal flags, they conserve beyond their sign use a "residue" which semiotic enquiry must take into account. One can blow one's nose on signal flags; on phonemes, one cannot, and even generated sentences are not big enough.

The speaker is a linguistic worker: in him is to be found the spring of linguistic operations, of the expenditure of linguistic labor-power. Such expenditure invests already existing products, united in the system of the language. As an extremely complex, human, social product, language offers to every linguistic worker an immediately accessible patrimony (a "constant capital") of linguistic materials, instruments, and "money." Using the artefacts of language, the linguistic worker is in a position subsequent, not anterior, to them. He carries out programs for the use of linguistic artefacts which are shown to him ready-made by those who teach him to speak (and thus back through the generations). The sense in which each speaker himself "reproduces" tokens according to models of production is a very attenuated sense; rather, he would be similar to one who picks up a hammer in his hand instead of leaving it in the closet. More than reproducing them, he *repeats* them, he *takes them up again*. This is the job of a machine, indeed, a computer, of still unequaled complexity, his organism. It was in this sense, perhaps, that Wittgenstein said that "everyday language is a part of the human organism and is no less complicated than it" (*Tractatus*, 4.002). This is also the site of possible confusion between the biological nature and the social nature of language. As a product of work, human language is *entirely social*; no contradiction arises when we add that, naturally, we are talking about hominoidea, that is, about extremely complex organisms. Not only doesn't the second evolution exclude the first; it presupposes it. The dialectic of work, product, and use as it applies in the field of language, and indeed of all social sign systems, accounts for current exaggerations of every linguistic worker's individual contribution, which according to some would be downright creativistic. It also helps to explain the opposition which we may encounter to the operation of placing work at the foundation of language.

Not only is the production model unconscious, but so is the repetition of tokens. Tokens are used (usually in the very act in which they are repeated) according to programs which are unconscious in their turn. To become aware of the programs for the use of linguistic artefacts we have to study the operation of things which are already produced. The single linguistic worker rarely goes back from the programs for use to the production models, crossing backwards over the artefacts, though this is not impossible. It usually happens only in research, in the invention of new words and phrases which satisfy a new social need, and in the case of so-called poetic or literary "creation" (modifications brought to programs, or even to a few production models).

The speaker repeats or takes up again tokens of linguistic artefacts, and uses them in new work which consists in the execution of social programs. No objection is made to the idea that in such execution we may also find small individual variations of the type found in the handling of the various utensils. In so doing, the speaker produces sentences and messages. Messages are sentences, or fragments or combinations of them, effectively transmitted.

Every message has its own end within it, the end of being received and interpreted, and possibly acted upon. In front of the multitude of messages, however, it is reasonable to extrapolate some common end, and distinguish it from the messages as products. This is how we come to the generalization that the primary ends of the speaker are to express himself and to communicate. The essential aspect of all this is that, exactly as occurs in the field of material production, the speaker uses the products of previous work even without being conscious of it, and usually considers these products natural (spontaneously *physiocratic conception* of language). At the most he arrives at considering the language as capital and speech as a sort of commerce (*mercantilistic conception* of language). When we apply the more mature theory of labor-value to language, we see in the articulations of work the appropriate design for beginning to explain some tangles of difficulties which up to now have remained mysterious, like the facility of language learning, reciprocal understanding among speakers, the "generation" of sentences, the relations between *langue* and *parole*, the spontaneous flow of speech, and many others.

Between material artefacts like wooden planks, shoes, or automobiles, and linguistic artefacts like words, sentences, or discourses, a constitutive homology can be traced. It can be baptized with the brief expression *homology of production*. If we use 'production' in its general sense, the homology is internal to it, and thus present *between* the two types or branches of production here distinguished as fundamental.

Man has never produced linguistic artefacts without producing material artefacts at the same time. Wherever we look, we find artefacts belonging to the two classes existing together. A civilization which is "only material" or "only linguistic" does not exist in reality. No definition or characterization of man is as radical as that which places in the *definiens* his capacity to produce material (*faber*) and linguistic (*loquens*) artefacts. But indeed, that material artefacts may be produced without the concomitant production of linguistic artefacts, and vice versa, is not even *thinkable*. Man would not have been able to work on any object without communicating with other workers, at least with rudimentary languages, at the beginning bordering on gestures. Conversely, verbal communication presupposes a world of real objects to which language refers, and thus the advent of the capacity to distinguish and manipulate such objects. Those particular animals that come together in communitary groups and, with the passage from unity to plurality, little by little become men, operate in a basically similar way when they organize all their sign systems, as different as these systems may seem at first glance. It would be strange if the opposite were true, since sign systems express the relations of social organization as it grew from the beginning. There would be no division of labor without the existence of some form of communication; communication, however, would not arise without the division of labor.

Linguistic production and material production develop according to parallel modalities and levels of complexity for which unitary explanations may be given. There is no reason why the internal articulations of work shouldn't be valid for both. When we reconstruct the phases of production in a parallel way we find that for every linguistic level (distinctive features, phonemes, monemes, words, phrases, sentences, and higher units of discourse) there is a corresponding level of nonverbal linguistic work, that is, a corresponding phase in the elaboration of nonsound material – this from the standpoint of language. But we can also take the opposite standpoint, and recognize in language the moments and levels of the various processes of "material," nonverbal, production.

In the following section ten levels of production are distinguished.

9.2 Homology of Production

9.2.1 First Level: Presignificant Items

Where and how does work begin? Any external material work can be broken down into simple operations. These must be operations that a human organism can perform upon objects that constitute his immediate environment. The most simple real operations one can imagine are operations like pulling, pushing, adding, taking away, turning, tracing, pressing; and like superimposing, overturning, heaping, flattening, sharpening, breaking, splitting, scraping, curving, spreading, reuniting, inserting, piercing. Notice that these must be operations carried out directly by the organism, not only without utensils but also without instruments and, indeed, without any intermediary. At a certain stage man (like other animals before him) is able to make some distinction and some modifications *between* and *in* the physical materials existing in nature, the former being results of perceptive operations and the latter of manipulative operations. All results belonging to this level, i.e. the most elementary modifications brought by man to his own natural external environment, will be called hereafter *matteremes*.

If we look for equally elementary elements in the field of linguistic production, we find that the first modifications made on sound material by the speaker are precisely the ones the linguists call *phonemes* as the minimal distinctive units traceable in a spoken chain. Matteremes and phonemes can in turn be broken down. Phonemes can be broken down phonetically into acustico-articulatory "coefficients" or pertinent "features"; matteremes into movements of the human members and displacements of the objects upon which they act (we could talk here about visual-motor coefficients and pertinent features in nonsound material). What interests us are minimal working units producing minimal distinctive units. *Both* in the flow of vocal emission *and* in the flow of corporeal movements, we single out some identifiable units which function as pigeon-holes able to accommodate individual variants.

These first results of work lend themselves to various considerations.

First of all, we cannot go below them and continue talking about work. A material object, whether a sound object or not, which bears not even one of the modifications able to make it a mattereme or a phoneme, is part and parcel of the field of "mere nature," it belongs to the world of the "unmanipulated." The reference to mere nature as unmanipulated can be understood either in the sense of what Hjelmslev calls substance (of the *signatum* as of the *signans*), or as the postulation of an undifferentiated level anterior to any human intervention. The notion of a substance not formed by man lets us glimpse the totality of materials virgin in nature; it belongs to disciplines which are not specifically semiotic, like physics, chemistry, and biology. If we postulate instead a level of the undifferentiated, we find that the passage to the differentiated can be caught in three ways: in the realm of genetic psychology (animal as well as human), or as the first moment in a doctrine of the formation of consciousness (Hegel, Husserl), or as the basic step for a theory of the scientific grasp of reality (the *Ergreifung des Wirklichen*, according to a posthumous formulation by Dingler). The study of any substance, whether in Hjelmslev's sense or not, naturally requires that the substance receive forms, and therefore that the level of *originary* differentiations be abandoned much earlier. This also amounts to saying that not even the substance of the *signatum* – in spite of its pre-sign indifference – can be studied without systems of signs coming into play. Thus the difference emerges between the study of things upon which work has been done and things upon which work has not been done, taking for granted that the study itself requires complex products of (sign and non-sign) work. It is submitted that the status of the genetic code may perhaps be reconsidered from this angle. Anything that is studied by humanity is studied at the level attained by humanity.

In the second place, the number of matteremes and phonemes is limited. It is surprising to notice how these first building stones of every successive material and linguistic working process appear in both fields in approximately the same number or quantity. Man is able to articulate, recognize, and use within natural sound material some few tens of phonemes because his articulatory and acoustic apparatuses are what they are; in the same way, he is able to articulate, recognize, and use only some few tens of matteremes as basic modifications operated on the nonsound material furnished to him by nature. His hands, his senses, and his brain are what they are (even if they can be modified precisely as a consequence of his work). The number of matteremes as well as of phonemes is also limited in view of the kinds of working processes that will have to be done upon them.

In the third place, matteremes and phonemes have no other signification than that of being destined to serve as elements in further units which are only slightly more complex than they are. These further units are the first human products to be endowed with a stable and independent signification. The elaboration of simple elements into elements which are step by step more complex is perhaps going to have a more familiar look in the field of linguistic production than in that of material production. And still we are always dealing with one and the same thing. We can discern here one of the senses in which work – as Hegel put it – is "appetite held in check," desire under control. In order to carry out a piece of work, man needs a utensil; in order to build the utensil, he must pass through various stages previous to it, beginning with the stage at which he has to effect in nature modifications which lack an independent signification, and which will assume their proper function only when they are further combined with one another.

At this level we can also catch the first irreducible differences between man and the other animals. Matteremes and phonemes have the simplicity and the availability of mere intermediaries or at most of quite elementary instruments. They are therefore remote from utensils proper. Nonhuman animals too use intermediaries and quite elementary instruments. They move a branch to bring a piece of fruit nearer, i.e. they obtain the fruit through the mediation "moved-branch," which makes an intermediary of the branch; they use a stone to crack nuts, that is, they work on the nuts with the elementary instrument of the stone (which, one will notice, recedes into the un-worked-upon as soon as it ceases being used: it has simply been assumed as an elementary instrument). To the same order of considerations belongs the fact that nonhuman animals also communicate, often in complex ways. These have only begun in the last few years to be subjected to systematic enquiries which probably have many surprises in store for us. There don't seem to exist any animals other than man, however, that produce modifications lacking a stable signification of their own *for the purpose* of combining them later on by means of a working synthesis, in this way producing artefacts endowed with a signification that begins to become specific and stable. Leaving aside minor exceptions about which very little is known, and while we are waiting for empirical discoveries which will demonstrate the contrary, it turns out that a proper *activity of combining by successive levels* is after all typical of man alone. This activity is *work*.

As soon as we leave the first level and move toward the second, we cross the zone in which Martinet's "second articulation" takes place: the articulation of monemes in phonemes and, as we shall see, of objectemes in matteremes.

9.2.2 Second Level: Irreducibly Significant Items

At this level we encounter stable, characterizing, and completed modifications made on materials by means of combinations of matteremes or of phonemes. At this point separate, independent new items have been created in the matter of the world. Each of these items already has some sort of signification, it is already a "significant unit" different from all the others. It cannot be broken down without destroying its signification; nor can this signification be traced back to significant elements that precede it at a more elementary level. However, we are not dealing here (if not in a minority of cases) with such completed significations as those we shall begin to encounter only at the next level, the third. The set of these pieces or significant units forms the first articulation of utensils and sentences, as will become clearer for both of the fields of production just as soon as we have all the levels up to that of sentences and utensils laid out in front of us.

Let's examine a hammer. It is composed of a head and a handle. According to artisan terminology, the head is in turn composed of a face, a peen, and an eye. The peen is the tapered striking end of the head opposite the face; sometimes it is divided into a claw and serves as a lever for extracting nails. The eye is the hole into which the handle is introduced; it can be circular, oval, or square. The face is the flat part used for hitting: it is that part of the whole head, and thus of the whole hammer, that enters into direct contact with the nail or any other object one is working upon. Let's call these three significant aspects of the head of the hammer *objectemes*.

Objectemes are at one and the same time parts and functions. They *are* parts – or, this is the aspect of them that emerges – every time it is easy to distinguish the objectemes from each other within the higher level unit to which they belong. Whenever this discrete aspect does not emerge we consider them, instead, as functions. Is there anything like a hierarchy among the parts making up the head of a hammer? There seems to be one in this sense: since the hammer is mainly used for hammering and you hammer specifically with the face, this is the principal significant unit, while the others concur to make its workings more precise, or equip it with additional signification in various ways. Let us call the part or aspect or function that bears the principal signification a *lexobjecteme* and the others *morphobjectemes*. The face of the head of the hammer is a lexobjecteme; the peen and the eye are morphobjectemes.

In the field of linguistic production the significant units described above are pieces of a complexity inferior to or, at the most, equal to that of the word. We are going to use Martinet's term *monemes* for such pieces or significant units in linguistic production. We can also apply here what we have learnt about material objects, and specify that monemes subdivide into *lexemes* (also called *semantemes*) when they constitute the significant nucleus, and *morphemes* when they serve to modify the nucleus (in American terminology: *morphemes* divide into *free* and *bound*). Thus 'love' and 's' are both monemes; but the former is a lexeme, the latter a morpheme (as a completed word, 'loves' belongs instead to the third level of this schema). It belongs to the nature of objectemes and monemes that they can be taken apart, for each of them is the result of combinations made with results of previous operations. The working process leading to any given moneme or objecteme is always the same. Thus the moneme 'love' can be analyzed into phonemes, as the objecteme face (of the hammer) into matteremes. As categories or pigeonholes, phonemes and matteremes cannot undergo any change; or better, a change brought to phonemes and matteremes would affect to some extent the whole of whatever sign system is built upon them. Their combination gives rise to a high number of monemes, and of objectemes respectively, usually several thousand or tens of thousands for every historical language and for every objectual, nonverbal sign system of a given community.

The signification of all the products described up to this point lies in the first place in this, that they are all *products of work*. This includes the way in which they are produced, the functions which they must be able to carry out and their lending themselves to different uses for different ends, the relations into which they enter with other products of work, and so on. Just these, and not others, are the factors that constitute their signification in the general sense. Let us think for a moment instead about the consequences we would have to face if we wanted to attribute to products a signification *that accompanied them*, that is, if we wanted to think of them only as *signantia* and started searching for their respective *signata*. With things put in these terms, signification ought to join the products of work in a different realm from that of matter. This would mean resorting to a dualistic conception of human activity. It is certainly legitimate to ask oneself what is the signification (what they are used for) of the monemes constituting the word 'loves,' i.e. 'love' and 's'; in the same way, it is legitimate to ask ourselves what is the signification (what they are used for) of the parts constituting the head of the hammer, i.e. the peen, the eye, and the face. But we would never dream of relegating the signification of these "material" pieces to a different realm; in the same way it is advisable not to try to do it with "linguistic" pieces.

9.2.3 *Third Level: "Completed" Pieces*

If we go on toward more complex units, in the field of material production we find, *in the first instance*, the pieces constituting a utensil, those whose parts we have so far described as objectemes. With restrictions which we will specify later, let us call these "completed" pieces; and since we lack a specialistic term we will keep on using this expression even when it seems unsatisfactory.

Often, perhaps in the majority of cases, these pieces are more or less easily separable from each other: for example the head and the handle of a hammer, the vamp and the sole of a shoe, the lens and the frame of a pair of glasses. A hammer is a complete utensil (more about this later on); the head and the handle are the "completed pieces" which make it up; the face, the peen, and the eye are the objectemes in which the head consists. The difference between an objecteme and a "completed piece" is clear in cases like these. A stable modification made by man in nonsound matter, endowed with a generic signification and able to be used in various ways, for example a wooden plank of a given form, is an objecteme. A semi-finished product which already lends itself, and is limited, to a particular use or working process, for example a wooden plank that has been reinforced, varnished, and accurately smoothed, and under which legs can be attached to obtain a table, is a "completed piece." Here various objectemes have been joined to each other in such a way as to form units which in turn are immediately able to give rise to finished utensils. In fact, putting two or more "completed pieces" together usually suffices to give us a utensil in its turn complete and ready for use. By this we do not at all mean to exclude that there may be utensils made up of a single "completed piece" (for example, a walking stick made from a single piece of wood, without other additions). However, we must distinguish carefully between utensils made up of a single "completed piece" and the isolated use of a "completed piece," perhaps as a substitute for a utensil which we lack. Nor should we ignore the existence of groups of "completed pieces" which may even be fairly complex but which are not yet organized in such a way as to constitute a utensil proper.

Things are not that simple, however. For expository purposes we have used some examples rather than others, and in so doing the situation has undergone a process of simplification. The combination of matteremes in objectemes, of objectemes in "completed pieces," and of "completed pieces" in utensils is obvious in the case of the hammer as in all artefacts which are at the same time equally simple and equally easy to take apart. It is not at all obvious for other, less simple utensils, or for utensils which are equally simple but not equally easy to take apart. A tree cultivated in the garden, regularly fertilized, pruned, and protected from the cold, is an artefact too. There is a sense in which we can say that a tree in flower is the sum of its own natural growth, plus the fertilizer, the plastic that protected it during the winter, and the pruning operations. But the sense in which we are dealing with component parts which have been pre-produced and then put together is different from that of the hammer. A big oil jar appears to us as a single piece. If we wanted to distinguish "completed pieces," objectemes, and matteremes in it, we certainly wouldn't succeed with the same comfortably discontinuous progression that we find in other cases, and perhaps we would not even succeed in doing it convincingly. Its matteremes have been resolved step by step into objectemes, which have been resolved in turn into "completed pieces," which, without a break in continuity, constitute the finished artefacts, the utensil jar. A plastic toy of a complex shape but stamped out by a single operation does not possess matteremes and objectemes independent from those belonging in an ideal way to the project according to which the matrix used in the stamping machine has been realized. Sailor's knots, from the simplest to the most incredibly complex, are artefacts realized by operating on a single "completed piece"; we can use a longer or shorter stretch of rope, the only limits to this being that there must be enough rope for tying and using the various knots; the objectemes of the rope are a large number of intertwined fibers.

Examples could be multiplied. Those offered here are already sufficient for raising a number of points which limit or alter the notion of "completed pieces," and in part also the notion of objectemes, as well as the relations between the two. There are artefacts produced by letting natural forces develop, or by assisting them. There are others in which no separation or difference can be found between matteremes and objectemes – artefacts, that is, in which the production of matteremes slowly assumes the status of a production of objectemes without a break in continuity. There are still other artefacts in which continuity is to be found in the process by which objectemes become "pieces" of the finished utensil (pieces which are therefore no longer "completed" *by themselves*). Others in which it is difficult or even impossible to distinguish between the level of objectemes and that of "completed pieces." There are also artefacts in which the objectemes that go together to form "completed pieces," or some of these objectemes, can be traced only as *functions* present in the "completed pieces," this being clear sometimes only from the vantage point of the finished utensil. And there are even artefacts where the level of the utensil seems to be reached directly by mere accumulation of matteremes.

All this shows how the level of "completed pieces" – as products at an intermediate stage between objectemes and utensils – may even be a sheer abstraction by which we are trying provisionally to fix some stage of the very complicated processes of material production. At this point it is useful to distinguish various families of objectual sign systems. Some utensils belong to families that we may call analytic, where every "completed piece," so to say by "isolating" itself, tends to remain always the same, as such always distinguishable from all the others; the difference between "completed pieces" and objectemes here tends to disappear. Then there are families where "completed pieces" which are homologous to each other are produced by means of different objectemes. These objectemes carry out the same function (even without having anything else in common) only because of the way in which they are fixed in constant objectual nuclei, that is, in lexobjectemes. And there are families where, instead, the objectemes are the ones that always remain equal to themselves, so that they reappear with the same function in the formation of different "completed pieces" by being so to say pasted on to each other in different ways. The different "completed pieces" can here be reduced to constituent objectemes of a clearly inferior level (this is the family to which the hammer belongs). One of the conclusions to be drawn when we consider the multiplicity of the families of objectual artefacts, is that they harbor remarkable differences in the relations between objectemes and "completed pieces." We can imagine that, given an objectual sign system, the *ratio* between the number of the objectemes and the number of "completed pieces" may be calculated, and that the result may offer an index of the analyticity of the utensils belonging to that family. The closer such *ratio* is to 1, the less one will be able to distinguish between objectemes and "finished pieces," and the more the utensil will be composed directly of objectemes.

These and other similar particularities of the various arts and trades have certainly been well recognized throughout the millennia by their respective master artisans, even though they would set them out and comment on them almost exclusively in their own language, practicing and refining the nonverbal codes of their arts, and verbally talking about them only for the purpose of handing the art down to others. The masters of the verbal arts, shut up as they were in a class isolation which convinced them of the superiority of intellectual over manual labor, certainly did not pay attention to the way in which the master artisans of the nonverbal were aware on their own of what they were doing all the time. Recently things have changed, however. Part of the immense complexity and variety of production seems to have made an impression on the masters of verbal arts also. We face difficulties very similar to the nonverbal difficulties described in the last few pages in the linguistic field as well, just as soon as we begin to deal with "completed pieces" of a level higher than that of monemes, like so-called "words" and other "linguistic units" (syntagms, locutions, dictions, phrases). Thus, for instance, recognized masters of the verbal arts explain how the difference between a completed word and a moneme, for example between the English word *unacceptable* and the three monemes *un, accept,* and *able*, may seem at first glance just as acceptable as instead it turns out to be unacceptable as soon as we try to establish general rules capable of explaining the exceptions and liable to be extended beyond the limits of any individual historical language. This is not the place to take up current discussions about the nature of words and other units in which it may seem convenient to subdivide the spoken chain. The variety of human languages, we must admit, is almost as great as the variety of objectual sign systems – even if we mustn't forget that in the latter very different bodily residues come into play, because their *signantia* are made of multiple substances instead of being limited (perhaps in a slightly monotonous way) to sound (or at the most graphic) substance.

Not directly relevant for the immediate ends of our classification by successive levels – which in turn only has the purpose of setting forth the homology of production – are the different ways in which, in the various languages, distinctions can be drawn within the *continuum* that goes from a word-moneme constituted by a single phoneme up to an extended and complex syntagm. Before going ahead to the level of sentences and utensils, we must only recall one more thing, i.e. that it is within the last two levels distinguished, the second and the third, that the "first articulation" takes place. This is the articulation of utensils and sentences in "completed pieces" and/or objectemes, and, respectively, in words and/or monemes. In a general theory of material production it is necessary to renounce the naïve view that utensils are always and only the combinations of prefabricated pieces – almost as if there were a sort of universal lexicon of such pieces, so that to obtain utensils it would be enough to apply constant rules to equally constant classes of pieces. Contemporary linguistic theory has arrived at a similar renunciation and is now a long way from maintaining that there are rules operating directly upon word-classes and that sentences are generated by applying such rules to all the lovely ready-made words listed in the dictionary. The fact remains that the utensil and the sentence occupy a recognizedly central position in their respective productions and that they are, after all, reducible to simpler elements.

9.2.4 *Fourth Level: Utensils and Sentences*

This is the first level in an order of rising complexity at which we encounter fully finished though still very simple artefacts lending themselves to *uses* or *working processes* which are complete in their turn. Let's call artefacts at this level *utensils*, generalizing the term somewhat; and, respectively, *sentences*. Sentences are verbal utensils, so that it may be said that all utensils divide into material (or, nonverbal) and linguistic (or, verbal) utensils, and that the latter are also called sentences. For clarity's sake, however, we shall mainly use 'utensils' for *material utensils*, and 'sentences' for *linguistic utensils*; and in using 'utensils' for both we shall always imply the clause 'whether material or linguistic,' or 'whether nonverbal or verbal.'

Examples of various types of simple material utensils are hammers, sickles, flags, stilettos, bottles, shoes, handkerchiefs, pots, spoons, pipes, tobacco pouches, cages, stools, chairs; and so are lawns and the trees and bushes in the garden insofar as they comply with the double character of being products of work and objects for use (even if one doesn't usually call them utensils). Simple pieces of more complex machines, like gears or inner tubes of tires are also simple utensils, although they are usually employed only within more complex totalities. Examples of simple sentences are: 'the water is hot,' 'the daisy is a flower,' 'the apple is tasty,' 'the sun will shine,' 'it's raining,' 'Amelia laughed,' 'the children were playing,' 'children like toys,' 'Eve ate the apple,' 'Adam ate the apple too,' 'the snake smiled,' 'hurray for Europe!,' 'down with Europo-centrism!,' 'he came here,' 'come here!,' 'are you coming here?,' 'aren't you coming here?,' 'why don't you come here?,' 'why didn't you come here yesterday?,' 'she didn't want to come,' 'they will not be able to get there,' and so on. These are sentences in the traditional sense. Let us say in traditional jargon that they are all composed of subject, verb, and predicate, or of a subject and intransitive verb, in some cases with slight syntactical complications which are not supposed to involve any necessary reference to *other* sentences.

Simple utensils, whether verbal or nonverbal, present the differential character with regard to previous products, of possessing *in se* the *form* of the use or of the working process to which they lend themselves. Instead, the "completed pieces" and/or the objectemes of which they are made up, although lending themselves to various uses, do not possess this form. With the finished utensil, as simple as it may be, the material productive process has arrived at its first halt; a working cycle has reached a conclusion, though a provisional one. The same can be said for verbal utensils, i.e. for simple sentences: as complex and as diverse as their genesis may be in the various languages, sentences possess, differently from words and/or monemes, the form of the use to which they lend themselves – whether it is a question of using them just as they are as messages, or instead of combining them with other simple sentences to obtain complex sentences and then discourses. If I say 'laughed' I don't yet know how was laughing *or not laughing*, while if I say 'Amelia laughed' I know that a person of the female sex did *not* do any of the many things that are excluded by the indication of the thing she was doing, that is, laughing.

Common to all the pieces of the first three levels (putting it in a unitary way: previous to the utensil, and respectively to the sentence) is the fact that they are not usually used alone; they are not ends in themselves. They are *instrumental pieces* whose ends lie outside themselves, serving precisely and solely the production of pieces of a higher level, beginning with the level which we have here distinguished as the fourth, i.e. with utensils and sentences. Nobody ever set himself the task of producing sixty-six hammer handles without any regard to their respective heads, without at least supposing that somebody else was going to produce the heads; nobody ever went about plowing thirty-three acres of land with the certitude that he would never be able to sow it, or in total ignorance of the existence of seeds. Nobody repeats a given moneme, well identified as such, ninety-nine times without ever going on to combine it with others. When things like this do happen we talk about pathology, or we have to construct very complicated explanatory contexts. We *usually* don't have any use for an isolated word or piece of utensil. It does not at all follow from this that we don't know what their signification or function is. But the idea of the utensil must be operating for anybody to be able to go back to the first level and then come down again through the second and third, following the flux of work, to the fourth, where the realization of the idea itself takes place. In the same way, we can isolate and discuss words and monemes only if we possess the idea of the sentence. In a different sense, however, the utensil and the sentence presuppose their own parts.

The fact is that the notion of what is presupposed must not be made absolute. To begin with, the notion of a generative idea must not be made absolute, as is typical in old and new idealisms, since even the idea that it seems indispensable to possess cannot itself have avoided being formed little by little in the course of social evolution. As far back as we try to go, we will still have to stop at the period in which the type of activity called work appeared on the planet, insofar as the appetite of certain primates was held in check and between their needs and the respective satisfaction of these needs (Hegel) something universal was inserted. It is in fact tautological that there are no *human* ideas previous to homination. It is a little ridiculous to imagine that one fine morning, even if we may concede that he had slept on a fortuitous bed of fronds, a single anthropoid merrily woke up *with* the idea of a sentence or a utensil all formed in his brain. (A geometrical idea, as Husserl says in Appendix III of the *Krisis*, would make the performance particularly stirring; but also the idea of nothing more than a pot would do.) And that that very anthropoid went about realizing his idea by *facing an intact nature for the first time.*

But on the other hand, not even the notion of the elements of the lowest level should be made absolute. For, unless we indulge in a sort of childish evolutionistic mechanicism, it would be almost insane to suppose that first man produced matteremes and phonemes without doing anything else, and only afterwards dedicated himself to the production of objectemes and monemes, passing over to the production of "finished pieces" and words at a still successive stage. And then again, perhaps after having rested for some tens of thousands of years, he made the further step of starting to combine the previous products (which meanwhile had lain there waiting for him) into utensils and sentences.

The central character of the utensil and of the sentence in the process of production, and thus also in the process of social reproduction as a whole, lies precisely in this duality of reciprocity: they each presuppose the pieces that go together in forming them, and are in turn presupposed by them. Of utensils and sentences, and of these alone, we can say that they are the finished items of the lowest level, in which the reciprocity of presupposition is fully present. That is: it is fully present, as we will mention, also in items of a higher level. Moreover it is also present, but not *fully* present, in the relation between monemes and words and between phonemes and monemes, and respectively between objectemes and "completed pieces," and between matteremes and objectemes.

All this amounts to saying two complementary things: the first, that sentences and utensils have been developed together with their own component pieces; the second, that the quality of being utensils and sentences is not an absolute quality but rather a relative quality. There are available sentences and utensils that are always such, but also utensils and sentences that *become* such in given circumstances but stop being such when those circumstances dissolve. Thus the sailor's knots are utensils with respect to the rope that functions as a "completed piece"; but the rope is a utensil with regard to the strands of which it is composed. 'It's a lovely day for fishing trout' is a sentence; but so are, if taken by themselves in given circumstances, 'it's a lovely day,' 'a day for fishing,' 'fishing trout,' and even 'trout!'

These considerations bring us to the next level of our schema.

9.2.5 Fifth Level: Aggregates of Utensils

In addition to simple utensils there are also compound utensils. The notion of compound utensil is in turn a compound notion. Space and time, to which the real responsibility must be attributed for the accidental death of the passer-by hit by the Hegelian roofing-tile, manifest their domination even here. Compound utensils may be implements with multiple uses, which always remain what they are themselves but are built in such a way as to be applicable in different working processes; or they may rest on the joint use of two different utensils which must be applied, either contemporaneously or one after the other, to the same working process, or to two working processes one of which is subordinate to the other or both of which concur to one purpose. Some examples are: a sofa bed, a complete suit made up of trousers, jacket, and vest, simple gardening tools seen as a whole, a group of weights for a scale, a wallet for documents, notes, and coins. In the field of linguistic production we have sentences combined or interconnected in various ways, like those in the following discourse: 'Rome is the capital of Italy, it has more than three million inhabitants, it is situated about halfway between Florence and Naples, it possesses many beautiful monuments, the traffic is terrible there, it is the seat of both the Papacy and the largest Communist Party in the West.'

One soon realizes that the distinction between simple utensils and sentences and compound ones is much more arduous than it may seem at first glance, or than it may emerge in the examination of a single group of examples. If the disjunction of the levels is to be measured on the yardstick offered by such substantial differences as those between matteremes and objectemes (respectively between phonemes and monemes), or the difference between objectemes (or "completed pieces") and utensils (respectively, between monemes – or words – and sentences), we might perhaps decide to renounce distinguishing the fifth level from the fourth. There is not an equally important leap here between simple and complex. What is simple and what is complex with regard to utensils and sentences depends upon too many criteria. Probably only the application of distributional criteria to a single "text" of objectemes or monemes, or even better, to the totality of an objectual or verbal sign system, would permit us at the present stage of research to provisionally stratify categories of utensils and sentences according to a larger or smaller degree of complexity.

Still, once two or more utensils, or two or more sentences which are distinct from each other have been joined in some way for an end which cannot be accomplished by a single utensil or a single sentence, a situation arises which we do not have the liberty to ignore. What we are concerned with here is this, that the two or more utensils or sentences *have entered into a relation with each other*. At a certain point the working process coagulates in an artefact which then remains there like a river-lock or synapse, conditioning every other working process by its own presence. Utensils and sentences are the most typical examples of artefacts endowed with this character. When two or more utensils or sentences are related, the dialectic internal to a single utensil or sentence *begins* to become a dialectic external to each of them. This amounts to saying that a new totality *begins* to form, dialectically posterior to that of the utensil or sentence. The dawning of this new totality had to be pointed out somehow to the reader, and this is the sense of the distinction made between the fourth level and the fifth. As soon as a dialectic *external* to the utensil or sentence has *fully* emerged, we have reached a further level, the sixth: we are, in fact, at the threshold of a fascinating stage, that of mechanism.

Once we have reached and recognized the utensil – either material or linguistic – as the central unit of all production, everything that follows it in order of complexity is a combination of utensils. The property of being useful for something, as we know, does certainly not belong to utensils alone: it belongs to all artefacts, and is the most general matrix for possessing a signification. The utensil is "only" an artefact at an intermediate level, between the first elementary modifications which man brings to nature and his highest constructions. At the same time, the utensil is the definitive sign of the irreversible separation of man from all other animals, not only because it is a finished product of work and requires the dialectic of exchange, but also because, more specifically, it has been obtained through a double selection of instrumental artefacts of a lower level, and therefore presupposes the use of communitary codes. As Hegel says: "The plough is nobler than the immediate pleasures which are procured through it and which are the aims. The tool preserves itself, while the immediate pleasures vanish away and are forgotten" (*Wissenschaft der Logik*).

9.2.6 *Sixth Level: Mechanism*

The first new totality built by man after the utensil is the mechanism. We shall describe a material (nonverbal) mechanism as a *machine*, and a linguistic (verbal) mechanism as a *syllogism*. Machines are utensils combined and organized for an end, endowed with the capability of working in a uniform way, even prescinding from how and where they are used and from who uses them. When it has assumed the rank of a mechanism, the artefact is called upon to carry out a working process which is already present or anticipated in its structure. The relation between working process and structure has become so close that the working process is at this point more or less obligatory; other working processes are excluded because they are impossible, or have an effect incompatible with the one expected, or are absurd. Consider, in the field of material production, the way in which looms "work," and bicycles, record players, lathes, electric saws, typewriters. What we aim at describing here is the system of the differences between such artefacts and the more simple artefacts we have so far discussed as belonging to lower levels. Not that the advent of the mechanism has excluded the worker; it continues to require him. But while at previous levels the worker had to carry out the whole working process himself, here it suffices that he put the machine he has decided to use in motion. Naturally, he has to have learned this too; but the machine functions "on its own," in one way and not in another, according to an operational cycle fixed beforehand. While external material operations done by anyone who uses a simple utensil still have an internal material guide, the working operations of a machine no longer need a guide of this sort for the good reason that they *are* themselves external material operations carried out according to a plan. The functioning of a machine appears as something pseudo-natural which has been generated by society. The machine bears its own programs and imposes them. Man, not satisfied with programming himself as an individual, has come to the point of programming the behavior of pieces of matter external to him. The modifications which a material machine has to be able to bring about in the world if it functions well, are constant and impersonal modifications: the loom always weaves, impersonally. The worker has gone outside of himself, he has inscribed himself in nature, he has ordered her to guide his own working steps.

Between the level of the utensil and that of the mechanism, then, we have a real substantial difference, a qualitative leap due to the formation of a new totality. Just as the totality "utensil" is not reducible to the pieces of which it is composed, neither is the totality "machine." We can of course think of the vanishing point where a utensil is used as a machine; and there can be cases of utensils that so to say shade off into machines as well as cases of machines used as utensils. For example, the literature is uncertain whether to call a plow a utensil or a machine; and the expression 'machine-tool' is in current usage. The complexity of production compels us – as the case arises – not to forget these prudential remarks. Still the new totality of mechanism imposes itself. Using a screwdriver merely as a weight for a scale is not only using it in an improper way, but also wasting it. What need is there to use a specific utensil like a screwdriver for its weight alone, one can ask oneself. But the waste and the regression are immeasurably more serious if the weight is a high precision, water-proof, self-winding watch.

In what, then, does a machine that is no longer a utensil consist? What "additions" must the structure of the utensil receive for a new totality of a higher level to be born? Does a minimal level of mechanism exist beneath which we cannot talk about machines and revert instead to utensils?

I want to hazard an answer, or better a proposal, as abstract as it may sound. So that an artefact may proceed to the rank of a machine, there must be at the start (at least) two pieces which condition each other reciprocally. Each of these two pieces must have a recognizable sense and a precise function. In brief, there must be (at least) two utensils. Now, if the two utensils confined themselves to contrasting with one another, one of the two might take the upper hand, or there might not even be any decisive action between the two. Nothing new would be formed. The two utensils must instead (i) find themselves in *opposition*, and (ii) this opposition must be overcome dialectically, that is, it must give rise to a synthesis. The kernel of mechanism lies precisely in this, that an artefact in the position of synthesis carries out the role of at least two utensils in opposition to each other. The two elements must become three, and binarism give way to dialectic. Let's take it up again. Two utensils act upon each other; this reciprocal action, whether or not it is physically represented by a third artefact of a higher level, is the dialectical sum of the work that the two utensils can carry out separately (or of essential parts of this work). The two elements have become three. When this happens, the mechanism dawns.

Thus, for example, the archer draws the string of a bow and thus bends the wood, storing up energy which will later be discharged all at once into the arrow. In the first phase the string acts upon the wood, in the second, the wood upon the arrow through the string. The string so to say belongs to the bow when it is drawn, and belongs to the arrow when it is released. The string is the mediating element. Although they are processed in such a way as to work together, wood, string, and arrow can be useful for something and be considered utensils each on its own account; but the machine "bow-and-arrow" (one of the most primitive machines) consists of the sum of the *two actions* of drawing and releasing, and cannot be reduced to one of them alone. Notice that the two actions are similar but certainly not identical; indeed, the machine "bow-and-arrow" benefits precisely from the way they differ. They are moreover separated in time; finally, the man who has accumulated energy by drawing the bow can release it at his discretion, triggering the machine without otherwise intervening in the process.

A similar mechanism is to be found in the oar and the rowlock: one rows by applying a force to the arm of a lever, which, resting on a fulcrum, transmits it to the resistance of the water and thus moves the boat. The oar and the rowlock are utensils, the whole made up of the two together is a machine.

Let us consider now the wheel-and-axle and its differences from a mere roller. The roller is among the most primitive of utensils, at the confines of the mere instrument, even when it is produced on purpose. If one uses the trunk of a tree which has been struck down by lightening as a roller, the level of the utensil is not even reached and what one is using is only an instrument which then is abandoned there, left to itself like a cry which serves only once for attracting attention. The roller comprehends in itself the functions of both wheel and axle, but in a still undistinguished manner. In the wheel-and-axle instead the two functions have been externalized for they have been embodied in two materially independent artefacts. An internal dialectic has become external. Man has discovered and extracted it and is by now able to reproduce it and make it work at his orders. At this stage, *post eventum,* he can also look backwards and say that that dialectic was present already in the roller, though in an undistinguished and indeed "undistinguishable" manner. The wheel-and-axle is manufactured according to a plan and carries out its function insofar as the wheel rotates on the axle, which in turn forms one piece with a cart. In this way the cart is easier to push. Because of its exploiting in this way rotary motion, the wheel-and-axle deserves to be considered a primitive machine.

Another example could be that of a pot filled with water and put over a fire of wood which has been arranged under it and lighted on purpose. Much human knowledge already goes into this simple procedure. Used in this way for boiling something, the pot is not just a mere container. It acts on the fire because it arrests the flame and receives it according to its shape and structure; the fire, naturally, acts on it by heating it. The water can be heated by the fire by virtue of the pot; and the pot can avoid getting burned by virtue of the water to which it transmits the heat received from the fire. Pot-and-water is the mediating element. Hot water is the result of the operation within this machine, much as the hurled arrow within the machine bow-and-arrow. An arrow, then, is expected to hit some target as hot water is expected to boil raw food: with these achievements the machine has been successfully applied. There is, then, a reciprocal action between the water-filled pot and the fire which is synthetically overcome by the operation of boiling. It is remarkable that the whole operation is described in terms of what happens primarily to the water. One boils something by putting a water-filled pot and a proper fire in the above relation and letting this elementary machine do its job.

Other primitive machines, just a little more complicated than utensils, are traps, bow drills (both derived from the bow or kin to it), bellows and blow pipes, bolas (which already require a complex play of forces). Generally, all so-called "simple machines" of elementary physics and their derivatives are primitive. Every simple machine is a device in which a resistant force is counterbalanced by a motive force. The machine is the result of *the play* of these *two forces*.

In the field of linguistic production, the difference between the level of mechanism and previous levels can be struck in the bull's-eye as soon as one considers the *syllogism*. The syllogism starts from two sentences (from the enunciation of two propositions), which are put to work together. The conclusion is the dialectical sum of the two premises. The content of the conclusion was present in the premises, but it emerges from them on the condition of their entering into reciprocal action. We cannot have less than three pieces if we want to talk about a syllogism. The elementary form of the syllogism, indeed of the various possible syllogisms, is homologous to the elementary form of the various possible mechanisms in the field of material production. One has to distinguish here in both fields between the study of pure and elementary forms and the study of whatever is actually produced in reality. As they are nonexistent or extremely rare in material production, pure and elementary forms are also rare in the field of linguistic production. This amounts to saying that we are not expected to find and discuss the mechanism only in the formalized study of mechanics or logic, but rather all along the variety of everything that assumes some sort of mechanical power in either field.

For a verbal mechanism to begin emerging, a more or less correct and complete argument, or just any grouping of sentences organized for some end, capable of communicating something in at least a relatively unambiguous way to any interpreter, are sufficient. One important requirement is that a double disconnection take place: the group of sentences must function *regardless* of (i) their immediate, actual use by whoever has emitted them, whether or not he is responsible for having organized them in that way; and (ii) the context they belonged to originally or in which they happen to be placed later on. This means that a given message, usually a non rudimentary one, is already inserted in the structure of the linguistic mechanism in such a way that it cannot avoid being received as such by whomsoever receives it, independently of the circumstances. Or, to put it negatively: we are by now a long way from the contingent and indiscriminate use of a simple sentence for the aims of immediate expressive and communicative contact. The needs that are satisfied by using linguistic mechanisms are sophisticated needs which can only be thought of as forming in a well organized (though "primitive") culture. Sound material has received a type of elaboration which constitutes a new level with regard to all previous levels.

The first linguistic mechanisms probably developed together with the emergence, if not of writing itself, at least of consolidated techniques for the oral handing down of knowledge. One can assume that their development was parallel to the production of the first material machines. If men had not learned to make a group of utensils function by itself, impersonally, it is unlikely that they could have learned to report anything in an equally impersonal way, regardless of the immediate performance of individual linguistic workers i.e. speakers. As we said, any connection among sentences apt to form a whole is sufficient for a linguistic mechanism to emerge. We can see this when examining any narrative passage in which a number of sentences of the factual kind (statements) are linked together in such a way that each of them is specified by the simultaneous presence of all the others and a global effect is obtained. Any grouping of sentences organized in this way functions by itself precisely because it becomes a communicative mechanism which stands alone. A small chain of interconnected sentences, *prima facie*, can seem much more simple than a formal syllogism. The opposite is true. If I say 'it's raining,' 'water gets you wet,' 'I want to go for a walk,' 'I don't want to get wet,' and 'I go back in the house,' I am using several disconnected sentences. But if I say 'I wanted to go for a walk, but as soon as I went out, I came back in again because it was raining,' I communicate in an unambiguous way a remarkable quantity of information which presupposes an already rather crowded network of formal relations between the various sentences. The simple group of sentences 'I wanted to go for a walk, but as soon as I went out, I came back in again because it was raining' already functions as a complete, impersonal, communicative mechanism. This doesn't have anything to do with the fact that it is you or I or somebody else who is making that utterance.

As often in these cases, the field of infantile language learning offers good examples. Whether we are dealing with material or linguistic mechanisms, it takes many months for a child to learn how to make a mechanism that the environment makes available to him function properly. Meanwhile he already knows how to express himself by using phonemes, monemes, words, syntagms, and finished sentences; in the same way that he already knows how to get about with matteremes, objectemes, "completed pieces" of utensils and their aggregates, and finished utensils. The machine and the syllogism, by objectifying the world, mark the advent of rationality.

Going ahead in the direction of increasing complexity, our schema offers four more levels. We can deal with these more rapidly because we have already met all but one of the dialectical leaps which are most important for us. These are the leaps between intact nature and matteremes; between matteremes and objectemes; between objectemes and utensils; between utensils and machines; and thus for linguistic production. We shall examine one more leap, leading to automated machines and program-bearing codes, presently. Apart from such a leap, at the higher levels which remain to be seen we find material and linguistic artefacts a thorough examination of which would take us far beyond the limits of the present essay. Moreover, the complexity of the artefacts renders the distinction between levels more and more uncertain.

9.2.7 Seventh Level: Complex and Self-sufficient Mechanisms

Here we find machines able to carry out multiple working processes. Their difference from simple machines is usually only quantitative, but as such it can be enormous. The whole historical development of technology from the origins up until a few decades ago enters into it. As examples we give automobiles, automatic looms, printing machines, office calculators. In the field of linguistic production we find all artefacts usually described as lectures, speeches, essays, books. Hundreds or thousands of sentences and syllogisms, and respectively of utensils and mechanisms, are organized here with an eye to sets of ends which can vary remarkably from case to case with regard to their different applications. The human performer, however, is still there. For the program to be carried out, the erogation of human labor is still required from beginning to end, though relieved by the presence of mechanism. In other words, there is still, at this level, a difference – which will instead disappear at level nine – between the program and its various executions. A professor can teach the same things, or extremely similar things, an indefinite number of times, repeating the same course. In much the same way, the artisan operator of an automatic loom can always weave according to the same program, producing the same type of material. Not for this is the loom operator reduced to that type of material, or the lecture operator to that course. They both have alternative programs in their pockets. Many different types of material can be woven, and of lectures delivered, by using the same complex mechanism. But further comment on the artefacts belonging to this level is unnecessary for our aims.

9.2.8 Eighth Level: Total Mechanism or Automation

We can consider this level as a development of the level of simple mechanism, from which it is distinguished by a new qualitative leap. It is listed here after the level of complex mechanism because it presupposes its *quantitative* presence, its historical accumulation. One does not get to automation immediately by starting from a simple machine. Between the abacus and the computer there is not only a qualitative leap but also a difference of quantity. We could also say that the quantitative accumulation of technological development has its outlet in a qualitative level of departure. In terms of our schema: level eight is a dialectical return to level six, that is, a recovery of level six at a higher level, and this is made possible by the development described as belonging to level seven.

Here we find *self-regulating* automatic machines, capable of substituting man entirely in complex and protracted working processes which previously were not conceivable as detached from continuous human intervention. Such machines are not made up only of a plurality of complex and self-sufficient mechanisms, like those encountered at the previous level; they also include all the programming necessary for passing from one mechanism to another according to a plan, for example: (i) subjecting a product to successive and independent working processes; (ii) putting semi-finished products aside to take them up again later together with other semi-finished products; (iii) taking account of the fact that each artefact, as soon as it is produced at any given stage of the total program, immediately possesses a reality of its own; (iv) respecting the qualitative leaps whenever they occur; and so on. The elements of the working process and the diverse levels of work are here all part of the machine. It is precisely because of this that at the level of total mechanism the machine is able to substitute man in an entire cycle of production, thus inserting itself in the very process of social reproduction. Think of the *possibility* of a program beginning with geological prospecting and the excavation of minerals and arriving at the stage where airplanes ready for use are manufactured.

Now let us ask the usual question: what do we find in the field of linguistic production that corresponds to a completely automated machine? The interesting answer is that we could even not find anything: it may be that we have already found everything there was to find. In fact, just as soon as we set foot on the ground of material automation, we find ourselves already on the ground of linguistic production as well. At the level of automation material and linguistic production are reunited, as it were, and exhibit their homology up to the point of beginning to resolve it in identity. This happens for *one sector* of linguistic production in correspondence to *one sector* of material production. In other words, there is a sector where the two overlap – the special technical or formal language which is realized in the matter of the machine as an integral part of it. It is the zone of the relations between hardware and soft-ware. The typical case is of course the computer.

Still we can hit on an independent linguistic production at this level as well. It is a question of self-sufficient codes functioning in social reality in such a way as to condition and absorb more or less completely the individuals who use them. If by deliberate abstraction we want to remain on the ground of language alone, we shall be dealing with subcodes or lexicons fed by a historical language: for example, ritual and ceremonial "languages," or literary production (but see level nine). These are portions of historical languages which become specialized for some separate aims forming relatively limited *postlinguistic sign systems* investigated by *semiology* as a sector of *linguistics* (which is, in turn, a sector of *semiotics*).

But as soon as we give up the abstraction of an independent language and widen our discussion to all verbal and nonverbal social sign systems having to do with the problem under examination, we find *communicative programs*. We shall then have to face not only ritual and ceremonial "languages" as something parasitic on a historical language, such as the ritual or ceremonial terminology belonging to the Navajo language; but also *nonverbal sign systems* of rites and ceremonies, pregnant with their non-sign residues and carrying all their typical power to absorb and condition the individual – a power often only very partially experienced by individuals at the level of consciousness.

Programs of communication, and sign systems in general, are self-regulating machines of a complexity which is *at least* equal to that of a perfectly automated material machine. When the enormous development of mechanical and electronic technology permitted man to realize these kinds of machines in matter, they were necessarily founded on sign systems proper. This is the sense in which reference to a totally automated machine automatically involves reference to a sign system with *at least* one program contained in it. The same point is more accurately made by saying that totally automated machines, in principle, have been able to develop only because verbal and nonverbal sign systems of an even greater complexity existed already. Machines have been built from the beginning by imitation of such systems. Before mechanical and electronic technology made it possible consciously to manufacture these complex machines in external matter, they *existed socially* – even if mainly at an unconscious level – in the form of verbal and nonverbal sign systems. Now, verbal and nonverbal sign systems require material processes internal to the individual; at the same time, since they are social, they constitute the form which matter has reached as the result of the stratification of human work for tens of millennia.

We insist on the fact that machines have been built from the start by imitating already existing human sign systems also in order to reassert their character as products and servants of man, while at the same time vindicating a structural continuity between producer and products.

9.2.9 Ninth Level: Nonrepeatable Production

We can relegate to this level, in both fields of production, artefacts which are usually considered *original*. While using the term 'original,' however, we are not entering into questions of value (whether artistic or of any other kind). The term is used only descriptively, the assumption being that there must be a recognizable kernel of objective originality at a stage less complicated than the stage at which any question of value is usually raised. One doesn't even begin talking about the original value of a shovel or of the sentence 'it is raining.' Original production in the descriptive sense is in the first place a single person's or individual group's production, projected and realized only once for ends and through modalities which are unique and, at the extreme, unrepeatable. The program is set out in the act of its realization; or, the model is one with the single token produced. In the field of material production this is the case of "unique prototypes." Instead of unique prototypes we may also have a very limited number of tokens, but then each token is cared for and modified individually, bears variants which are all original, and can itself be proposed as a prototype. This type of production is exemplified by a very special automobile or yacht made-to-order; an ocean liner or a nonconventional dam; or, at a higher level, enterprises like the transfer of the temple of Abū-Sìmbel following upon the creation of Lake Nasser. Altogether, every artefact which is the final result of purposely projected and realized working cycles and possesses a unique character can be described as belonging to this level.

In the field of language, this is the place of literary and scientific production viewed as the construction of special languages; while the production of nonverbal arts as well as that part of scientific production which cannot be reduced to scientific languages, exemplify nonrepeatability and originality within the respective nonverbal sign systems. It is worthwhile to add that the printing of the works of a poet leads us completely outside of the level under examination. The production of books is a production of tokens according to a material program and does not have anything to do with the production *of the text* (Macherey). The poet realizes his model in the very act in which he realizes the unique token of the model. The typographer takes only the nonsign body of the text as the model to be reproduced, while the text as such remains the unrepeatable model of itself. If things weren't like this, misprints would be welcome, or at least they would not arouse protest. With the necessary variations, much the same would hold good for the production of any original artefact as distinguished from the various ways in which it can be reproduced. That, on the other hand, any "original" literary text is the expression of a social group even without the author's knowing it, so that the author is in the position of acting as an individual channel for a collective work (Goldmann), confirms the social character of original production itself.

We can attempt to say that we find here a dialectic between levels not dissimilar from that found for automation. The products of level nine are a further development of those of level seven, but they are made possible by the quantitative accumulation of products of level eight. Even without entering into questions of esthetic or other assessment, there is something more to an original book than to a book which has only been compiled. It is in comparison with a current, average assembly line car that a special model Ferrari is something new; and if Nicholson, Stephens, or Harlé accepted to project and build a yacht for the America's Cup, it wouldn't cease being a yacht because of such special and highly competent planning. But the original book, the special model Ferrari, and the yacht for the America's Cup, because of their self-contained character and perfection, also presuppose the developments of total mechanism. This, at first glance, seems clearer in the field of material production than in that of linguistic production; but it becomes clear here too as soon as we recall how total mechanism was operating in the form of subcodes or lexicons even before it was able fully to manifest itself in the form of artefacts which are deliberately planned and manufactured in the external material world. This is the sense in which we say that every poet has his own self-contained and self-sufficient language; or that the Pyramids, the taming of the Yellow River, or mass anti-polio vaccination, are unique phenomena. In other words, original production arises in both fields as a sign subsystem which conveys in its way a vision of the world, partial as this may be, offering to interpretation all the richness of the layers accumulated in it.

9.2.10 Tenth Level: Global Production

We will only say a few words about our tenth and last level, although it is the one upon which one might enlarge the most. It is a widely varied level, or perhaps it is not just one level at all, but many; for our purposes, however, we don't need to examine them one by one. Let us locate here all artefacts that result in one way or another from the work of any historically real "productive unit." So we'd better have a look at this last notion. A productive unit can be a man, a more or less wide and/or permanent social group, a whole culture; the widest productive unit one can think of is mankind as the totality *hominum sapientum*. In other words, the overall production of a single individual, of various social groups, of various cultures, of mankind as a whole can be examined.

Social sign systems, whether verbal or nonverbal, belong by right to each of the last three levels we have distinguished. As we saw, they already appear at the level of complete mechanism; their originality and unrepeatibility show that it is convenient to consider them at level nine too; finally, their global character makes them an appropriate object of study for anybody who wants to see things from the point of view of productive units. A culture as a whole is a system of sign systems, a sort of enormous historical "language" transmitting messages to whom it may concern. That a whole sign system may be viewed from the outside is apparent, if only we concentrate in the appropriate manner on even very simple cases. A glance at a written page, without really reading and retaining anything of it, suffices for us to decree what language it is written in (provided we are at least a little acquainted with it, of course); and there are artefacts one single token of which suffices for the identification of a material culture. By considering, moreover, how a simple artefact abandoned in a desert place does inform us of the fact that man has worked near there, we can glimpse the methodological possibility of examining from the outside even the total production of humanity. A single artefact appears to be sufficient for distinguishing man not only from the other animals but also from everything nonhuman which has ever existed on the planet.

We mustn't forget that all these are comments made about *provisionally distinguished levels in an artificial schema*, the aim of which is to exhibit progressive homological complications of production in two expressly privileged fields. The *level of complication* at which *complete* sign systems begin to appear shouldn't be confused with the items that every sign system must include. A sign system does not *consist* only of automated mechanisms, but also of artefacts of previous levels. Verbal and objectual sign systems are already present in reality as soon as sentences and utensils begin to develop. As for organic sign systems (using the human body as the *locus* of codes), it would seem that they begin to form at even lower levels. It remains to be seen, however, whether or not they possess at least the two articulations that lead to sentences and to utensils and are therefore typical of the initial phases of verbal and objectual sign systems. But a structural comparison between the production of utensils and sentences and the production of "organic artefacts" lies entirely outside the scope of the present enquiry.

Which is, in conclusion, the relation between (i) a verbal sign system and a nonverbal sign system of an objectual type, and (ii), the homological schema of linguistic and material production? We shall try to say that the schema is a sounding-rod inserted vertically into any sign system and describing its stratification, with no claim to describing its width and coverage, as well.

Meanwhile, a table allowing a comprehensive glance at our ten levels may be of help for grasping some of their interconnections.

9.3 Plurality of Articulations

Let's examine one essential character of the homological schema of production again. Some passages between levels require proper qualitative leaps, others do not; or at least, some of the qualitative leaps are decidedly more important than others. The most important qualitative leaps are: from intact nature to matteremes and phonemes (the schema begins with matteremes and phonemes as *first results* of work); from matteremes and phonemes to objectemes and monemes; from objectemes and monemes to utensils and sentences; from utensils and sentences to mechanisms and syllogisms; from mechanisms and syllogisms to automated machines, that is, to nonverbal and

ARTICULATIONS

Artificial Scheme of Progressive Complexity	Material Production	Linguistic Production
Zero level: intact, unworked-upon nature	material nonsound substance	material sound substance
First level: presignificant items	matteremes	phonemes
	intermediary-noise	
Second level: irreducibly significant items	objectemes (lexobjectemes or morphobjectemes)	monemes (lexemes or morphemes)
	instrument-cry	
Third level: "completed pieces"	"finished pieces" of utensils; syntagms, expressions, parts of speech, phrases in the "language of things"	words; syntagms, expressions, parts of speech, phrases
Fourth level: utensils and sentences	simple utensils, i.e. material sentences	simple sentences, i.e. linguistic utensils
Fifth level: aggregates of utensils	compound utensils	compound sentences
Sixth level: mechanism	machines of a simple type, i.e. material syllogisms	syllogisms, organized groupings of interconnected sentences: i.e. linguistic mechanisms
Seventh level: complex and self-sufficient mechanisms	self-sufficient mechanisms	lectures, speeches, essays, books
Eighth level: total mechanism or automation	automated machines	subcodes and lexicons (postlinguistic)
	objectual and verbal program-bearing codes	
Ninth level: nonreportable production	special constructions, unique prototypes	"original" literary and scientific production
	objectual and verbal program-bearing codes	
Tenth level: global production	all objectual sign systems of a "productive unit"	all verbal sign systems of a "productive unit"

verbal program-bearing codes. Extrapolating these five levels means further simplifying an already simplified schema, paring it to the bone. This further simplification is useful for a new order of reflections which were already implicit in the exposition of the schema, and which we want do delineate more clearly now. As we shall presently see, even the schema "pared to the bone" appears to be a relatively complex one if we compare it to current tenets on the same basic issues.

For each of the levels in which a qualitative leap is realized, the artefacts, whose production is made possible by that leap and whose structure is characterized by it, so to say *pour out of the productive process* and *stay there waiting*. Let us try to see what the real processes are hinted at by these metaphors. Artefacts are all bound together, whatever level they belong to, by the general process of production. There is among them all a continuous dialectical play by virtue of which the modifications brought by work to artefacts of any one of the levels end up sooner or later by reverberating at all the levels. But most artefacts are new totalities superior to the sums of their parts; work is coagulated in them, furnishing them with a skin that opposes a more or less long-lasting resistance to the entry of new influences from the outside. Artefacts tend to remain what they are even when they are used in new productive processes. The more so, of course, they don't lose their properties if they are *not* used. Indeed this is necessary, otherwise any worker wanting to start a new piece of work at a given level wouldn't find anything ready to start working with and would always have to begin anew from scratch. Let us find an expression describing the condition of artefacts that have poured out of the productive process and of their forming groups by levels. *Faute de mieux* we choose *parking lots of artefacts*. New workers learn to use "parked" artefacts in new working processes, or else they simply consume them to satisfy a need. Generally, we use artefacts leaving aside the fact that they are arte-facts, i.e. products. The consumer goes to the parking lot, gets his car, and goes on about his business. A dialectical terminology avoids in its way the anticlimax introduced by talking about parking lots and cars: the artefacts are assumed "in their new immediacy," "in themselves and by themselves."

That artefacts pour out of the productive process, arrange themselves in parking lots, and are used in themselves and by themselves, is particularly evident when we are dealing with artefacts destined for immediate consumption (even if it should never be forgotten that *consumption is production anyhow*). One does not work any more on food which is ready to be eaten, if not in the possible but not essential sense, which is also an attenuated one, that usually men eat according to ceremonial or ritual programs. The parking lot of all food ready to be eaten is available to the market. The parking lot of all "units" ready to be used is available to the linguistic market. Less evident is the fact that there are parking lots of artefacts not destined for immediate consumption. If we take another look at the homological schema of production, concentrating on the five levels at which a qualitative leap occurs, we find that we have to list the following *parking lots of artefacts*:

– parking lot of matteremes and (respectively) of phonemes;
– parking lot of objectemes and monemes;
– parking lot of utensils and sentences;
– parking lot of mechanisms and syllogisms;
– parking lot of automated machines and of nonverbal and verbal program-bearing codes.

We are dealing with parking lots which are very different from each other in nature, structure, and use. Many considerations of a descriptive type could be made about them. For example, the lower the level, the more intersubjective is the parking lot in principle. A polished stone is less culture-bound than a mortar and pestle, and a simple mortar and pestle is less culture-bound than a carpenter's tools. Japanese and Italian phonemes are similar even if the two languages are very different. The most vast and multiform parking lots can be found at the fourth and the sixth levels of the schema: a curve developing along the axis of the abscissa and indicating the extent of the parking lots, would have its highest ordinates at these levels. The wealth and variety of forms, in fact, are greater for utensils and mechanisms and for sentences and syllogisms than they are for matteremes and phonemes at one end of the schema and for codes and programs (considered in their formal abstraction) at the other.

But these and other similar descriptive features, on which it would be easy to harp at length and minutely, are not central to our argument. What interests us here above all is that we have five levels of parking lots of artefacts, each of which is *composed of* artefacts of the previous level *plus* the work done to compose them, and will serve (together with new work to be done) to compose artefacts of the subsequent level. As we know, the process often takes place through quantitative accumulations realized at intermediate levels, i.e. at levels that are not marked by qualitative leaps themselves, or not by equally decisive ones. Thus objectemes and monemes are composed of matteremes and phonemes; utensils and sentences are composed of objectemes and monemes; mechanisms and syllogisms are composed of utensils and sentences; automated machines and nonverbal or verbal program-bearing codes are composed of mechanisms and syllogisms (and in them the two branches of production approach one another again up to the point of appearing reunited: the homology finds a ground upon which it may be resolved in identity).

At this point we must ask ourselves if the expression 'composed of' has the same sense at the various levels; or, in Oxonian jargon, we may ask what its "logic" is. But we'd better transform this way of putting it into a question about the real processes under examination, as distinguished from a question about the ways in which we describe such processes. The main question, then, is the following. Is the dialectic presiding over qualitative leaps always the same at the various levels, or is it at least a similar dialectic? Or, rather, is it a dialectic that changes substantially with the changing of levels? For example, when we pass from the level of sentences to that of syllogisms, are the operations presiding over this passage substantially similar or dissimilar from the operations by which we passed from the level of monemes to that of sentences? Is the work which brings together sentences in such a way as to build a syllogism the same sort of work which is applied to the task of bringing together monemes in such a way as to build a sentence? The answer to such questions – apart from anything that might be said at the level of linguistic usages, whether popular or donnish – is that *it must necessarily be a similar dialectic as far as the substantial part of the whole process is concerned.* And the substantial part is nothing else than the *articulation of work*. We know that all the objectemes and monemes we use are produced with a few tens of matteremes and phonemes. Moreover we know that it is with a few thousand objectemes and monemes that utensils and sentences we use are produced. *Hic Rhodus, hic salta.* Does a process of the same kind obtain when we produce mechanisms and syllogisms by means of utensils and sentences, and then automated machines and program-bearing codes by means of mechanisms and syllogisms? Is there in these two cases as well a parking lot of artefacts upon which production can draw – a parking lot, we mean, which can be held under practical, operational control because of its being numerically *limited* (even though it may be a very high number)? Obviously yes, as we have seen during the exposition of the schema. Thus the problem is resolved already. But it is worth our while to look at its facets a little longer.

The conventional reply to the last two questions we asked sounds more or less like this (try and see). The two questions don't make sense for language because there is an "infinite number" of sentences which are produced by the "free creative activity of individual speakers." So there is no parking lot of sentences, leaving alone syllogisms. As far as material production is concerned, the problem is not even raised. Thus *the progression of production is interrupted* on the linguistic side at the level of sentences, without even taking further developments into account. On the side of material production, the progression is *not even introduced.* In this way various pieces of knowledge are left to wander about on their own, without any attempt to bring them together; indeed, obstacles are erected against their unification. Suffice it to think of the programs governing every form of verbal and nonverbal communication. These programs are artefacts of the highest level and as such they presuppose the progressive and organic play of all previous levels. How in the world could we ever arrive at a theoretical foundation for the simultaneous presence of (i), the common use of language understood as the *free* production of sentences, and (ii), the programs *governing* every form of verbal communication from a level of elaboration higher than the level at which the very production of sentences takes place?

These are basic difficulties. In order to overcome them, or at least to face them on their proper theoretical ground, it is necessary to make great sacrifices, leaving the security of the sown field and hazarding into virgin territory. Let's say this, then. *Even in the case of utensils and sentences, and then of mechanisms and syllogisms, we can only be dealing with dominable parking lots which are numerically limited and subject to precise organizational choices.* Otherwise, it would be simply impossible to proceed to a higher level and produce more complex artefacts, for the techniques which are used in this as in any production could never have been invented and much less transmitted to new workers. Techniques exist only for what is selected and determined. You don't build anything with the indeterminate, or worse with the infinite.

Let's take up again the important case of sentences as materials for the construction of syllogisms. Sentences are all reducible in principle into tribes, families, and subfamilies, the structures of which are transmitted from generation to generation as an essential part of linguistic knowhow. Syllogisms can be constructed by man because he has succeeded in isolating some typical cases of sentence-making, choosing them from among all possible sentences and conferring an organization upon them. This is the most important point, lending itself to generalization as regards the constructive relations between artefacts of all the levels. As we saw in dealing with the level of mechanism, a syllogism occurs when at least two sentences are put in opposition and this opposition is overcome dialectically (binarism thus giving way to dialectic); and moreover, when one prescinds from both the immediately existential use of the sentences and the context they happen to belong to. In this way a permanent and autonomous formal relation, the syllogism, is instituted among sentences. Well then, we do not see any difference in principle between these operations of selection, freezing, and organization of reciprocal relations and the operations that govern the formation of linguistic artefacts of either a lower or a higher level.

Production is articulated in *four* main successive phases, those conjoining the *five* listed parking lots of artefacts. Production – material as well as linguistic – rests on a *quadruple articulation*. In order to grasp this articulation it is necessary to move continually back and forth along the schema. Articulation in fact is the relation of any given artefact to a number of artefacts that precede it; as such it is a passage from unity to plurality. This passage is possible, however, and makes sense, only insofar as there is a previous possession of that unity. Thus we shall say that every objecteme and moneme *is articulated in* a certain number of matteremes and respectively of phonemes. This means that *in order to build* a given objecteme or moneme, some matteremes and phonemes *are required* which have been selected and isolated from all other possible matteremes and phonemes and organized in a certain way. Work is necessary, too, of course: and indeed, the notion has already been introduced in terms of 'building' in general, and, specifically, in terms of 'selection,' 'isolation,' and 'organization.' Another aspect of articulation is that when we have an objecteme or a moneme, we have at the same time certain matteremes or phonemes. And since *these* matteremes and *these* phonemes do not and cannot exist without *the other* matteremes and phonemes that are produced by the community, the notion of the parking lots of matteremes and phonemes turns out to have been already introduced as well. Considerations of the same sort are valid for all the other articulations, up to the highest level. We shall also say, therefore, that automated machines and program-bearing codes are articulated in mechanisms and syllogisms. That is, certain sets of mechanisms or syllogisms which have been selected and isolated from all possible others and organized in a particular way are necessary for the construction of any given automated machine or program-bearing code. Thus when we have an automated machine or program-bearing code we already have those mechanisms and syllogisms and therefore we already have their relative parking lots.

Maintaining the existence of a quadruple articulation, and maintaining it both for the field of linguistic production and for that of material production, does not mean extending it to all possible sign systems; but it does mean moving away radically from the common doctrine according to which only a double articulation exists, and only with regard to language (of which it is held to constitute a differential characteristic, perhaps the most important one). To conclude this long essay, let us have a look at the two points separately.

First point. It is still a current conception that language is a system of words and expressions *by means of which* the speakers of a given linguistic community "express feelings and thoughts," "analyze experience," and "communicate with each other." This amounts to saying that language is an instrument which we use for further ends. But if that is what language is, then the place for locating the other three parking lots we distinguished is outside of language. An alternative would consist in extending the notion of language to include all five parking lots. In this case the notion of language would be stretched until it becomes identical with the notion of "verbal sign system." A verbal sign system, in fact, includes all five parking lots by definition, for it consists of codes and messages and thus of the program for realizing the messages, which also means that all lower-level parking lots are already involved in its construction and, of course, continue to be used.

Neither of the alternatives – restricting language to the first two parking lots or extending it to all five – seems sufficient to us. The problem is, instead, how to tie language to work in the proper ways. The precariousness of the Saussurian notion of individual *parole* begins to emerge here. It is a very partial conception of linguistic work, able only to put a two-parking-lot language in motion, but certainly not capable of justifying higher-level parking lots. If *parole* is individual work, whatever factor there is which binds the innumerable individual *paroles* in communion, thus making communication possible, remains totally unexplained. One doesn't understand how on earth the parking lots of sentences that all speakers learn to produce univocally, and then also more complex parking lots, were ever produced. Really, one doesn't even understand how the first two parking lots have ever been produced. There have been well known attempts to overcome these difficulties by enriching the two parking lots attributed to language (*langue*) with operative and generative rules and by introducing intermediate ideas for the purpose of linking individual *parole* to language (*langue*) as a collective patrimony. One of these "linking ideas" is the contradictory invention of a "speech pact" to which already-speaking-individuals adhere. The Saussurian opposition between a two-parking-lot collective *langue* and an individual *parole* has thus been substantially accepted. Remedies to its deficiencies have been proposed in the form of various corrections or integrations made for the purpose of sewing up again precisely that which had been irremediably lacerated from the beginning.

In order to put all the five parking lots of linguistic artefacts in motion, the overall power of linguistic work is required. According to the present writer, the first notion to introduce is that of a *collective parole or speech*. Making some sort of "terminological decision" and leaving it at that is of course of little importance. The basic task consists in *not interrupting* the continuity of articulations in favor of something abstract. And this instead is exactly what happens when language is postulated as a two-layer system of phonemes and monemes and all the rest of linguistic production is left vague; or else one "passes the buck" to other disciplines with the self-congratulatory excuse that it doesn't enter into the field of linguistics; or again, one loads it all onto that mean slice of linguistic work which is individual *parole*. Whether in the course of a reconstruction of the continuity of linguistic production the notion of language turns out to be extended, or whether its restricted notion is arranged within a vaster organism, may also be, from the point of view of basic theoretical decisions, a secondary question. What is important is to turn to the primacy of work.

The reconstruction of the totality of the articulations is intended to be a move toward a more faithful and pregnant representation of reality. A child immediately learns together with words the use of the most common sentences, just as he immediately learns the use of the simple utensils currently employed in the community to which he belongs. Moreover, a child does not just learn the use of sentences and utensils, but that of mechanisms and syllogisms as well, with a remarkable homology in this learning process of his. Thus he learns, for example, to recognize the generic sense of a little discourse, that is made to him with the purpose of inducing him to behave in a certain way, homologically to the way in which he learns the generic use of an everyday mechanism, let us say a watch. He will be able to use the watch and the little discourse in a superficial but practically adequate way much before he begins to look at all into the way they function, and much before he even glimpses anything of the principles guiding the construction and functioning of such complex mechanisms. Simple sentences present themselves to whoever is learning to speak together with their combinations – 'it's raining,' 'I'm going outside,' and 'I'll get wet' present themselves together with 'if I go outside when it's raining, then I'll get wet.' In a homological manner, complex machines present themselves together with the simple machines and with the utensils that make them up. Finally, the child immediately learns to execute, or at least to comply with, verbal and nonverbal programs so much so that one can assume that he is entangled in them from birth (Ivanov, Lotman, etc.). It is necessary to take account of all this in a unitary way and not by bits and pieces. We must acquire the capacity to face both philogenetic and ontogenetic homination in their totality.

There is a question which has been hiding between the lines so far, and which may seem futilely numerological, or at the most intellectually elegant; we want, instead, to attribute much importance to it. While adding *three* parking lots to the two which are usually recognized in language, we have only added *two* articulations. We have brought the parking lots of linguistic artefacts from two to five, but the articulations from two to four. Let us take a look into the reasons of this apparent asymmetry.

According to the doctrine of linguistic double articulation, sentences produced by speakers are traced back to parking lots of monemes in which they are articulated, but they aren't seen as forming a parking lot themselves. The speaker, according to the doctrine, produces sentences "freely" and in "infinite" number. Rules do exist which he has to follow somehow; but they are either immanent in the production of sentences – or they are biological features of the human organism, and with this the progression of production is interrupted in the most radical way. Consequently, parking lots of a level higher than that of monemes (or at the most of words) wouldn't exist. But our highest parking lot is instead that of program-bearing codes. Therefore we have to ask ourselves whether or not, above codes and programs, there may be working processes that have to program-bearing codes the same type of relation that sentences are supposed to have to the parking lot of monemes. If they did exist, they would be working processes not belonging to any parking lot but still traceable to the parking lot immediately previous to them, that of program-bearing codes. Then there would be a fifth articulation (to tell the truth, this would be the first articulation, all the others descending by one unit along the numerical scale), consisting in the articulability of verbal behavior (freely produced in infinite number) in what we could call "programmatic units," in the same way that sentences can be articulated in "meaningful units" (monemes). *Prima facie*, such an hypothesis would seem to fit into what is known about the programs of communication and their being reducible to sequences or aggregates of fixed and conventional units (Pike, Scheflen, etc).

The temptation to admit this fifth (first) articulation is remarkable, also because it may appear as necessary for the justification of the free human use of the codes and programs themselves, beginning with the work consisting in their production. We'd better renounce this temptation, however. Accepting the existence of behavior of a level higher than that of the parking lot of the highest level, does not so much mean affirming the freedom of that behavior as deferring to another parking lot the property of belonging to the highest possible level. In other words, we only make this property slide, leaving the rest as it is. Let us explain. Communication *is* the execution of programs. Behavioral units in which the behavior of those who execute programs is to be articulated, are by definition units of a *lower* level. By opening the door to a further level of linguistic production, we would then find an impossible choice in front of us. On the one hand, we could not avoid formulating the pseudo-problem of a further level, still higher than the level just produced; that is, we would run the risk of an infinite regression. On the other hand, it could happen that in order to get around the regression, we might not know how to refute a conception of man – of his most intimate and motivating portion – as an entity winging its way above his own parking lots of artefacts (to which, however, with a further contradiction, we would still have to resort for an explanation of what man himself was). But this would mean that we hadn't understood anything at all about communication as the execution of programs and that we were regressing to a romantic vision of human activity.

Let us therefore refuse these philosophical complications *toto corde* and state that the freedom of human behavior cannot reside in something that wings its way above all the parking lots of artefacts, but rather in conscious and original ways of using units of any level – up to the point of modifying from within the verbal and nonverbal sign systems to which we cannot avoid belonging. The very work that has produced codes, programs, and whole sign systems, if it is work, cannot have been exempt from programs. Original planning itself is either new use of sign systems, or doesn't make sense. If we want to find the fount of all human programming, we must look for it in needs and in the work done for their satisfaction, certainly not in something human precedent to work. Consequently, it seems more correct (and healthier) methodologically, to include all human behavior within the apparatus of the five parking lots here distinguished and the four articulations which join them internally.

All human communication takes place by using the parking lots of artefacts and the articulations *that can be distinguished*. Beyond the parking lots of artefacts and the articulations that can be distinguished, communication does not obtain. This is a definition, or if you prefer, a characterization, of communication, made in terms of elements that must be working together for it to exist at all. It should be clear that we are not in the least defending *a certain number* of parking lots and articulations. Empirical research and the work of theoretical systematization can always bring us to modify our descriptive data and their arrangement. For example, in the examination of a given language or objectual sign system, we might find it convenient to single out the level of words and "completed pieces," recognizing in it a qualitative leap as important as the leaps occurring at the levels we have selected in this essay, our present aim being the construction of a schema as general as possible. When this is the case, the parking lots will become six, and the articulations five. The same thing can happen with aggregates of sentences and of utensils. And so on. Questions of this sort should always remain open. What we have to defend, instead, from a general theoretical point of view is the notion of the *system of all parking lots*. This system should be viewed as an autonomous and irreducible block of interdependent levels. We are moving away from the conventional doctrine of the articulations also in this: that we don't defer to anything external, on the contrary, we contend that everything that happens within a given field is in principle capable of being explained with the conceptual instruments that define the field itself.

Second point. Not only is the articulation quadruple instead of double. It exists, and is quadruple, also in the field of material production. In this field as well there is a full realization of that thrift which linguists rightly insist on when they observe how a few thousand monemes suffice to produce an enormous number of sentences, and a few tens of phonemes suffice for the production of all the monemes of a language. If a utensil entirely new in all of its constituent parts, that is, different from every other artefact, were necessary for every material working process; and still worse, if entirely new modifications, different from all the others, were necessary for the construction of the parts of every distinct utensil, then there would never have been anything like technological development on the planet. This would simply mean that man would never have learned to dominate nature. Instead we know that a utensil is composed of objectemes which are in turn composed of matteremes, and that objectemes and matteremes have the homological level of monemes and phonemes.

The structural similarity of the parking lots of the same level permits us to find and recognize more or less the same artefacts in all equally developed cultures. This happens insofar as the artefacts are assimilated to one another by means of an operation which we could baptize "material translation." One finds, for example, that a given group of objectemes, taken as a whole, corresponds to another group of objectemes with a completely different origin. One can say then, that two different utensils belonging to two different cultures are equivalent: one of the two utensils has been "translated" into the other, so that it can be employed in the place of the other. Even the observation that the form of the *signans*, since it is articulated into phonemes void of *signata*, withdraws from the value of its corresponding *signatum* and in this way acquires a greater stability (Martinet), is an observation that is equally valid in the field of material production. Matteremes, in fact, as modification of the first level, are not significant by themselves. A mattereme is a modification that anyone can bring to formless material even independently of the use that he may make of it, if and when he combines it with other such nonsignificant elements, in this way forming a significant unit, i.e. an objecteme, which may in turn become the part of some utensil. A mattereme, moreover, is a stable modification. A piece of wood which has been cut and a polished stone remain cut and polished independently of the use that may be made of them – indeed, independently of their being later used or not used at all.

10. Sign Systems and Social Reproduction*

10.1 Social Reproduction as the Principle of All Things

Social reproduction is the whole set of the processes by means of which a community or society survives, develops, or at least continues to exist. The notion has strong economic connotations, as individuals must, as a minimum, eat, drink, and protect themselves from inclement weather. Thus, the heart of social reproduction lies in the production of goods for immediate consumption (at the initial level, in the appropriation of goods offered by nature). But there is no way in which, even at the primordial level, the activity producing such goods could entirely cover social reproduction. Even to satisfy immediate material needs, individuals must unite in groups, and by so doing they put other social processes into action at once; and the material goods themselves are not all consumed immediately, even at an elementary stage of social development, but rather, for the most part, they are put aside ("accumulated") for later consumption. This too involves forms of organization among the individuals of the group. All the principal processes acted out in society, and not just those which are directly productive, together form an integral part of social reproduction from the very beginning.

10.1.1 Social Reproduction, Social Practice, and History

How should we relate the notion of social reproduction to other very general notions which seem to indicate more or less the same field? We shall

---

* This essay [R.-L. 1978b] is Chapter 12 of *Between Signs and Non-signs*, a forthcoming collection of published and unpublished essays in English, 1952-1976. [For further information on this project as it was originally elaborated by R.-L. and as it has now been realized with the present volume, see my introduction.] Some of the ideas discussed herein appeared in Italian in "Criteri per lo studio ideologico di un autore," 1976[c], Sections 3 and 4 are also used in Part I of the booklet *Ideologia*, forthcoming [cf. R.-L. 1978c]. See also, in English, "Introduction to *Semiosis and Social Reproduction*," 1977. [This volume, Chapter 8.] This essay, however, is independent from the above texts, and aims at giving a short but self-contained exposition of the working of sign systems within social reproduction.

endeavor to answer this question by considering two other notions: *social practice* and *history*.

If we examine certain commonly used phrases, such as 'men make history,'[1] 'the forces which move history,' and others similar, we find history in the position of complementary object, as a product *of* work exercised *by* men, according to ways, and through instrumental phases which repeat themselves. The notion of social practice seems instead to refer predominantly to what men *do*, to their operation as members joined together in the community. Social practice is seen as the practice *of* men *as* subjects *of* history, as operators *upon* nature and *upon* themselves. This sort of reference considers men in and of themselves (by dialectical suspension from the rest), which means to a certain extent detached from nature. So much so that one of the essential moments of social practice is the appropriation and exploitation *of* natural resources. Not even nature is excluded from the notion of social reproduction, as society must use that which nature offers to it in order to reproduce itself.

From these considerations (there are others which are here left aside), it would seem possible to group these three notions as moments of social reality in general according to a tripartition based upon the elementary scheme of productive labor (workers and work; materials and instruments; products):

Social reality,

> *social practice*: work carried out by men in society. It uses men themselves, and nature already modified by them (that is past history), as both materials and instruments.
>
> *social reproduction*: an enormous machinery, that is, an instrumental organization, invented and constructed by men to produce history. The machinery comprises both the men themselves and nature, which are used within it as both materials and instruments.
>
> *history*: a product of social practice, produced by means of social reproduction; history, in its turn, comprehends men and nature as products.

Note that this tripartition comes from an immediate cut in the historical process of social reproduction. It represents synchronically every given instant of this process. The previous product is always already present both as material and as the instrument of new work. In this way it is possible to eliminate the apparent contradictions between such commonly used propositions as 'men ... who produce history,' 'men ... as instruments of superpersonal forces,' 'men ... as historical products,' and similar. In producing history, men produce and reproduce themselves by using themselves – *even if on the whole they don't know how*. Many useless squabbles would have been avoided if the elementary scheme of productive labor had been applied dialectically. Everything, in fact, *can* be *either* work, or instrument, or product; and can be the material upon which *new* work takes place.

Various other articulations are possible. As is well known, three essential moments – class struggle, practical domination of nature, and scientific research – are distinguished in social practice. Social reproduction articulates fundamentally in production, exchange, and consumption. We shall return to this below. History lends itself to an immediate tripartition into past, present, and future history, with the present mediating incessantly between past and future. Among other things, this last tripartition permits a clarification of the relationship between conservation and innovation, the real and the possible, ideology and utopia.

For the purpose of this essay, the aspect which interests us most is the instrumental moment represented in the scheme as social reproduction insofar as we can distinguish it from social practice and history. Nevertheless, it must be remembered that the three notions are often used as synonyms, separately, as able to encompass, or at least indicate by connotation, the entire field. Clearly one doesn't exist without the other, and the fact itself that the relationships they summarize are also always temporal, so that it is possible to keep them distinct only by using an immediate synchronic cut, shows how these notions do cover one another almost exhaustively. So it will be useful to adopt the syntagm 'social reproduction,' not just in the function of a *definiens* which accentuates its instrumental aspect, but also in the function of a *definiens* which renders it able to exhaustively represent the totality of which it is a part.

10.1.2 *The Idea of a Catalogue of Social Reproduction*

As soon as we turn our gaze to social reproduction as the machinery that produces history, trying to understand it globally in its essential lines, we remain breathless in front of its enormous complexity. There isn't anything which does *not* belong to social reproduction. This is true both in a descriptive sense and in principle. A descriptive approach to social reproduction would lead to the compilation of some sort of an enormous catalogue of all the principal human activities. This immediately poses the problem of distinguishing principal from secondary activities, and establishing relationships between them.

To begin working systematically on such a catalogue is not impossible, and even though it goes beyond the limits of this paper, it is worth remembering that it would have to include at least the following groups of general categories, as well as a study of their relationships, and working hypotheses about the type of society which would exist if one or another of these categories were to be subtracted from the described totalities.

1. Production, exchange, distribution, modalities of consumption of subsistence goods, beginning, obviously, with food.
2. Choice and use, or construction, of an environment in which the community members can live adequately.
3. Transmission to the children of the social patrimony of language, nonverbal and postverbal sign systems, rituals, folklore, customs, fundamental values, and every other code which is either useful to, or simply used by, the community.
4. Organization of relationships between the community members at all possible levels and for all possible ends.
5. Care of groups of persons in a special condition whether or not these are recurrent: infants, pregnant women, the old, the infirm, individuals who are abnormal or deviant (the latter, obviously, according to the ruling criteria of normality and conformity).
6. Favoring, controlling, making possible, or simply tolerating the transmission and development of other social activities such as the arts, music, literature or oral traditions, philosophies or world views, religions, scientific or prescientific research, various technologies.
7. (Doing other things which have simply been left out of this first list.)

The empirical-descriptive factor inherent in the idea of a catalogue may serve as a corrective to the abstractions and prejudices of models and other solely theoretical constructions. The models and constructions which survive the impact of a complete description of reality will be truly general rather than generic, constructive rather than simplifying.

10.1.3 *Social Reproduction as the Matrix of All Possible Categories*

Here let us turn to see, even if only briefly, in what sense it would be possible to affirm that all things, *in principle*, belong to social reproduction. It certainly isn't an idealistic sense. Social reproduction isn't consciousness, language or thought, but rather a totality of processes which are material in various manners, which really take place upon the planet Earth, and of which consciousness, thought, and language are but the products (see here the work of Trân duc Thao 1973). One is certainly not asserting that rocks and trees don't also exist "on their own account," as "external objects," or – as they used to say – "independently from thought"; nor that geological did not precede biological evolution, or the latter the social, in such a way that the first has a total temporal independence from the second, and the second from the third. The distinction itself between thought and reality is not in the least called into question, and neither are similar traditional oppositions and distinctions. Rather, what is asserted is that any and every object, whatever its order or type of existence, is always individuated, assumed and adopted, within social reproduction. All of these discourses, *beginning with the constitution of their objects*, are human discourses, as such belonging to social reproduction. The same conception of Nature as external to man, that man discovers in himself as a real and conditioning force from birth to death, is always a conception, a way of seeing and interpreting reality: always, in short, an object which man has created with his thought. It is in this sense that Nature is a human invention, unthinkable without Society, and as such it is in its turn conditioned by all that produces and conditions man. This is shown by the fact that there have been and continue to be many different conceptions of Nature. Even when we seek "direct and spontaneous contact with nature," the procession of our thoughts, or even just our feelings and attitudes, follows precise ideological tracks which have been constructed for us by the society we belong to. In other socio-historical contexts the problem of "entering into contact with nature" isn't even posed. Any theory, not just of nature, but also of man, society, history, and so on, is always internal to, never external to, social reproduction. Far from taking place *according* to some theory, social reproduction *produces* and employs theories which serve its own ends.

It is in this sense that social reproduction is the fundamental category, or, better, the matrix of all possible categories. It is the principle, both real and methodological, of all things. This principle is not a mere part of objectified reality, as was Thales' Water; neither is it entire reality reduced to nature, as in every form of naturalism; nor is it something which transcends nature once and for all, as in every type of spiritualism and idealism. The "principle" is the reality itself, as the sum of natural and historical factors: a sum which man has been constructing all the time, that he has been producing and reproducing himself in increasingly complex and conscious forms. This sum is subject to incessant changes in both time and space. These changes are not only obvious to all, but their negation is, in principle, inconceivable. It is impossible to get out of the process which changes in this way. The intention to "describe its events from outside" has no sense, and the sense of the propositions in which such an intention is expressed is, at best, irreducibly metaphorical. In a metaphysical and mystified form, bourgeois thought, culminating in Hegel, had already arrived at this conclusion. Thus the factors which must interest us most are the real forces which in every given case determine the process of social reproduction as the sum of natural and historical factors.

Even if provisional and generic, the conclusions arrived at may perhaps allow the substitution of the tripartite diagram put forward above by the following scheme. To simplify:

Social reproduction,   *social practice* as work,
comprising both social
reality and nature: *machinery* for the production of history with its internal articulations: that is, social reproduction itself seen in its instrumental moment,

history as product.

10.2 The Articulations of Social Reproduction

Given the level of generality of this paper, it is clear that simplified criteria are necessary if something more is to be said about social reproduction. It is a question of finding at the center of social reproduction some distinctions with sufficient content so as not to be vacuous, while being sufficiently formal to allow re-application independently from the incessant variation of socio-historical contents.

The outstanding contribution of historical materialism was the discovery of distinctions of this type; and it continues to develop them. Every system of distinctions obtained by applying appropriate simplifying criteria can take the form of a model for further research. Here we point out three models, distinct among themselves, but nonetheless interconnected, which may be useful to our aims. These are: the articulation of production, exchange and consumption; the opposition between structure and superstructure; and the tripartition of modes of production, sign systems, and ideologies. Whilst the first two models already belong to, and continue to be refined within, already existing disciplines, the third is an attempt at innovation or integration. We must repeat that it is a question of three models which, far from being mutually exclusive, aid each other by throwing into relief in a complementary way, various aspects of the same reality – or, rather, of reality itself.

10.2.1 *Production, Exchange, and Consumption*

The three principal moments of every concrete case of social reproduction are production, exchange, and consumption. It is possible to distinguish these three moments from each other at both the individual and the collective level. Someone who eats an apple is neither buying it nor producing it. One who works at constructing a car is neither selling it nor using it himself. He who buys, or exchanges, or sells any object can do it insofar as he is leaving himself apart as a producer or consumer of that same good. Different complexes of social activities correspond to these different positions of the individuals as the institutional developments of such positions. There are factories and industries; networks of distribution and shops; and consumers. Even though consumption comes to fruition ultimately in an individual act, this does not alter the fact that there are specifically social kinds of fruition, operable only in company, and that the beneficiaries always belong to social groups whose modes of consumption are to a large extent, even in the most minute detail, determined by production and exchange.

Production, exchange and consumption are inextricably connected in a more fundamental sense, as was shown definitively (to fix a date) in Marx's "Introduction" to *Grundrisse* of 1857. They belong to the same totality; one doesn't exist without the other. Their unity is dialectic, which is not to say that they are identical. Given this unity which underlies phenomenal diversifications, to operate in any one of these three moments means, *ipso facto*, operating in the other two. Thus he who consumes promotes production and exchange, he who exchanges promotes production and consumption, and he who produces promotes consumption and exchange. Mediations enter into play so that action in one reaches the other two. These mediations may in reality be slow, and subject to peripheral pulverization and phenomenological proliferation of every type. Nevertheless, it is always a question of preordered and inevitable mediations *in the substance.*

It must be stressed that the three moments do not refer solely to so-called material goods, destined to the physical subsistence of the human individual, but also to the so-called cultural and spiritual goods, which are not immediately material, such as language and other social institutions of every type, value systems, the distribution and organization of individuals within a social system. All is produced, exchanged and consumed. Nothing can subtract itself from being produced, exchanged and consumed. To make a semi-theological side-track: even the world and the angels were produced. Indeed God could be defined as the only Being not produced, as the Absolute Producer. Theogony denies itself. Naturally, all the well-known difficulties, and the well-known oddities and eccentricities follow from this, such as the conception of God as the greatest repressive tyrant, and as absolutely "capricious," because not subject to any conditioning.

It is in the moment of exchange that the principal root of communication lies: communication here being the exchange of both verbal and nonverbal messages. Just as with everything else, messages must be produced and consumed as well as being simply exchanged. Thus we have, *within the general dimension of exchange*, a *production*, an *exchange*, and a *consumption of messages* (see here "Omologia della riproduzione sociale" [R.-L. 1972c], "Articulations in Verbal and Objectual Sign Systems" [R.-L. 1974e], and Chapter 2 of *Linguistics and Economics* [R.-L. 1975b]). It is possible to introduce subdivisions of the same type for the other moments. In the third model below we will return to the moment of exchange of messages, reintroducing the notion of sign systems.

10.2.2 Structure and Superstructure

A fundamental opposition is given within social reproduction, which cuts across the tripartite scheme of production, exchange and consumption, and divides social reproduction into two coexisting halves. On one side we have the *modes of production*, which are in their turn subdividable into productive forces and relations of production. All this constitutes the *base*, or *structure*, in every instance of social reproduction. The base comprehends also that which Mario Rossi calls "the *existential* forms of living together and productive collaboration between individuals (for example, family relations and work relations)" (1974: 504; see also Dhoquoi, 1971: 256; also at the level of material relations, relations of ideas are to be found). On the other side, we have the so-called *superstructure*, that is, everything that does *not* regard the mode of production *in a direct way*, that is to some extent detached from it, and acquires a relative autonomy, developing itself *also* (even if never *only*) according to laws of its own. The superstructure is characterized by the ideological factor. It comprises all institutions which are neither directly economic-productive, nor simply existential, and all artistic, literary, scientific, religious, and political activities.

Between these two halves of social reproduction, there are complex and entangled relationships, and it cannot be said that the founders of historical materialism ever managed to unravel them completely. On the contrary, though they examined in depth both the structure on one hand, and various aspects of the superstructure on the other, they only hinted at their relations as such and their actual modalities. And despite the high standard of some later contributors (for example Lukács 1923), none of the successive interpreters have ever clarified these relationships in depth, or even approached them in a sufficiently systematic manner. As is well known, Gramsci subdivides the superstructure into *civil society* (schools, churches, associations, newspapers, political parties, market of ideas: the sphere of *ideology*, where a *hegemony* founded upon the so-called "free consensus" of the masses is produced), and *political society*, (government, police, armed forces, tribunals: the sphere of the *state*, where the direct exercise of *domination* takes place when "free consensus" is lacking). This subdivision contains elements which send us back toward the relations of production at the same moment in which it seems to subtract political society from ideology (although in this context see many of Gramsci's other remarks in the 1975 edition, pp. 433-434 and *passim*). In other words, as Bobbio (1968: 26) observes, Gramsci operates with *two dichotomies*, that between structure and superstructure and that between civil society and political society, but doesn't follow this to the point of using a trichotomous system. We will return to this in a moment. There are a few other examples of truly to the point analyses (such as Williams 1973); but the question remains in a magmatic state, still very open to various interpretations, to the point that one could hazard the hypothesis that a determinate social object may never be a structure or superstructure in its own right, but only *according to the way in which it is considered*, or according to the discourse in which it is situated.

Nevertheless, it does not seem that the opposition between structure and superstructure can ever be abandoned. There is no doubt that it touches upon something absolutely fundamental. Despite the variability in interpretations, there are some general points upon which a noteworthy agreement reigns. By a happy paradox, it is a question of precisely the most important points, which are also the most important for our discussion. The first is that every mode of production exercises a continual influence upon its superstructure and that this influence is the pre-eminent one. The second, that ideology belongs to the superstructure and indeed constitutes its main common element. The third, that the superstructure reacts (or at least, *can* react) upon the mode of production. It is in this sense that modes of production and ideological superstructures develop in a state of continual and reciprocal interaction but in an interaction which presents various asymmetries. A circle exists between the two halves, but the rhythm and the effects of this circulation are not always the same. The importance of these three points of agreement can be indicated as follows: the pre-eminence of the influence exercised by the mode of production upon all the rest has its roots in the economic heart of social reproduction (see above), and thus serves power in its self-perpetuation. In contrast, the retroaction of the superstructure permits innovational and revolutionary ideological projection, justifies putting politics first, and frees us from a mechanical-deterministic vision of history.

10.2.3 *Modes of Production, Sign Systems, and Ideological Institutions*

In order to begin to make some conscious mediations between structure and superstructure, in 1968 it seemed to me to be useful to introduce a third part or dimension, that of *sign systems*. This was at first timid and experimental, but it has increasingly become a practical framework. It is often said that communication occurs "by means of" sign systems. According to this approach, communication and sign systems are presented as separate entities. Sign systems exist, lie there waiting; communication intervenes, using them as instruments. We are even offered a sort of list of the pieces which intervene in the process: emitters and receivers, sign systems, contexts, channels, and then communication itself, which is the putting into action of all the above elements. I have already argued extensively against the instrumental conception of sign systems in general, and of language in particular, from the time when I wrote *Il linguaggio come lavoro e come mercato* [cf. R.-L. 1968h; English transl. 1983b]. Here, I will only point out that, according to a realistically enlarged conception of any sign system, this comprehends not only a code and the rules for its use, that is, also the materials upon which one works which are themselves the products of preceding work (including the rules as products), but also all the messages which are exchanged, and which can, in principle, be exchanged, within the universe of discourse put into action by the system itself. The code is thus only a part of the sign system.

Further, by using yet another realistic enlargement, we see that every sign system also contains the individuals and social groups who operate it. It is, therefore, also possible to say that they are operated by it. In this sense a sign system is a slice of reality and is a form of social planning. Now, as already mentioned, communication has its main root in the moment of exchange, intermediate between production and consumption. By putting together these considerations, and measuring them against the two preceding models, one can say that the third model constitutes an attempt at mediation and synthesis between the first two. Social reproduction would, consequently, take place at three levels: mode of production, sign systems and superstructures. Between this triad, which comprehends the bipartition of the second model, and the triad of the first (production, exchange and consumption), there would be an intimate correspondence already in part evidenced by current terminology and which we are trying to bring to light in these pages.

The ideological factor is present at all three levels, but it manifests itself, and can be spotted, principally at the superstructural level, that is, in human institutions and activities. By considering that any activity requires already institutionalized structures (as a minimum in the form of a superpersonal code) if it is to take place significantly, it is possible to have the notion of human activity absorbed by that of social institutions. Simplifying, we will therefore talk about *ideological institutions*, not to distinguish them from other institutions which wouldn't be ideological, but rather to emphasize a constant and indeed basic character of theirs. In other words, the syntagm 'ideological institutions' describes reality in a unitary way. Thus conceived, ideological institutions are none other than articulations of the superstructure. Their correspondence to the moment of consumption justifies the idea that men must continually feed off them. Consumption, permitted by exchange, "produces" production. Thus the circle closes and renews itself, and retroaction is justified.

Sign systems, originating in the moment of exchange, occupy predominantly an intermediate position between modes of production and ideological institutions. They can, however, be mediated in their turn. The most common situation is the one described, in which sign systems mediate modes of production by means of ideological institutions, or the latter by means of the former; but one can also postulate, and find in reality, all the other theoretically possible cases of mediation.

10.3 Sign Systems in Social Reproduction

Let us now examine some aspects of the tripartition of social reproduction into modes of production, sign systems and ideological institutions, paying particular attention to the newcomers, sign systems, and starting from the mere fact of their presence.

10.3.1 The Presence of Nonverbal Sign Systems

The verbal sign system of every community has developed over the centuries through the work of common speakers and other more specialized linguistic operators (such as witches, priests, poets, writers, technicians, and organizers of every type). In this way special, or even "ideal" languages have been formed, detached from common speaking but nevertheless fed by it and in circulation with it. Their totality constitutes the first and most obvious sociohistoric conditioning of a speaker as such. The special languages of the various operators correspond in part to what is understood by the term "subcode." Although this is a very fashionable subject, it isn't the one we must concern ourselves with at the moment.

Our point is rather that neither common speaking, nor the various special languages are sufficient in and of themselves to determine the world-view of the speaker, as the idealistic supporters of the so-called "linguistic relativity" school used to maintain (see here my essay of 1968 [R.-L. 1968h]). On the contrary, they aren't even able, taken by themselves, to determine their own use, as they don't exist *in isolation from* the other sign systems practiced in the community, those which are nonverbal only in the strict sense of the term in relation to verbal sign systems (i.e. *preverbal, paraverbal*, and *postverbal*) and those which are not in the least verbal insofar as they are founded upon codes which have nothing to do with the articulated sounds constituting the code of a verbal sign system, or that are distinguished from these because they are not originally systems of sounds but rather systems of other objects.

The second group is by far the most complex and the least known. Our entire life, from the origins onward is interwoven by nonverbal sign systems. It was necessary to renounce the anthropomorphic and, in the final analysis, classistic privilege traditionally conferred upon verbal sign systems before nonverbal sign systems could emerge as "new" objects of study. This is not the place to even sketch a classification of nonverbal sign systems. We will only note that one distinguishes *objectual* or *instrumental* types of nonverbal sign systems whose code consists of objects found in nature or produced by men for some aim, from *organic* nonverbal sign systems, whose code is found in the organism itself of the user, under the form of body position and movements, and of nonverbal behavior of various types. A third great class is that of nonverbal sign systems of the *institutional* type, whose code is made up of the articulation of social institutions. Furthermore, one can distinguish between nonverbal sign systems of a human, animal, or otherwise natural type, although obviously here the notion itself of an "only natural" sign system immediately poses the delicate problem of the *status* of its interpreters.

10.3.2 *The Influence of the Nonverbal upon the Verbal*

From the origins of society onwards, at all levels of complexity, there are clearly continual and profound reciprocal influences between verbal and nonverbal sign systems. Without denying the influence of the verbal sign system upon nonverbal sign systems, it will be useful to show here how nonverbal sign systems have influenced the very structuring and level of abstraction arrived at by a verbal sign system. As I have already devoted myself at some length to this subject in other publications, here I will simply use a couple of examples from other authors.

Let us take up the classic principle that "nothing exists in consciousness that hasn't first existed in social reality." This is true for both the formation of attitudes, ideas and conceptions as reflections of real social relationships, and the verbal formulation of preceding nonverbal situations. Ambrogio Donini concentrates more upon the first than the second of these aspects. The two exemplary formulations which follow come from his work *Lineamenti di storia delle religioni*:

> The *mind-body* dualism intervenes ... as a reflection of the scission which has been produced in man's way of living. To the measure in which new relationships of production make the domination exercised by some minorities possible, thus creating the dualism of ruling and subordinate classes, the need to satisfy in another sphere, in another world, and ultimately in another life those demands that unjust social conditions no longer allow to be guaranteed to all within the existing social organization is born ... Men had first to experience the limitations that the new social structure imposed upon their daily lives before the division in classes brought forward the need for a spiritual element – spiritual in the sense that theologizing and idealistic philosophies give to this term, as opposed to nature, to the body, to the "material." (1964: 42-43)

> The idea of a superior being, and much less of a personalized divinity, couldn't have begun to impose itself before the supremacy of a privileged group, of a leading caste, of a social class, had been affirmed among men. (*ibid.*: 53)

Thus the real social relationships *produced, projectively*, superstructural relationships and entities for predominantly compensatory motives, according to various modalities of reflection. Such superstructural relationships tend to be verbalized much more than the structural ones, although the latter are also full-fledged sign relationships.

Applying the same principle of the priority of social reality over consciousness, but at least implicitly emphasizing the second aspect more than the first (that is, the transition from nonverbal to verbal situations), George Thomson (1949, 1955) and Alfred Sohn-Rethel (1970, 1971) analyzed in depth the conceptual consequences of the formation of a *monetary economy*. The Parmenidian conception of a unitary Being, whose value was that of existing thoroughly, of "being there," independently of its internal differences which are liable to be severed by the senses and modified by manual labor, emerged for the first time in Greece with the appearance of this economic formation. It seems that the same development took place in a parallel manner in China and India.

The conceptual implications of a monetary economy are as follows. In a world subject to continual change, the *value* of gold and silver coins doesn't change, doesn't "flow," insofar as it is guaranteed by the political authorities who impose it. Any doubts could only arise in relation to the physical body of the coin, which is subject to deterioration. But then political power sees to it that new coins, "fresh from the mint," replace the old ones. Thus, whatever happens to the body of the coin, its value is guaranteed by the very system of social relationships stemming from power. The coin, social invention *par excellence*, is a first outcome in the process of abstraction through which commodities are exchanged without regard for their use-value. A second outcome is money. Gold and silver coins still preserve their use-value. It is their generalized exchange-value which is supported socially. The support of money is, instead, entirely social. Every possible use-value here has practically disappeared (or would be reduced to things like blowing one's nose with or writing notes upon, a banknote). The social support is a social practice imposed and rendered necessary. It seems that, in the last few years, the Swiss have used the devalued Italian coins of 100 lire to make the backs of watch cases: an exchange-value superior to the original one of the coins was obtained through a readaptation of their bodies, and this, in a certain sense, revalued them. This is why so many of the coins disappeared from circulation.

The essential point is that the exchange of commodities, as with every type of exchange, is already a nonverbal sign system, which becomes more complicated and reaches higher levels of abstraction with the institution first of coins and, later, of money. The structures of this nonverbal sign system are reflected in language. In this way the possibility of knowledge detached from manual labor comes into being. Abstract, empty and formal concepts begin to take form in language, which then in the course of time permit the construction of a science of objectified nature such as Galilean physics. Just as the idea of a unitary Being could not have been formed if coins hadn't existed previously in social reality, so too the paradigm of uniform rectilinear motion required the social pre-existence of the qualitative uniformity of money, of its total lack of internal differences. In commodity exchange, we have the movement of bodies in space and time without material change, with only quantitative mutations. We have, in short, abstract matter in movement. And this is the foundation of modern science. Money, a supreme social invention, in which every possible exchange is generalized, permits a physical science of a quantified and objectified nature (Sohn-Rethel 1971: 118-119; 1972 (second edition): 98-115, 150-173). As Marx said, "Damn it! Logical categories really do come from 'our commerce'!" (letter to Engels, 25th March 1868).

10.3.3 The Position of Language in the Structure-superstructure Circle

Here we can find a (proposal of) clarification of the long-debated question of the "position of language" within the structure-superstructure circle, a question to which neither Marr nor Stalin, at the time of the polemic of the latter against the former, managed to give a satisfactory solution. We will approach this by considering a number of interconnected points:

i. The question of the position of language in the structure-superstructure circle cannot be detached from the question of the position of all *sign systems* within the same circle. It is even surprising that such an obvious idea has not received the attention it merits, or it would be surprising if it were not for the fact that language has always been kept isolated from the other sign systems;

ii. All modes of production and all ideological institutions are *also* sign systems. This is an aspect of their nature. It *does not exhaust it*, as a certain recent and burgeoning bourgeois "semiotic panlogism," of an idealistic rather than materialistic, literary rather than scientific, stamp would like to believe. This train of thought ends up by taking the form of the description and exaltation of capital as the sum of all possible exchanges, and of these exchanges and their organization considered separately from the feared and despised materiality of work. Modes of production and ideological institutions "are" sign systems, but in the dialectic sense in which it can be said that production and consumption "are" exchange, much as exchange "is" production and consumption, within the social totality to which they all belong. As we have already seen, dialectic unity does not mean identity. Nothing prevents us from keeping the various moments distinct within an organized discussion;

iii. Sign systems are far from possessing either an infrastructural or hypostructural *virtus*, and are not reducible to being either only modes of production or only ideological institutions. On the contrary, they are constantly open to every influence of social reproduction, of which they are one integrating part from the very beginning of a production which can be called human, and, indeed, is already present at the level of the higher animals. As an aside here, we must add that this is not to say that there aren't signs and communication at the primordial animal level as well, or even in the vegetable world;

iv. At the same time, without contradicting the above points, one can affirm that sign systems enjoy a certain measure of independence, which allows them to develop *also* according to their own laws, through pulsations and articulations internal to the totality that they constitute. In this sense they are related to the ideological institutions;

v. The verbal sign system, or language in the proper sense, species-specific to man, very quickly reaches a level of complexity so high that the laws which regulate it present themselves as even more independent from the rest of social reproduction. It is also true that language is the main instrument of education, of the production of consensus, and the exercise of domination. All this tends to generate the illusion, common even today, especially among scholars who are only concerned with language, that the laws regulating language are completely independent of social reproduction. One thus daydreams about language, as if the rest of reality didn't exist and didn't influence it, or served only as material to permit the functioning and exhibition of this amazing machine.

10.3.4 Planning at Three Levels of All Behavior

From the viewpoint of human group or individual behavior, the fact that social reproduction takes place at three levels means that behavior itself is planned on the same three levels. Groups and individuals learn to carry out their activities on three planes: mode of production, sign systems and ideological institutions. This can happen at any stage on the scale which goes from the most lucid awareness to the most total unawareness, to the threshold of the "merely biological." At this point the intricate problem of unconscious, involuntary learning, to which one passively submits, presents itself.

The planning of behavior, conscious or unconscious as it may be, for the programmer, the programmed, or for both, always takes place, and only takes place, within a totally determined situation. There is no alternative. The very notion of a socio-historical situation makes it unavoidable that determination is always total. If at a certain point we discover that "there is also another factor," we do nothing other than enrich the same situation: the new factor (which is new only because we didn't *know* about it before) also and inevitably contributes to it. From this it follows that every social action, in principle, reverberates everywhere. Thus, on each of the three planes, those of the social forces which find themselves in the condition of acting more efficaciously, affirm themselves. These we call the dominant forces. This is the way in which, at every level, power plans its own perpetuation.

10.3.5 Sign Systems and the Production of Consensus

Sign systems serve power above all as producers and organizers of *consensus*. Gramsci was certainly well aware of this. Obviously he reasoned about it in completely presemiotic terms, but he can hardly be blamed for this. The times and the conditions in which he wrote were what they were. On the contrary, his observations on language continue to be stimulating (the entire page 3217 in the "Subject-matter Index" in the critical edition lists relevant references). It is necessary to bear various factors in mind in order to grasp the importance of sign systems in social planning as the main mediators between the mode of production and the ideological institutions, and as organizers of consensus. We will touch upon three of the principal ones here.

In the first place, there is the factor of the *enormous variety and complexity of sign systems*, not just the verbal but also the nonverbal ones, whose emergence constitutes a new fact, typically contemporary, of which nobody could take account *ante eventum*.

The second factor is that of the *unconscious and superpersonal character of sign systems*, particularly nonverbal ones. Here 'superpersonal' is accompanied by 'hypopersonal' in the sense that if personality identifies itself in an essential portion with individual consciousness, all that which evades the grasp of the individual mind, or rather of the plurality of individual minds, must necessarily place itself below the level of the consciousness of every single individual. We distinguish two principal ways in which sign systems, particularly nonverbal sign systems, are to a large extent unconscious. In many cases, we know only that we are using some sort of sign system, but we do not in the least know how it functions. In very many other cases, we don't even know that we are using a sign system. Both situations, but especially the latter, underline the observation mentioned above that *it is the sign system that uses us*. Our own consensus can consequently seem not only "spontaneous" but downright "natural" to us. It is only in the last few decades, with the advent of the theory of communication, new linguistics, and above all semiotics, which were in their turn promoted by the formation of mass communication and every day exchanges at a planetary level (both of which are expressions of neocapitalism and neoimperialism), that sign systems have *begun* to come to the attention of scholars. The fact that men, as Marx said, continue "to do things they don't know they are doing," illustrates the importance of the study of sign systems as forms of planning at the unconscious level. The bringing to consciousness of the things that formerly were done unwittingly has demystifying functions, and, therefore, favors the formation of *new* social plannings. In this way neocapitalism, as already with classical capitalism, has brought to the surface and made available adequate instruments for its own destruction.

The third factor to remember is the *difficulties always encountered* when examining *the relationships between structure and superstructure*, between modes of production and ideological institutions. It is our hypothesis that the study of sign systems as mediating elements may help in the explanation of such complicated phenomena as the co-presence of a determinate ideology, whatever its institutionalized form with a certain mode of production, whatever its level of development. *In what way* does society institute a given ideology *starting from* a given mode of production? *In what way* can an ideology duly constructed *retroact* upon the mode of production? Using the useful abstraction of a Social Mind which plans, in a superpersonal manner, things which the individual unconsciously accepts within himself, and manages to discover only by means of specific liberating work, one could say that the Social Mind constructs sign systems and imposes them, mediating in this way between the two levels of mode of production and ideological institutions. That which is common among the three levels permits transmission; that which is distinct among them allows each of them to operate at one level only, and the intermediary function that sign systems mainly possess makes them the most important instrument of the entire planning operation.

Usually intermediate sign systems are carriers of the structures of the mode of production, with them permeating the ideological institutions, which then serve to justify it. But well-timed political work can use sign systems to permeate the dominate mode of production with new ideological values.

Note

1. It is apparent that formulations such as this one could be seen to imply a sexist bias. This is not the authors intention, but the task of providing alternatives for such phrases faces difficulties that await a satisfactory resolution.

References

Bobbio, N. 1968. "Sulla Nozione di 'società civile'." *De homine* 24-25: 19-36.
Dhoquoi, G. 1971. *Pour l'histoire*. Paris: Anthropos.
Donini, A. 1964(5). *Lineamenti di storia delle religioni*. Rome: Editori Riuniti.
Gramsci, A. 1975. *Quaderni dal carcere*. Critical edition of the Istituto Gramsci directed by V. Gerratana, in 4 vols. Turin: Einaudi.
Lukács, G. 1923. *Geschichte und Klassenbewusstsein. Studien über marxistische Dialektik*. Berlin: Malik. English transl. by R. Livingstone. London: Merlin, 1971.
Marx, K. 1953. *Grundrisse der Kritik der politischen Ökonomie* (1857-1858). Berlin: Dietz. English transl. by M. Nicolaus. Harmondsworth: Penguin Books, 1973.
Rossi, M. 1970. *Da Hegel a Marx*. Milan: Feltrinelli. New edition in 4 vols. 1970, 1970, 1974, 1975.
Rossi-Landi, F. [See the general bibliography of his writings at the end of this volume.]
Sohn-Rethel, A. 1970. *Geistige und korperliche Arbeit*. Frankfurt: Suhrkamp, 2nd ed. 1972.
———. 1971. *Waren und Denkform, Aufsatze*. Frankfurt-on-Main: Suhrkamp. (See also Sohn-Rethel, 1972. "Mental and Manual Labour in Marxism." In P. Walton

and S. Hall, *Situating Marx*. Human Context Books; and Sohn-Rethel, 1973. "Intellectual and Manual Labour." *Radical Philosophy* 6, Winter 1973).

Stalin, J. 1951. *Marxism and Linguistics*. New York: International Publishers.

Thomson, G. 1949. *The Prehistoric Aegeans* (= Studies in Ancient Greek Society, vol. 1). London: Lawrence and Wishart.

———. 1955. *The First Philosophers* (= Studies in Ancient Greek Society, vol. 2). London: Lawrence and Wishart.

Trân Duc, T. 1973. *Recherches sur l'origine du language et de la conscience*. Paris: Editions sociales.

Williams, R. 1973. "Base and Superstructure in Marxist Cultural Theory." *New Left Review* 82: 3-16.

11. Ideas for the Study of Linguistic Alienation

11.1 Introduction

This paper [cf. R.-L. 1979i] is a very schematic exposition of some main features of a theory of sign production and sign alienation on which I have been working since the early sixties.

The emphasis here is on alienation rather than on production and on language rather than on nonverbal codes. It should be clear, however, that languages in the proper or restricted sense are only the verbal subclass of human social codes. *Nonverbal codes are equally important.* They remain outside this paper only for the reason that their examination raises additional problems I have no room to deal with here. But the main principle is that all human social codes, or indeed all codes without restrictions, should lend themselves to unitary treatment. Semiotics is straining toward this end.

My starting point is the well-known Marxian principle that man is characterized by his own work – indeed, he is its product. If man himself is a product, so must be everything that man produces. Human languages, too, can be explained in terms of human work. What we produce with them, verbal messages, certainly don't exist "in nature" like stones or trees. But neither does the activity of speaking which requires instead a long social evolution and which cannot be isolated from the instruments and materials by which it is exercised. Reflection on this situation brought me to develop a number of interconnected ideas, some of which I shall briefly group here, in nuclear form, as follows:

i. The so-called activity of speaking is itself better described as work. The most fundamental component of language is human work;

ii. All that is done with languages can be viewed as linguistic production, and it is strictly related to the production of tools and other artefacts, i.e. to so-called "material" production. These two branches of production are basic in the very formation of social life under the division of labor. It is illuminating to study them together – they throw light on one another;

iii. Actually, a comparative study of linguistic and material production shows that they are *homologous* in their essence (although they cannot be expected to be *analogous* in their manifestations). What I mean is that they develop according to modalities and degrees of complexity which are amenable to unitary explanations. Two French scholars have recently written interesting books in this direction (Baudrillard 1972 and Goux 1973). In my own view, the homology is founded on the human work expended in both cases ("Il linguaggio come lavoro e come mercato," 1965, now in the book with the same title, 1968[h]). Work is always work – it cannot fail to articulate itself in materials on which it is exerted, instruments utilized and products. As shown by Marx in Chapter 5, Book 1 of *Kapital*, nothing is an instrument, material or product in its own right. A product can be used as an instrument or as material; an instrument is always a product of previous work and can be worked upon as new material; material can be used as an instrument and is always also a product itself (the stage of *direct* contact with a virgin nature having been overcome hundreds of thousands of years ago). It is refreshing to approach language dialectically in these terms: Dialectic causes many of the tools traditionally used by intellectuals in the study of language and communication to explode;

iv. Indeed, the conceptual framework and apparatuses developed by Marx and others in the study of material work and production can be used in the study of language (see Ponzio 1972 and 1973, for commentaries, my writings since 1961, and Thomson 1949-1961). Since the products of material work constitute nonverbal codes the study of which is a highlight of contemporary semiotics, the above operation is to some extent complementary to the rather common operation of applying to nonlinguistic codes a conceptual apparatus of linguistic origin. For example, commodities can be approached as messages, and messages can be approached as commodities. The conjunction of the two complementary approaches and their systematic developments generate a *Marxist semiotics* as an anti-separatistic theory of all social codes, viewed in terms of work and production;

v. Bourgeois semiotics, pseudo-Marxist or not, is prone to the danger of a new sort of panlogism: If we view everything as a sign, it is difficult to set limits to the field of semiotics. To avoid this danger, it is necessary to keep the study of signs as such severed from the study of the *various kinds of bodies capable of functioning as signs*; we can thus proceed to distinguish the various "manners of production" which bring about the various kinds of bodies. Bodies capable of functioning as signs can exist "in nature," like meteorological signs; or they can be produced by man for other aims, like most objects of daily use, which also signify in various ways; or they can be produced exclusively for the purpose of bearing signs, like phonemes. We start with signs as totalities and then proceed dialectically to discard by determinate negations the sign function from the body, in this way coming to face something which I have labeled 'the bodily residue of signs' ("Sul linguaggio verbale e nonverbale," 1966[a], now in *Il linguaggio come lavoro e come mercato* [1968h; English transl. 1983b]; see also "Signs about a Master of Signs," 1975[c]). This procedure is of course especially important in the study of nonverbal codes; but since verbal and nonverbal codes interact continuously, we have to apply it in the study of verbal codes as well;

vi. Once the idea of linguistic production is grasped, one can develop it step by step and come to consider highly complex notions like "linguistic private property," "linguistic exploitation" and "linguistic alienation." To do so in a systematic manner, one has to go through such notions as *linguistic* workers, needs, materials, instruments, money, capital (constant, variable, and total), working process, products, work vs. use in language, linguistic use-values, exchange-values, surplus value, market, consumption, consumerism, and many others.

In this paper I shall expand a little on some of these notions. But let me first add some words of warning. If we look at the above notions in an interdisciplinary way rather than contrasting them with current discussion in any specialized discipline, especially linguistic theory, we find that their scientific *status* varies very much and that some are already used in some fields while being ignored in others. Just to give a few examples, "linguistic needs," "linguistic money" and "linguistic alienation" are discussed by psychiatrists but are usually ignored by linguistic theory; the syntagm 'linguistic needs,' however, is being used more and more by philosophers of language. The "linguistic working process" consists in the dynamic relationships among the various elements of language as used by individuals or groups: It turns out to be a notion unifying the field investigated by generative grammars, the field known as psycholinguistics, and part of the field known as sociolinguistics. That there is a "linguistic market" may sound awkward to some chaste ears but it is an easily understandable thing to people working in the fields of mass media and propaganda or investigating the formation of ideologies and the political background of education. There is a long tradition in the study of various kinds of values in language, and the opposition between "use-values" and "exchange-values," first brought to full light by Marx in the study of the commodity, is of help in clarifying many traditional issues. The notion of "linguistic capital" was brought up by the fact that various linguistic categories, whose interrelationships unavoidably build up the more general category of linguistic capital, were already emerging one by one in different fields of enquiry. That speakers are used by the sector of society which is language, for instance, is an insight almost present in Marx himself; it can certainly be found in Lukács, in the Frankfurt School and in a number of contemporary students either of Marxism or of semiotics or of both (cf. Schaff's works).

11.2 Linguistic Capital, Constant

Language-in-general (*langage*) can be viewed as a capital we use when we speak, within which we speak and which uses us as speakers. We are going to consider all these aspects as belonging to one and the same totality. The capital of language, or linguistic capital, consists of a constant and a variable portion. Within its constant portion we can distinguish linguistic instruments, materials, and money. While the instrumental view of language is widespread, linguistic materials and linguistic money are less commonly recognized, at least by professional linguists, and *pour cause*. In this paper we shall deal only with linguistic materials.

According to the instrumental view of language, we use the system of a language (*langue*) *in order to communicate*, that is, to construct, transmit, receive and interpret messages. The language in its entirety has an instrumental character, and we work *with* the language *on* something else *for* something else. The language is thus inserted in a broader totality of which it constitutes a part alongside other parts. What is supposedly the nature of these other parts? What is their relationship to the part constituted by the language? If a language is declared to be an instrument, the other parts must be materials and products. According to this point of view, materials are not allowed to be linguistic, otherwise they would turn into instruments. The construction of messages by means of the language would then lie in working on nonlinguistic materials by means of linguistic instruments. And as for the nature of messages, it would be partly linguistic and partly nonlinguistic – linguistic because messages are products of linguistic work but also nonlinguistic insofar as nonlinguistic materials enter into them. Things of this sort, particularly the nonlinguistic nature of materials, are contained in the current definitions of a language as an instrument for organizing and communicating "feelings, thoughts, and experiences," that is, precisely materials that a majority of linguists willingly abandon to other fields of study.

However, the "feeling or thoughts or experiences" extraneous to language, on which the instruments of language are supposed to act, are scarcely liable to accurate nonlinguistic identification. They form and become distinguishable only insofar as one learns to speak. They can be properly described only linguistically. They vary to some degree precisely as a function of one's mother tongue, or even as a function of the language one happens to be speaking at a given moment.[1] Besides, no instrument of a language is an instrument in the absolute. Each instrument must be a product of previous linguistic work; and, moreover, it must be susceptible of becoming a material again. There are no limits to the ways in which a language can be worked upon. If a language consisted of instruments that always remained instruments, no such elaboration would be possible. Indeed, if instruments were not in their turn products, and were never able to become materials again, we would be forced to the awkward conclusion that the language's entire supply of instruments had been furnished to us once and for all. Always equal to itself, unable to evolve, this supply of instruments would serve to encapsulate and transmit "feelings, thoughts, and experiences." All the variations in the produced messages would then depend solely upon the variation of the undescribable nonlinguistic materials which happen to be worked upon. At the most, they could also depend on small personal variations in the use of superpersonal, irremovable instruments.

These difficulties seem to indicate that the conception of language as an instrument doesn't hold water. It is, of course, a predialectic conception which opposes an over-rationalized linguistic machinery to an only-irrational world of experience. We overcome it by admitting that not only instruments but also materials are essential to every language and that both are the products of previous linguistic work. In using a language we work with linguistic instruments on materials which are (at least partially, but necessarily) linguistic themselves. An important consequence of this is that one has to overcome the traditional opposition of *langue* and *parole*. Another is the recognition that we carry along with us traces of the whole linguistic experience of the species. Each child, when it begins to speak, is already using highly complicated materials and instruments. It is using them as products of previous linguistic work. The same obtains with material production: As soon as a child begins to crawl around and manipulate objects, it is already using materials and instruments which are immensely removed from the condition of sheer natural items.

11.3 Linguistic Capital, Variable

In the case of language, variable capital consists in the value of the linguistic labor-power expended by men who speak and understand a given language, who express themselves and communicate in it – whether they are in the position of speaker or writer (transmitter) or in that of listener or reader (receiver). When we talk about constant linguistic capital, we certainly do not wish to imply an ontological fixity or even only a naturalistic one, but rather to indicate a difference in comparison with variable capital. Constancy and variation are both relative, and one can grasp them very well by considering the permanence of a language from generation to generation. Speakers are relatively a variable item in front of their own language as a relatively constant item. The point is, however, that constant and variable capital always exist together. If we *take away* variable capital we are left with only materials, instruments and money, which without labor are dead things. Before being dead, a language must have been alive; it is precisely the notion of a dead language that *we arrive at* when variable capital is taken away. On the other hand, *the addition* of variable capital to constant capital appears clearly when we consider the case of a linguist who succeeds in interpreting a dead language: He is like one who enters an abandoned factory and little by little starts up the machinery, whose workings he has learned to understand, and reuses the materials which have been left there waiting.

For the capital of language (*langage*) to continue to operate, it is necessary that not only its constant portion, that is, *the* language (*langue*), but also its variable portion, that is, the linguistic workers, survive.[2] But how does one produce linguistic workers? The answer, which is only apparently obvious, is that they are produced by language (*langage*), that is, by their being a portion of linguistic production, a controllable and exploitable element of it. If we carry out the operations that, in economics, make us sort out wages from other prices, and if we consider the working class as a commodity, then we are struck by this fact, that we are dealing with a *talking commodity*. The language, in conclusion, must continue to function; for this to happen, those who speak it must continue to exist; by handing the language down from generation to generation, linguistic alienation is also handed down (cf. Section 11.5 below).

The *organic structure* of linguistic capital, i.e. the relationship between constant and variable linguistic capital, lends itself to interesting considerations. We can assume that a truly primitive language made up a constant capital of little value, which as such allowed a certain freedom to the speakers. The very conversational parsimony of the primitives is an indication of a certain nearness to the specific linguistic elaborations with which we obtain *linguistic use-values*, that is, to the relative independence and integrity of the craftsman. As constant capital grows, any interruption or defect or modification in the working of machines endangers an ever greater value. The more complex and regulated the structure of constant linguistic capital, the more the speaker is atomized, reduced to the condition of an individual who works without freedom inside an immense machine. At this point, as Marx says in *Grundrisse*, the worker's activity

> is limited to mediating the work of the machine ... (it is an activity which is) determined and regulated in every direction by the machinery's motion ... The accumulation of knowledge and talent of the general productive forces of the social brain, is thus, with regard to work, absorbed in the capital and manifests itself therefore as a property of capital, and more precisely of *capital fixe* (French in the German text), to the extent in which this enters into the productive process as a real means of production. (Marx 1953: 584, 586; translation from the German text)

It would seem that the extreme stage one can reach is that of coming once *again* to believe that a language is something only natural, a force which cannot be opposed, a necessary condition. At this point *linguistic exchange-values* put themselves forward again as linguistic use-values. The worker's resignation is complete since it is no longer even felt as resignation. The transition from capitalism to neocapitalism, linguistic as well as nonlinguistic, is accomplished.

11.4 Total Linguistic Capital

Communication at large is the production, circulation and accumulation of messages within a linguistic community, on a communicative market. Communication is thus the operation of *total* linguistic capital, that is, of a language as constant linguistic capital together with its speakers as variable linguistic capital. The process must be viewed as something unitary and circular: There is no speaker without a listener, nor listener without a speaker, nor speaker and listener without messages which go from one to the other, nor comprehensible messages without a code in common, nor a code in common without previous linguistic-communicative work. The whole situation takes shape little by little as a whole; it is only much later, at a relatively advanced stage, that an individual can distinguish himself as an individual (in the sense of Marx's *Vereinzelung*) within such a situation and come to assign to himself a particular position in it. This is an instance of the principle that an individual is the product of its own society, that social relations determine consciousness and are precedent to concepts.

Communication being the operation of *total* linguistic capital, it is not possible to characterize it as a function of only a portion of that capital. If, for example, one said that communication took place *by means of language*, that is, with only the constant portion of capital, and then one added that the language *is made use* of by the speakers, one would be describing language and speakers as separate items. What would then get lost would be the reciprocal influence of two parts of the same totality.

When one studies a language by itself, as a relatively immobile structure and as such as capable of being isolated as an object of attention, the fact is that in this, as in other cases of separatistic make-believe, it is not at all possible to eliminate work. When one believes one has eliminated work, one is at least reintroducing it oneself as a scholar, whether or not he is aware of the fact. Nevertheless, what often happens is precisely that the language and the speakers are presented as *separate entities which meet in the act of speech*. Here instead we are proposing as primary and foremost a totality comprehensive of both the language and its speakers, including their economic and other determinations, as its intrinsic and constitutive parts. Total linguistic capital is a reality which proceeds with its own motion, a motion which includes both the language and its speakers – the constant as well as the variable portion of total linguistic capital. Neither the language nor the speakers exist by themselves in reality. Let us then start from the real thing, the totality of language-in-general, and *then* proceed to see what its parts are and how they work.

Communication is made up of messages, and in each message the totality of language is present if only embryonically. Messages can exhaust themselves in the act of reception, upon linguistic consumption or fruition. In this case they act mainly on their receivers. Or else, they can retroact on the constant capital of a linguistic community, bringing about modifications in the units and in the aggregates which form the language and in the rules for the use and combination of both. Another path that messages can follow is that of their piling up and organizing themselves in the form of higher-level capital, remaining available for further and more complex linguistic elaborations to be undertaken on the basis of that language within that community. Here I am referring to the ceremonial, ritual, folkloristic, literary patrimonies, both oral and written; and I believe that here we could bring out elements homologous with financial capital.

Inside the limits within which translating is possible, all these patrimonies exert reciprocal influences. Beyond the national linguistic markets corresponding to the various languages, the plurality of the languages and the exchanges that take place among them determine various international linguistic markets and create tensions among them, the general tendency being the building up of one planetary linguistic market. The ways in which we receive and absorb messages translated from other languages, and the difficulties of these operations, present in fact remarkable similarities with the ways in which we absorb commodities imported from other markets.

One final point about linguistic capital in general. If we were always to use 'capital' in the strict historical sense of a mode of production which only affirmed itself during the last few centuries, then it would be immediately obvious that no such use can apply to language. For language, indeed, existed long before the capitalistic mode of production ever arose (that some critics felt it necessary to point out this important piece of truth to me even before seriously reading my books is one of those surprises every author attempting independent thinking must be prepared for). The answer is, of course, that material production and alienation *also* existed long before the capitalistic mode of production arose, and so did linguistic production and alienation. We may avoid the terminological difficulty by using 'patrimony,' or 'asset,' or 'wealth' instead of using 'capital.' Nobody will deny that language as a patrimony or asset or wealth, shared to some extent by all who are born into any given linguistic community, is handed down from generation to generation, and always was. But then, why try to avoid a *terminological* difficulty?

There is, in fact, much more to it than sheer terminology. While studying the capitalistic mode of production, Marx was doing both historical and theoretical work (he was primarily doing *political* work, of course; but here we are concentrating on his scientific method and results). Historically, he was describing the internal structure of the capitalistic mode of production; theoretically, he was applying and developing materialistic dialectic. Now materialistic dialectic cannot be accepted in one case and denied in another. It is, and must be, a universal method; and the fact that some of its features were only discovered in recent times and within a given field of study cannot prevent us from applying it even to previous epochs and in different fields. When Marx stated, rather cryptically, that "in the anatomy of man there is a key for the anatomy of the ape," he was hinting precisely at this. The *mature situation* represented by fully developed capital ('the anatomy of man') made it possible to unravel the structure of social reproduction which nobody could perceive at a stage when its constituent parts had not yet grown together into a full totality and so to say lay scattered in different zones of reality ('the anatomy of the ape'). While discovering the structure of historically determined capital, Marx was also discovering some permanent features of human life at large. This amounts to saying that he was operating on (at least) two different levels of abstraction. There are precise indications to this effect in *Kapital* itself, but much more in the *Grundrisse*, a text which cannot by now be ignored by any student of *Kapital* for it gives a more general framework within which even the immense structure of *Kapital* must find its own particular place.

To conclude, I recommend that my attempt at viewing language as a capital, and at describing its internal structures in Marxian terms, be understood as an attempt at applying materialistic dialectic and Marx's own discoveries concerning human social life in general to the field of language and communication (the most systematic treatment so far is to be found in "Omologia della riproduzione sociale," 1972[c], and in *Linguistic and Economics*, 1975[b]). It isn't certainly an attempt to transplant some historically determined notions into a field subject to different historical determinations at the same level of abstraction. Whether or not a language does work as *constant* capital, and whether or not the speakers of that language are being used as *variable* capital, is to be decided by the study of reality at the appropriate level of abstraction.

11.5 Linguistic Exploitation

As I have tried to show in some chapters of *Semiotica e ideologia* [1972i] and of *Linguistics and Economics* [1975b], in every linguistic communicative market the ruling class privately possesses the language in the three dimensions of (i) control of the code or codes and the modalities of codifications;

(ii) control of the channels, that is, of the modalities of the circulation of messages; (iii) control of the modalities of decodification and interpretation. The ruling class increases the redundancy of the messages which confirm its own position and attacks with noise, or if necessary with disturbance, the decodification and circulation of messages which could instead invalidate it. The subordinate class is placed in the position of being able to decode with particular ease and thus to consider as "real" or "natural" those messages which are sufficiently redundant to overcome the noise or disturbance which could falsify their reception, or else, those messages which are transmitted to it by means of codifying modalities and through communicative channels particularly exempt from noise or disturbance. For such messages, the operation of subtracting spurious information from total information is either unnecessary or is reduced to a minimum. On this basis, we can propose a semiotic definition of 'ruling class' as the class which possesses the above controls.

One might object that redundancy is not due to the free choice of the transmitter but to the statistical rules which govern the use of the signs in question – in our case, of words. This does not change anything. In fact, here in the position of transmitter we find the ruling class itself, which imposes on itself and on other classes the acceptance of certain systems of signs instead of certain others; alternatively, we find subordinate transmitters who, being forced to endure the dominion of the ruling class, limit themselves to using those codes *or else keep silent*.

The individual speaker, who has no control over the codes and the channels, finds himself in a position analogous to that of the individual non-linguistic ("material") worker. The worker no longer shares in the working and productive process to which he nevertheless belongs. The phases of a given working process, which once made up the personal work of the craftsman, are now distributed in an equal number of phases external to the person; it follows that first the factory and then the entire capitalistic production become on an ever broader scale a sort of inhuman reproduction of man as a worker. We can say similarly that the linguistic working process and, the more so, the whole process of linguistic production and circulation become external to the individual linguistic worker precisely with the taking on of the institutionalized form of a linguistic capital and a linguistic market which no speaker can change at will. The speaker, so to say, *is hired by the society in which he is born*: He is obliged to expend his linguistic labor-power in preestablished modalities he is forced to accept and learn. Reciprocal though limited and severely controlled understanding is the wage paid to him for his labor. A large part of linguistic behavior, in fact, consists in using *already existing* products, in consuming them, unconsciously reproducing them according to models which as a result are confirmed and perpetuated. The speaker must transmit certain messages and not others; he is able to understand only certain messages and not others. His whole linguistic activity is programmed, and the ultimate program is that enforced on society by the ruling class with the aim of keeping in power.

11.6 Linguistic Consumerism

The freedom of the individual is limited to the use of everyday objects in both fields of production, the material production of commodities and the linguistic production of messages. When an individual speaker succeeds in refusing the models imposed on him by society, and operates within himself a sort of linguistic-communicative inversion, the penalty he must pay is his expulsion or marginalization by the linguistic community. Anyone who does not learn to speak like the others, or who starts out to speak a language personally deviated from the models, is no longer understood. His wages are suspended, and paraphrasing Shakespeare we can say that he will loose his life for want of language.

Production as the mere use of products – this is what is handed down. The materials assumed in the process of linguistic production are handed down just as they are without an ulterior return to the working process of which they were the products. Thus the separation of man from nature and of man from man fulfils and perfects itself, hands itself down, institutionalizes itself and becomes definitive. Man has been transformed into a Consumer. The road is barred along which he could try to go back to that relationship for which a separation has been substituted. And it is a perfect road-block, constructed by making available – immediately and easily available – the product of the above relationship, not however as products but instead as something natural upon which man no longer intervenes. That man *has* intervened on them, and that without such an intervention those products would never have emerged, is precisely what is ignored. And since the intervention we are discussing here, that of language in the division of labor, is a factor in man's make-up, the overturning of the real situation causes man to deny himself as man. Within the pseudo-totality in which this negation takes place, this means that man establishes himself then as a mere cog-wheel, as a spokesman, repeater, and victim of the social process of linguistic production. Since his own products have organized themselves in a system above and against him, his thrashing about under their weight pushes him further and further down — toward a situation which, insofar as it is *not fully* linguistic any longer, necessarily becomes either subhuman or mechanically pseudo-human. As Marx put it, man is limited to being either a thing, or a phantasm.

Within revolutionary movements throughout the world the new desire can be traced to give back meaning to words and to set up new constructive mediations between the linguistic and the nonlinguistic or to find again mediations that have been lost. This amounts not only to an initial recognition, intuitive but collective, of linguistic exploitation and alienation; it amounts also to the forming of a conflictuality directed against the exploitation of codes by ruling classes and nations and the alienation of language and communication. Linguistic disalienation, in fact, belongs to the future; it necessarily requires revolutionary praxis. No real operation on language can be only linguistic. To operate on language, one has to operate on society. Here as everywhere else, politics comes first.

Rome, 1973

Notes

1. This is meant to be a *partial* recognition of some factors usually studied under the label "linguistic relativity." My own views on this matter are to be found in *Ideologies of Linguistic Relativity*, 1973[d] (Italian original 1968[g], now in *Semiotica e ideologia* [1972i]).

2. Here more than elsewhere I feel the lack of a phenotypic distinction in English between "language-in-general" (corresponding to the French *langage* and the Italian *linguaggio*) and "*a* or *the* language" (corresponding to the French *langue* and the Italian *lingua*). If we accept the notion of the constant part of linguistic capital, in French and Italian it is obvious that this constant part is *la langue* or *lingua*, while total linguistic capital, if anything, is *langage* or *linguaggio*. *Speech* wouldn't do, for *speech* indicates precisely the activity which is expended by means of *a* language: One speaks (in) English, or (in) Italian. *Speech*, if anything, is the French *parole*, Italian *parlare* or *parola*. But then, all these traditional concepts are open to unlimited criticism. To say the least, each of them covers a number of distinctions to be unraveled.

References*

Adorno, Theodor and Max Horkheimer. Cf. Horkheimer.
Baudrillard, Jean. 1972. *Pour une critique de l'économie politique du signe.* Paris: Gallimard.
Goux, Jean-Joseph. 1973. *Freud, Marx. Économie et symbolique.* Paris: Seuil.
Horkheimer, Max and Theodor W. Adorno. 1947. *Dialektik der Aufklärung, Philosophische Fragmente* (1942-1944). Amsterdam: Querido. Italian transl. of the revised ed. 1947 as *Dialettica dell'illuminismo,* by L. Vinci. Turin: Einaudi, 1966.
Lukács, György. 1923. *Geschichte und Klassenbewusstsein. Studien über marxistische Dialektik* (1919-1922). Berlin: Malik. French transl. by K. Axelos and J. Bois. Preface by K. Axelos, Paris: Minuit, 1960. Italian transl. by G. Piana, with a new introd. by the Author, Milan: Sugar, 1967. English transl. as *History and Class Consciousness: Studies in Marxist Dialectics,* by R. Livingstone. London: Merlin, 1971.
Marx, Karl. 1962-1964. *Das Kapital* (1867-*posthumous*). Now in *Werke,* vols. 23, 24, and 25, Berlin: Dietz. English transl. of Book 1 by E. and C. Paul (= Everyman's Library, 848 and 849), 2 vols. London: Dent, 1957.
———. 1953. *Grundrisse zu einer Kritik der politischen Ökonomie* (Rohentwurf, 1857-1858). Berlin: Dietz. Bad French transl. as *Fondements de la critique de l'économie politique,* by R. Dongeville, 2 vols. Paris: Anthropos, 1967. Good Italian transl. as *Lineamenti della critica dell'economia politica,* by E. Grillo, 2 vols. Florence: La Nuova Italia, 1968-1970. Some passages have been translated into English by J. Cohen in K. Marx. *Pre-capitalist Economic Formations.* Ed. and introd. by E.J. Hobsbawm. New York: International Publishers, 1965. There is also a short anthology by D. McLellan, *Marx's Grundrisse.* London: Macmillan, 1971. A complete transl. by M. Nicolaus appeared in 1973. New York: Vintage Books.
Ponzio, Augusto. 1972. "On Language as Work and Trade." *Semiotica* 6, 4: 378-389.
———. 1973. *Produzione linguistica e ideologia sociale. Per una teoria marxista del linguaggio e della comunicazione.* Bari: De Donato.
Rossi-Landi, Ferruccio. [See the general bibliography of his writings at the end of this volume.]
Saussure, Ferdinand de. 1967-1968. *Cours de linguistique générale.* Critical ed. by R. Engler, vol. 1 and 2, 1967, vol. 3, 1968. Wiesbaden: Harrassowitz. English transl. by W. Baskin of the previous French edition. *Course in General Linguistics.* New York: McGraw-Hill, 1966.
Schaff, Adam. 1962. *Introduction to Semantics.* Transl. of the Polish original, *Wstęp do semantyki* (1960), by O. Wojtasiewicz. Oxford: Pergamon.

* Some of these references have been brought up to date in proofs (April 1976). Extended bibliographies can be found at the end of Chapter 7 of *Il linguaggio come lavoro e come mercato* (2nd ed. [cf. R.-L. 1968h], of Chapter 10 of *Semiotica e ideologia* [cf. R.-L 1972i], and of *Linguistics and Economics* [cf. R.-L. 1975b].

———. 1964. *Język a poznanie*. Warsaw: Państwowe Wydawnictwo Naukowe. German transl. as *Sprache und Erkenntnis*, by E. M. Szarota. Vienna-Frankfurt-Zurich: Europa-Verlag, 1967. French transl. as *Langage et connaissance*, followed by six *Essais sur la philosophie du langage*, by C. Brendel. Paris: Anthropos, 1967.

Thomson, George. 1949-1961. *Studies in Ancient Greek Society*. Vol. 1, *The Prehistoric Aegean*, 1949, 1954(2). Vol. 2, *The First Philosophers*, 1955, 1961(2). London: Lawrence and Wishart.

IV

SIGNS AND MATERIAL REALITY

12. Signs and Bodies*

In this short paper I shall put forward five abstract propositions in two groups and then briefly try to comment upon them. The propositions are:

    A, All signs are bodies;
    B, Not all bodies are signs;
    C, All bodies can be signs.

And

    D, Signs are not bodies;
    E, All bodies are signs.

The two groups of propositions represent two highly simplified models which have been reached through much discussion. However, there is no finality about them. If a proposition doesn't work, it will be changed. The idea is to use the terms 'signs' and 'bodies' in *some* of their possible relations, and see what happens. Whether or not they change their meaning in the various propositions, and if so, to what extent, is something to be ascertained through a process of analysis, rather than something to be decided upon from the start. The alternative, at the very beginning to decide what their meaning must be, would send us back to the previous possession of a fully formulated theory of what both signs and bodies are. Moreover, *initial* definitions, when they are meant really to precede the discussion, always run the risk of isolating the *definienda* from their contexts. It is as if each of the *definienda* showed up by itself, came to us, and said to us, "I am a *definiendum*, Sir: Why don't you define me? Haven't you got a lovely *definiens* to wrap me up with?"[1]

    In my books and essays, I have, of course, commented on some current definitions of 'sign' and related terms, and even tried to submit some new definitions or characterizations of semiosic processes in terms of work, product, and use, within a Hegelo-Marxian theory of social reproduction [cf. R.-L. 1968h (2nd ed. 1973), 1972i, 1973a, 1973d, 1974f, 1975b]. But this is not my

---

* Paper presented at the First Congress of the International Association for Semiotic Studies (Milan, June 2-6, 1974) [cf. R.-L. 1979b].

present concern. I want to proceed here by intellectual trial and error, and am asking the reader to join me in the venture. As speakers of at least one natural language, we all distinguish between "signs" and "bodies" to some extent. We would never say that that girl on the first floor has got a beautiful *sign*, or that she made me a *body* that I can enter the front door and reach her. All we need to add at this stage is that 'bodies' in the widest sense must refer to all conditions of matter, including energy, and that 'signs' stands for semiosis in general. In a much more extended version of this paper many pages are dedicated to an examination of the internal structure of both signs and bodies, and some similarities and dissimilarities between the two are indicated; there is no room for any such examination in this very reduced congressual version.

My main working hypothesis is that the first model, composed of the first three propositions, is the basic model of *materialistic semiotics*; while the second model, composed of the last two propositions, is the basic model of *idealistic semiotics*. According to this hypothesis, materialistic semiotics starts with bodies, and by realizing that bodies can be *or not be* signs, comes to consider signs as a subclass of bodies-in-general; while idealistic semiotics works the other way round, i.e. starts with signs, and while insisting on the differences between signs and bodies, reaches the apparently contradictory conclusion that, after all, all bodies are signs. We shall come back to this apparent contradiction of idealistic semiotics later on.

There are two *provisos* to hint at before going any further afield. The first is that the tone of what I am saying is ontological, not historical (let's hope that my mentality doesn't succumb to my tone). What I mean is that I am here talking about things as I think they are, not about the historical process of human knowledge. In the course of such a process, in fact, man has acquired the capacity to distinguish both signs and bodies as objects of thought and discourse. If we took the historical process of knowledge as a description of how things are, we would find ourselves stating that bodies and signs exist together, which in a sense is of course true; but we may also come to the wrong conclusion that there is no sense in starting with bodies in order then to single out signs, or vice versa. Confusion between a description of how things are, or are supposed to be, and the historical process that has brought man to the point of being able to describe them, it should be noticed, accounts for the following strange fact. Contrarily to what one could think, the demystification of idealistic semiotics must itself start with signs, not with bodies. The reason is that it is much more difficult to show step by step how bodies *become* signs while remaining bodies, than it is to show that signs are *also* bodies, and that not all bodies are signs. In the former case one takes it upon oneself to single out and describe processes that bring us to new totalities, while in the latter one puts oneself in front of an already constituted totality, enters into it, and describes its parts. While having attempted myself the first and more difficult course somewhere else, I shall stick here to the easier one: I shall welcome my totalities as they arise in front of me.

The second *proviso* is that the two models are not equally fair. Let us confess that the villain of my story is idealistic semiotics. I shall be accusing it of committing a number of tricks. What I am not contending, however, is that there must be any idealistic semiotician so completely silly as to openly endorse the two propositions of the model we are dealing with. Even an idealistic semiotician will probably find that the first model is adequate, while the second isn't. The reason why I have nevertheless put forward my second model is that I believe that propositions D and E, or some cognate propositions, are to be found underneath most open declarations of idealistic semioticians. They are, so to say, the deepest structure on which idealistic mistakes must rest. Or better, I am advancing the working hypothesis that they are; or at least that they can be of help in grasping that structure.

Let us now comment a little on the five propositions. What happens is that idealistic semiotics, whether declared or not, cynically enjoys the ailments from which proposition A is apparently suffering. What are these ailments? Firstly, that various classes of signs, according to some usages of the terms, do not seem to be endowed with any sort of corporeality; and secondly, that no sign is *only* a body. These two ailments impair the validity of proposition A up to the point that some people believe A to be a dead and done with proposition and put D in its place. But this is running into the opposite extreme. In fact, A and D are not perfect contraries. When you say that *all* signs *are* bodies, what you want to exclude is the existence of incorporeal, immaterial, "mental" signs in the ontological sense of 'mental.' You are taking here an anti-idealistic, anti-mentalistic stance; you are stating that signs are things belonging to this world of ours and not to some other world. When you deny instead that signs are bodies, you are vindicating some other dimension whose absence would prevent us from grasping something as a sign instead of grasping it as a mere body. The point is, what is this other dimension? In my opinion, the only possible answer from the point of view of materialistic semiotics is that a sign is a sign because it is the center of a network of social relations, or because it belongs to such a network.[2] The logic of this statement is similar to the logic of the statement that *a commodity is not a material thing because it is a social relation*. From this it doesn't follow that a commodity doesn't have a material body – indeed, without a material body, the bearer of its use-value, no piece of goods would ever be able to enter the social relations which make of it a commodity.[3] This is a historico-materialistic approach. What happens instead with idealism – including its semiotic species, mentalism – is that a mental dimension is substituted for the social dimension. Idealists tend to call mental what they find inconvenient to accept as social.

Moreover, idealistic semiotics tends to ignore the distinction between proposition *B* (*Not all* bodies are signs) and proposition *C* (All bodies *can be* signs). Both propositions are substituted by *E* (All bodies *are* signs). In this way *C* is ignored by affirming the contrary to *B*. The logic of these substitutions is rather intricate. When *C* is ignored, in fact, the *process* by which men and other living beings make a body into a sign, or read a sign in a body, is forgotten. Everything is a sign *already*. This is a basic step for (i) escaping from a social interpretation of signs, and (ii) affirming that there is something else one cannot escape from, namely signs themselves. Mind as an item isolated from the rest of the world pays for its pseudo-freedom by entering into a sign-prison of its own.

If we consider now the idealistic model by itself, i.e. if we concentrate on propositions *D* and *E*, we find a contradiction. How do all bodies manage to be signs, if signs are not bodies? This contradiction, however, is more apparent than real; or rather, it is leveled out by the idealistic procedure of creativism. All bodies are signs because we are continuously and unavoidably making them into signs: this is the contention an idealist would either openly state or secretly accept. Our creativistic activity of reading signs everywhere would transform bodies into signs, and these signs wouldn't be bodies any longer as a result of the transformation. According to this approach, signs are not bodies precisely because all bodies are signs – what *remains* a body is of no interest. In this exaggeration, it should be noticed, there is an important kernel of truth. That there are no signs without interpreters is a generally agreed upon statement. But the point is that the intervention of the interpreter, necessary as it is, does not suppress the materiality of bodies, nor does it transform into a sign what is not a sign.

As a result of the moves described, idealistic semiotics tend to convert and nullify our world into mere semiosity, much as traditional idealism would convert and nullify the world into thought. If traditional idealism could reach the metaphysical level of Panlogism, semiotical idealism is certainly able to reach the metaphysical level of Semiotical Panlogism.

Semiotical Panlogism, whether hidden or outspoken, whether partial or total, is a danger to our studies. It should be carefully criticized, and dispensed with. Bodies, and not signs only, are the world's furniture. Bodies are to be met both outside of signs and within signs themselves. Interpreters are bodies with needs, desires, illnesses, etc., and not only bodies capable of using signs. If you put a man into jail, what you put into jail is not only an interpreter, but a physical body as well. If you kill a man, you kill a man, and not only an interpreter. Social life, while being entirely covered by sign systems up to the point that without signs it wouldn't be social and, possibly, it wouldn't even be life, consists also of something else.

But does a general semiotics correspond to a general theory of society? Let's make a geometrical metaphor. If you put a small cylinder on top of a taller cylinder, the two coincide when their diameters are the same. The area of the base is then the same, but the height and volume of the cylinders are different. Semiotics, while overlapping with the theory of society, is like the small cylinder. These differences ought to be kept in mind. It is by acknowledging its own limits that semiotics can fortify itself and avoid the danger of converting itself into some sort of new philosophical superscience in the old sense.

To conclude, it is clear that the five propositions I have so briefly discussed contain an enormously complicated network of relations. This network derives from the potential of meanings enshrined in the two recurrent key-terms, 'signs' and 'bodies.' Such complication reminds one of, although doesn't amount to, the complication of the relations which obtain as soon as one starts playing with propositions pivoting on the terms 'man,' 'nature,' and history.' Unraveling the various senses in which man is and is not (only) nature, and is and is not (only) history, is a job which has engaged generations of scholars. If one has at all ever begun this job of unraveling, one must know how thin the zones are which divide positions which are very different or even opposed intellectually, ideologically and politically. It is enough to change very slightly the use of even only one of the three fundamental terms in order to shift to a position which cannot be reconciled to the position endorsed before the change. The categorial value of each of these terms could be compared to a beam of light investing different zones of reality; and these zones become more detached from each other if only you turn the projector just a little on its axis.

In the case of signs and bodies, in spite of the vast literature already existing on signs, we are only at the beginning. A literature on bodies as related to signs doesn't exist, or it hasn't been unified. In my opinion, to reinforce the foundations of materialistic semiotics we should in the first place enquire into bodies from the point of view of signs, classify bodies in terms of the various classes of signs which are usually attached to them. A comparison with commodities may again be of help. By studying bodies from the point of view of signs one comes across a dialectic similar to the dialectic which one comes across when studying the use-values *of* (i.e. related to) the exchange-values which *are* (happen to be) attached to them. Economics doesn't center on use-values as such, but necessarily presupposes them. And similarly semiotics with bodies. Insofar as the two subjects of enquiry correspond (but indeed, economics proper can be viewed as a sector of semiotics), the dialectic of what the two enquiries both discard and presuppose, presuppose and discard, is bound to be the same dialectic. The main point here is that neither economics nor semiotics can fully fly its own flight *as if* what it presupposes didn't exist. Semiotics needs bodies much as economics needs use-values. Neither is a complete theory of society; but no theory of society can avoid being founded on them. And, whatever the approach, the world continues to exist.

Rome, May 1974

Notes

1. And why don't linguists furiously sleeping with definitions when they are in bed on Saturdays ever read "old" philosophical essays which have already taken care of some of their basic difficulties, such as – just to give one example – Isaiah Berlin's "Logical translation" (*Proceedings of the Aristotelian Society*, vol. L, 1949-1950: 157-188)?

2. Animal relations also are social relations, though in an attenuated sense; the extent to which this sense is attenuated is itself a big chapter in semiotics. We are dealing here, however, especially with human social signs.

3. In the case of so-called "spiritual commodities," like a record or a painting, the use-value cannot be properly described as "material" according to the *prima facie* use of this word; the dialectic between use-value and exchange-value is nevertheless always there. See on this Marx himself, especially in the *Grundrisse* and in the *Theorien über den Mehrwert*.

13. Ideas for a Manifesto of Materialistic Semiotics*

Terminological remarks have a healthy tendency to become remarks about our way of using words and phrases, and the latter have an even healthier tendency to become remarks about our way of using concepts and conceptions. Let us begin, then, with some terminological remarks about our title. Since all the other words are of more or less common usage, and even the existence of some endeavor to be called 'semiotics' is here out of discussion, our attention must concentrate on the single term, 'materialistic.'

It is an historically determined use. Now all pieces of language are always used within, and not certainly outside, an historically determined situation. But when a piece of language is a term laden with conceptual implications, it seems that historical factors are even more conditioning. Let us give an example. Water is always water, much as it is *Wasser* or *eau* or *woda* or *víz*, with a measure of independence from the moment and circumstances in which you are using the word. There is here a *continuum* of different cases, and their systematic description is certainly an attractive task for every semiotician; one could say straight-off, however, that at the opposite extreme a term like 'materialistic' does change its denotation and connotation almost entirely according to the person, group, place, country, natural language, cultural tradition, and historical moment in which it is used. Which is, then, *our* use of it in this sketch of a manifesto?

It is, of course, the post-Hegelian usage enacted by Feuerbach, Marx, and Engels and then further developed by all the main masters of the various Marxist schools and also by thinkers of other descriptions (suffice it to think of G.H. Mead who was the main direct master of Charles Morris, the founder of twentieth-century semiotics and certainly a nonmechanistic materialist though not a Marxist). This use of 'materialistic' involves a complete rebuttal of all sorts of idealism, including its semiotic branch part of which used to be

---

* [Originally published as R.-L. 1979g. In the reference section originally appended to his *Manifesto*, Rossi-Landi indicates the following as the main books and articles in which he develops the views sketched in this paper: R.-L. 1968h, 1972i, 1974f, 1975b, 1975c, 1976c, 1977, 1978b, 1978c, 1978e, 1979c.]

described as 'mentalism'; but it also involves a refusal of what within that tradition is called 'mechanicistic materialism.' Our use does *not* involve that man is not the actor of history, or that "matter" is all there is to society. Quite to the contrary, it contains an attempt at striking a balance between "natural" and "social" factors in order to preserve the continuity between men and the other animals while at the same time properly assessing the qualitative leap that distinguishes man from the rest of the universe known to us. A defence of such continuity refuses any *ontological* leap, while the assertion of a *qualitative* difference refuses the biologistic reduction of men to other animals which is common among mechanicistically-oriented materialists. The complex and heavy phrase, 'dialectical-historical materialism,' when properly used within its historical context, helps to bring out some of these ideas in a nutshell.

A materialistic semiotics must be a semiotics founded on social reality, on the actual ways in which men interact among themselves and with the rest of the living and nonliving world. It cannot examine sign systems apart from the other social processes with which they are functioning all along. It cannot make everything rest on signs by themselves. It must discover and work out its proper collocation as against a more general background which will also give it a feeling of its own boundaries and only relative importance. In other words, it cannot become a sort of *panlogism*.

The best way known to me to describe social reality at large is to approach it in terms of *social reproduction (gesellschaftliche Reproduktion)*. Social reproduction is the totality of the processes by which any society – from a primitive tribe to contemporary highly developed societies – proceeds in time, preserving itself while at the same time administering some changes to its own internal structure. Whenever it happens that one of the basic processes is not performed with sufficient accuracy, the society is destined to disappear. A brief list of some of the main processes will make the issue clearer. A society – any society – must at least feed its members, shelter them from inclement weather, organize them against the forces of nature and of other societies, hand over to new generations the social patrimonies of language, nonverbal sign systems and common lore, accept or further artistic and other "ludic" activities, protect people in special conditions (newly born babies, pregnant women, the old and the sick), build up, and keep working, material and symbolic communicative channels, develop one or more basic visions of the world, control people who are not considered "normal" from the established point of view or find special accommodations for them; and so on, one would say, almost endlessly. That a distinction between basic and nonbasic processes can at least in principle always be drawn, however, is itself a basic feature of social reproduction. Nobody would say that a society in which no more bridge is played is doomed, while it is difficult to imagine the survival for more than two generations of a society in which infants were no longer taught to speak.

The very reduced list given above is already able to raise a number of problems. I have examined some of them in various publications. Suffice it here to propound a few general points:

i. Semiotic studies are deeply involved in the study of social reproduction. In fact, social reproduction is also, necessarily, the reproduction of all sign systems. Even in those sectors or moments of social life where no work in the material sense is performed, *sign work* of which linguistic work is a species continues to be expended, whether consciously or not (the latter, not the former, being the normal case). But usually students interested in sign systems give little importance to social reproduction, and vice versa. Thus there are Marxist scholars who know everything about social reproduction, except ... that it is also, necessarily, the reproduction of sign systems (an extreme example of a totally asemiotic and therefore presemiotic approach is Althusser's). And there are semioticians who tackle sign systems as something existing independent of social reproduction, without ever dreaming that for sign systems to exist there must be other social processes going on as well;

ii. The sign systems reproduced within social reproduction are both verbal and nonverbal. No consideration of verbal languages by themselves would be sufficient from the point of view of social reproduction. The difference between linguistics as the science of verbal sign systems and semiotics as the general science of any sign systems whatsoever becomes here particularly evident. A proper approach to the sign factors of social reproduction cannot be but a *fully semiotic approach*. No merely linguistic approach would ever do. The internal weakness of Sapir's and Whorf's theories concerning so-called "linguistic relativity" is evidence of the inadequacy of *linguistic* intellectual tools to cope with society at large. *Semiotic* tools are required instead;

iii. Everything that goes on in social reproduction is *also* a sign process. The production of corn in the fields or of cars in an assembly line is also sign production. By this we mean, almost tautologically, that nothing *made by man* can be exempt from signs *at the human level*. Also animals use signs; but stating that corn or car production is human does not seem to be irrelevant when measured against common ecological literature on animal behavior and natural settings. There is, therefore, a *semiotics of material production*. Sign processes which accompany or are at work even within material production are themselves a huge chapter in the semiotic enterprise;

iv. However, it seems that the semiotic approach acquires its full strength when applied to nonmaterial production, i.e. to the production of superstructural items such as legal systems, religious and moral sets of rules, arts and poetry, philosophies and ideologies. Notice that, for instance, rituals and rules are nonverbal sign systems independent from whether or not they are also verbally expressed. In other words, not even at the superstructural level is a merely linguistic approach sufficient. But then the economic base and the superstructures are developing together in a condition of continuous reciprocal influence;

v. Consideration of some of the above difficulties – more of those which have here remained between the lines than of those I have openly hinted at – has brought me to an attempt at introducing sign systems as a "third item" in-between the economic base and the superstructures. This acquires perhaps more sense if we call the former mode of production and the latter *ideological* superstructures. It would appear that passing from a dichotomy to a trichotomy is of help here. "Civil society" as defined by Gramsci would be the most proper place for the study of sign systems, whether verbal or nonverbal. This is the zone of social reality where *consensus* is produced. It would then also appear that the semiotic endeavor can acquire a demystifying power. It does not follow that it should not extend to other zones.

To sum up, semiotics should be fully materialistic, and this means that it should not confine itself to the study of sign systems as such – as formal structures detached from the social and historical realities in which alone they are allowed to develop and to become available to common usage. Moreover, semiotics should extend itself to the totality of social reproduction. Finally, and as a limitation to the previous point, semiotics should concentrate on those aspects of social reproduction which lend themselves to it with particular intensity, that is to sign systems as a machinery mediating between the mode of production and the ideological superstructures. This is, of course, only the beginning of a long and rather intricate argument.

14. Toward a Theory of Sign Residues*

14.1 Introduction: Sign Systems and Social Reproduction

The two main notions to be discussed in this introductory section are "sign systems" and "social reproduction" (*gesellschaftliche Reproduktion*). Sign systems, the object of *semiotics*, are characterized by semiosis, viz. by the functioning of signs which are always organized in systems. We can speak of "sign systems *and* social reproduction," or of "sign systems *in* or *within* social reproduction." Social reproduction is the totality of the processes by which any given society proceeds in time from generation to generation, keeping itself going in history (or prehistory, as the case may be) while both preserving its internal structure and administering some changes in it. These practices may be relatively simple in the case of a very primitive, prehistoric community bordering on the tribe; or immensely complicated, as is the case with contemporary societies. To continue to exist, a society must obviously produce and exchange goods, teach children to speak and to interpret nonverbal sign systems, build a suitable environment, organize the relations among its members, take care of groups of people in special conditions (such as infants, pregnant women, and the old), transmit some basic values, and so on.

All these various processes can be grouped into vast categories according to different criteria. One usual and fruitful grouping consists in opposing the *economic base* or *structure* to the *ideological superstructure* (a *Basis* to an *Überbau*). The economic structure comprehends all the processes required for the production of goods and can be basically described in terms of the prevailing *mode of production*. A mode of production is the sum of *productive forces* and *relations of production*. The ideological superstructure comprehends all sorts of institutions, such as legal systems, religions, or folklore, and

---

* This essay is the English translation and arrangement for oral presentation of part of the material prepared for a private seminar on semiotics held by a group of friends in Spring 1974. About half of the English text was read at the "Third Viennese Symposium on Semiotics" held on August 25-27, 1977. A German translation is forthcoming in *Kódikas* (Tübingen) [cf. R.-L. 1979c].

all "cultural or intellectual life," such as philosophy, the arts, or literature. The basic feature of any given ideological superstructure, however, rests on its dominating ideology. An ideology is a *social design* of a general type, over the long term, concerning society as a whole: It is the general framework within which all the programs of the society must fit. Economic structures, or modes of production, determine to some extent ideological superstructures. Ideologies, however, retroact on the modes of production, so that there is a circle between the two levels. The last deep treatment of these problems is to be found in Schaff 1977.

In other published and unpublished writings (cf. References [In the reference section originally appended to this essay, R.-L. lists the following: 1961d, 1968h, 1972i, 1975b, 1977, 1978b, 1978c, 1978e, *Between Signs and Non-signs* (now this volume), and *Dall'analisi alla dialettica*. For further information concerning the latter, see the introduction.]), I am trying to introduce sign systems as a third vast category in-between modes of production and ideologies. What is the function of semiosis in social reproduction? And since *semiosis, in its turn, is socially reproduced*, what are the influences of modes of production and of ideologies upon it? Obviously, for a society to reproduce itself also sign systems must be reproduced. Sign systems can be first introduced as mediating between modes of production and ideologies, but they can also be considered as being mediated in their turn by either modes of production or ideologies. In other words, one can either start with sign systems, oppose them to ideologies, and mediate between the two in terms of modes of production, or start with modes of production, oppose them to sign systems, and mediate between the two in terms of ideologies. This dialectical terminology represents the fact that a third item has been introduced into a previous two-item totality, and expresses the author's approach to a *materialistic semiotics* as a portion of a general science of man.

The available literature shows us that the relations between semiotics and philosophy have never been properly and finally assessed, and that the limits and purposes of semiotics as distinguished from other scientific endeavors are far from being clear. Sometimes semiotics is presented as one scientific discipline among others; but then, since there are signs everywhere and it is very difficult to say what is *not* a sign, semiotics seems to expand to cover the whole field of human knowledge. This would bring us to the opposite conclusion that semiotics is only a sort of superimposed awareness, or a set of new methods that scholars of various fields are invited to learn in order to then apply them to their own individual pieces of research. Difficulties of this kind are also felt in the history of the subject. It is, for instance, almost impossible to decide the extent to which Peirce's semiotics is independent from his metaphysics and valid even without it; and there are two very different conceptions in Charles Morris's main books – the conception of semiotics as psychobiological science and the conception of semiotics as a new organon for science in general, namely of semiotics as the present stage of what used to be called philosophy, taking its twentieth century "linguistic turn" into account.

Let us proceed from the idiom of disciplines to the idiom of subject-matters. Our question will then be: What are the relations between sign systems and social reproduction? In one main sense of the umbrella term, 'behavior,' non meaningful behavior simply does not exist. No man can operate without consciously or unconsciously using sign systems, and it is in fact with the whole of his social organization that man communicates. In other words, every human action, whatever else it may be, must also be sign action. This is why it is social; or perhaps, with a more conservative formulation, this is the main reason why we call it social. (Notice that "private actions" are themselves just a species of the kind "social actions"; in fact, the very opposition between "private or individual" and "public or collective or social" is a social opposition.)

What is, then, the relation between a general theory of signs and sign systems, or semiotics, and a general theory of social reproduction? Two solutions seem to be theoretically possible; and indeed, they are dominant in the literature with which I am acquainted. It can be maintained that sign systems exist *within* social reproduction. In the most obvious sense of 'within' this is certainly true. No human activity exists outside of social reproduction. Thus the statement that sign systems exist within social reproduction is unimportant. Or, one has to be careful. If, by stating that sign systems exist *within* social reproduction, we mean to divorce sign systems *from the rest of* social reproduction, we may lose sight of the fact that the whole of social reproduction is also, necessarily, the reproduction of sign systems; and even more so, that social reproduction could not even take place *without* sign systems. Some scholars take the opposite view that all there is to social reproduction is the reproduction of sign systems. This amounts to saying that sign systems are themselves the social reality, namely, that there is nothing more to social reality than sign systems. When this latter solution has its root and justification in the refusal of the consequences of the former, it can even be taken as a serious effort to find a way out of them. Its danger, however, is that it is easily transformed into an idealistic solution. A sort of "semiotic panlogism" is then born. Much as Hegel's "Idea devoured Reality," now the "Sign devours Society." I have dealt with these fantastic developments elsewhere. I shall say here only that, in my view, semiotic panlogism must be given the sack straight away. What we need here is preventive repression. Paraphrasing a Chinese proverb reported in Latin by the Jesuit Fathers, let us proclaim that *In semioticam aulam nefas introducere panlogismum.* Social reproduction is based on need, work, exchange, class division, exploitation: that is, on factors that brutally beset the very body of man in its psycho-physical materiality, and not just the sign systems practiced by him. Signs are immensely important; but the furniture of the world does not consist of signs alone, and there is something of the ideology of total control in the contention that it does.

My point of view is the point of view of social reproduction, not the point of view of sign systems. If we succeed in clarifying to any extent the location and function of sign systems in social reproduction, to that very extent we shall have learned something about semiotics as distinguished from the other social sciences and from philosophy as well.

14.2 The Typology of Signs as a Function of Social Reproduction

Once the position of sign systems within social reproduction has at least been glimpsed, we can afford to state that every typology of signs is necessarily a function of social reproduction. What is common to all cases of social reproduction will produce common elements in all sign systems, while what is different in the different cases of social reproduction will produce different elements in the same sign systems and also sign systems which are altogether different from one another. If there is one metaphysical belief which is invalidated at its root by this approach, it is the belief that it may be possible ever to discover a typology of signs independent from social reproduction, a typology valid for all times and places, and perhaps common to all living beings. From this it does not follow, however, that common elements in various instances of social reproduction, or in the reproduction of human and other animals, cannot be discovered and usefully investigated.

Sign systems should not be lifted above the reality of social reproduction, or viewed as its sign skeleton. They must be approached as social reproduction themselves. But since we are dealing here with sign systems rather than with social reproduction at large, we shall have to find a clue. What I have in mind is that somewhere must lie the end of a skein of social reproduction, the pulling of which may allow us to perform a double operation: on the one hand, to talk sign systems as such with a view to proposing a typology of them, while on the other hand respecting the basic principle that nothing exists outside of social reproduction and that sign systems themselves are a constant factor of it.

14.3 The Totality "Sign," and "Sign Residues"

The end of the skein that I propose to begin pulling on this occasion is the methodological notion of "sign residues." According to both common sense and the majority of investigations in the field, a sign is no simple entity; it is, instead, something composite. This means, to begin with, that every sign must contain in itself both sign and non-sign portions which can be investigated on their own account and more often than not survive the extinction of the sign. This is a first, very rough presentation of the notion of sign residues. I shall phrase the situation by saying that each sign is always a *totality* of a peculiar sort. Let us submit these initial statements to a little dialectical probing:

i. If a sign is a totality, then there must be some parts, at least two, which constitute the totality. A one-part totality would be a contradiction in terms;

ii. Such parts may exist in some way before the formation of the totality. Alternatively, they must be reciprocally present at the moment when the totality comes into being. In other words, even in cases when the parts do not exist in any conceivable manner before the totality is born, they must be there for the birth to take place. We shall say that in such cases the parts are being produced or reproduced by the same process by which the totality itself is produced or reproduced;

iii. Whether pre-existing or not, no part as such can in any way perform the job performed by the totality, or represent it on the stage of communication. However, it is reasonable to admit that once a part of the totality is recognized and remembered as such, the idea of its totality is also evoked or the idea that there must be a sign totality arises. Here there are subtle difficulties, some of which we shall return to;

iv. The complexity of the parts as such and the procedures by which they are produced or reproduced are irrelevant to the functioning of their totality. Or at least, irrelevance is the usual case. Let us give an example: the procedures by which a car is built are certainly not taken into any account when we identify a car in a parking lot and this informs us of the presence of the driver in the vicinity, or when a luxury car informs us on the social *status* of its proprietor;

v. Once the totality "sign" dissolves, there can be residues of the parts, residues in the sense that something survives the passing away of the totality. We can also, so to speak, destroy the totality with a mental experiment, precisely in order to find out whether or not there are residues, and what they consist of. In the majority of the cases one can think of, such residues do in fact exist and they can be studied in their own right. This is a second, slightly more refined presentation of the notion of "sign residues." The car in the example given above, for instance, continues to exist after subsiding in its function as a sign;

vi. We have spoken so far of a totality and of *at least two parts*. But how do the two parts get together, and how do they remain united for the totality to function at all? There must be some human work by means, and as a result of which, two or more parts get together to the effect of bringing into being, or producing, the totality "sign." Moreover, the parts *are not* allowed to sever from each other if the sign which comprehends them is to function at all. The reference to human work is by no means simple or unitary. We must, in fact, distinguish at least the following items: a) The specific social work which has phylogenetically produced the various sign totalities since the first dawning of human communities. b) The social work necessary to continue to produce each sign totality as a distinguished entity within the global sign production of the sign community. c) The work of transmitting sign totalities from generation to generation. Teaching is a substantial part of this transmission. d) The individual work of reproduction of sign totalities. Each of these four kinds of work is liable to be subdivided into various families, each of which should be investigated in great detail. For a discussion of these possibilities, and in general for a theory of sign production as a part of a theory of the articulations of work and of social production and reproduction, all I can do here is to refer to my own writings since the early sixties. I have been using the notion of linguistic work since 1961, and that of sign production since 1965. It is, however, a pleasure to add that several scholars have found this approach useful and have added to it. For instance, to limit myself to my own countrymen, in 1973 and 1974 Augusto Ponzio developed several social aspects of sign production, while in 1975 Umberto Eco submitted individual sign production to a close and brilliant scrutiny.

Human work, however, in spite of all its internal complication, certainly does not cover all that goes into the formation of any sign – into the great set of all processes which govern what I would more pompously call in Italian *il divenire segnico*, and in German, perhaps, *das Zeichenwerden*. To begin with, physiological and chemical processes are obviously intervening in all human sign production. Besides, nonhuman animals also produce signs, and the genetic code is a sign process on which all living beings depend, or from which they derive. Furthermore, nonhuman and even nonliving processes contribute to the formation of the parts which enter into the totality "sign." But since my main concern is with human social signs, it is on human work that I shall limit myself in this paper. No objection is made toward the extension of human sign facts to the sign facts of other animals, or vice versa.

What we start with, then, is the sign as a totality. Paring it to the bone, we know that every sign is expected to be composed of at least one *signans* and one *signatum*. These recently revived Augustinian terms are supposed to avoid the mentalistic ambiguity of Saussure's *signifié*. The *signans* "stands for" the *signatum*. The whole operation can also be described by saying that the sign "contains" a *renvoi*, and this may help to avoid another ambiguity, that between *signans* and sign, between one part of the totality and the totality itself.

This last ambiguity, however, is a recurrent one (even in Saussure's and Morris's texts), and it is difficult to expunge it entirely from everyday language. A current expression like "being a sign of ...," for instance, should either be substituted by "being a *signans* of ...," or taken to describe the use of the whole sign as a new *signans* for a new *signatum* (connotation).

Signans and *signatum* are to be found in the sign which has been transmitted and received, i.e in the *message*. But they are not to be found in the *signal*, for the signal is a *signans* traveling from a transmitter to a receiver. When the signal arrives, the *signans* re-embodies itself into the sign if and only if the receiver possesses a code sufficiently similar to the code of the transmitter. Common rules to use the code and contextual and existential conditions must also be sufficiently similar. I have dealt with these problems especially in my 1961 book *Significato, comunicazione e parlare comune* (Meaning, Communication, and Common Speech) which is now being reprinted [cf. R.-L. 1961d, second edition 1980]; and I am hinting at them now to explain why I deem it preferable to begin my argument on the residues of signs with signs themselves and not with either signals or messages.

In one sense, in fact, the signal is doubly removed from the sign: one returns from the signal to the sign only by going through the message, and the message in its turn requires codes and contexts. This situation has been reinforced by extrinsic but not intrinsic similarity by the fact that in a normal communicative situation the signal appears as something both precedent to, and less complex than, the sign. A simple signal is just a bit of information – there can be no internal structure in it. In this sense we speak of signals traveling in the universe not only at the level of life but also at the preorganic level.

Thus we do not start with signals because a simple signal cannot be a totality. But why don't we start with the totality "message"? The reason is that messages are more complicated than signs because they can only be explained within the complete network of a real communicative situation. The sign has the advantages of being both a totality and of lending itself to direct investigation. At the beginning there was not a message, but a sign: *Logos* by itself, not a transmitted, and received, and properly interpreted *logos*. Or, if you prefer, at the beginning there was a prehuman need. Human signs abide socially and thus become universal; they emerge together with human work to satisfy human needs. In other words, when needs become human both work and signs must be present.

Two further cautionary propositions before being reduced to our residues. Actually, these propositions are an anticipation of the theory of sign residues, but I prefer to propound them here to avoid misunderstandings. First: If no reference to the *referent* or *Bedeutung* was made so far, it is only because we shall find these most important items within the residues of the *signatum*. Second: Both *signans* and *signatum* are both material and social, but they are material and social in different manners, and the implications are different.

To sum up. We start with the sign as a two-part totality; the two parts are usually called *signans* and *signatum* and they are put and/or kept together by human work of various descriptions. We are now ready to bring forward a fundamental pair of methodological questions: what are the residues of the sign in the direction and on the side of the *signans*? and what are the residues of the sign in the direction and on the side of the *signatum*? We shall have to examine the two cases separately since they afford very asymmetric developments. We shall continue to speak of *signantia* and *signata* because we are talking signs and decided to start with the totality "sign." It should be clear that once such a totality passes away, in either direction we shall find items that are *not signantia* and *signata any longer*, although they might and usually are liable to reassume their status (in which case we may find ourselves saying that they are *not yet signantia* and *signata*). The time dimension is oozing all the time, but the fact is that it also oozes back. Signs can be past, present, or future; there are ghostly creatures which I would call ex-signs, or would-be-signs, or quasi-signs. A sign can squirt out from nowhere and immediately vanish, sometimes leaving behind a sulphureal scent. Paradoxically, we then have to construe the scent itself as a sign.

14.3.1 Residues on the Side of Signantia

We consider as residues on the side of a *signans* all the material which went into the construction of the sign-vehicle. The term, 'material,' takes here advantage of its own ambiguity: it refers to the notions of the materials upon which work is expended, but it also refers to the material character, or corporeality, of the sign-vehicle. I have dealt at length with the Morrisian notion of sign-vehicle elsewhere. I shall say here only that it should not be confused with, or worse reduced to, the Saussurian notion of *signifiant*. We are using it precisely because of its immediate materiality. But we are interested in the materiality of these vehicles insofar as they are the vehicles of signs, while we are not interested here in the materiality of a wheelbarrow which carries stones and other objects and therefore is a vehicle but not, in its normal and proper use, a sign-vehicle.

It is interesting to inspect the materials of different sign-vehicles. In the case of spoken language we have sounds which become graphs when the language is written. But while the sounds must be much the same whether the speaker is a human being or a machine, in the case of writing the materials can change remarkably – the shapes can be designed with ink on a sheet of paper or they can be engraved with a chisel on a leveled stone. Very different is the *status* of the materials used in ostensive communication. When a lady receives flowers as a token of love, she will probably admire them and smell their perfume, and the fact that they are beautiful and perfumed is part of the message she is receiving; but it is a secondary part, as is shown by the usual notion that love is shown by the action of sending flowers and not by the quality of the flowers themselves. Moreover, some poor wild flowers may have much more importance than the most magnificent box of orchids. The most important features of the materials under examination, however, are others still. The flowers continue to perfume even when nobody smells them, and within some days they wither and one throws them away. A host of different cases have been examined by various semioticians. It is easy to imagine them. A yacht is a high-level artefact, but its complexity is only very indirectly taken account of when the yacht functions as a sign of the wealth of its proprietor. Street signs are made of wood, glue, colors, or other materials which are irrelevant to their sign functions. A gesture can have a very precise meaning in a given context, but nothing remains of it unless you filmed it, and apart from the fact that both actor and spectator can remember and perhaps repeat it.

Our present concern, however, is not the enumeration of many different cases, but rather the methodological procedure that consists in entering the sign, leaving aside the *signatum*, concentrating on the *signans*, and proceeding, as it were, in the direction indicated by the *signans* as such. By so doing we come to face all the materials which could be used as signs since they could be used as *signantia*. These materials are bodies: pieces of matter, or energy as a different form of matter. They are, of course, more often than not, *socialized* bodies insofar as social work must have been expended upon them. The vanishing point here is that an object or event can be assumed as a *signans* in an instantaneous and totally nonmediated manner. We shall come back to this last point in a moment.

Becoming aware of what I have labeled since 1965 "the corporeal, or bodily, residues of signs" as materials of their *signantia* opens the road to various classifications of signs and is, in my view, a fundamental instrument for their typology. I shall list here four different possibilities of classification, with the *proviso* that they are complementary and may partially overlap. As for the difference between typology and classification, I would say that the latter is an empirical, *a posteriori* procedure, while the former retains something of what used to be called the *a priori* approach. The theory of sign residues should be an instrument for tracing back classifications to typologies.

14.3.1.1 Typology of signs according to the different materials which have gone into their signantia. This classification is empirically endless: there are signs which are "made of" sounds, gestures, paper, flowers, wood, stone, iron, flesh, bodies, movements, and so on; and we all know that sounds are not wood, flowers are not iron, flesh is not paper, and movements are not stone. Only a moment's reflection on this classifying procedure will easily convince us that all bodies and events can, in principle, function as a sign, which means that each of them can be used as material of a *signans*. However interesting, this classification is simple, or I would say simple-minded, because it is merely descriptive. One just has to sit down and list all that can be used as *signans*.

14.3.1.2 Typology of signs according to the permanence/presence of the above materials before, during, and after the actual functioning of the sign. This is a much more subtle and complicated typology. When we compare as *signantia* such very permanent objects as the marble of temples which are signs of cults etc. and such very transient objects as phonemes or gestures, we are already facing a number of problems. To begin with, the distinction between legisign and token is involved, for a temple is both a token and a legisign, while the transiency of phonemes only concerns tokens. But much more is involved. Take the case of the fire set by Herostratus to the Temple of Artemis in Ephesus in 356 B.C. If we isolate this deed, it is the sign, and a gigantic one, of Herostratus' folly. The use of "a sign ... of ..." is an example of the ambiguity between "*signans*" and "sign" hinted at above. The fact is that the isolation of Herostratus' deed is the result of a process of abstraction of which we are responsible. During the fire, as long as it lasted, a *signans* was being destroyed. The *signans* was a complex construction, and a permanent one before the sign we are considering came into being. But once the sign arose, the materials of the *signans* lasted as long as the sign. The ashes or remains also continued partially to act as *signans* of the same *signatum*, Herostratus' folly. Later on, when even the ashes and remains of the original *signans* failed to be there to foster the original sign, the sign as a totality passed over into the verbal code of oral tradition, storytelling, chronicle, and historical writing.

Thus, it would seem, the permanence of the bodily residue tends to decrease proportionally with the increase of a factor which could be called "the specificity of production." Stones and trees last more than the majority of artefacts, especially when artefacts are very refined. Vegetable and animal life, moulded and reproduced by nature without human intervention, last longer than anything which is linked in one way or another with such intervention. Mustangs as a species last longer than thoroughbreds. Weeds are transient when compared with the stone of which a temple is built, but in the long run they will submerge the temple. Artefacts, on the other hand, last longer than articulate sounds.

The more we proceed from *signantia* with natural bodies to *signantia* the bodies of which were produced for non-sign aims, and then to *signantia* whose bodies are produced precisely in order to work as *signantia*, one has the impression that matter becomes more refined, and the bodily residue recedes toward the background.

14.3.1.3 Typology of signs according to the ways in which the materials have entered the signans, and by so doing entered the sign. This third classification unifies some elements of the previous two and introduces a criterion which, in my opinion, is the most important one: The modalities of production of the *signans* and thereby of the sign itself. As I have had the opportunity of saying in several writings since 1965, we can in fact distinguish at least the following cases:

a. *Signantia pre-existing in nature*, neither produced nor manipulated by man independently from sign production. Take the case of a tree. A tree is perfectly liable to serve as a *signans* while being a natural item to the extent to which it does not belong to human cultivation; it continues to be at least partially natural even when it has been the object of human activity since it was a seed. The problem, here, is how to distinguish what is solely natural from what is natural-social – a problem well known to anybody who has given proper attention to the analysis of commodities and of money. Suppose that two explorers are wandering in virgin territory, and one says to the other, "if you want to reach a spring of fresh water, you have to turn to the right at the third tall tree that you meet after fording the stream." It is clear that that tree is "natural" in the sense of having grown on its own without being aided by manure and pruning and even without ever having been photographed or even perceived by men – with the exception of the explorer who found the spring of fresh water and conferred upon the tree the property of being a *signans*. But what about the process of isolating that tree by perceiving and numbering it in a row? The point is – is this, or is it not, human work, which makes the tree abandon pure naturality and enter a relation with man? Is perception not an operational process governed by socially induced rules? Is the very technique of numbering objects something that adds to the tree a character that nature had not supplied to it? We are here on the dividing line of traditional discussions between idealists and realists. We can get across that line and abandon those discussions, by saying that there is a sense in which the tree does remain natural in its very body, in the matter it is compounded of, while in another sense the same tree, as a sign, is a human social fact brought into existence by the two explorers as well as by us who are talking about them. Except that the work expended by men when they turn a tree into a sign *has not modified the signans as such*: not even one atom of material substance has been either substracted from, or added to, the tree (as Marx would say about the "transformation" of a good into a commodity).

Why then are we continuing to talk in terms of *signantia*? Could we not, in a simpler way, just talk about bodies which become signs when they are used in certain ways? The answer to this query is that we started with signs as totalities and entered them. If we want to keep to this procedure, we must see the bodies through the *signantia*. But in order to avoid misunderstandings as for the human social work which transforms a body into a *signans* and thereby into a sign, we must remember that we are always dealing with the body of the *signans*, of the sign-vehicle as a vehicle. To sum up, or repeat, every body or event existing by itself in nature can function as a *signans* and thereby as a sign. We have been talking so far about natural bodies or events which are not signs by themselves; in fact, they are not even *signantia*. The more natural a body or event is, the more human social work is usually required to transform it into a *signans*.

b. *Signantia produced for other aims*. These are not natural bodies in the sense of the tree of the previous example. They are produced bodies, i.e. goods of some description: They are *produced as* bodies, not as signs. This is the case in which man introduces into reality bodies which did not exist at all before his intervention. In the case of the tree used as a sign, instead, the intervention was limited to using an already existing body. In the case of flowers, we produce them in the sense that we cultivate them for other aims, and then we can also use them as signs. The previously non-existing bodies introduced into reality by man's work are all the artefacts of any complexity, from a sharpened pebble to a computer. It is obvious that the measure in which artefacts did not exist before man's production can vary very much. In some cases they partially existed, if only as materials which are then assembled by human work; in other cases their whole existence, if one can say so, depends on human intervention. For instance, a plastic model of the Parthenon cannot certainly be thought of as pre-existing to human intervention.

Now, the point is that every material artefact, even when it was not produced as a sign (and this is, after all, the majority of cases), can function as a sign. The material of the *signans* is extraneous to the sign as such, as was the tree; but on the other hand, man must have intervened upon nature with his own work at a previous stage, otherwise the *signans* itself would not exist and nothing would be available for the functioning of a sign. Man produces things also for aims which are not sign aims; but he can make the things produced work as signs, or recognize them as signs. This additional performance by them, however, is not necessary to their original production.

We are not going to consider in this paper the following additional cases: (i) Sign products which function as signs at a higher level of semiosis independently from the processes and aims for which they had been produced; (ii) the presence of sign processes even within the non-sign processes of material production.

c. *Signantia produced especially as such*, that is, bodies or events produced or manipulated or enacted only insofar as they are destined to work as *signantia*: articulate sounds, graphic shapes realized by means of colors, gestures, photographs, and so on. In these cases man does not limit himself to enacting codes out of pre-existing materials; he builds up the codes from entirely raw materials – even the material support is produced.

14.3.1.4 Typology of signs according to the level of socialization reached by the signans. This typology produces classifications which overlap with the previous ones to a remarkable extent. For brevity's sake, I shall hint only at some connections within the examples already given. Natural trees get socialized only when they are used as *signantia*, while phonemes are social items at the very beginning of their production. A car or a yacht are highly socialized already, and undergo further socialization of a different kind when they are used as *signantia* of someone's presence or of someone else's status. The materials out of which they had been originally produced as bodies, however, had reached different levels of socialization: seasoned-timber is in a way less removed from nature than GRP (glass-fiber reinforced polyester). Moreover, one would be tempted to say that the more it belongs to complex codes, the more a *signans* is socialized. This last point would perhaps offer a clue for the description of some differences between human and animal codes.

14.3.2 Residues on the Side of the Signata

If we enter the sign, break it into its two minimal components, and then proceed in the direction of the *signatum*, we are going to meet a much more tangled situation. *Signantia* are relatively easy items, *signata* are almost unbearably complex entities or processes. There are some traditional and still continuously rediscussed distinctions concerning the realm of entities and processes to be found on the side of the *signatum*. They usually cope with only a little part of that realm. We cannot attempt here a typology of *signata*, not even at the provisional level of the typology of *signantia* sketched above. But in order to identify the field of research we are referring to, and before commenting a little upon it, it is necessary to hint at three main groups of notions which traditionally accompany the term '*signatum*.'

14.3.2.1 The *signatum* as interpretant, that is, either as a modification in the behavior of the interpreter, or as a modification *within* the interpreter, in his internal structure. This is what used to be called the concept. Saussure's *signifié* is a modern instance of it. The notion of the *use* of a sign also belongs to this group. Using a thing amounts to behaving with, or with respect to, it. If we accept the notion of the sign as a totality of *signans* and *signatum*, however, the expression 'use of a sign' should be substituted by the expression 'use of a *signans*.' The use of a given *signans* is then its *signatum* and the sign is the totality consisting of a *signans* and its use. Notice that with this group of notions one begins already, at least partially, to get out of the sign. This exit is either mentalistic or (in a large sense) behavioristic: some steps are made in the direction of the interpreter as a sign operator.

14.3.2.2 The *signatum* as λεκτόν, as *Sinn* as distinguished from *Bedeutung*, as *reference* as distinguished from *referent*, as *intension* vs. *extension*, as *signification*. There is in all these notions an antipsychologistic, antimentalistic, anticonceptualistic demand. What is felt is that, independently from what is happening within or with the interpreter, for the *signans* to be what it is there must be "something objective" that accompanies it. This "something objective" was often construed in terms of ontological entities, but I believe that it can be better construed as a focus of social relations. The present group of notions pertains better than any other group to the structure of the sign as such. Also in this case, however, there is something external to the minimal structure of the sign totality in which we identified the end of the skein to be pulled.

14.3.2.3 The *signatum* as *denotatum, Bedeutung, referent*, or *extension*: a physical or nonphysical object, something that "really exists" in some manner of existence and in some sense of 'really.' Here the exit from the totality "sign" is total: We are beginning to deal with the non-sign world, with all that can be the object of non-sign work or that existed in nature independent from human sign or non-sign work. But we are, of course dealing with all these things insofar as they were, or can become again, *signata*.

Let us point out two asymmetries. This manner of "getting out" of the sign is different from the manner described in 14.3.2.1 because the interpreter is necessary to the sign while the *denotatum* is not. There are, in fact, signs which have no *denotatum* while there can be no sign without an interpreter (at least in terms of the transmitter alone, or of the receiver alone). The second asymmetry concerns the exit from the sign into the world on the side of the *signans* and on the side of the *signatum*. A complete lack of matter, if only in the form of perceivable energy, makes it impossible to have a *signans*. A *signans* therefore always has a bodily aspect which can be detected before, during, and after the functioning of the sign (the minimal requirement being that it must be there during such functioning). A *signatum*, instead, can be something nonmaterial in the sense in which a feeling, a logical relation, a commodity are not material objects. To exit the sign totality on the side of the *signans* is to describe the objective furniture of the world; to exit it on the side of the *signatum* amounts to extending our sight to the subjective and social worlds.

Things, in fact, are more complicated; but all I can add here is that they are probably amenable to dialectical treatment. It falls entirely outside the scope of this paper to examine the splendid intricacies of all that goes under the term '*signatum*,' or is connected to *signata*, so to speak, on their side. Suffice it to say that such intricacies have not yet exhausted their fertility in promoting scholarships, presidencies, colloquia, and other cultural facilities all over the world. Which should be, however, the path possibly leading us to some unifying factor? – a factor unifying *signata*, if anything, at the level of generality at which one can state that *signantia* must be bodies upon which the capacity to stand for something else is conferred by human sign work? I believe that we should begin to look at society as a totality of individuals communicating with one another. Animals become human members of a human social group insofar as they learn to communicate with one another in new ways. With this we are leaving aside the so-called "natural signs," and animal signs as well; as stated above, our boundaries are those of human social life. And after all, also natural and other-animal sign systems are studied by means of human sign systems within which they are retransmitted and reinterpreted.

This point can be made clearer by drawing attention to one important and perhaps difficult feature of social reproduction. Social reproduction includes biological reproduction, while biological reproduction does not include social reproduction. Once the reproduction is social in the full human sense of the term, biological reproduction must be seen as a part of it, and not the other way round. Social reproduction includes, of course, (i) the biological reproduction of human individuals; but also (ii) the biological reproduction of domesticated animals, and (iii) the biological reproduction of all life relevant to the human species and to the animals it uses. This was always true, to some extent, since the first emergence of human settlements and of constructive relations between men and animals (although the animals themselves, we must admit, may not always feel that such relations are constructive). In our present, ecologically threatened world, it can be said that social reproduction must take care of, and can be affected by, practically all that happens to animal and plant life at large. As soon as the most primitive, originary level of immediate appropriation of the spontaneous product of nature is abandoned, social reproduction must include much more than the mere survival of life, whether human or animal or vegetable. Biological and nonbiological dimensions have grown more and more interconnected. Not even the survival of life at the human level could now be assured without the intervention of nonbiological processes. This is one of the senses in which the formal and natural sciences are themselves an expression and a part of social reproduction.

In the light of these remarks, it is methodologically plausible to use as a foundation of knowledge what is done by us – men reunited in society. Biological and psychological processes are always present within social reproduction. But social processes take the upper hand if what we are looking for is a proper methodology of our endeavor. What is, then, the unifying element of all that goes with the *signatum* either within the totality "sign" or, outside of it, in the direction indicated by the *signatum* as opposed to the *signans*? The answer is – *social substance*: Human actions of any description, institutions, relations of men among themselves and with nature at large. The *signatum* is the coagulation of a piece of society. The residues on the side of the *signatum* are social residues to be classified in terms of social reproduction. It is also on the side of the *signatum* that we pass from signs to non-signs; and it is irrelevant whether the materials entering a given sign are themselves signs or non-sign materials before they enter it.

14.4 Signs as Mediating between the Material and the Social

We have seen that the sign is a synthesis of *signans* and *signatum* which floats, on the side of the *signans*, on an inexhaustible world of material bodies and, on the side of the *signatum*, on an inexhaustible world of social actions and institutions. Both material bodies and institutions are viewed as residues; or better, they can be systematically reached and described in semiotic terms by going through sign residues in both directions.

To conclude, let us try to submit the following definition or characterization of the sign: The sign is a mediation between the material (in the usual sense of this term) and the social. In dialectic terminology, what happens when a sign is used is that a "social thesis" is mediated by means of a "material antithesis." The *signans* as antithesis has immobilized that social piece and it has brought it to a new level as a *signatum*; by doing this, it has identified it. The antithesis is a piece of matter which is used socially (and this sense is itself socialized) in order to identify the thesis as something which had reached the social level already. The antithesis as a *signans* exercises its essential power of negation by blocking the free oozing of the only-social, imprinting it with the mark of a relative immobility. Under the impact of the antithesis, the "only-social" undergoes a change, is subjected to a new and different restriction. It accepts, so to speak, a different kind of "only." It becomes, or is reduced to, the component of a sign. Now, since the body of the *signans as signans* (though not necessarily, as we have seen, the *body as body*) is matter at a less organized stage than the *signatum*, one could suspect than within this dialectic the antithesis can only operate at a lower level than the thesis. In a sense this is true, for a sign is always a limited piece of reality. But since, by means of its lower stage of organization, the *signans* is imposing its own restricting power on the *signatum* as its opposite, the contradiction between two different levels of organization is overcome, and the provisional "peace" of a synthesis is reached. This synthesis is *the social result that we call "a sign."* In its capacity to identify bodies, society is thus being used by its own products with the aim of better identifying itself. Society provides the human individuals who are its members – i.e. it provides itself insofar as it is internally subdivided – with systems of bodies capable of preserving and handing down systems of social relations which are the syntheses of previous sign work. But the place for these difficult dialectical developments is elsewhere.

References

Eco, Umberto. 1975. *Trattato di semiotica generale*. Milan: Bompiani. English transl. as *A Theory of Semiotics*. Bloomington: Indiana University Press, 1975.

Ponzio, Augusto. 1973. *Produzione linguistica e ideologia sociale*. Bari: De Donato.

──. 1974. *Filosofia del linguaggio e prassi sociale*. Lecce: Milella.

Rossi-Landi, Ferruccio. [See the general bibliography of his writings at the end of this volume.]

Schaff, Adam. 1977. *Entfremdung als soziales Phänomen*. Vienna: Europa Verlag. Italian transl. as *L'alienazione come fenomeno sociale*, by G. Mininni. Introd. by A. Ponzio. Rome: Editori Riuniti, 1979.

Writings by Ferruccio Rossi-Landi

This bibliography was compiled by Ferruccio Rossi-Landi up to 1975 and is revised and updated by Augusto Ponzio and Susan Petrilli.

N.B. The date refers to publication; when the time lapse is considerable the original date of writing is also indicated in square brackets. This information was provided by Rossi-Landi.

1949a. "Considerazioni semantiche sulla musica." *La rassegna musicale* XVIII, 2: 113-122.
1949b. "Bernard C. Heyl e l'estetica del relativismo." *Lettere italiane* I, 3: 129-144 (with the addition of four "Notarelle").
1949c. "'Libertà semantica'?" *La rassegna d'Italia* IV, 9: 930-933.
1949d. *Storia filosofica della scienza.* Italian transl. (with S. Ceccato) of Hugo Dingler, *Geschichte der Naturphilosophie.* Milan: Longanesi.
1950. Critical notes, reviews and discussions in *Methodos* 1950 and 1951.
1951a. "De la communication d'une langue au point de vue épistémologique et au point de vue opératif." [1949]. Congrès International de Philosophie des Sciences, Paris, Sorbonne, 1949. *Actes* I° (= Epistemologie), 177-182. Paris: Hermann.
1951b. "Problemi di metodologia e analisi del linguaggio." *Aut Aut* I, 1: 76-80.
1951c. "Il Manuale di Richard von Mises." *Rivista di filosofia* XLII, 4: 424-439.
1951d. Review of *Value: A Cooperative Inquiry*. Ed. by R. Lepley. New York: Columbia University Press, 1949. *Methodos* III, 9: 65-68. In Rossi-Landi 1992.
1951e. Review of *Logic and Language*. Ed. by A.G.N. Flew. *Methodos* 3: 208-210.
1951f. Review of Silvio Ceccato, *Language and the Table of Ceccatieff. Methodos* 3: 132-137.
1952. "Sugli scritti di Eugenio Colorni." *Rivista critica di storia della filosofia* VII, 2: 147-153.
1953a. *Charles Morris*. [1951-1952]. (= Storia universale della filosofia, 21. Series directed by Mario Dal Pra). Milan: Bocca. (Reprinted in 1975d.)
1953b. "Towards an Analysis of Appraisive Signs in Aesthetics." [1952]. *Methodos* V, 18: 103-120. This volume, Ch. 5.
1953c. "La nozione di unità in arte." XIème Congrès International de Philosophie, Brussels, 1953. *Actes* X: 253-258.

1953d. "Socialità nella filosofia inglese contemporanea." *Comunità* VII, 17: 43-45.
1953e. "La filosofia come analisi del linguaggio." XVI National Congress of Philosophy, Bologna, 1953. *Atti*, 674-680. Rome: Bocca.
1953f. "Riserve di un anglofilo." *Occidente* IX, 3/4: 192-222.
1954a. "Del non-traducibile." Congress of Methodological Studies, Turin, 1952. *Atti*, 112-117. Turin: Ramella.
1954b. Review of *Le basi fisiche del pensiero*. By various authors. Turin: Einaudi, 1953. *Rivista critica di storia della filosofia* IX, 4: 405-412.
1954c. Review of Francesco Barone, *Il neopositivismo logico*. Turin: Edizioni di Filosofia, 1953. *Rivista critica di storia della filosofia* IX, 6: 631-635.
1954d. *Lineamenti di una teoria dei segni*. Introd., transl. and comment by Charles Morris. *Foundations of the Theory of Signs* (= Biblioteca di filosofia e pedagogia). Turin: Paravia.
1955a. *Lo spirito come comportamento*. [1953]. Revised Italian ed. with an introductory essay by Gilbert Ryle. *The Concept of Mind* (Biblioteca di cultura filosofica, 19). Turin: Einaudi.
1955b. "Sulla mentalità della filosofia analitica." *Rivista di filosofia* XLVI, 1: 48-63.
1955c. "La filosofia analitica di Oxford." *Rivista critica di storia della filosofia* X, 1: 69-84.
1955d. "L'eredità di Moore e la filosofia delle quattro parole." *Rivista di filosofia* XLVI, 3: 304-326.
1955e. "La filosofia analitica." Six letters exchanged with L. Lombardo-Radice. *Il Contemporaneo* II, 50: 10-11.
1955f. "A proposito di Caiumi e di Croce." Four letters exchanged with Renato Treves. *Occidente* XI, 6: 539-544.
1956. "Di alcune modalità del filosofare." *Rivista di filosofia* XLVII, 3: 267-295.
1957a. "Some Modern Italian Philosophers: 1° The Knife-Grinders, 2° The Pontiffs." [1956]. Conversations held on the third Program of the BBC, December 1956. *The Listener* LVII, 1450: 59-61; 1451: 97-98.
1957b. "Osservazioni sul nuovo corso della filosofia italiana." *Rivista di filosofia* XLVIII, 3: 298-304.
1957c. "Attività umane e momenti dello Spirito." Paper presented at the Philosophical Convention of Bologna, April 1957. Now in *La ricerca filosofica nella coscienza delle nuove generazioni*, 38-51. Bologna: Il Mulino.
1957d. "Sul carattere linguistico del filosofare." *Aut Aut* 39: 268-284.
1957e. Giovanni Vailati. *Il metodo della filosofia*. Introd. notes and ed. by F. Rossi-Landi. Bari: Laterza. (Revised reprint, 1967.)
1957f. Una nuova lettura di Giovanni Vailati. *Cultura moderna* 30: 17-19.
1958a. "Universo del discorso e lingua ideale in filosofia." [1956]. *Il pensiero americano contemporaneo*, 2 vols. Ed. by F. Rossi-Landi. Vol. I: 133-182. Milan: Edizioni di Comunità.
1958b. "Filosofia della scienza." [1956] (with Vittorio Somenzi). *La filosofia contemporanea in Italia. Società e filosofia di oggi in Italia*. Ed. by Rossi-Landi *et al.*, 407-432. Asti-Rome: Aretusa.

1958c. "Materiale per lo studio di Vailati." *Rivista critica di storia della filosofia* XII, 4: 468-485; XIII, 1: 82-108.
1958d. "Universi del discorso." *Rivista di filosofia* XLIX, 3: 396-421.
1958e. "Aspetti della riforma logico-linguistica in filosofia." Reworked text of a paper presented at the Sodalizio Glottologico Milanese, May 1957. *Atti* of the S.G.M., Milan, 16-32.
1958f. "La polemica contro lo storicismo." *Nord e Sud* V, 40: 104-112.
1959a. Gustav Bergmann. "The Contribution of John B. Watson." Transl. and notes by F. Rossi-Landi. *Rivista di psicologia* LII, 4: 311-325.
1959b. "Critica metafisica e filosofia analitica." *Rivista di diritto civile* V, 2: 201-215.
1959c. "L'estetica del divenire nell'ultimo libro di Gillo Dorfles." *Notiziario Einaudi* VIII, 1: 18-19.
1959d. Translation and revision of the Proceedings of the IV world Congress of Sociology. *Atti. La sociologia nel suo contesto sociale*; *Sociologia: applicazioni e ricerche*. Milan-Stresa, September 1959. Bari: Laterza.
1959e. "La sociologia torna in Italia." *Cultura moderna* 5, 43: 12-14.
1959f. Denis Mack Smith. *Garibaldi*. Transl. introd. and notes by F. Rossi-Landi. Milan: Lerici.
1960a. "La costanza del parlare comune." *Rivista di filosofia* L, 4: 465-483.
1960b. "'Costanza' e 'fluenza' logico-linguistiche." *Atti*, vol. IV: 295-301. Florence: Sandron.
1961a. "Rigorizzazione del concetto di verità e tolleranza intellettuale." XVIII National Congress of Philosophy, Palermo-Messina, March 1960. *Atti*, vol. I: 442-450. Palermo: Palumbo.
1961b. *Sapere scientifico e sapere filosofico*, (Padua-Magistero, 1960), 112-118, 149-153, 193-194. Florence: Sansoni.
1961c. "Husserl sulla comunicazione." *Nuova corrente* 22: 37–46.
1961d. *Significato, comunicazione e parlare comune*. Padua: Marsilio; 1980(2), with an introduction of 1979.
1965. "Il linguaggio come lavoro e come mercato." *Nuova corrente* 36: 5-43.
1966a. "Sul linguaggio verbale e non-verbale." *Nuova corrente* 37: 5-28.
1966b. "Per un uso marxiano di Wittgenstein." *Nuovi Argomenti* N.S., I, 1: 187-230.
1966c. Giovanni Vailati. "La grammatica dell'algebra." Presentation by F. Rossi-Landi. *Nuova corrente* 38: 131-132.
1966d. "Schema per una dialettica del teatro d'avanguardia." *Nuova corrente* 39/40: 285-292.
1967a. Entries: M. Calderoni, C. Cattaneo, E. Colorni, H. Dingler, F. Enriques, G. Peano, G. Vailati. [1964]. *Encyclopedia of Philosophy*, 8 vols. Ed. by P. Edwards. New York: MacMillan & Free Press.
1967b. "Note di semiotica: 1. Perché 'semiotica'; 2. Su enunciato, proposizione e contesto; 3. Sul pregiudizio contrattualistico." *Nuova corrente* 41: 90-109.
1967c. "Uso e significato di parole ed enunciati." *Ricerche metodologiche* III, 1: 33-45.

1967d. "Lavorando all'omologia del produrre." *Nuovi Argomenti* 6: 70-83.
1967e. "Il teatro e il suo procedimento." *D'Ars Agency* VIII, 35: 98-99.
1967f. "Ideologia come progettazione sociale." *Ideologie* 1: 1-25.
1967g. Presentation of three writings by Charles Morris. *Nuova corrente* 42/43: 113-117. Now "Sul modo in cui è stata fraintesa la semiotica estetica di Charles Morris." In Rossi-Landi 1972i: 64-70.
1967h. "Il centro-sinistra cibernetico." *Paese Sera* XVIII, 340: 3.
1967i. "La scienza dei segni." *Paese Sera* XVIII, 353: 3.
1968a. "Questions concerning: Elio Pagliarani. Difficoltà ideologiche del lavoro poetico." *Ideologie* 2: 94-98.
1968b. "Guevara e la scienza dell'uomo." *Paese Sera* XIX, 15: 3.
1968c. "Teatro come azione sociale." *Paese Sera* XIX, 35: 3.
1968d. "Una figliastra della borghesia." *Paese Sera* XIX, 57: 3.
1968e. "Significato, ideologia e realismo artistico." *Nuova corrente* 44: 300-342.
1968f. "Editoriale: per un rinnovamento dell'elaborazione ideologica" (with Mario Sabbatini). *Ideologie* 3: 3-8.
1968g. "Ideologie della relatività linguistica." *Ideologie* 4: 3-69; Spanish transl. 1974c; English transl. 1973d.
1968h. *Il linguaggio come lavoro e come mercato*. Milan: Bompiani. (= Nuovi saggi italiani, 2), 1973(2), 1983(3). The third edition includes (in order): 1966b, 1965, 1966a, 1967f, 1967d, 1970b, and an unpublished paper; English transl. 1983b; Spanish transl. 1972a; German transl. (unreadable) 1972j; German transl. of the 2nd ed. 1974a; partial translations into Hungarian and Portuguese available.
1968i. "Note di semiotica: Sui segni del mare interpretati dai naviganti; Sui programmi della comunicazione non-verbale." *Nuova corrente* 46/47: 296-319.
1968j. "Editoriale" (with Antonio Melis and Mario Sabbatini). Special issue of *Ideologie. Le radici storiche della rivoluzione cubana. Ideologie* 5/6: 3-6.
1969a. "Cervelli, calcolatori e sistemi semiotici." Intervention on a paper by Vittorio Somenzi presented at the colloquium on "L'automazione elettronica e le sue implicazioni scientifiche, tecniche e sociali," Rome, Accademia Nazionale dei Lincei, October 16-19, 1967. *Atti*. Quaderno n. 110, 238-241. Rome: Accademia Nazionale dei Lincei.
1969b. "Neofeudalesimo finanziario-tecnocratico e nuovo contropotere politico." Reply to the questionnaire, "Partiti, sindacati, contestazione dal basso e nuova sinistra" (with Mario Sabbatini). *Questitalia* 130/131: 78-83.
1969c. "Dialettica e alienazione nel linguaggio." Conversation between Enzo Golino and Ferruccio Rossi-Landi. *Paragone* (= Letteratura) XX, 234: 78-160.
1969d. "Editoriale: Rivoluzione e studio." *Ideologie* 9/10: 4-16.
1969e. "Extension de l'homologie entre énoncés et outils." X Congrès International des Linguistes, Bucharest, August 28 – September 2, 1967. *Actes*, vol. I: 503-508. Bucharest: Éditions de l'Académie de la République Socialiste de Roumanie.

1969f. "Remarks on Prof. Jakobson's paper." cf. 1969e: 112-113.
1970a. "Russell filosofo." *Paese Sera Libri* XXI, 36: 1-2.
1970b. "Problemi dell'alienazione linguistica." *Linguaggi nella società e nella tecnica*. Colloquium held at the Museo nazionale della scienza e della tecnica, Milan, October 14-17, 1968, 83-112. Milan: Edizioni di Comunità. English transl., 513-543 as "Linguistic Alienation Problems"; now in Rossi-Landi 1992.
1970c. *Dizionario teorico-ideologico*: "Premessa," 3-6; "Calcolatori e cervelli," 6-10; "Corpo" (with Giuseppe Di Siena): 11-20; "Semiotica," 38-44. *Ideologie* 12.
1971a. "Editoriale. Produrre uomini nuovi." *Ideologie* 15: 3-7.
1971b. *Dizionario teorico-ideologico*: "Premessa," 10-12; "Dialettica dello scambio esogamico," 12-15; "Lavoro e attività," 21-23; "Ominazione," 23-25; "Scambio non-mercantile," 38-41; "Strutture del lavoro," 41-49. *Ideologie* 15.
1971c. "Editoriale: Le nostre forze e la Rivoluzione cinese." *Ideologie. Per lo studio della Rivoluzione cinese* 13/14: 5-12.
1971d. "Premessa" to *Testi di revisionisti sovietici. Ideologie. Per lo studio della Rivoluzione cinese* 13/14: 345-350.
1971e. "Sul contributo di Mao alla dialettica." *Ideologie. Per lo studio della Rivoluzione cinese* 13/14: 519-540. German transl. 1972h.
1972a. *El lenguaje como trabajo y como mercado*. Caracas: Monte Ávila. Spanish transl. of 1968h.
1972b. *Dizionario teorico-ideologico*: "Programmazione sociale dei comportamenti," 18-22; "Programmi della comunicazione," 22-36; "Sistemi segnici," 36-42. *Ideologie* 16/17.
1972c. "Omologia della riproduzione sociale." *Ideologie* 16/17: 43-103.
1972d. *Scritti programmatici di Ideologie*. Edizioni di Ideologie.
1972e. "Kapital und Privateigentum in der Sprache." Transl. by K. Steinbacher. *Ästhetik und Kommunikation. Beiträge zur politischen Erziehung* III, 7: 36-46.
1972f. "Programación social y comunicación." *Casa de las Américas* 71: 20-35. Includes revised editions of items from *Dizionario teorico-ideologico*, cf. 1970c and 1972b.
1972g. "Semiótica; Programación social de los comportamientos; Ampliación de la homología entre enunciados y utensilios; Autonomía de los sistemas sígnicos no-verbales." *Santiago. Revista de la Universidad de Oriente* 6: 7-43. Includes revised editions of items from *Dizionario teorico-ideologico*, cf. 1970c and 1972b, and other materials now in *Semiotica e ideologia* (1972i).
1972h. "Über Mao's Beitrag zur Dialektik. Deutsch von Arno Widmann." *Ästhetik und Kommunikation* III, 8: 72-83. Transl. of 1971e.
1972i. *Semiotica e ideologia*. Milan: Bompiani, 1972. (= Uomo e società, 21), 1979 (2). The second edition includes (in order): 1967b, 1967c, 1968c, 1967e, 1966d, 1969e, 1967g, 1968i, 1973b, 1968g, 1968i, 1969c, 1970c. German transl. available in two separate volumes (Munich: Hanser; Frankfurt: Makol, 1973a). Partial transl. available in English (The Hague: Mouton). Spanish transl. in three volumes (Buenos Aires: Nueva Visión, 1974c).

1972j. *Sprache als Arbeit und als Markt*. Ed. by K. Steinbacher. Munich: Hanser. German transl. of 1968h. See also 1974a.

1972k. "Per lo studio della rivoluzione cinese." Letter by Ferruccio Rossi-Landi and Giuseppe di Siena to the Director of *Politica ed Economia*. Published in *Politica ed economia* with a reply from Adriano Guerra, III, 6: 161-163.

1972l. "Trabajo y cambio." *Santiago. Revista de la Universidad de Oriente* 9: 40-69. Includes revised editions of items from *Dizionario teorico-ideologico*, cf. 1971b.

1973a. *Dialektik und Entfremdung in der Sprache*. Transl. by A. Widmann. Frankfurt: Makol. Includes (in order): 1969c and 1968g.

1973b. "Commodities as Messages." Paper presented at the *Symposium de Varsovie*, August 25 - September 1, 1968. *Actes: Recherches sur les systèmes signifiants*, 625-631. The Hague-Paris: Mouton.

1973c. "Scienza, tecnica e società: neutralità e responsabilità dello scienziato." *Ricerche metodologiche* VI, 1/2: 79-81.

1973d. *Ideologies of Linguistic Relativity* (= Approaches to Semiotics, Paperback Series, 4). The Hague: Mouton. Reproduces 1968g with a supplementary bibliography.

1974a. *Sprache als Arbeit und als Markt*. Transl. of the 2nd ed. of 1968h. Ed. by B. Kroeber. Munich: Hanser. See also 1972j.

1974b. "Sul denaro linguistico." *Follia e società segregativa*, 96-123. Congress held in Milan, December 13-16, 1973. Milan: Feltrinelli. (Bibliography, 303-308.)

1974c. *Ideologías de la relatividad lingüística*. Transl. by J. A. Vasco. Buenos Aires: Nueva Visión. Spanish transl. of 1968g.

1974d. *José Martí*. Anthology of texts and criticism. Introd. and ed. by C. Vitier. Italian ed. F. Rossi-Landi (ed.). E. Clementelli and L. Acerbi (transl.). In collab. with the Editiorial Committee of *Ideologie*, with a "Premessa" by the Direction. Rome: Edizioni di Ideologie.

1974e. "Articulations in Verbal and Objectual Sign Systems." (Centro Internazionale di Semiotica e di Linguistica dell'Università di Urbino). *Working Papers* 38/39. This volume, Ch. 9.

1974f. "Linguistics and Economics." [1970-1971]. Part eight of Volume XII, *Linguistics and Adjacent Arts and Sciences. Current Trends in Linguistics*, tome 3: 1787-2017. The Hague: Mouton. (Published also as an independent volume in the series Janua Linguarum, Series Maior, 81, same publisher, cf. 1975b).

1975a. [1964-1966]. Eugenio Colorni. *Scritti* (= Biblioteca di cultura, 126). Ed. by F. Rossi-Landi. Introd. by N. Bobbio. Florence: La Nuova Italia.

1975b. *Linguistics and Economics*. [1970-1971]. (= Janua Linguarum, Series Maior, 81). The Hague: Mouton, 1977(2). Reproduces, with revisions and addition of indexes, 1974f.

1975c. "Signs about a Master of Signs." [1973]. A review article of Charles Morris, *Writings on the General Theory of Signs* (= Approaches to Semiotics, 16). Ed. by T.A. Sebeok. The Hague: Mouton, 1971. *Semiotica* XIII, 2: 155-197. (Revised and enlarged Italian ed. in 1975d). This volume, Ch. 2.

1975d. *Charles Morris e la semiotica novecentesca* (= Semiotica e pratica sociale, 1). Reproduces 1953a, the Italian ed. of 1975c [1973], and an "Avvertenza." Milan: Feltrinelli.

1976a. "On Absurdity." [1963]. With a "Head Note" of 1975. *Semiotica* XVI, 4: 347-367. This volume, Ch. 6.

1976b. "Ideen zum Studium sprachlicher Entfremdung." *Soziolinguistik*. Ed. by A. Schaff, 171-198. Vienna: Europa Verlag.

1976c. "Criteri per lo studio ideologico di un autore." *Quaderni latino americani* 2: 5-32. Now in Rossi-Landi 1985a: 167-192.

1977. Introduction to *Semiosis and Social Reproduction*. [1974]. (Centro internazionale di semiotica e di linguistica dell'Università di Urbino). *Working Papers* 63. This volume, Ch. 8.

1978a. "Ontologia sociale delle proprietà e primo articolarsi della falsa coscienza." *Psicoanalisi e classi sociali*, 21-43. Transactions of the homonymous Colloquium held in Milan in December 1977. Rome: Editori Riuniti.

1978b. "Sign Systems and Social Reproduction." [1976]. *Ideology and Consciousness* 3: 49-65. This volume, Ch. 10.

1978c. *Ideologia*. Milan: ISEDI. 2nd revised, enlarged ed. Milan: Mondadori, 1980; English transl. 1990.

1978d. "On the Overlapping of Categories in the Social Sciences." [1972]. Ninth International Congress of Anthropological and Ethnological Sciences, Chicago, August-September 1973. *Language and Thought. Anthropological Issues*. Ed. by W.C. McCormack and S.A. Wurm, 391-403. The Hague: Mouton. This volume, Ch. 7.

1978e. "On Some Post-Morrisian Problems." *Ars semeiotica* 3: 3-32. German transl. by A. Eschbach in *Zeichen über Zeichen über Zeichen. 15 Studien über Charles W. Morris*. Ed. by A. Eschbach, 235-266. Tübingen: Narr, 1981; Italian transl. in Charles Morris, *Segni e valori*. Transl., introd. and ed. by S. Petrilli, 201-231. Bari: Adriatica, 1988. This volume, Ch. 3.

1979a. "On the Dialectic of Exogamic Exchange." [1972]. Ninth International Congress of Anthropological and Ethnological Sciences, Chicago, August-September 1973. *Towards a Marxist Anthropology*. Ed. by S. Diamond, 141-150. The Hague: Mouton.

1979b. "Signs and Bodies." [1974]. *A Semiotic Landscape*, 356-359. Proceedings of the First Congress of the International Association for Semiotic Studies, Milan, June 1974. The Hague: Mouton. This volume, Ch. 12.

1979c. "Towards a Theory of Sign Residues." Paper presented at the third Austrian Symposium of Semiotics, Vienna, August 1977. Subsequently published in *Versus* 23: 15-32; German transl. by J. Bernard and G. Withalm. "Aug dem Wege zu einer Theorie der Zeichenresiduen." *S. – European Journal for Semiotic Studies. Dialectics, Semiotics, Materialism. In Memoriam Ferruccio Rossi-Landi* 3, 1/2 (1991): 205-277. This volume, Ch. 14.

1979d. "Introduzione" to the new edition of *Significato, comunicazione e parlare comune* (1961, 2nd ed. 1980). Prepublished in a non definitive form with the title "Per la ristampa di un mio vecchio libro." *Science umane* 2: 147-167.

1979e. "Wittgenstein e l'alienazione." Paper presented at the Congress of Studies on Wittgenstein: Linguaggio e conoscenza come realtà sociale, Rome 1979. *Scienze umane* 1: 135-145; German transl. in the Proceedings of the Colloquium. *Sprache und Erkenntnis als soziale Tatsache.* Ed. by R. Haller, 108-118. Vienna: HPT, 1981.

1979f. "Aspetti biologici e aspetti sociali del linguaggio nella loro interrelazione" (with Massimo Pesaresi). *Scienze umane* 3: 37-96.

1979g. "Ideas for a Manifesto of Materialistic Semiotics." *Codice* 2: 121-123. This volume, Ch. 13.

1979h. "Zeichenproduktion." Partially republished as "Das semiotische Modell der (Zeichen-)Produktion." See 1983c.

1979i. "Ideas for the Study of Linguistic Alienation." *Social Praxis* 3, 1/2: 79-92. This volume, Ch. 11.

1980. "I residui dei segni." [1974]. *Scienza, linguaggio e metafilosofia*, 267-279. Naples: Guida.

1981a. "Wittgenstein, Old and New." [1979]. Contribution for the series "The Viennese Heritage" presented at the Second Congress of the International Association for Semiotic Studies, Vienna, July 1979. Republished in *Ars semeiotica* IV, 1: 29-51. This volume, Ch. 4.

1981b. "Gondolatok a nyelvi, elidegenedésröl." *Szemiotikai Tanulmányok. Semiotic Studies* 59: 117-131.

1983a. "Uso sociale e uso personale dei sistemi segnici." [1982]. *Il gioco impari*, 29-32. Milan: Angeli.

1983b. *Language as Work & Trade. A Semeiotic Homology for Linguistic & Economics.* South Hadley (MA): Bergin & Garvey; English transl. by M. Adams *et al.* of 1968h, 1973(2).

1983c. "Das semiotische Modell der (Zeichen-)Produktion." *Didaktische Umsetzung der Zeichentheorie. Akten des 4. Symposiums der Osterreichischen Gesellschaft fur Semiotik, Linz 1981* (= Angewandte Semiotik, 2). Ed. by J. Bernard, 93-111. Vienna-Baden: OGS.

1985a. *Metodica filosofica e scienza dei segni.* Milan: Bompiani. Includes revised editions (in order) of: 1971b, 1972c, 1978d, 1980, 1976c, 1978a, 1979f.

1985b. "L'autore fra riproduzione sociale e discontinuità." Seminar held at the Institute of Philosophy of Language, Bari University, April 19, 1985. *Lectures* 15: 149-174.

1985c. "Il segno e i suoi residui." Paper presented at the Facoltà di Lingue e Letterature Straniere, Bari University, April 19, 1985. In A. Ponzio, *Ferruccio Rossi-Landi e la filosofia del linguaggio*, 263-291. Bari: Adriatica, 1988.

1985d. "Concerning Some Aspects of Communicating Something New" (with Haimo I. Handl). *Semiotische Berichte* 9, 1/2: 30-35 (parts of an interview held on June 18, 1984).

1986. "Semiosi e riproduzione sociale." Paper presented at the Institute of Philosophy of Language, Bari University, May 7, 1976. *Idee* 2/3: 87-97.

1987. "La 'non-filosofia'." *Il Progatora. Per Ferruccio Rossi-Landi* 11-12. Ed. by S. Petrilli, 191-194.

1988. "A Fragment in the History of Italian Semiotics." [1984]. *Semiotic Theory and Practice. Proceedings of the Third International Congress of the IASS, Palermo, 1984*. Ed. by M. Herzfeld and L. Melazzo. Berlin: Mouton de Gruyter, 1988; Italian transl. by S. Petrilli in A. Ponzio, *Rossi-Landi e la filosofia del linguaggio*, 243-261. Bari: Adriatica, 1988. This volume, Ch. 1.

1990. *Marxism and Ideology*. Oxford: Clarendon; English transl. by R. Griffin of 1978c.

1991. "Work, Signs, and Some Uses of Language." *Zeichen/Manipulation. Akten des 5. Symposiums der Osterreichischen Gesellschaft fur Semiotik, Klagenfurt 1984* (= Angewandte Semiotik, 6). Ed. by J. Bernard. Vienna-Baden: OGS.

1992. *Social Practice, Semiotics and the Sciences of Man. The Correspondence between Charles Morris and Ferruccio Rossi-Landi*. Introd. and ed. by S. Petrilli. *Semiotica* 88, 1/2.

Index Auctorum

A.
Abbagnano, N.: 12
Acerbi, L.: 306
Adler, A.: 49
Adorno, T.W.: 266
Alston, W.: 147, 154
Althusser, L.: xxiv, 279
Anscombe, G.E.M.: 108, 168
Anshen, R.N.: 47, 48
Aristotle: 53, 88, 155
Artemis: 291
Augustine, St.: xxii, 287
Austin, J.: 154
Axelos, K.: 266

B.
Baillie, J.B.: 168
Bakhtin, M.M.: xii, xxiv, xxvi, 65, 83
Bally, C.: 56
Barone, F.: 12, 83
Baskin, W.: 56, 266
Baudrillard, J.: 266
Beavin, J.H.: 155
Bentham, J.: 9
Bentley, A.F.: 81, 96-97, 106
Bergin, T.G.: 11
Bergmann, G.: 303
Berkeley, G.: 9
Berlin, I.: 11, 15, 107, 168, 276
Bernard, J.: xxvi, 128
Biancofiore, A.: xvii, xxiv, xxvii
Biemel, M.: 54
Boas, F.: 95, 106

C.
Cacciari, M.: 91, 106
Cairns, D.: 54
Calabrese, O.: xxvii
Calderoni, M.: xiv, 12, 15, 60, 83, 303
Calogero, G.: 83
Campa, O.: 15, 83
Caputo, C.: xxvii
Carnap, R.: 21, 62, 97
Casetti, F.: xxvii
Cassina, U.: 84
Cattaneo, C.: 11, 15, 60, 83, 303
Ceccato, S.: 12-13, 18, 60, 83, 96-97, 106, 128, 154
Ceres: 149-150
Cesare, G.: 84
Chaple, S.: 54
Chatterjee, R.: xxvii

Bobbio, N.: xxv, 12, 251
Boehm, R.: 54
Bois, J.: 266
Boselli, M.: 91, 108
Boudon, R.: xxiv, xxvii
Bourdieu, P.: xxiv, xxvii
Bradley, F.H.: xiv, 14
Brendel, C.: 56, 84, 267
Brentano, F.: 90
Brewster, J.M.: 47
Bridgman, P.W.: 96-97, 117, 128
Bryson, L.: 47
Burke, K.: 51
Burks, W.: 55

Chomsky, N.: xiv, xxv, 154
Churchill, J.S.: 54
Clementelli, E.: 306
Cohen, J.: 266
Colli, G.: 107
Colorni, E.: xiv, xxv, 12, 15, 60, 83, 303, 306
Condillac, E. Bonnot de: 10
Corti, M.: 65, 83
Croce, B.: xiv, 12-13

D.
Dal Pra, M.: 85, 301
De Crescenzo, G.: 83
Descartes, R.: 30, 68, 123
Democritus: 10
De Morgan, A.: 135
Destutt de Tracy, A.-L.-C.: 55, 84
Dewe, J.A.: 51
Dewey, J.: 21, 62, 67, 81, 83, 96-98, 106
Dhoquoi, G.: 251
Diamond, S.: 307
Díaz-Diocaretz, M.: xxiii
Dingler, H.: xiv, 96-97, 117, 128, 195, 303
Di Siena, G.: 305
Dongeville, R.: 266
Donini, A.: 245, 251
Dorfles, G.: 303
Dunham, A.M.: 47

E.
Eco, U.: xxv, xxvii, 52, 54, 65, 83, 93, 106, 287, 299
Edwards, P.: 303
Eiduson, B.T.: 49
Einaudi, L.: 107
Emerson, C.: xxvi
Engels, F.: 89, 106-107, 166, 168, 185, 277

Engler, R.: 38
Enriques, F.: xiv, 12, 15, 60, 83, 303
Eschbach, A.: xxix, 307

F.
Faccani, R.: 107
Facchi, P.: xxv
Fatta, C.: 83
Feuerbach, L.: 277
Filiasi-Carcano, P.: 12
Finkelstein, L.: 47
Fisch, M.H.: 11
Fischer, S.: 107
Fleischer, M.: 54
Foucault, M.: xxiv
Frege, F.L.G.: 12
Frescobaldi, G.: 151
Freud, S.: xix, xviii, 89, 91, 100-104, 107-108

G.
Galilei, G.: 247
Gambarara, D.: 84
Gentile, G.: xiv, 12, 128
Gerratana, V.: 15
Geymonat, L.: 12, 83
Goldmann, L.: xi, 218
Golino, E.: 304
Goux, J.-J.: 266
Gramsci, A.: 13, 15, 68, 83-89, 241, 249, 251, 280
Grillo, E.: 266
Guerra, A.: 306

H.
Hall, S.: 128
Haller, R.: 308
Hamilton, D.J.: xvi
Handl, H.I.: 308
Hartshorne, C.: 55

Hegel, G.W.F.: xv, 2, 14, 28, 68, 83, 103, 159, 168, 175, 184, 195-196, 205, 208, 238, 271, 284
Heidegger, M.: 108
Heijerman, E.: xxvii
Herder, J.G.: 15
Herostratus: 291
Hervey, S.G.J.: 52
Herzfeld, M.: 309
Heyl, B.C.: 128
Hitler, A.: 88
Hjelmslev, L.: 195
Hobsbawm, E.J.: 266
Holquist, M.: xxvi
Holton, G.: 48
Homer: 151
Hook, S.: 48
Horkheimer, M.: 266
Hull, C.L.: 27, 66
Hume, D.: 9
Husserl, E.: xiv-xxv, 52, 54, 195, 205
Huxley, J.: 84

I.
Ivanov, V.V.: 229

J.
Jackson, D.D.: 155
Jakobson, R.: 30, 51, 54
James, W.: 12, 21, 47, 62
Jones, L.V.: 48
Jonson, R.: 47

K.
Kallen, H.M.: 47, 48
Kant, E.: 14, 28, 155, 183-184
Kaplan, A.: 47
Kelemen, J.: xxv, xxvii
Kepes, G.: xxviii, 48, 49
Klibansky, R.: xxvii

Kloesel, C.J.W.: 15
Kluckhohn, C.: 48
Koerner, E.F.K.: 54
Kokoschka, O.: 90
Konvitz, M.R.: 48
Kosík, K.: 68, 83
Kovanda, K.: 83
Kraus, K.: 90
Kristeva, J.: 51-55, 65, 84

L.
Laguna, G.A. de: 50
Lanaro, G.: 16, 85
Lanuë-Villène, G.: 50
Lasson, G.: 83
Latzke, M.: 84
Leakey, L.S.B.: 84
Lenneberg, E.: 165, 168
Lepley, R.: xxviii, 48, 301
Lévinas, E.: 54
Lézine, I.: 51, 55
List, E.: xxvi, 93, 279
Livingstone, R.: 251, 266
Locke, J.: 9, 183
Lombardo-Radice, L.: 15, 83, 302
Loos, A.: 90
Lorenz, K.: 80, 84
Lotman, Y.M.: 51, 55, 95, 107-108, 229
Lukács, G.: 88-89, 107, 241, 251, 256
Luperini, R.: xxv

M.
Mace, C.A.: 56
Mach, E.: 12, 90
Macherey, P.: 218
MacIver, R.M.: 47
Maldonado, T.: xvi
Malinowski, B.: 182
Mao Tse-tung: 28
Marcus, S.: 51, 55

Markey, J.F.: 50
Marr, N. Ja: 247
Martí, J.: 306
Martinet, A.: xx, 187, 197-198, 232
Marx, K.: xix-xv, xx, 2, 10, 14, 28, 45, 88-89, 91, 100-107, 134, 161-162, 166, 168, 185, 187, 239, 247, 250-251, 254, 256, 259-262, 265-266, 271, 276-277, 293
Marzaduri, M.: 107
Masters, R.D.: 6, 30, 55
Matejka, L.: 85
McGuiness, B.F.: 155
McLellan, D.: 161, 168
Mead, G.H.: 19, 21, 27, 47, 55, 62, 66, 95, 107, 277
Meddemmen, J.: 84
Meek, P.: 49
Meinong, A. von: 90
Melazzo, L.: 309
Meletinsky, E.: 55
Melis, A.: 304
Miceli, S.: xxvii
Mill, J.S.: 9
Miller, D.L.: 47
Mininni, G.: xxvii
Miscevič, N.: xxvi, xxvii
Mises, R. von: 147, 154
Mondadori, F.: xxvii
Monteverdi, C.: 151
Montinari, M.: 107
Mooney, M.J.: 16
Moore, C.A.: 21, 62
Moore, G.E.: 21, 62
Morris, C.: xiv, xvi, xix, xxiii, xxv, xxvii-xxviii, 1, 8, 11-13, 15-44, 46, 51-53, 55, 57, 59-79, 82, 84, 97-99, 107, 111-116, 118, 120, 124, 126, 128, 174, 277, 283, 287
Mucci, E.: xxvii
Mukařovský, J.: 51, 55
Mulder, J.W.F.: 52, 55

Murray, H.A.: 48
Musil, R.: 90

N.

Nagel, E.: 49
Nagt, L.: xxvi
Navarro, D.: 51, 55
Neurath, O.: 51
Nicolaus, M.: 161, 168
Nietzsche, F.: 91, 104, 106-108
Nyíri, C.: 92, 107

O.

O'Donovan, D.: 49
Ogden, C.K.: xxv
Orwell, G.: 78
Osgood, C.E.: 49

P.

Paci, E.: 12, 84
Pagliarani, E.: 304
Papastamatin, B.: 55
Papini, G.: 83
Parmenides: 246
Parsons, T.: 182
Passeron, G.C.: xxvii
Paul, C.: 266
Paul, E.: 266
Peano, G.: xiv, 60, 84, 303
Pears, D.F.: 108
Pêcheux, M.: xxviii
Peiffer, G.: 54
Peirce, C.S.: xxii, xxv, 1, 12, 14-15, 21, 29-30, 35, 37, 39, 52, 55, 62, 174, 283
Pelc, J.: 52, 55
Perlini, T.: 108
Pesaresi, M.: 308
Petrilli, S.: xxviii, 299
Piaget, J.: 128-129, 149-150

INDEX AUCTORUM

Piana, G.: 266
Picasso, P.: 149-150
Pike, K.L.: 230
Plato: 10, 53, 88
Pompa, L.: 11, 15
Ponzio, A.: xvii, xxi, xxiii-xxiv, xxviii, 154, 266, 286, 299
Posner, R.: xxv, xxix
Premoli, O.: 57, 85
Preti, G.: 12
Price, H.H.: 43, 55
Prieto, L.: xvi, 84

Q.
Quaranta, M.: xxviii, xxix, 16

R.
Rastier, F.: 25, 55, 65, 84
Ratner, J.: 67, 83
Rella, F.: 108
Retamar, R.F.: 51, 55
Révzina, O.G.: 52, 55
Rey-Debove, J.: 55
Rhees, R.: 57
Ricardo, D.: 134
Ricci, U.: 16, 57, 85
Richards, I.A.: xxv
Riedlinger, A.: 56
Riverso, E.: 12, 91, 108
Robering, K.: xxix
Rossi, M.: 240, 251
Royce, K.: 83
Ruesch, J.: 52, 56
Russell, B.: 46, 155, 304
Ryle, G.: xiv, 1, 8, 56, 113, 138-140, 146-147, 152, 154-155, 166, 168

S.
Sabbatini, M.: 304
Sapir, E.: 279

Saussure, F. de: 2, 13, 37-39, 53, 56, 61, 266, 287, 295
Scarpelli, U.: 12, 84
Schaff, A.: xvi, 24, 52, 56, 84, 266, 282, 299
Scheflen, A.E.: 230
Schiller, F.C.S.: 46
Schilpp, P.A.: 49
Schlick, M.: 21, 62, 97
Schmid, G.: xxvi
Schmidt, J.: 83
Schmitz, W.H.: xxvii, xxix
Schopenhauer, A.: 91
Schrag, C.O.: 54
Sciadini, F.: xxviii, 49
Sebeok, T.A.: xxv, xxix, 56, 84, 93, 108
Sechehaye, A.: 56
Sechi, G.: 91, 108
Segal, D.: 56
Segre, C.: 65, 84
Sellars, R.W.: 51
Semerari, G.: xxv
Senofonte, C.: xxix
Sertoli, G.: 108
Sheldon, W.H.: 113, 127, 129
Shils, E.: 182
Skékeley, D.L.: 49
Skinner, B.: 49
Slama-Cazacu, T.: xxv, 154
Smith, D.M.: 134
Smith, T.V.: 134
Sohn-Rethel, A.: 246, 251-252
Solar, C.: 154
Solomon, M.: 55
Somenzi, V.: 302
Spaier, A.: 50
Sraffa, P.: 88, 89, 93
Stalin, J.: 247, 252
Steinbacher, K.: xxix
Stevens, S.S.: 129
Stout, G.F.: 51
Strachey, J.: 107

Strada Janovič, C.: 107
Stravinsky, I.F.: 149-150
Strong, C.A.: 51, 99
Suzuki, D.T.: 49, 50
Szarota, E.M.: 56, 267

T.
Tagliacozzo, G.: 11, 15
Tarski, A.: 127, 129
Tentori, T.: xxv
Thales: 237
Thomson, G.: 252, 267
Tinbergen, N.: 80, 84
Titunik, I.R.: 85
Tolman, E.C.: 27, 66
Trân duc, Thao: 237, 252
Treves, R.: 302
Tucker, W.B.: 129
Tynianov, Y.: 51, 56
Tyson, A.: 107

U.
Uspensky, B.A.: 51, 56, 107-108
Umiker-Sebeok, J.D: 55

V.
Vacca, G.: 16, 57, 85
Vaccarino, G.: 12, 84, 154
Vailati, G.: xiv, xxv, xxix, 8-9, 12-13, 15-16, 39, 57, 60, 85, 160, 168, 302-303
Vasco, J.A.: 306
Vaughan, G.: 67, 85
Verene, D.Ph.: 11, 16
Verón, E.: 25, 52, 65
Vico, G.: 11-12, 14, 16
Vinci, L. da: 266

Vitier, C.: 306
Vodicka, F.: 57
Voloshinov, V.N.: 65, 85

W.
Wahl, J.: 51
Waismann, F.: 21, 62, 97
Walton, P.: 251
Ware, E.E.: 49
Warnock, G.J.: 155
Watson, J.B.: 27, 66, 303
Watzlawick, P.: 155
Weiss, P.A.: 55
Welby, V.: xxv, xxix, 12
White, H.V.: 11, 16
Whorf, B.L.: 279
Widmann, A.: 305, 306
William, J.: 129
Williams, R.: xxix, 252
Wisdom, J.: 154-155
Withalm, G.: xxvi, 307
Wittgenstein, L.: xiv-xvi, 4, 8, 13, 21, 38, 52, 57, 62, 87-108, 127, 131-132, 154-155, 166, 168, 192
Wojtasiewicz, O.: 56, 84, 266
Wolman, B.B.: 49
Wright, G.H. von: 92, 108
Wright, W.K.: 46

Y.
Yamaguchi, S.: 49
Young, K.: 4, 51, 57, 89, 91

Z.
Zavala, I.M.: xxiii, xxiv-xxix
Žinkin, N.I.: 52, 57

Index Rerum

A.

absurdity: xvii, 131-156;
— and logical types: 151-153;
types of –: 142-151.
alienation: ix-x, 3, 103-106;
linguistic –: 89, 103-106, 253-265.
American philosophy: *see* philosophy.
analytical philosophy: *see* philosophy.
anthropology: 9, 100, 182, 183.
artefacts: xix, 190-194 (definition of –), 219-220;
parking lots of –: 222-224, 229-231;
typology of –: *see* homology of production.
articulations:
— in signs and objects: xix, 189-251;
double –: xx, 189, 198;
plurality of –: 220-232.
audience: 10-12.
author: xi-xii, xxiv, 8, 136, 218.
automation: 215-217.
axiology: *see* value.

B.

behavior: 26, 30-34, 41, 66, 74, 79-82, 95, 111, 115-117, 121, 125, 132, 163, 166, 249, 280, 283;
— and communication: 31-34, 164-165, 168;
linguistic –: 31;
non-sign –: 33-34, 76;
nonverbal –: 166; (*see also* non-verbal sign systems);
sign – and – as communication: 30-35, 43-45, 66, 74-79, 115, 120, 127, 165;
social –: xxiv, 53;
value –: 115; (*see also* value).
behaviorism: 21, 27, 29-31, 61, 66-67, 75, 79, 111, 114-116, 117.
bodies:
— and signs: xxi-xxii, 30, 40-41, 254-255, 271-276, 285-294, 298-299.

C.

capital:
cultural –: ix-x, 184;
linguistic –: xi, 256-262;
constant –: 255-258;
total –: 255, 259-262;
variable –: 255, 258-259.
capitalism: ix-xii, 45, 179, 184-185.
categories: xxii, 75, 236-238;
— and social reproduction as their matrix: 236-238;
— as paired terms: 158-160;
— in the human sciences: 157-168;
overlapping of –: 157-168;
variation of –: 157-158.
civil society (Gramsci): 68, 241, 280.
classes:
social –: 66, 105.
code-and-message-semiotics: *see* semiotics.

commodities:
- as messages: 44, 102, 190-194; (*see also* linguistics and economics; *and* semiotics and economics).

common speech: *see* speech.

communication: 3-4, 7-11, 13-15, 30-35, 43, 45, 52, 67, 74-79, 95, 104-106, 157, 164-167, 179, 193-194, 213, 227, 230, 283;
- as behavior: *see* behavior and –.

consciousness: 29, 32-34, 103, 165, 185, 260;
false –: 103.

consumerism:
linguistic –: 264-265.

consumption: 61, 160-162, 186, 222, 239-240, 243;
non-sign material –: xx;
sign –: xx.

context: 7-9, 135;
meaning and –: *see* meaning.

D.

denotatum: 72-73, 296; (*see also* referent).

designatum (significatum): 20.

distribution: 161.

dialectical materialism: *see* materialism.

dimensions of semiosis: *see* semiosis.

discourse: 64-65.

E.

economic base: *see* structure.

economics: *see* linguistics and –; *and* semiotics and –.

empiricism: 21-22, 24-28, 62-63, 98-99.

essence and phenomena: *see* phenomena.

esthetics: xvi, 24, 64-65, 111-130;

esthetic value: *see* value.

ethology: 80-82.

exchange: xix, 61, 67, 102, 178-179, 186, 239-240, 243;
- values: 102, 134, 190, 256, 273;
sign –: xx.

experience: 9, 257.

exploitation: 69, 100, 255, 262-265; (*see also* linguistic alienation).

F.

false: *see* true/false;
- consciousness: *see* consciousness;
- praxis: *see* praxis;
- thought: *see* thought.

fetishism: xxii, 102.

finis Austriae: 87, 92.

H.

homology: xix, xxi, 3, 189-194; (*see also* homological method);
- of production: 189, 194-232;
levels of the –: 194-220;
schema of the –: 220-221.

human sciences: *see* sciences.

I.

ideology: ix-xii, xxi, xxiv, 8, 45, 103, 135-136, 166, 172-173, 183-184, 255, 280, 281-282;
ideological institutions: 240-243.

interpretant: 25, 27, 29, 36, 41, 66, 69.

interpretation: 9, 25, 33, 70, 89, 104, 132, 135.

interpreter: 25, 36, 41, 69, 274-275.

Italian semiotics: *see* semiotics.

L.

language: 8, 10-12, 14, 21, 25, 42, 62, 65, 68-69, 72, 78, 97-98, 100, 103-105, 125, 128, 131, 133-134, 136, 142, 153-156, 163, 165-166, 179, 189-194, 219, 227-228, 253, 256-265, 272, 277, 278; (*see also* linguistic work);
– and thought: 165-166;
– in stuctures and superstructures: 247-248;
philosophy of –: *see* philosophy;
– and semiotics: *see* semiotics;
theory of –: 11.
linguistic alienation: *see* alienation.
– consumerism: *see* consumerism.
– philosophy: *see* philosophy.
– relativity: 104, 279.
– work: *see* work.
linguistics and economics: 89, 131, 133-134, 172-173, 186-187, 190-194, 198, 202-206, 227-232, 240, 256-265; (*see also* semiotics and economics; *and* homology of production).
literary production: *see* production.
logic: 9, 21-22, 29, 62, 98, 100, 118, 186; (*see also* syllogism).

M.

market: *see* trade.
Marxism: xxiv, 2, 28, 45, 59-60, 88-89, 100-103, 134, 161-162, 166, 185-187, 239-240, 247, 253-265, 271, 277.
material and social: 298-299.
materialism: 27, 30, 61, 66-67, 81, 277-280; (*see also* reality);
dialectical –: 27, 30, 45, 132, 162-163, 267, 280.
materialistic semiotics: *see* semiotics.
materiality: xxv, 66, 166-167;

physical, socio-historical and semiotic –: xxii.
material reproduction: *see* reproduction.
meaning: 62, 71-73, 91, 118, 132, 134, 141, 287, 294-298; (*see also* signifiant/signifié, semantics);
initial – and additional –: 134-135;
– and context (and historical milieu): 9-10, 135; (*see also* context);
– and semiosis: 26, 40, 42-43, 69-74;
three dimensions of –: 39-43.
mentalism: 116, 133, 273, 278.
messages: 8-10, 14, 30, 131-133, 135, 192-193, 219, 260, 287.
metalinguistic disciplines: 24, 64.
method: 22, 99, 111, 114-116, 119, 127, 132, 142, 181-184, 186-187; (*see also* methodics);
homological –: xvii-xviii; (*see also* homology).
mind: 62, 95, 119, 157, 250-257.

O.

oneiric work: *see* work.
operationalism (operational approach): 13, 96, 116-126, 128, 133.

P.

phenomena and science: 167-168.
philosophy:
American –: 11-13, 17-53, 59, 82;
analytical (linguistic) –: 12, 14, 17, 59-60, 90-93, 104, 131, 136-140;
– and semiotics: *see* semiotics and –;
– of language (*see also* semiotics and –): 11, 13.

practice: (*see also* praxis);
  – and history: 233-235, 236-238;
  social –: 14, 25-28, 65-69, 71, 79, 81, 157, 176-178, 180-181, 233-238;
    – and personal therapeutic –: 101-102.
pragmatics: 21, 40, 43; (*see also* semiosis: dimensions of –).
pragmatism: 11, 13, 21-22, 62-63, 97-99.
praxis: (*see also* practice);
  false –: 103;
  social –: 67;
  therapeutic –: 101-102, 104.
private and public: *see* public and private.
production: xix-xx, xxii, 26, 28, 45, 61, 68-70, 91-117, 133, 160-162, 179, 186, 189, 222, 239-240, 243, 253, 264;
  global –: 219-220;
  homology of –: *see* homology;
  linguistic –: 133, 194, 212, 227; (*see also* linguistic work; *and* homology of –);
  modes of –: 242-243, 281-282;
  nonrepeatable –: 217-219;
  original, literary, and scientific –: 217-219;
  sign –: xx, 25-27, 70, 286-287.
program: xviii, xxiv, 32, 45, 61, 95, 176, 186, 189, 192, 225, 229-230, 282.
public and private: 157, 162-164, 174.

R.

rationalism: 22, 63, 98.
reality: 28, 69, 157, 184-186, 298;
  material – and signs: 273-299;
  social –: 26, 186, 233-235, 298-299.

referent: 288, 295-298; (*see also* denotatum).
reproduction: xxii, xxiv, 26;
  material – and social –: 298-299;
  material – and symbolic –: xxi;
  social –: ix-xii, xx-xxi, 3, 60, 171-187, 272, 278-280, 281-285, 297;
    articulations of –: 238-243;
    catalogue of –: 235-236;
  – and semiosis: 171-188;
  – and sign systems: 232-251.
residues:
  sign –: xxi, 191, 285-299;
    – and non-sign –: xxi, 44;
    – on the side of the signata: 294- 298;
    – on the side of signantia: 289-294.

S.

sciences: (*see also* categories in the human –);
  biological – and semiotics: *see* semiotics;
  human –: 19, 79, 99, 173;
  social –: 59, 61, 80, 104, 171-173, 157-168, 182.
science of signs: *see* semiotics; *and* signs: theory of –.
scientific production: *see* production.
semantics: 21-22, 24, 41, 43, 63, 98, 133.
semiology: 38, 216, 227-228.
semiosis: 39-41, 44, 60, 70-72, 171-187; (*see also* meaning and –);
  dimensions of –: 21-22, 35-37, 40-41, 63, 72-74, 99-100;
  factors of –: 25.
semiotics: 9, 12-13, 17, 19-23, 25-26, 28-29, 42-43, 59-61, 63-64, 69, 72-74, 79, 81, 87, 93-95, 97-99,

131, 171, 173-174, 216, 254, 271-280, 282; (*see also* signs: theory of –);
code-and-message–: 9-14, 227-228, 257;
Italian –: xiv, 7-16, 60, 119;
masters of –: 17-53, 87, 94-95;
materialistic –: xxii, 173, 271-276, 277-280, 282; (*see also* materialism);
– and biological sciences: 23, 26-27, 29-30, 43, 51, 59-60, 63, 115, 174;
– and economics: 44-45, 133-136, 171-187, 220-232, 238-251, 253-265, 275-276; (*see also* linguistics and –);
– and philosophy: 20-25, 28, 52, 60, 61-64, 98, 123, 271-276;
– and philosophy of language: 7, 60, 93-100;
– and social reproduction: *see* reproduction;
– and theory of value: 21-25; (*see also* value: theory of –).
sign: 22, 24-26, 33, 35-39, 42, 44, 61, 63, 65, 73, 81, 98, 100, 174-175, 191, 254, 274-276, 281-299;
– and non-sign material consumption: *see* consumption;
– as a totality: 85-89;
– behavior: *see* behavior;
– consumption: *see* consumption;
– exchange: *see* exchange;
– production: *see* production;
– work: *see* work.
signans: 71, 102, 199, 202, 232, 287, 289-296, 298-299; (*see also* residues: sign –);
signatum: 71-72, 102, 199, 232, 287, 290, 294-299; (*see also* residues: sign –).
signifiant/signifié: 35-39, 287.

significance: 123-125;
– and signification: 124.
signification: *see* significance and –.
significatum: 72-73; (*see also* designatum).
Significs: xxv.
signs: (*see also* systems; *and* residues);
– and bodies: *see* bodies and signs;
– and values: 23, 64-65;
– as a totality: 285-289;
– as terms of mediation: 298-299; (*see also* structural and superstructural);
– in general: 22, 24-26, 33, 35-39, 42, 44;
theory (science) of –: 18-19, 24-29, 35-39, 35-39, 127; (*see also* semiotics);
typology of –: 284-285.
sign-vehicle: 30, 35-39, 41, 43, 52; (*see also* sign residues on the side of signantia; body and signs);
social behavior: *see* behavior;
– classes: *see* classes;
– institutions: *see* thought;
– reality: *see* reality;
– reproduction: *see* reproduction;
– sciences: *see* sciences.
social and material: *see* material and social.
speech:
common –: xiv-xv, 2, 14, 97, 131, 135;
methodics of common –: xvii.
structure (economic base) and superstructure: 17, 45, 60-61, 172-173, 177, 185-186, 240-242, 247-248, 250-251, 280, 281-282.
syllogism as a linguistic (verbal) mechanism: 208-214, 220, 225-226.
syntactics: 41-43, 74, 98; (*see also* semiosis: dimensions of –).

systems:
  sign –: xx, 26, 28, 30, 45, 66, 69, 82, 171, 174, 175, 179, 189-251, 281-284;
    – and ideological institutions: 242-243;
    – and production of consensus: 249-251;
    – and social production: *see* social production;
    – and systems of value and ideology: 24, 65;
  nonverbal –: 34, 66, 189-190, 244-245, 253-254;
    – and verbal –: 34, 69, 245-247.

T.
terms:
  paired –: 158-160.
thought: 29, 91, 98, 103, 157, 257;
  false –: 103;
  – and language: *see* language and thought;
  – and social institutions: 166-167.
token and types: 35, 37.
trade (market):
  linguistic –: 132, 255.
true/false: 100-101, 103, 140.

V.
value: xvi-xvii, xix, 23, 24, 65, 111, 114-115, 124, 126-127, 276;
  economic –: 115;
  esthetic –: (*see also* esthetics), 111, 117-126;
  exchange –: *see* exchange;
  labor –: 193;
  linguistic –: 258-259;
  theory of – (or axiology): 21-24, 62, 98;
  use –: 132, 134, 256, 276;
  – and signs: *see* signs and values;
  – behavior: *see* behavior.
vehicles: *see* sign-vehicle.
verbal and nonverbal: *see* systems: sign –.

W.
words:
  combination of –: 142-151.
work: 27-28, 67-68, 118, 190-194, 220-232, 234-238, 253-254; (*see also* production; *and* reproduction);
  alienated work: xviii; (*see also* alienation);
  linguistic – (and linguistic production): xv, 3, 12, 71, 131-132, 191-194, 220-230, 253- 265;
  oneiric –: xviii-xix;
  sign –: 278, 286-288;
  – and activity: xviii.

In the CRITICAL THEORY series the following titles have been published thus far, and will be published during 1993:

1. DÍAZ-DIOCARETZ, Myriam and Iris M. ZAVALA (eds): *WOMEN, FEMINIST IDENTITY AND SOCIETY IN THE 1980's*. Amsterdam, 1985.
2. DÍAZ-DIOCARETZ, Myriam: *Translating Poetic Discourse: Questions of Feminist Strategies in Adrienne Rich*. Amsterdam, 1985.
3. DIJK, Teun A. van (ed.): *DISCOURSE AND LITERATURE. New Approaches to the Analysis of Literary Genres*. Amsterdam, 1985.
4. ZAVALA, Iris M., Teun A. van DIJK and Myriam DIAZ-DIOCARETZ (eds) coordinated by Bill DOTSON SMITH: *APPROACHES TO DISCOURSE, POETICS AND PSYCHIATRY: Papers from the 1985 Utrecht Summer School of Critical Theory*. Amsterdam, 1987.
5. HELBO, André: *THEORY OF PERFORMING ARTS*. Amsterdam, 1987.
6. SEIDEL, Gill (ed.): *THE NATURE OF THE RIGHT. Feminist analysis of order patterns*. Amsterdam/Philadelphia, 1988.
7. WODAK, Ruth (ed.): *LANGUAGE, POWER AND IDEOLOGY. Studies in political discourse*. Amsterdam/Philadelphia, 1989.
8. MEESE, Elizabeth A. and Alice A. PARKER (eds): *THE DIFFERENCE WITHIN: FEMINISM AND CRITICAL THEORY*. Amsterdam/Philadelphia, 1989.
9. PARKER, Alice A. and Elizabeth A. MEESE (eds): *FEMINIST CRITICAL NEGOTIATIONS*. Amsterdam/Philadelphia, 1992.
10. ROSSI-LANDI, Ferruccio: *BETWEEN SIGNS AND NON-SIGNS*. Amsterdam/Philadelphia, 1992.
11. PONZIO, Augusto: *SIGNS, DIALOGUE AND IDEOLOGY*. Amsterdam/Philadelphia, n.y.p.